# Wisdom in Transition

## Act and Consequence in Second Temple Instructions

*By*

Samuel L. Adams

BRILL

LEIDEN • BOSTON
2008

This book is printed on acid-free paper.

**Library of Congress Cataloging-in-Publication Data**

A C.I.P. record for this book is available from the Library of Congress.

ISSN 1384-2161
ISBN 978 90 04 16566 3

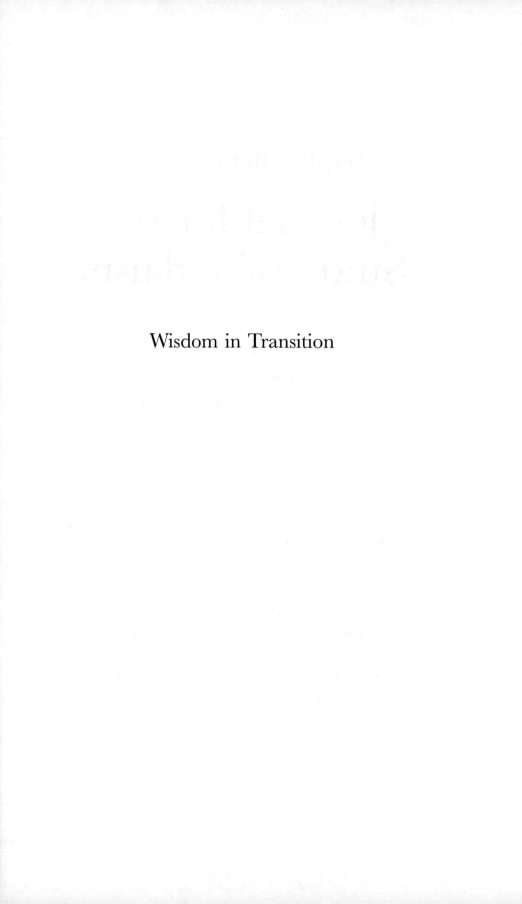

Wisdom in Transition

ˇSupplements to the

# Journal for the Study of Judaism

*Editor*

John J. Collins
The Divinity School, Yale University

*Associate Editors*

Florentino García Martínez
Qumran Institute, University of Groningen

Hindy Najman
Department of Near and Middle Eastern Civilizations,
University of Toronto

*Advisory Board*

J. DUHAIME — A. HILHORST — P.W. VAN DER HORST
A. KLOSTERGAARD PETERSEN — M.A. KNIBB
J.T.A.G.M. VAN RUITEN — J. SIEVERS — G. STEMBERGER
E.J.C. TIGCHELAAR — J. TROMP

VOLUME 125

FOR HELEN

# CONTENTS

# ACKNOWLEDGMENTS

This study, a revised version of my dissertation submitted to Yale University, grew out of an abiding interest in the Wisdom literature of the Hebrew Bible and ancient Near East. The Graduate School of Arts and Sciences at Yale generously supported me with a dissertation fellowship and the chance to learn from a group of brilliant, accessible scholars. I will always be grateful for the opportunity to pursue doctoral work in such a setting. Prior to his retirement, I took a yearlong course on the Egyptian instructions with William Kelly Simpson. His kind attention to our work helped me a great deal. Other specialists in Egyptology, especially David Klotz, have answered my questions over the years and continued a meaningful dialogue. H.W. Fischer-Elfert read a draft of chapter 1 and offered valuable suggestions. Matthew Goff went over much of the study with care and gave helpful feedback. Special thanks go to my dissertation committee members: Robert Wilson, Steven Fraade, and John Collins, who has served as the primary advisor.

I have been working with Professor Collins since my first M.Div. course at the University of Chicago, and he is an exemplary model for me. He considers his tireless efforts with students to be an essential aspect of his scholarly work. He is a generous and fair advisor, and his comments are always incisive. John Collins has taught me the importance of this vocation and the need to pursue it with intensity and creativity.

Brill has graciously agreed to include this book in the *Journal for the Study of Judaism Supplement Series*, and I thank Mattie Kuiper at Brill for her prompt response to questions and her help with finalizing the manuscript. Here at Union Theological Seminary and Presbyterian School of Christian Education in Richmond, Virginia, where all of the revisions were done, I am grateful to New Testament doctoral student William Robinson for his careful help with indexing and proofreading matters, and to Dean John Carroll for his support.

My parents, Alfred and Joanna Adams, have supported me throughout my life and encouraged me to ask questions about God and the Bible. My wife Helen and two children, Virginia and Charlie, have been my greatest source of strength throughout this process. They remind me each day about present possibilities for joy. Helen has been steadfast in her devotion to me and my pursuit of this study, which I dedicate to her with much love.

Finally, I am grateful to the sages who wrote these ancient instructions. These authors struggled with justice, death, and the nature of God, and they were willing to challenge each other and offer new ideas about important matters (sometimes with a sense of humor). I remain thankful for the preservation of their discussion and the privilege of being able to study it.

Richmond, Virginia
September 15, 2007

# ABBREVIATIONS

This study will follow the abbreviation guide in Patrick Alexander et al., *The SBL Handbook of Style* (Peabody: Hendrickson, 1999). The following abbreviations do not appear in the guide:

| | |
|---|---|
| ADAI.K | Abhandlungen des deutschen archäologischen Instituts, Kairo |
| ÄUAT | Ägypten und Altes Testaments: Studien zur Geschichte, Kultur und Religion Ägyptens und des Alten Testaments |
| BAe | Bibliotheca Aegyptiaca |
| BLS | Bible and Literature Series |
| CBOTS | Coniectanea Biblica Old Testament Series |
| *DSSSE* | Dead Sea Scrolls Study Edition |
| FThSt | Freiburger theologische Studien |
| GOF | Göttinger Orientforschungen |
| HBS | Herders biblische Studien |
| *JANES* | *Journal of the Ancient Near Eastern Society* |
| *JARCE* | *Journal of the American Research Center in Egypt* |
| MÄSt | Münchner ägyptologische Studien |
| PÄ | Probleme der Ägyptologie |
| *RdÉ* | *Revue d'Égyptologie* |
| WAS | Wiener Alttestamentliche Studien |
| YES | Yale Egyptological Studies |

# INTRODUCTION

> I have seen the business that God has given everyone
> to be busy with.
> He has made everything suitable for its time;
> moreover he has put a sense of past and future into
> their minds,
> yet they cannot find out what God has done from
> the beginning to the end.
>
> *Ecclesiastes 3:10–11*

## 1. *Klaus Koch and the* Tun-Ergehen-Zusammenhang

If cultural and religious systems are to flourish and have lasting significance, they must be able to address fundamental questions for the
ordering of individual lives and the larger society. Within many contexts,
the affirmation of predictability is an essential requirement, especially
in relation to human behavior and the expected outcomes. The assertion is often made that righteousness brings manifold blessings, and
wickedness leads to misery. Such a guarantee can create cohesion and
stability for societies, since it encourages members to conduct themselves with integrity, both in the family unit and the public sphere. The
promise of benefits functions to preserve the status quo, as individuals
are enjoined to respect the system in place and wait for guaranteed
rewards. Such a framework is frequently illustrated through sapiential
discourse, where culturally relevant sayings describe human behavior
and its anticipated consequences.[1] Through colorful images and pithy
language, members of a society or religious group are presented with
maxims on the particularities of life and how to achieve and maintain
success. Such proverbial material is often compiled into instructional
texts, which have humanity as the basic point of orientation.[2] In these

---

[1] The assumption of predictability does not necessarily indicate an infallible principle of justice, even when isolated sayings seem to suggest as such. See Michael V.
Fox, "World Order and Maʿat: A Crooked Parallel," *JANES* 23 (1995), 40, and the
discussion below.

[2] James L. Crenshaw, *Old Testament Wisdom: An Introduction* (rev. and enl. ed.; Louisville: Westminster John Knox Press, 1998), 10, explains the perspective of the Wisdom
books, which are usually anthropocentric and interested in social harmony. It generally

collections of observations and warnings, larger issues are also considered, such as divine justice, the natural world, and the intricacies of
human relationships.

For the cultural world of the ancient Near East, particularly in
Egypt and Israel, Wisdom literature became an important means of
shaping communal life, posing theological questions, and speaking to
the inherent need for predictability. In a famous essay ("Is There a
Doctrine of Retribution in the Old Testament?"), Klaus Koch pointed
to an underlying principle in these instructions, especially the book of
Proverbs:

> What we do find repeated time and time again is a construct which
> describes human actions which have a built-in consequence. Part of this
> construct includes a conviction that Yahweh pays close attention to the
> connection between actions and destiny, hurries it along, and "completes"
> it when necessary. The wisdom literature reflects on and articulates the
> close connection between the Good Action-Blessings-Construct and the
> Wicked Action-Disaster-Construct as this applied to individuals.[3]

Koch posits a framework in the Wisdom books in which events happen
of their own accord, as part of a process set in motion by a deity whose
role is more like a "'midwife who assists at a birth' by *facilitating the
completion of something which previous human action has already set in motion.*"[4]
As a result of the fair and self-perpetuating system in place, bad events
befall evil people, and fortunate occurrences await those who adopt
a reverential mindset (usually called "fear of the Lord" in Israelite
instructions). Many sayings seem to support this reading, such as Prov
11:18: "The wicked earn no real gain, but those who sow righteousness
get a true reward." An individual's fate hinges on understanding the
system in place and heeding the call of Wisdom: "For waywardness
kills the simple, and the complacency of fools destroys them; but those
who listen to me (Wisdom) will be secure and will live at ease, without
dread of disaster" (Prov 1:32–33).

---

follows that optimism lies at the heart of the sapiential message, although there is also
a lively tradition of more complex, speculative works (e.g., the Dispute between a Man
and His *Ba*, Qoheleth).

[3] Klaus Koch, "Is There a Doctrine of Retribution in the Old Testament?" trans.
T.H. Trapp, in *Theodicy in the Old Testament* (ed. J.L. Crenshaw; IRT 4; Philadelphia:
Fortress Press, 1983), 64; originally published as "Gibt es ein Vergeltungsdogma im
Alten Testament?" *ZTK* 52 (1955): 1–42.

[4] Koch, "Is There a Doctrine of Retribution in the Old Testament?" 61.

Koch's seminal discussion produced a number of responses, as commentators have built on the identification of an act-consequence nexus (*Tun-Ergehen-Zusammenhang*) and how this model can clarify the content of ancient Near Eastern instructions. An important corrective to the original proposal is that Koch did not adequately emphasize the social aspect of ancient Near Eastern instructions. One primary goal of these texts is to foster mutual solidarity, as Carl-A. Keller, Jan Assmann, Lennart Boström, and Bernd Janowski (among others) have clearly demonstrated.[5] According to the maxims in these compilations, persons are supposed to rely on one other, since benevolence is ultimately beneficial to the purveyor of a kind deed. Another issue relates to the role of God in determining outcomes. Koch's "midwife" argument pointed to the lack of divine initiative in the instructions, particularly in the context of judgment.[6] Yet the fact that judicial language is used sparingly in Proverbs and other texts does not indicate the absence of a larger retributive principle or a deity whose role in human events is removed or in any way inconsequential. A saying in which God is not mentioned does not presuppose a lack of divine agency, including the capacity for judgment.[7] In a number of sayings in these proverbial collections, the Lord can freely intervene and "return" a deed back upon the person who committed it (e.g., Prov 24:12).[8] For a person who deals kindly with an enemy, "the Lord will reward (יְשַׁלֶּם) you"

---

[5] Carl-A. Keller, "Zum sogenannten Vergeltungsglauben im Proverbienbuch," in *Beiträge zur alttestamentlichen Theologie: Festschrift für Walther Zimmerli zum 70. Geburtstag* (ed. H. Donner and R. Hanart; Göttingen: Vandenhoeck & Ruprecht, 1977), 223–38; Jan Assmann, *Ma'at: Gerechtigkeit und Unsterblichkeit im alten Ägypten* (Munich: Beck, 1990); Lennart Boström, *The God of the Sages: The Portrayal of God in the Book of Proverbs* (CBOTS 29; Stockholm: Almqvist and Wiksell International, 1990); Bernd Janowski, "Die Tat kehrt zum Täter zurück: Offene Fragen im Umkreis des >> Tun-Ergehen-Zusammenhangs <<," *ZTK* 91 (1994): 247–71. For a recent review of Koch's thesis and how it can be applied to the Wisdom books, see Georg Freuling, *>>Wer eine Grube gräbt...<< Der Tun-Ergehen-Zusammenhang und sein Wandel in der alttestamentliche Weisheitliteratur* (WMANT 102; Neukirchen-Vluyn: Neukirchener Verlag, 2004).

[6] Koch, "Is There a Doctrine of Retribution in the Old Testament?" 59, argues that an explicit judicial process must be described if one is to speak of "retribution."

[7] Elizabeth Huwiler, "Control of Reality in Israelite Wisdom," (Ph.D. diss., Duke University, 1988), 68.

[8] This type of understanding also occurs in the Egyptian texts such as Ptahhotep: "Do not stir up fear in people, or God will punish in equal measure" (P 99–100). Translation is from William K. Simpson, ed., *The Literature of Ancient Egypt* (3d ed.; New Haven: Yale University Press, 2003).

(Prov 25:22).[9] In this respect, Koch's narrow understanding of "retribution" has required modification. According to Janowski, this concept in the instructions does not simply mean "payback" for evil deeds, but appropriate outcomes for all actions.[10] The current study takes divine retribution to mean "reprisal" or "recompense," the rendering of just consequences based on an individual's actions/character. Boström has also shown the hortatory value of act-consequence language, as the sages created incentives for righteousness.[11] By lauding the benefits of virtuous living, ancient sages sought to construct an orderly society, marked by reverence towards God and honesty in human relationships. Finally, these works do not necessarily demonstrate the belief in an elaborate "world order" built into the fabric of the universe. This was argued by several commentators subsequent to Koch's original proposal.[12] Roland Murphy, Michael Fox, and a number of other commentators have added important nuance to this discussion.[13]

When surveying the discussion on the ancient Near Eastern Wisdom texts, it is clear that Koch's thesis has sparked a lively debate and a better understanding of the instructions. In some cases, scholarly proposals of this sort can be unwieldy constructs that do not illuminate the source material. Yet the *Tun-Ergehen-Zusammenhang* is a window into the sapiential worldview and the larger purpose of the Wisdom books. As analysis moves forward, the act-consequence framework continues to be a useful means of studying these works and drawing important new conclusions about them. Several factors demonstrate the ongoing

---

[9] Janowski, "Die Tat kehrt zum Täter zurück," 269–70, deals with Koch's thesis and the issue of divine agency. He claims that in the book of Proverbs, "JHWH steht zwar in Relation zum Tun-Ergehen-Zusammenhang, die Freiheit seines Willens bleibt davon jedoch unberührt."

[10] Koch, "Is There a Doctrine of Retribution in the Old Testament?" 78, posits a "sphere of influence" around each person according to this literature, so that consequences happen automatically without a larger retributive principle. For an analysis of this thesis, see Janowski, "Die Tat kehrt zum Täter zurück," 255–66, who offers a more balanced understanding. According to Janowski, the retributive concept in the Israelite instructions is based on a belief in connective justice. "Retribution" can simply mean service (or justice) returned for each act (whether mediated by the deity or not). In the case of positive payback, some type of "remuneration" is in order, and when sinful acts occur, "punishment" becomes more appropriate terminology.

[11] See, for example, Boström, *God of the Sages*, 120–26.

[12] For example, see Hans H. Schmid, *Gerechtigkeit als Weltordnung* (BHT 40; Tübingen: Mohr, 1968).

[13] Roland E. Murphy, *The Tree of Life: An Exploration of Biblical Wisdom Literature* (3d ed.; Grand Rapids: Eerdmans, 1990), 116, distinguishes between "accepted regularities" and a "world order" built into the universe; cf. Fox, "World Order and Ma'at," 37–48.

value of the model. First, the ancient authors use causality language themselves to unpack their understanding of the created order and human destiny in particular. Instructions offer rewards for conformity to the various requirements and punishment for neglecting them. In some cases, God is the arbiter of human conduct, and in other instances events seem to happen on their own. For example, the Jewish sage Ben Sira (ca. 190 B.C.E.) begins his teaching by associating proper reverence with blessings: "The fear of the Lord delights the heart, and gives gladness and joy and long life" (Sir 1:12). The *Tun-Ergehen-Zusammenhang* is not a fanciful construct, for it often explains the internal logic of the sages' language. The Hebrew of Prov 10:24 posits a basic connection between character and consequence:

מגורת רשע היא תבואנו ותאות צדיקים יתן

> What the wicked dread will come upon them, but the desire of the righteous will be granted.

Similarly, the pupil of the Egyptian instructions whose actions reflect honesty and mutual solidarity (i.e., the concept of Ma'at) is promised benefits. In the Teaching for Prince Merikare, the royal addressee is presented with a clear formula: "Observe Ma'at, that you may endure long (*w3ḥ.k*) upon the earth" (47).[14] Most stable societies offer a series of expected links between what people do and how they will fare in their daily lives. The authors of ancient Near Eastern instructions make great efforts to underscore the benefits of honesty and the certainty of recompense through their use of specific constructs.

There is a third reason for the usefulness of this act-consequence model. An important transition took place during the late Second Temple period among Jewish sages, a reassessment of longstanding typologies for reward and punishment. Certain figures began to question the viability of earlier Wisdom, especially the gap between the promise of reliability and actual human experience. Qoheleth and Job are the authors usually associated with this later phase in the tradition, although there could have been others. Not only does a figure like Qoheleth question the validity of longstanding assumptions, but his writings also reflect a thematic shift from the earthly focus of Proverbs

---

[14] For the primary text of Merikare, see Joachim Friedrich Quack, *Studien zur Lehre für Merikare* (GOF 23; Wiesbaden: Otto Harrassowitz, 1992). The main source is a papyrus from St. Petersburg (1116A). The use of the subjunctive in this statement (*w3ḥ.k*) expresses purpose.

to a more serious engagement with the implications of human mortality. This sage is exasperated by the frequent unfairness of existence and the finality of death (a shadowy state in Sheol) for even the most righteous persons. This leads Qoheleth to a rejection of the somewhat facile understanding of act and consequence in Proverbs, especially in relation to death: "Then I said to myself, 'What happens to the fool will happen to me also; why then have I been so very wise?' And I said to myself that this also is vanity" (Qoh 2:15; cf. Job 14:10–12). Qoheleth dares to reflect on the absurdities he finds "under the sun," particularly the transience of life. Moreover, it is likely that he had contemporaries with revolutionary ideas about this issue. The entire wisdom tradition was being challenged by a radical new proposal, which Qoheleth and other figures, including Ben Sira, vigorously opposed: fulfilling the act-consequence relationship through eschatological means.

## 2. *Second Temple Instructions and the "Eschatologizing" of Wisdom*

In certain sapiential texts from the Hellenistic period, most notably 4QInstruction (from the corpus of the Dead Sea Scrolls) and the Wisdom of Solomon, the concept of Wisdom becomes "eschatologized" in a sense.[15] The proposition of individual salvation for the righteous

---

[15] 4QInstruction is a fragmentary text, preserved in multiple copies (1Q26, 4Q415–418, 423). For the critical edition, see John Strugnell and Daniel J. Harrington, *Qumran Cave 4.XXIV: Sapiential Texts, Part 2. 4QInstruction (Mûsār Lĕ Mēvîn): 4Q415ff. With a re-edition of 1Q26* (DJD 34; Oxford: Clarendon Press, 1999). Reference to the "eschatologizing" of Wisdom can be found in several recent discussions of instructional literature. John G. Gammie, "From Prudentialism to Apocalypticism: The Houses of the Sages amid Varying Forms of Wisdom," in *The Sage in Israel and the Ancient Near East* (ed. J.G. Gammie and L.G. Perdue; Winona Lake, Ind.: Eisenbrauns, 1990), 489, has noted a shift during the early Hellenistic period to a "more vivid eschatology and acceptance of what may be called a temporal dualism," which he defines as a contrast between the challenges of present existence and otherworldly possibilities. Armin Lange, *Weisheit und Prädestination: Weisheitliche Urordnung und Prädestination in den Textfunden von Qumran* (STDJ 18; Leiden: Brill, 1995), argues that the apocalyptic perspective in Judaism grew out of the sapiential tradition, and in this sense Wisdom is "eschatologized." Lange builds on the original proposals of Gerhard von Rad, *Old Testament Theology* (trans. D.M.G. Stalker; 2 vols.; OTL; Louisville: Westminster John Knox Press, 2001). Von Rad had argued that Wisdom literature is the background for the development of apocalyptic constructs. Matthew J. Goff, *The Worldly and Heavenly Wisdom of 4QInstruction* (STDJ 50; Leiden: Brill, 2003), devotes an entire study to the otherworldly vision of 4QInstruction and how this text combines sapiential and apocalyptic elements; cf. John J. Collins, "The Eschatologizing of Wisdom in the Dead Sea Scrolls," in *Sapiential Perspectives: Wisdom Literature in Light of the Dead Sea Scrolls. Proceedings of the Sixth International Symposium of the*

and eternal punishment for the wicked offered a radical, neat application of the *Tun-Ergehen-Zusammenhang*, particularly when compared with the earlier framework. With the help of apocalyptic constructs and in some cases the philosophical ideas associated with Hellenistic thought, certain authors modified or abandoned the earthly framework of their predecessors. The descriptions of the heavenly realm and the belief in a final judgment in *1 Enoch* provide further evidence for an emergent belief system during this period, one that included eternal possibilities for the human spirit. In these later works, the horizon for act and consequence is extended into the afterlife, so that proper results are guaranteed by means of an evaluation at the end of days. When compared with the more limited outlook of earlier Wisdom, this move represents a fundamental shift. According to Gammie, such a development "permitted a radical rethinking in the design of the houses the sages constructed to afford their compeers protection from anomie and attacks that suggested that the cosmos was without divine justice."[16]

The discovery of 4QInstruction, the longest and best-preserved sapiential text found near Qumran, is a critical indicator of this new framework for retribution and belief in individual immortality. The content of this text does not signify a chafing against older assumptions in the manner of Qoheleth, but a major shift in emphasis. The division of humanity into two camps, one destined for heavenly reward and the other for eternal punishment in Sheol, represents a different perspective. With a distinct lack of confidence in the possibility of present prosperity, the author of 4QInstruction offers a different vision of reality and human possibility. As Matthew Goff has shown in his recent studies of this work, the combination of admonitory and apocalyptic formulations makes for a unique form of sapiential discourse, particularly in relation to earlier texts.[17] 4QInstruction provides much-needed evidence for the "eschatologizing" of Wisdom, and its availability invites a comprehensive examination of Wisdom and retribution in ancient Near Eastern instructions. This new model would reverberate across later generations, as beliefs about individual immortality became central for many Jewish and early Christian communities. When studied

---

*Orion Center for the Study of the Dead Sea Scrolls and Associated Literature, 20–22 May 2001* (ed. J.J. Collins et al.; STDJ 51; Leiden: Brill, 2004), 49–65.

[16] Gammie, "From Prudentialism to Apocalypticism," 489.

[17] See also Matthew J. Goff, *Discerning Wisdom: The Sapiential Literature of the Dead Sea Scrolls* (VTSup 116; Leiden: Brill, 2007).

alongside the Enochic books and other texts from this period, including other scrolls, 4QInstruction proves that a variety of individuals began to discuss the afterlife as an "inheritance" for good behavior. The shift within the wisdom tradition was apparently a broad one, influencing the author of 4QInstruction as well as the Alexandrian Jew who wrote the Wisdom of Solomon.[18]

As a contribution to the work done in recent years regarding the content and meaning of 4QInstruction, this study will seek to contextualize the developments that occurred during the early Hellenistic period and the positions of the various sapiential authors on causality and the type of retribution one could expect. In addressing this topic, it is necessary to examine the earlier instructional literature in order to determine where the tradition stood prior to any reevaluation. A large degree of confusion has characterized scholarly assessments of the act-consequence relationship in the Egyptian instructions and the book of Proverbs, and one cannot attempt an accurate analysis of later texts like Ben Sira and 4QInstruction without clarifying the assumptions of earlier sages. It is impossible to explicate any "departure" models unless the previous understandings are outlined. Moreover, any resistance to the eschatologizing of Wisdom merits careful attention. The otherworldly vision of 4QInstruction, *1 Enoch*, and the Wisdom of Solomon did not represent the majority position at first. It is apparent from Ben Sira and Qoheleth that the combination of earthly advice with speculation about the heavenly realm and the afterlife was a controversial move, a shift that was closely related to the social location of specific authors and their intended recipients.

## 3. *Layout of the Present Study*

This study will proceed with an analysis of the relevant instructions in chronological order. Chapter 1, "Act and Consequence in Egyptian Instructions," will address the rich heritage of sapiential literature from Egypt. The sages responsible for this material relied on the all-important concept of Ma'at (usually translated as "justice" or "truth") to regulate earthly behavior and prevent the "chaos" (*jzf.t*) that threatened the

---

[18] Wisdom of Solomon, written around the turn of the era, also posits a belief in the immortality of the righteous soul (e.g., 3:1–9).

possibility for social cohesion. Our discussion will seek to demonstrate the remarkable consistency of Egypt's wisdom tradition in associating probity with earthly benefits and wickedness with punishment and the breakdown of social solidarity. In assessing major works like Ptahhotep, Merikare, and Amenemope, we will take up the popular theory that a more unpredictable "personal piety" replaced the traditional understanding of justice (Ma'at) during the New Kingdom.[19] According to this hypothesis, the Instruction of Amenemope signifies a move from the impersonal understanding of act and consequence (i.e., Ma'at) to a more arbitrary framework based on the will of God. The present study maintains that this theory reflects an oversimplified reading of both early and late Egyptian instructions, and it has led to some erroneous conclusions about the tradition that influenced these Israelite sages. The hypothesis rests on the faulty assumption that divine freedom and a more impersonal understanding of causality are mutually exclusive in the Wisdom texts. Egyptian instructions from all periods reflect a complicated dynamic between the "free will" of the deity and a more self-regulating system. As astute observers of the human situation, Egyptian sages recognized that a mechanistic framework for causality does not exist. Our analysis of these important antecedents to the tradition in Israel will demonstrate a complex discourse in Egypt, where the type of statement being offered depended on the rhetorical strategy of the author and the lesson being imparted in a particular maxim. We will seek to demonstrate that there was no "crisis of Wisdom" precipitated by the abandonment of Ma'at. In addition, this discussion will point to the earthly focus of the Egyptian instructions. For a culture with an elaborate view of death and the afterlife, the lack of engagement with human mortality and its implications is a noteworthy feature of these texts.

Chapter 2, "Act and Consequence in the Book of Proverbs," will outline the understanding of causality in the collection that became foundational for the wisdom tradition in Israel. Although the bulk of the sayings in Proverbs demonstrate the belief in a consistent act-consequence relationship, there are still open questions regarding this book. The date for the various units in Proverbs is one of the more

---

[19] See the study of Hellmut Brunner, "Der freie Wille Gottes in der ägyptischen Weisheit," in *Les Sagesses du Proche-Orient Ancien, Colloque de Strasbourg 17–19 mai 1962* (Paris: Presses Universitaires de France, 1963), 103–20.

difficult and consequential issues and will receive careful attention in our discussion. Like most commentators, we see a distinction between Proverbs 1–9 and the shorter sayings that follow. Some of the sayings in Proverbs 10–30 reflect circumstances under a functioning monarchy and should therefore be situated prior to the exile. In addition, this discussion will counter the assertion that a later redactor added a "Yahwistic" layer to a secular collection.[20] Although it is plausible that sayings involving the deity coincided with the development of postexilic religious beliefs, there was never a pietistic moment in which the compilers of Proverbs moved from the predictable, God-as-midwife framework, to an arbitrary, Yahwistic worldview. Like the Egyptian texts, references to both a self-regulating system and divine freedom can be found throughout this collection, including units from earlier periods. Finally, one of the most critical and overlooked features of Proverbs will be discussed: the lack of interest in physical death and its ramifications. Consistent with the larger religious tradition, Proverbs places no hope for continued existence beyond Sheol. The sages responsible for this collection instead focus on the idea of a qualitative rather than natural death. In their framework, a fool has already perished through his idiocy, while a wise man can choose the "path of life" that leads "upward" (e.g., Prov 15:24). "Life" in such an example indicates that an individual has developed the required mindset for virtuous behavior. For our discussion, it is significant that the outlook in Proverbs is removed from a later discussion during the Second Temple period about death and the afterlife. The anxious concern with death in Qoheleth and Ben Sira is foreign to the thought-world of Proverbs, and this suggests an earlier date for the finalizing of this more traditional collection.

With the book of Ecclesiastes (Qoheleth), death overwhelms all other topics: this text will be taken up in Chapter 3, "Wisdom in Transition: The Book of Ecclesiastes." Unlike the compilers of Proverbs, Qoheleth views all reality through the darkness of Sheol. For the author of this work, human mortality cancels every perceived accomplishment, and all persons and occurrences are ultimately forgotten in a cyclical world. This chapter will argue that the era of the Ptolemies is the most likely setting for such a perspective, when a number of issues relating to death

---

[20] See, for example, the schema of William McKane, *Proverbs* (OTL; Philadelphia: Westminster, 1970).

and retribution were being debated and recast. Jewish and Greek texts from this later period contain descriptions about the ascent/survival of the soul after death, and this belief seems to be the background for a pivotal section in Qoheleth on the possibility of an afterlife (3:16–22). In considering this and related passages, the author's level of indebtedness to outside influences (Egyptian, Babylonian, Hellenistic) is a major issue. Moreover, the authorial integrity of the book continues to be a topic of central concern in recent studies, particularly the relationship between the epilogue (12:9–14) and the "words of Qoheleth" (1:1–12:8). Our discussion will argue that the epilogue and certain verses in the main body of text do not cohere with the original author's perspective and almost certainly derive from a later, more "orthodox" source. Through an examination of the sage's ethic and views on death, we will attempt to clarify the specific context and purpose of the book of Qoheleth, basing our conclusions on the major preoccupation in the text. Qoheleth's engagement with this topic of human mortality seems to represent a forceful contribution to a nascent debate on death and eschatology during the era of the Ptolemies.

The debate over Wisdom continued during the period of Ben Sira's career. Chapter 4, "Ben Sira's Apologetic Response," will assess the memorable writings of this fierce defender of the tradition. Ben Sira affirms the basic suppositions of his predecessors and takes issue with developing beliefs on the afterlife. Both apocalyptic formulations and philosophical understandings had begun to influence sapiential discourse, and Ben Sira opposes all efforts at speculative Wisdom (e.g., 3:21) and refutes the idea of individual immortality. This discussion will explicate the sage's considerable efforts at defending the justice of God without post-mortem possibilities. In order to accomplish this task, he insists on an eternal reputation for all righteous persons and a moment of reckoning at death for the wicked. Speaking to a class of aspiring officials and other interested pupils, he counters the otherworldly perspective found in books like *1 Enoch*, while at the same time promising his pupils that life and the sapiential worldview have consistency and meaning. In this pursuit, Ben Sira struggles with the difficult relationship between human inclinations, divine determinism, and the presence of evil in the world. His perspective is invaluable for tracing major developments during this period, because he attempts to defend the longstanding paradigm against an array of new opponents, especially those with eschatological proposals. Sirach's apologetic response involves several related claims: all events happen according to a divine scheme, only humanity is responsible for evil, and a good name lasts in a way that nothing else can, including the human spirit.

Chapter 5, "Wisdom in Transition: Mystery and Eschatology in 4QInstruction," will consider the longest instructional text from the corpus of the Dead Sea Scrolls. After a brief examination of the structure of this fragmentary document and the possibility that its diverse content reflects a composite text, we will discuss the framework for retribution in 4QInstruction. Those who are wicked will be sentenced to eternal punishment in the "everlasting pit" (4Q418 69 ii 6), while the righteous elect (the "spiritual people") achieve a state of "glory everlasting and peace eternal" (4Q418 126 ii 8). In 4QInstruction, the description of eschatological judgment and the contrasting fates of two types resembles the Enochic corpus, Daniel, and other passages from the Dead Sea Scrolls, and stands in contrast to Proverbs and Ben Sira. In addition, the central concept of 4QInstruction, the "mystery that is to be" (רז נהיה), has parallels in texts with explicitly apocalyptic interests. Yet 4QInstruction also contains admonitions that could easily be found in any of the earlier Wisdom books we have been discussing. This combination invites an examination of the relationship between the generic categories of Wisdom and apocalypticism and how different ideas were brought together during the Hellenistic period. By combining earthly and otherworldly elements, 4QInstruction represents a fundamental alteration of the *Tun-Ergehen-Zusammenhang*. The addressee, if he commits himself to a present life of "meditating" upon the mystery and avoiding iniquitous behavior, can look forward to eschatological reward.

As we examine this transition through a diachronic study of the relevant instructions, several pertinent issues will be revisited with every text. The structure and literary integrity of each instruction are essential topics. Important issues can be clarified through structural analysis, such as the identification of units that do not cohere with the overall thrust of a particular text. Moreover, this discussion will be attentive to the social setting for the various Wisdom books. Theological assertions are always made from a specific context, and it is incumbent upon the modern interpreter of sapiential literature to locate the material as precisely as possible. Of particular interest for this study will be the pattern that emerges regarding social location and the affirmation of predictability. For earlier sages in Egypt and those responsible for Proverbs and Ben Sira, prosperity and the possibility for advancement within existing social structures are a real possibility. In contrast, the poor addressees of 4QInstruction cannot hope for a successful scribal career or some of the traditional rewards associated with "fear of the Lord" (wealth, social advancement, etc.). The peripheral status of the community responsible for 4QInstruction (and *1 Enoch*) necessitates a different model/vision. This study will endeavor to determine the nature of this new vision, the diverse reasons for it, and its impact on sapiential discourse.

CHAPTER ONE

## ACT AND CONSEQUENCE IN
## EGYPTIAN INSTRUCTIONS

### 1. *Introduction*

The tradition of instructional literature flourished in Egypt more than in any other ancient Near Eastern setting. The sheer number of texts and the perennial presentation of favorite topics demonstrate the importance of this type of discourse in Egyptian society. The authors and compilers of instructions were astute observers of the human situation and offered memorable advice on matters large and small. Their warnings and reflections have a timeless quality that surely contributed to the faithful transmission and lasting appeal of these compilations. By lauding such qualities as discretion, respect before a superior, and honesty in one's business transactions, Egyptian sages sought to frame communal life among particular segments of the population and instill a specific set of behavioral patterns. They also addressed larger issues about justice, appropriate rewards for virtuous individuals, punishment for the wicked, and the role of the deity in determining human fate. The consideration of major theological propositions alongside commonplace observations would become a staple of ancient Near Eastern instructions in a variety of contexts. These issues and the question of an act-consequence relationship in the Egyptian texts will be the focus of the present discussion.

### 1.1 *Background on the Instructions*

Before proceeding with an analysis of causality in some of the major instructional documents, we must briefly address the parameters of Egypt's Wisdom literature and the basic focus of the material. With regard to delineating a specific corpus, the process of determining what constitutes Egyptian "wisdom" is surprisingly difficult. Many narratives and biographical texts contain parenetic elements and mundane advice, and scribes did not make absolute demarcations according to genre.[1] Significantly, there is no Egyptian term for "wisdom" equivalent to Hebrew חכמה. Yet there is a body of literature that shares a common heading: sbȝy.t ("instruction"). The sbȝy.t is generally cast as indispensable advice from a father to his son and placed in the mouth of a senior official.[2] In many cases, this attribution was probably a pseudepigraphic device that lent gravitas to the instruction.[3] The principal goal was to teach pupils the right attitude and behavior, the proper "way of life."[4] Such a task could be undertaken through a series of pithy statements on human existence, together with colorful warnings about how to avoid various pitfalls. As with Israelite instructions, the focus in these texts is generally anthropocentric and related to interpersonal activity, covering such matters as speech, public interactions, and relationships with superiors. The social aspect of these texts is their most salient feature: the Egyptian instructions demonstrate an abiding concern with how a person speaks and acts towards others. The concept of Ma'at, usually translated as "justice" or "truth," offers an all-important blueprint for behavior in the public realm. Ma'at is a foundational principle for the instructions and much of Egyptian literature. The aspiring official or other young pupil who strives "to know" (rḫ) justice, whose actions are a living embodiment of Ma'at, will reap considerable benefits.

With regard to format, Egyptian instructions are organized in cluster groupings of related sentences, often called "maxims" or "chapters." In many cases, maxims are arranged topically to emphasize a specific behavioral trait or real-life situation. For example, the Instruction of Amenemope contains thirty chapters of admonitions and advice on a

---

[1] For example, the poetic petitions in the Tale of the Eloquent Peasant offer admonitions, advice, and perorations on the concept of Ma'at. Such content correlates with a formal instruction like Ptahhotep. Ronald J. Williams, "The Sages of Ancient Egypt in the Light of Recent Scholarship," *JAOS* 101 (1981): 1–13, considers a text like the Eloquent Peasant to be an example of "speculative wisdom," since it moves beyond the basic instructional rubric (i.e., maxims on a variety of themes). While "speculative wisdom" is admittedly a more fluid category, the tone and content of these texts are frequently similar to the sbȝy.t.

[2] There are also "royal testaments," where the future ruler is instructed in matters of state and personal conduct. Two examples are Merikare and the Teaching of Amenemhet I for His Son Senwosret.

[3] See Miriam Lichtheim, "Didactic Literature," in *Ancient Egyptian Literature: History and Forms* (ed. A. Loprieno; PÄ 10; Leiden: Brill, 1996), 244.

[4] On the importance of this phrase, see Pascal Vernus, *Sagesses de l'Égypte pharaonique/présentation, traduction et notes* (Paris: Imprimerie nationale, 2001), 42 n. 77.

host of issues: the dangers of the "hot-headed man," greed, corruption, and theft.[5] Although the subject matter varies, the format is relatively consistent within individual texts.[6] Negative imperatives appear in all of these instructions, and the two-line unit is the most common form for a particular saying.[7] Parallelism such as one finds in the book of Proverbs (e.g., synonymous, antithetic) is also a prominent feature. For the most part, individual maxims had no fixed length in the Egyptian texts, and the sages often introduced new material to make a related point. It is often through secondary statements and incidental references that one glimpses underlying theological beliefs.[8]

## 1.2 *Purpose of This Chapter*

While this discussion cannot provide an exhaustive treatment of Egyptian Wisdom texts, an evaluation of the assumed connection between an act/behavioral pattern and its consequence offers a window into the sages' ethical and theological assumptions. Some nexus between deed and result is essential in this type of literature: a sapiential work would be pointless (or reflect a crisis point) if it did not guarantee at least a modicum of success for adhering to specific sayings and prohibitions.[9] Our task is to determine the type of causality envisioned in these works, whether mechanistic, contingent upon the "free will" of the

---

[5] Some instructions, such as Ptahhotep, have continuous text with no chapter headings.

[6] Miriam Lichtheim, *Late Egyptian Literature in the International Context: A Study of Demotic Instructions* (OBO 52; Fribourg/Göttingen: Universitätsverlag/Vandenhoeck & Ruprecht, 1983), 2–3, notes the tripartite form for the 37 maxims in Ptahhotep: (1) conditional clause; (2) series of imperatives; (3) summarizing statement(s) that amplify the issue at hand. The introductory conditional clause is not always present, becomes less frequently used over time, and disappears altogether in Amenemope and the Instruction of Anii. The layout of Demotic instructions differs considerably, since the advice is placed in monostich form.

[7] Kenneth A. Kitchen, "The Basic Literary Forms and Formulations of Ancient Instructional Writings in Egypt and Western Asia," in *Studien zu altägyptischen Lebenslehren* (ed. E. Hornung and O. Keel; OBO 28; Fribourg/Göttingen: Universitätsverlag/ Vandenhoeck & Ruprecht, 1979), 254. On the negative imperative and other forms in these texts, see also William McKane, *Proverbs* (OTL; Philadelphia: Westminster, 1970), 75–150.

[8] For more detailed background on the forms found in the *sbꜣy.t* and the history of its development, see Vernus, *Sagesses de l'Égypte pharaonique*, 9–43.

[9] Michael V. Fox, "World Order and Maꜥat: A Crooked Parallel," *JANES* 23 (1995), 40: "We can hardly imagine a didactic literature *without* the assumption of predictability."

deity, or perhaps a more nuanced understanding.[10] In addressing this topic, several related questions will be considered. What is the relationship between "the god" (*pꜣ nṯr*) of Egyptian instructions and Ma'at?[11] What, specifically, can an individual who lives in accordance with Ma'at hope to gain? For a culture with a complex set of beliefs regarding the afterlife, how does the prospect of eternal reward shape the advice offered in the instructions? Our discussion will also take up the lively debate among scholars concerning the *Tun-Ergehen-Zusammenhang*. The popular theory that a New Kingdom move towards "personal piety" led to the dissolution of any act-consequence framework in the later instructions, particularly Amenemope, is a major component of many modern assessments of these works. This discussion will maintain that the Egyptian texts, including New Kingdom instructions, are remarkably consistent in their depiction of appropriate behavior, expected outcomes, and the role of the deity in determining an individual's fate. A fundamental breakdown of the basic understanding of causality never occurred, and this continuity is significant for our understanding of this literature and its impact on Israelite sages. These Egyptian texts focus on shaping human behavior in the earthly realm, particularly among younger addressees, and in this pursuit the main incentive is the promise of earthly prosperity (rather than eternal reward) in exchange for uprightness. While later instructional texts began to use more explicitly

---

[10] Fox, "World Order and Ma'at," 40–41, explains that mechanistic "world orders" operate independently of any deity: "This order must be a natural force like gravity, that automatically and indifferently links consequence to deed."

[11] Egyptian instructions frequently use the singular *pꜣ nṯr* ("the god") in reference to the deity. The use of the singular form has sparked a number of theories about implicit assumptions. This designation does not necessarily reveal a monotheizing tendency, since there are many passing references to specific deities (Re, Amun, Thoth, etc.), indicating an acknowledgement of the Egyptian panoply of gods. Note the full list of references to various deities in the Egyptian instructions provided by Joseph Vergote, "La notion de Dieu dans les Livres de sagesse égyptiens," in *Les Sagesses du Proche-Orient Ancien: Colloque de Strasbourg, 17–19 mai 1962* (Paris: Presses Universitaires de France, 1963), 170–86. Erik Hornung, *Conceptions of God in Ancient Egypt: The One and the Many* (trans. J. Baines; Ithaca: Cornell University Press, 1982), 56, argues that the sun god is implied in many instructional texts. In addition, Hornung claims that the Egyptian authors chose the singular, neutral term (*pꜣ nṯr*) to suit varying locales (p. 59). While this seems to be an accurate assessment, there is another important factor at work in the frequent use of *pꜣ nṯr*. These instructions are anthropocentric and interested in the divine as it relates to human affairs. Any effort to distinguish or depict specific gods is usually done in the service of a statement about human destiny (e.g., the allusion to Thoth in chapter 15 of Amenemope). We generally see language about the deity in Egyptian instructions when an author wishes to comment on how "the god" shapes earthly events, especially the consequence of human actions.

religious vocabulary, the pedagogical thrust of this literature continued to be part of Egypt's wisdom tradition.

## 2. Ma'at and the "Free Will of God"

At a 1962 conference in Strasbourg, Hellmut Brunner argued for a major transition in Egyptian instructions during the New Kingdom, from a mechanistic, "Ma'at-driven" belief in reward and punishment to an understanding of human fate as subject to the (arbitrary) will of the deity.[12] According to Brunner, early instructions like Ptahhotep have a more reliable act-consequence principle, with Ma'at functioning as the guidepost for human conduct.[13] Then a "sea-change" occurs in texts such as Amenemope, with the result that divine agency supercedes all other factors and Ma'at is abandoned. According to Brunner, a consistent relationship between virtue and reward became obsolete:

> «Nach seinem Belieben» verteilt Gott die menschlichen Lose—nicht also nach dem Verhalten des Menschen. Die Maat wird hier nicht mehr genannt, und es muss sonderbar mit ihr bestellt sein, wenn Gott «nach seinem Belieben» schaltet.[14]

For Brunner, the shift towards *persönliche Frömmigkeit* and away from an impersonal understanding of the universe had a major impact, as Egyptian texts began to express humanity's relationship with God in more intimate terms. Such a theological move signified a more elevated deity, who stands over Ma'at and the created order and acts "unabhängig von jedem Werk des Menschen."[15] Brunner argues that the later sages dispensed with any notion of indirect causation, so that during the New Kingdom, prosperity or punishment depended solely on the free will of God.

---

[12] Hellmut Brunner, "Der freie Wille Gottes in der ägyptischen Weisheit," in *Les Sagesses du Proche-Orient Ancien, Colloque de Strasbourg, 17–19 mai 1962* (Paris: Presses Universitaires de France, 1963), 103–20.

[13] The date for Ptahhotep is debated. The text is ascribed to an aging vizier under the rule of Isesi, although this is probably a pseudepigraphic attribution. Miriam Lichtheim, *Ancient Egyptian Literature, Volume 1: The Old and Middle Kingdoms* (Berkeley: University of California Press, 1973), 62, locates the text during the Sixth Dynasty, near the end of the third-millennium. Based on the number of Middle Kingdom forms in this text, other scholars propose a date as late as the Twelfth Dynasty. See below for further discussion.

[14] Brunner, "Der freie Wille Gottes," 108.

[15] Brunner, "Der freie Wille Gottes," 108.

Brunner arrived at such an ambitious thesis by positing an impersonal understanding in the earlier instructions, and then a decisive shift from the Eighteenth Dynasty onwards. The earlier framework is found in numerous texts. He cites a passage from Merikare that is pivotal to his argument:

> Verily destruction is detestable.
> It is pointless for a man to repair what he has destroyed
> Or to rebuild what he has torn down.
> Beware of such!
> Affliction will be requited in kind,
> And every deed committed has its consequence (121–123).[16]

Brunner understandably cites the importance of the last line, where a consistent principle seems to be offered: "And every deed committed has its consequence" (*mḏd pw jr.wt nb.t*). A passage from the Instruction of Anii (early New Kingdom) represents a similar outlook:

> Behold, I give you these useful counsels,
> For you to ponder in your heart;
> Do it and you will be happy,
> All evils will be far from you (5.4–5).[17]

Although he is careful not to argue that such language implies automatism (analogous to the Hindu understanding of karma), Brunner does posit a reliable act-consequence understanding in these texts, with Ma'at as the baseline concept.

According to the thesis, this type of framework breaks down in later texts, beginning with Amenemope: "Bei Amenemope wird also durch Einbruch des Gedankens von Gottes freier Wahl nach unberechenbarer Liebe der Tun-Ergehen-Zusammenhang wesentlich aufgelockert."[18] Brunner points to several famous passages in support of this claim:

> Man is clay and straw,
> And God is his potter;

---

[16] The issue at stake in this passage is the plundering of This by the Herakleopolitan army without the king's authorization. Although this statement refers to a specific historical circumstance, the logic behind it surely applies to other situations. Unless otherwise noted, this discussion will use the Egyptian translations in William Kelly Simpson, *The Literature of Ancient Egypt* (3d ed.; New Haven: Yale University Press, 2003).

[17] Translation is from Miriam Lichtheim, *Ancient Egyptian Literature, Volume 2: The New Kingdom* (Berkeley: University of California Press, 1976), 138.

[18] Brunner, "Der freie Wille Gottes," 111.

He overthrows and He builds daily,
He impoverishes a thousand if He wishes (24.13–17).

Chapter 21 of Amenemope contains similar language: "Indeed, you cannot know the plans of God; You cannot perceive tomorrow" (22.5–6). According to Brunner, such language represents a decisive shift, since control of human destiny in Amenemope is shaped directly and completely by the deity, as opposed to the impersonal understanding based on Ma'at. Consequently, the authors of later instructions cannot seek to motivate pupils through earthly incentives; specifically, they cannot guarantee success for virtuous behavior. The sages can only claim that God desires goodness. An individual should avoid sin, because it is repugnant to God. Yet the sinner might escape divine judgment for his or her actions in certain cases. Brunner claims that such an arbitrary framework represents a "rupturing" (*Einbruchsstelle*) of standard sapiential thought in ancient Egypt.[19]

This argument has sparked a variety of responses, as scholars have attempted to determine the ethos of Egyptian instructions, and by extension, how these texts influenced Israelite sages. Uncertainty about the Egyptian context has added to the confusion of clarifying the relationship between automatic processes and divine intervention in Israelite instructions. When Brunner originally offered his proposal, Hartmut Gese questioned whether such a rigid dichotomy between early and late texts is possible.[20] Similarly, Jean Sainte Fare Garnot warned against neat classifications and oversimplifications, citing the complexity of the instructions and the polyphonic nature of Egyptian cultural and religious beliefs: "Dans l'univers des Anciens Égyptiens l'existence d'un certain «ordre» n'est point inhibitrice, bien au contraire; il y a place pour des dieux libres et pour des hommes libres."[21] Such reactions present an important critique of Brunner's argument. Since they are not systematic theological treatises, the Egyptian instructions cannot be expected to clarify every contradictory statement about God and the adjudication of human conduct. The larger point of these works is to shape human behavior. Nevertheless, a number of scholars have

---

[19] Brunner, "Der freie Wille Gottes," 116.

[20] Hartmut Gese, response to Brunner, "Der freie Wille Gottes," in *Les Sagesses du Proche Orient-Ancien*, 117.

[21] Jean Sainte Fare Garnot, response to Brunner, "Der freie Wille Gottes," in *Les Sagesses du Proche Orient-Ancien*, 120.

accepted this hypothesis as normative, using it as a template for evaluating the sapiential literature of Egypt *and* the influence of this material
on the Israelite texts, particularly the book of Proverbs.

In assessing the type of development suggested by Brunner, we
must give particular attention to Maʾat, which serves as a core ethical
principle in Egyptian instructions. The work of Jan Assmann is critical
here: his analyses have elucidated this multivalent term, both in the
sapiential works and the entire range of Egyptian literature.[22] According
to Assmann, Maʾat cannot be defined as the expression of an axiom-
atic link between a good deed and its reward. If previous discussions
had described Maʾat as more of an impersonal force that expresses a
reliable "world order," Assmann highlights the social dimension.[23] He
claims that Maʾat relates to *public* justice and the need for mutuality
in human relationships. In Egyptian literature, it often denotes "kommunikative Solidarität/Reziprozität." The "justice" (Maʾat) that the
instructions speak of is "connective justice," which becomes manifest in
the arena of human interaction and public discourse. Although Maʾat
is depicted in different forms of Egyptian literature as a goddess and
cosmic counterpoint to "chaos" (*jzf.t*), such levels of meaning should
not detract from the more practical connotation (particularly in the
instructions) of a "connective justice" that creates "social solidarity."[24]
Maʾat is an integral component of Egypt's didactic literature, since the
quality of one's public interactions determines whether an individual
is leading a righteous existence. This social aspect of justice and virtue
is also important for understanding sapiential texts from ancient Israel,
a topic we will address in subsequent chapters.

---

[22] Jan Assmann, *Maʿat: Gerechtigkeit und Unsterblichkeit im alten Ägypten* (Munich: Beck,
1990); idem, *Maât, l'Égypte pharaonique et l'idée de justice sociale* (Paris: Julliard, 1989).

[23] For the more traditional understanding, see Siegfried Morenz, *Egyptian Religion*
(trans. A.E. Keep; London: Methuen and Co., 1973), 113: "Maat is right order in
nature and society, as established by the act of creation, and hence means, according
to the context, what is right, what is correct, law, order, justice and truth." Cf. Henri
Frankfort, *Ancient Egyptian Religion* (New York: Columbia University Press, 1948), 63–64;
Hans Heinrich Schmid, *Wesen und Geschichte der Weisheit: eine Untersuchung zur altorientalischen
Weisheitsliteratur* (BZAW 101; Berlin: A. Töpelmann, 1966), 17–20.

[24] Jan Assmann, "State and Religion in the New Kingdom," in *Religion and Philosophy
in Ancient Egypt* (ed. W.K. Simpson; *YES* 3; New Haven: Yale University Press, 1989),
63–64, addresses the cosmic implications of this concept and the relationship between
king and cosmos: "The creator installed the solar cycle as an institution of cosmic
government, developing Maat and dispelling Isfet, in precisely the same way as he
installed the pharaonic kingship in order to do the same on earth."

The person who actualizes Ma'at through integrity has the potential for prosperity. Assmann outlines the manner in which this can occur in the earthly realm, according to the Egyptian instructions. The public expression of Ma'at involves three basic features: solidarity, reciprocity, and retribution. The solidarity aspect is straightforward, since an individual who communicates well and acts kindly towards others becomes a living embodiment of truth.[25] The second component, reciprocity, demands cooperation in a diverse society. Ma'at does not express a mythical substance that binds humanity together; it functions as a contract encouraging individuals to seek harmony and social cohesion.[26] "Greedy" behavior (*'wn jb*) represents the antithesis of reciprocity, since avarice fosters self-serving acts at the expense of community. Yet Assmann is careful to distinguish his definition from altruism, since the pursuit of Ma'at has a self-interest component. A person should act justly towards others because it is the right thing to do, but also out of a conviction that good deeds lead to future kindness. With regard to the last element, retribution in the Egyptian instructions does not involve a private judgment between an individual and God or an impersonal cosmic force, but rather "einer eminent zivilisatorischen Sozialordnung, einer Ordnung des Aneinander-Denkens und Füreinander-Handelns."[27]

Other scholars have provided similar definitions. Fox claims that Ma'at is not actualized by automatic forces in the universe (a "world order"), but through individual actions: "Ma'at is not an automaton maintaining justice by impersonal processes."[28] In the Egyptian literature, "justice" and "truth" are revealed by the choices of gods, kings, and people. According to Fox, when a king or individual "lives on Ma'at," this expression relates to personal volition and not predetermined cosmic force. He cautions against any effort to define this term through a "grand theological construct of modern design."[29] Citing the work of Miriam Lichtheim, Fox understands Ma'at to be a principle of justice in the public sphere. Honest relationships are the essence of Ma'at: "Far from being a blanket term for virtuous behavior, Maat

---

[25] The virtue of listening is especially important (e.g., chapter 39 of Ptahhotep).
[26] Assmann, *Ma'at: Gerechtigkeit und Unsterblichkeit*, 89–90.
[27] Assmann, *Ma'at: Gerechtigkeit und Unsterblichkeit*, 66.
[28] Fox, "World Order and Ma'at," 41.
[29] Fox, "World Order and Ma'at," 42.

meant specifically veracity and fair dealing."[30] Such an understanding
is confirmed by the Egyptian instructions, which emphasize this justice
concept as a bulwark against the pitfalls of errant speech, greed, and
other corrupt behavioral patterns.

The boldest of Brunner's claims-that the "disappearance" of Ma'at
fundamentally altered Egypt's wisdom tradition-is one of the most
critical issues in the debate over the *Tun-Ergehen-Zusammenhang* and
the nature of Egyptian influence on Israelite sages. Assmann supports
Brunner's thesis and has taken the argument to a more comprehensive
conclusion.[31] According to Assmann, Old and Middle Kingdom texts
(particularly the instructions) reflect a system of causality in which
divine agency does not play a pivotal role. In these earlier texts, the
primacy of Ma'at leads to a system of indirect causation, so that the
"free will" of the deity does not directly shape human events.[32] According to the earlier paradigm, the state plays a role in the maintenance
of a just society. The state functions as *the* vehicle for expressing Ma'at
and therefore operates to protect the oppressed and the needy. Such a
requirement is confirmed by various texts, including Merikare, where
the ruler exists "to raise up the backs of the weak" (136). Yet the ethical foundations of this vision were shattered by theological revolution.
Assmann attempts to substantiate a post-Amarna shift towards "personal
piety."[33] According to the theory, later instructions such as Amenemope
indicate a more uncertain principle, as divine freedom becomes the
main factor in determining human outcomes. With God's will as the
operative force, even the king is placed under a new rubric. Events occur
or do not occur according to this new model. Ma'at no longer serves
as the underlying ethical principle, so that the logic of the *Tun-Ergehen-
Zusammenhang* disappears.[34] According to Assmann, this development

---

[30] Miriam Lichtheim, *Maat in Egyptian Autobiographies and Related Studies* (OBO 120;
Fribourg/Göttingen: Universitätsverlag/Vandenhoeck & Ruprecht, 1992), 37.

[31] Jan Assmann, "Weisheit, Loyalismus, und Frömmigkeit," in *Studien zu altägyptischen
Lebenslehren* (ed. E. Hornung and O. Keel; OBO 28; Fribourg/Göttingen: University
Press/Vandenhoeck & Ruprecht, 1979), 47, reaches the same conclusion as Brunner:
"Wir sind vom Tun-Ergehen-Zusammenhang ausgegangen und sind in diesem Tra-
ditionszusammenhang zu einer Konzeption geführt worden, die Frömmigkeit als ein
Tun, ein Handeln für Gott, bestimmt."

[32] Assmann, "State and Religion in the New Kingdom," 76, provides a chart to
illustrate the two different principles.

[33] For background on the Amarna period, see Jacobus van Dijk, "The Amarna
Period and the Later New Kingdom," in *The Oxford History of Ancient Egypt* (ed. I. Shaw;
Oxford: Oxford University Press, 2000), 272–313.

[34] Assmann, *Ma'at: Gerechtigkeit und Unsterblichkeit*, 254.

marked a "Copernican" change in sapiential literature and the larger culture: "Dieses Weltbild, das 'das Geschehende' in Gottes Hand legt, radikalisiert die Vorstellung von der *mutabilitas mundi*."[35] Like Brunner, Assmann cites Amenemope as the watershed text.

Many scholars have accepted this theory as an interpretive key for evaluating the instructions *and* the influence of Egypt's Wisdom literature throughout the ancient Near East. For example, Steiert has analyzed Egyptian instructions and the biblical book of Proverbs in light of Brunner's argument.[36] According to Steiert, the major change that occurred in Egypt should not be underestimated, since the age of "personal piety" signified a different understanding of reward and punishment.[37] While he does not substantially alter the hypothesis set forth by Brunner and Assmann, Steiert points to its implications for Egyptian-Israelite comparative work. If Ma'at no longer functioned as a key principle in a text like Amenemope, then any attempt to posit an Egyptian-Israelite connection based on this concept is flawed. One should instead examine "personal piety" passages in Proverbs for possible Egyptian influence.[38] Boström argues that the Egyptian departure from Ma'at occurred before any conceivable period of influence on Israelite sages.[39] Finally, Harold Washington's comparative study of Amenemope and Proverbs maintains that the changing economic conditions of the late Ramesside period had made social mobility a more realistic possibility among the lower scribal classes. During this turbulent era, Ma'at had become anachronistic in a text like Amenemope, and prosperity or poverty happened "according to his (God's) will ($n\ mr.f$)" (Amenemope 24.16). Such a belief matched the economic fluidity of the Ramesside era, when Amenemope was written. According to Washington, $n\ mr.f$ reflects an arbitrary framework: "Here the act-consequence relation is severed entirely."[40]

---

[35] Assmann, *Ma'at: Gerechtigkeit und Unsterblichkeit*, 256.

[36] Franz-Josef Steiert, *Die Weisheit Israels: ein Fremdkörper im alten Testament?: eine Untersuchung zum Buch der Sprüche auf dem Hintergrund der ägyptischen Weisheitslehren* (FThSt; Freiburg: Herder, 1990).

[37] Steiert, *Die Weisheit Israels*, 57.

[38] Steiert, *Die Weisheit Israels*, 31.

[39] Lennart Boström, *The God of the Sages: The Portrayal of God in the Book of Proverbs* (CBOTS 29; Stockholm: Almqvist and Wiksell International, 1990), 96.

[40] Harold C. Washington, *Wealth and Poverty in the Instruction of Amenemope and the Hebrew Proverbs* (SBLDS 142; Atlanta: Scholars Press, 1994), 102.

This proposed development, particularly the rejection of any type of act-consequence principle in Amenemope, is highly questionable.[41] While evidence for a heightened religiosity during the New Kingdom seems unassailable, the theory of a "crisis of Wisdom" does not withstand further scrutiny. A basic counter to this school of thought is that Amenemope presents many of the same positions as earlier texts with regard to Maʾat and the reward for virtue. We must reject the supposition that later instructions abandon a mechanistic framework in favor of a belief in unpredictability. Such a development contradicts the very enterprise of didactic literature and is not borne out by the actual texts. Fox explains the basic problem with the thesis:

> While the tone of humility and deep piety in Amenemope and Anii is new, none of the sayings in NK Wisdom that supposedly show the eclipse of Maʿat are unparalleled in earlier Wisdom. It is true that in the NK Wisdom does not assume a simple *Tun-Ergehen-Zusammenhang*, but it never did.[42]

Fox's assessment is confirmed by earlier instructions, which recognize the power of divine agency and a degree of unpredictability in human events. There is a tension in most Egyptian instructions between the advancement of a consistent principle of causality and an acceptance of the unknown. This dialectic is common to the entire corpus of ancient Near Eastern instructions, as the ancient sages attempted to motivate pupils *and* acknowledge the ultimate authority of God. In most instances, the decision to privilege one model (indirect causation) over the other (divine agency) is a matter of situational ethics or simple rhetorical choice as opposed to emergent theological doctrine. What is noteworthy about Egyptian instructions is not a decisive shift towards uncertainty during the New Kingdom, but a sustained effort to maintain some sort of act-consequence nexus in the wake of profound religious and political developments. A careful reading of some of the major texts will verify this complex relationship between divine freedom and a more impersonal principle of justice, and the basic problems with Brunner's thesis. We will also point to the lack of engagement with death and the possibility of an afterlife, a characteristic feature that also marks the biblical book of Proverbs.

---

[41] For a creative reading of this passage, see Hans Goedicke, "The Teaching of Amenemope, Chapter XX. (Amenemope 20, 20–21, 20)," *RdÉ* 46 (1995): 99–106, and the discussion below.

[42] Fox, "World Order and Maʿat," 43.

### 3. *Old and Middle Kingdom Instructions*

#### 3.1 *Instruction of Ptahhotep*

The Instruction of Ptahhotep, one of the classic texts of Egyptian literature, provides an early perspective on Ma'at and causality. Other texts from the Middle Kingdom such as the Instruction of Hardjedef and the Teaching for the Vizier Kagemni offer similar insights, but these are less thorough in their treatment of ethics and morality.[43] Whether Ptahhotep dates as early as the Fifth Dynasty is an open question. Many Egyptologists have argued that the language and grammar are reflective of the Middle Kingdom, even if much of the content echoes the spirit of the Old Kingdom.[44] Ptahhotep is cast as indispensable advice from an aging vizier under the ruler Isesi, and the larger purpose is set forth in the prologue: to transmit the "wisdom (*sḥr.w*) of those who have lived in earlier ages" for the benefit of the vizier's "son" (P 31).[45] This young pupil is to receive instruction for right living and appropriate behavior, from good table manners to the benefits of silence. The opening lines convey urgency, as the vizier must act before the onset of senility precludes the sharing of advice. The moment has arrived for an essential imparting of advice; these maxims *must* be passed on to preserve Ma'at for the coming generation. In the prologue, the speaker declares, "Permit your humble servant to appoint a staff of old age (*mdw jȝw*)" (P 28). If a vizier became demented or otherwise incapacitated, a transitional figure could be appointed, known in these texts as a "staff of old age." This individual guaranteed that the tradition would continue.[46] This scene

---

[43] Kagemni is preserved with Ptahhotep in Pap. Prisse, which dates from the Middle Kingdom. Line numbers for Ptahhotep correspond to the ones assigned by Eugene Dévaud and Zybnek Žába. See Zybnek Žába, *Les Maximes de Ptahhotep* (Prague: Editions de l'Académie Tchécoslovaque des Sciences, 1956).

[44] See Vernus, *Sagesses de l'Égypte pharaonique*, 70–71; Eckhard Eichler, "Zur Datierung und Interpretation der Lehre des Ptahhotep," *ZÄS* 128 (2001): 97–107.

[45] While *sḥr.w* generally denotes "plans" or "thoughts," the translation "wisdom" in Simpson, *The Literature of Ancient Egypt*, 131, is defensible. The connotation in this passage is the passing down of accumulated sayings for the addressee.

[46] Elke Blumenthal, "Ptahhotep und der 'Stab des Alters'," in *Form und Mass: Beiträge zur Literatur, Sprache und Kunst des alten Ägypten: Festschrift für Gerhard Fecht zum 65. Geburtstag am 6. Februar 1987* (ed. J. Osing and G. Dreyer; ÄUAT 12; Wiesbaden: O. Harrassowitz, 1987), 84–97, provides other attestations of this phrase to demonstrate the critical value of a "staff of old age." Also referred to as the "son," this individual basically served as the aging official's substitute, and then the apprentice could transition to the formal vizierate. This person might be the biological child of the ailing figure, his student, or another suitable successor. The descriptions of this process demonstrate a commitment

and literary device frame the main content of Ptahhotep and provide the occasion for the sharing of these maxims. Within this context, the safeguarding of justice is the primary aim: one must "cling" (*nḏr*) to Ma'at (P 151), and favorable results will follow. Such a goal represents the central aim of Ptahhotep: "clinging" to Ma'at provides the best (and only) opportunity for success in life.

The significance of Ma'at is apparent in the opening sections of Ptah-hotep. Chapters 2–4 outline appropriate behavior in a public tribunal, depending on whether one is in the presence of a superior, equal, or subordinate. The beginning of chapter 5 exhorts the one who leads (*sšmy*) to act with fairness. The praise of Ma'at in this maxim represents the ethical core of the instruction:

> Great is Ma'at, the effect is long-lasting,
> It has not been confounded since the time of Osiris.
> The transgressor of laws is punished,
> but it is an oversight in the eyes of the greedy.
> It is baseness which takes away riches,
> and wrongdoing has never brought its venture to port.
> He (the greedy man) might say, "I will acquire for myself."
> He cannot say, "I will acquire because of my effort."
> In the end, Ma'at will endure (P 88–95, translation mine).

In this section, the sapiential author provides a vivid contrast between Ma'at and avarice and cautions against any hope for advancement through corrupt means. Dishonesty may provide ephemeral profit, but the greedy individual (*ꜥwn jb*) cannot achieve (literally "moor") lasting success. One should strive to live in accordance with Ma'at, because failure is the only alternative. This description supports Assmann's understanding of Ma'at as a "connective justice." A righteous person can actualize Ma'at through honesty and fair dealing in the public realm.

In a detailed study of chapters 5 and 19 in Ptahhotep, Gerhard Fecht has posited a dual meaning for several Egyptian terms, indicating a possible allusion to the afterlife.[47] This is particularly true of P 92–93, where Fecht claims that *ḥꜥ.w* can mean either "riches" or "lifetime," and *jtt* can be read "to take" or "to last." According to this proposal, *zp.s* ("its

---

to having knowledgeable figures at all times, who could transmit the necessary advice that prevented chaos (*jzft*) and preserved "justice" (Ma'at).

[47] Gerhard Fecht, *Der Habgierige und die Maat in der Lehre des Ptahhotep (5. und 19. Maxime)* (ADAI.K 1; Glückstadt: J.J. Augustin, 1958).

venture") also represents the verbal form *zpj* ("to remain"). Rather than
"to bring to port, moor," *mnj* can mean "to die." According to Fecht,
these alternatives render a radically different translation: "Die Bosheit
(zwar) währet die Lebenszeit, (doch) nie ist das Vergehen unversehrt
(im Jenseits) gelandet."[48] Similar language can be found in chapter 19,
which offers a stern warning against greedy behavior (*'wn jb*): "A man
lasts when Ma'at is his exactitude...but the greedy man will have no
tomb" (P 312–315, translation mine). This proposal has implications for
the act-consequence presentation in Ptahhotep, especially if the imbal-
ance between evil behavior and unwarranted prosperity can be rectified
in the afterlife.[49] Yet Fecht is judicious in ascribing a fully developed
belief in universal judgment to Ptahhotep, and Assmann doubts the
validity of a double-sense meaning in chapters 5 and 19.[50] Whatever
the force of this unit, the larger instruction consists of prosaic advice
for the earthly sphere, with no sustained interest in the afterlife as a
reward for good behavior. This is not the case with Merikare, where
the author makes a more direct appeal based on the promise of eternal
existence for the ruler (see below).

While Ptahhotep does not promote an infallible *Tun-Ergehen-Zusammenhang*, this instruction offers a largely predictable framework based
on Ma'at *and* the involvement of the deity in the human realm. A few
examples demonstrate the understanding of causality in the various
maxims. Good character brings favorable results, as in chapter 35:

> The property of one man may (pass) to another,
> But the integrity of a gentleman is always beneficial to him,
> And a good character will be his monument (P 492–494).

In chapter 6, God responds in accordance with human conduct: "Do
not stir up fear in people, or God will punish in equal measure (*mjtt*)"
(P 99–100). The use of *mjtt* ("in equal measure" or "accordingly")
implies proportional punishment for the recalcitrant individual, with
God functioning as the retributive agent, the one who "brings back" the

---

[48] Fecht, *Der Habgierige und die Maat*, 27, 33.
[49] Fecht, *Der Habgierige und die Maat*, 28.
[50] Assmann, *Ma'at: Gerechtigkeit und Unsterblichkeit*, 92–97, focuses on the numerous
tomb references in the autobiographical texts. An individual's allegiance to Ma'at
and the material witness of the stone perpetuate a good name. This is confirmed by
P 314 of Ptahhotep and the phrase *jm.t pr* ("testament"). According to Vernus, *Sagesses
de l'Égypte pharaonique*, 126 n. 157, the righteous person can avoid premature death and
pass on his good deeds, his "testament."

deed upon a person "in equal measure." This is similar to the concept
of God "returning" or "repaying" wrongful actions back upon the
perpetrator in the book of Proverbs (e.g., 24:12). The "intervention"
of God here is not an intrusive element, but a logical extension of the
act-consequence relationship.[51] When considering the implications of
this presentation, the prominence of divine agency in one of the earlier
instructions undercuts the scholarly argument for a later shift from a
Ma'at-based framework to a belief in the "free will of God." Both
automatic processes ("the integrity of a gentleman is always beneficial
to him") and divine intervention ("But what God determines comes
to pass") are clearly mentioned in this early instruction. As Lichtheim
explains, "Wisdom and piety were partners in the endeavor to formulate
and teach the right kind of living."[52]

This issue of the deity's role and an act-consequence nexus must be
pursued further, since Ptahhotep contains numerous references to the
divine will and its consequential impact on human affairs. In chapter
8, an abundance of crops is cited as a gift of God (P 162); in chapter
13, the sage claims that the deity rewards officials in a public tribunal
(P 229). Another relevant passage can be found in chapter 10, where
the servant of a wealthy and powerful master receives instructions
about his superior:

> If you should learn that he was once of low estate,
> Do not be disdainful toward him
> Because you have learned about his past.
> Respect him in accordance with what he has made of himself,
> For wealth does not come of its own accord,
> But it is the ordinance of the gods for one whom they favor (P 177–
> 182).

In these examples, human success in the earthly realm derives from
the deity, and this casts doubt on the argument for a pioneering shift
in Amenemope. This hypothesis is also weakened by the division of
humanity into two camps in Ptahhotep: "Great of heart are those
whom God has established, But he who listens to his stomach is his
own worst enemy" (P 247–248). In this maxim (14), the sage counter-
balances "those whom God has established" with the human tendency
towards selfishness and baseness. Such examples demonstrate the pivotal

---

[51] The same point is reaffirmed later in the maxim from Ptahhotep: "But what God determines comes to pass" (*wḏ.t nṯr pw ḫpr.t*) (P 116).

[52] Lichtheim, *Maat in Egyptian Autobiographies*, 100.

role of the divine will in Ptahhotep: God is the guarantor of a system based on social solidarity and the potential for advancement. The effort to distinguish an automatic principle from the role of the deity as a retributive agent is understandable, but this early instruction uses both models as a means of encouraging righteous conduct.

The content of chapter 12 is also pertinent to our discussion of divine agency. In a contrast between the good and bad son, the insolent figure receives a strong rebuke:

> Punish him for all his talk,
> For he who has extended his arm against you is hateful to the gods.
> Surely evil was fated for him from the womb,
> For he whom the gods guide is one who cannot err,
> And he whom they leave stranded is unable to cross the river (P 215–219).[53]

In this section, the author seems to suggest an elect status at birth for certain individuals.[54] Does this signify a belief in predestination? The vocabulary and constructs of systematic theology can be misleading in assessing the content of ancient Near Eastern instructions. Egyptian sages, like their Israelite counterparts, practiced situational ethics and often tailored their advice for maximum effect. A principle or goal of uniformity did not prevent them from making a forceful point about the nature of God, even if it contradicted an earlier maxim. The issue in chapter 12 is a practical one: the rearing of disciplined children and the pitfalls of failure.[55] This is a hyperbolic explanation for why some children have behavioral problems. The insolence of minors would continue to be a popular theme in later instructions (e.g., Prov 10:1); the sages believed that thoughtful attention to child rearing is incumbent upon every parent. In particular, parents must teach their children the art of listening. In a message to parents, the epilogue of Ptahhotep declares, "He who listens is favored of God, But he who is hated of God does not listen" (P 545–546). In this section from chapter 12 and in many other passages, God is cited as the controller of human fate,

---

[53] The third-person verbal suffixes (.sn) clearly refer to "the gods."

[54] The emphasis on God's role at birth is common in ancient instructions. Ben Sira offers a similar claim: "Like clay in the hand of the potter, to be molded as he pleases, so are all in the hand of their Maker, to be given whatever he decides" (33:13).

[55] Unlike most translations, we render P 198 as a command: "Have (jr.k) a son who will make God well-disposed." This text emphasizes the obligatory nature of thoughtful parenting and the passing down of good values.

and both parents and children are to respect the system in place, even if they do not fully understand it. This is a standard motif in Amenemope and also in the Demotic instructions. The refrain in Papyrus Insinger describes the relationship in the following terms: "The fate and the fortune that come, it is the god who sends them."[56]

Yet rhetorical flair about divine power and deterministic language in Ptahhotep are counterbalanced by an appeal to personal initiative. A command in the prologue about the educational process mitigates the more deterministic passages: "Instruct him, for no one is born wise (s3w)" (P 41). This observation implies that self-improvement can be cultivated; attentiveness to wisdom yields positive results; a person who "clings" to Ma'at will reap benefits. Such a pursuit requires diligence: "For no one has ever attained perfection of competence, And there is no craftsman who has acquired (full) mastery" (P 55–56). Much of the subsequent material in the various maxims functions as a self-help manual for bureaucratic functionaries, members of the upper classes, and other interested citizens on how to become wise and successful.

Certain Egyptian terms and motifs illustrate this pursuit of self-improvement, including *jkr*. The basic meaning of *jkr* in Ptahhotep is "skillful" or "virtuous." Although modern translations often associate this term with material prosperity, *jkr* generally describes the "virtue" that *leads* to prosperity.[57] The disputant in chapter 2 is one who is "more skilled than you" (*m jkr r.k*, P 61). In chapter 12, the *z(j) jkr* probably refers to a "virtuous" rather than a "wealthy" individual (P 197). This maxim encourages the good son to emulate his father's "character" (*ḳd*, P 199), not his affluence. Chapter 21 begins with a statement in the subjunctive: "If you would be virtuous (*jr jkr.k*), may you establish your household" (P 325, translation mine).[58] Here and elsewhere in Ptahhotep, an individual's "skill" or "virtue" becomes a prerequisite for

---

[56] Translation of Papyrus Insinger is from Miriam Lichtheim, *Ancient Egyptian Literature, Volume III: The Late Period* (Berkeley: University of California Press, 1980). Hereafter, citations from this series will be abbreviated with "*AEL*." The connection between chapter 12 of Ptahhotep and other instructions is discussed by Aksel Volten, "Der Begriff der Maat in den Ägyptischen Weisheitstexten," in *Les Sagesses du Proche-Orient Ancien: Colloque de Strasbourg 17–19 mai 1962* (Paris: Presses Universitaires de France, 1963), 73–101.

[57] For example, Raymond O. Faulkner, *The Literature of Ancient Egypt* (ed. W.K. Simpson; New Haven: Yale University Press, 1972), generally takes *jkr* to be "wealthy." For a more nuanced translation, see Vernus, *Sagesses de l'Égypte pharaonique*, 72–112.

[58] This is a quotation from the Instruction of Hardjedef. Most translations read *grw.k pr.k* as a continuation of the protasis.

prosperity. In the warning against gossip in chapter 23, "the one who is in front of you" is a person who "can discern what is trustworthy" (P 355). Both this maxim and the advice in chapters 2–4 praise a silent, measured person as the ideal or "skilled" type, who is a *z(j) jkr*. A later chapter (24) confirms the accuracy of this translation:

> If you are a skillful man (*z[ j] jkr*),
> who sits in the council of his lord,
> set your heart on virtue (*bw jkr*).
> Your silence is more beneficial than chatter (P 362–365, translation mine).

In all of these examples, the possessor of *jkr* exhibits prudence and skill, particularly in public settings.[59] According to Ptahhotep, self-discipline (primarily through silence) embodies *jkr*, and this ultimately leads to success.[60]

Several "heart" expressions in Ptahhotep are also relevant to our discussion. The sage(s) responsible for this text utilizes multiple *jb*-compounds.[61] Of particular interest are *šms-jb* and *hrp-jb*. With regard to the first expression, there is a much-debated passage in chapter 11:

> Follow your heart (*šms-jb*) as long as you live,
> Do no more than is required (lit. "said"),
> Do not shorten the time of "follow-the-heart,"
> Trimming its moment offends the *ka* (P 186–189).[62]

The meaning of *šms-jb* here has perplexed commentators. Some examples of the phrase in Egyptian texts clearly reflect a call to seek pleasure; the Jewish sage Qoheleth has a parallel expression about the need to enjoy the period of one's youth ("Follow the inclination of your heart," הלך בדרכי לבך, 11:9).[63] Yet *šms-jb* seems to be a multivalent

---

[59] A similar passage can be found in the epilogue (P 566–567).

[60] We should also note the stelae associated with Deir el-Medina that contain *ȝh jkr* and an individual's name. See Robert Johannes Demaree, *The ȝh jkr n Rʿ Stelae: On Ancestor Worship in Ancient Egypt* (Leiden: Nederlands Instituut voor het Nabije Oosten, 1983).

[61] Alexandre Piankoff, *Le «cœur» dans les Textes égyptiens depuis l'Ancien jusqu'à la Fin du Nouvel Empire* (Paris: Librairie orientaliste Paul Geuthner, 1930), reviews major "heart" expressions in ancient Egyptian literature.

[62] Translation here is from Lichtheim, *AEL*, 1:67.

[63] Nili Shupak, *Where Can Wisdom Be Found? The Sage's Language in the Bible and in Ancient Egyptian Literature* (OBO 130; Fribourg/Göttingen: Universitätsverlag/Vandenhoeck & Ruprecht, 1993), 303. For the reading that this is a call to pleasure, see Jan Assmann, *Death and Salvation in Ancient Egypt* (trans. D. Lorton; Ithaca: Cornell University Press, 2005), 275–76. Piankoff, *Le «cœur» dans les Textes égyptiens*, 86, reads *jb* in this maxim as a reference to the conscience.

expression, and it is unlikely that its usage in Ptahhotep relates to satisfying desire. While some have proposed a hedonistic reading of chapter 11, there are cogent objections. In Ptahhotep and related texts, the heart serves as the seat of the conscience, so that "following" one's heart means engaging in righteous behavior and remaining attentive to daily responsibilities, presumably approved by the deity.[64] There are multiple Egyptian phrases where the heart leads an individual down the proper path.[65] This is the likely sense of the expression in Ptahhotep, which is not a text that counsels the addressee to seek material pleasures in excess. The admonitions in Ptahhotep encourage pragmatism and modest behavior as prerequisites for success. In this case, "following" one's heart involves devotion and honesty in daily activities.

Another difficult *jb*-expression can be found in chapter 2: "If you meet a disputant who is driven of heart (*ḫrp-jb*) and more skillful than you..." (P 60–61, translation mine). In the Obelisk Inscription of Hatshepsut and in Sinuhe, there are similar examples of the heart "driving" a person to appropriate action.[66] Brunner has demonstrated the Egyptian belief in God communicating through an individual's heart, so that the "driving of the heart" implies direct contact with the divine plan and therefore Wisdom.[67] According to Shupak, the heart remains "the residence of divine inspiration in man, the organ that transmits God's will."[68] In Ptahhotep, a person with a receptive heart is able to "hear" God and attain success. There is also an element of personal initiative in this expression: divine guidance must be met with

---

[64] See David Lorton, "The Expression *šms-jb*," *JARCE* 7 (1968): 41–54. Lorton views the "conscience" reading as more consistent with the thrust of Ptahhotep (p. 43). His study provides an impressive range of additional passages in support of this interpretation.

[65] Shupak, *Where Can Wisdom Be Found*, 308.

[66] The Obelisk Inscription of Hatshepsut (Urk. IV, 305): "That my heart led me to make for him Two obelisks of electrum" (*jb.j ḥr ḫrp.j r jr.t n.f tḫnwj m ḏ'm*). See Lichtheim, *AEL*, 2:27. Similarly in Sinuhe: "My feet scurried, and my senses overwhelmed me (*jb.j ḥr ḫrp.j*), with the god who decreed this flight" (B 229). For the primary text, see Roland Koch, *Die Erzählung des Sinuhe* (BAe 17; Brussels: Fondation Égyptologie Reine Elizabeth, 1990). These and other heart expressions are addressed in David Klotz, "The Use of *jb*-Compounds in Ptahhotep," (paper presented at Yale University Near Eastern Languages and Civilizations panel, 5 December 2001).

[67] Hellmut Brunner, *Das hörende Herz: kleine Schriften zur Religions- und Geistesgeschichte Ägyptens* (OBO 80; Fribourg/Göttingen: Universitätsverlag/Vandenhoeck & Ruprecht, 1988), 3–4. This understanding also sheds light on the biblical account of the exodus, where the "hardening" of Pharaoh's heart (חזק את־לב פרעה) relates to the impairment of the Egyptian ruler's cognitive abilities.

[68] Shupak, *Where Can Wisdom Be Found*, 308.

an individual's willingness to acquiesce to God's plan and lead a virtuous existence. The person who is "driven of heart" must be internally motivated. In Ptahhotep, the disciplined son reaches old age because of his heart:

> It is the heart which causes its possessor to be
> One who hears or who does not hear.
> The "life, prosperity, and health" of a man are his heart (P 550–552).

The presumed addressee(s) of Ptahhotep is also pertinent to our discussion. Topics such as table manners at banquets, the handling of wealth, and the responsibilities of public officials seem to indicate an elite group. Yet the various titles and references in the text point to a more diverse audience than is commonly assumed by many commentators. Ptahhotep targets a broader swath of society than Merikare and Amenemhet (the future ruler), Khety (future scribes), and the Loyalist Instruction (an elite leader). According to Vernus, "il est écrit apparemment de manière à concerner un large éventail sociologique, alors que la plupart des sagesses ne visent qu'un groupe particulier de personnes."[69] The addressee might be a "ruler" (sšmj: chapters 5, 16, 17), a person of good birth (z³-z[j]): chapters 28, 34), a "powerful" or "wealthy" individual (wsr: chapter 25), a "weak" or "poor" individual (ḫz: chapter 10), or someone in an inferior position (chapters 8, 15, 24, 26).[70] Nearly all of the maxims in Ptahhotep focus on hierarchical relationships and the complex dynamics between persons of unequal status. Much of the senior sage's advice describes how a more junior official can attain success. If an individual learns good comportment before his master, he will receive sustenance (chapter 27). Social mobility remains a possibility (chapter 10), and a person should not be boastful once he has wealth (chapter 30). Like most ancient Near Eastern instructions, Ptahhotep is conservative in orientation. The author affirms the status quo, does not advocate the emendation of existing social structures, and offers a generally optimistic assessment of human potential. This instruction emphasizes the possibility for advancement through the exhibition of virtue. As with the biblical book of Proverbs, a person who controls his

---

[69] Pascal Vernus, "Le discours politique de l'*Enseignement de Ptahhotep*," in *Literatur und Politik im pharaonischen und ptolemäischen Ägypten* (ed. J. Assmann and E. Blumenthal; Paris: Institut Français D'Archéologie Orientale, 1999), 143.

[70] Vernus, "Le discours politique," 143–47.

selfish instincts and adopts a measured, honest approach will succeed: "In the long run, it is Ma'at which endures."

### 3.2 *Teaching for Merikare*

With its promise of eternal existence and guarantee of an act-consequence relationship, the Teaching for Prince Merikare also merits attention. Merikare is a didactic text that should be classified as a "royal instruction" or "testament."[71] Whereas Ptahhotep was addressed to individuals with varying degrees of social status, the advice in this text comes from a king of the Herakleopolitan line to his son and successor Merikare. The backdrop of the First Intermediate period reflects unsettled conditions, which we do not find in Ptahhotep.[72] As Tobin explains, "There is in this text little of the high optimism of the Old Kingdom, and there is a strong stress on the actual sense of responsibility of the monarch as opposed to his privileges."[73] The father (Khety) is a pragmatist who warns his son about the responsibilities and dangers of leading. A ruler must monitor dissent, eliminate seditious elements, fortify his borders, and tend to the cultic needs of the community. Above all, the king must "Shepherd the people, the cattle of God, For it is for their sake that He created heaven and earth" (131).[74]

---

[71] Merikare is not formally a *sbȝy.t*, since it is addressed to the future ruler. See Lichtheim, "Didactic Literature," 247.

[72] Many scholars believe Merikare to be a product of the Tenth Dynasty period it describes, since the king is warned about political instability. Other interpreters conclude that this is a pseudonymous work with a later date. The Twelfth Dynasty is the usual suggestion. Vernus, *Sagesses de l'Égypte pharaonique*, 135–37, views the Tenth Dynasty to be the most likely possibility, since there are precise historical references in the text. Some commentators argue that this didactic work was written by an official within the court of Merikare as a propaganda piece. For a review of other options, see Joachim-Friedrich Quack, *Studien zur Lehre für Merikare* (GOF 23; Wiesbaden: O. Harrassowitz, 1992), 114–36, who himself posits a later date.

[73] Vincent A. Tobin, introduction to "The Teaching for King Merikare," in *The Literature of Ancient Egypt* (ed. W.K. Simpson; 3d ed. New Haven: Yale University Press), 152–53. The historical context of the First Intermediate period and the tenuous political dynamics of the Herakleopolitan kingship are major factors in the advice, even if the text derives from a later period.

[74] The allusion to the people as the "cattle of god" is noteworthy, particularly in an instructional text for the king. In pWestcar 8,17, the people are called a "noble flock" (*tȝ ʿw.t šps.t*). For the primary text, Aylward M. Blackman, *The Story of King Cheops and the Magicians Transcribed from Papyrus Westcar (Berlin Papyrus 3033)* (ed. W.V. Davies; Reading: J.V. Books, 1988). References to a person created in the "image" of God are usually reserved for the king. See Hornung, *Conceptions of God*, 138.

A connection between deed and recompense is apparent in Merikare, and the author of these colorful exhortations retains an essential place for Ma'at. Several passages cite the benefits of Ma'at, including an extended section that offers a clear principle of causality:

> Speak Ma'at within your palace,
> So that the officials who are over the land may respect you,
> For an upright heart is becoming to a lord;
> It is the front of a house which creates respect for the back.
>
> Observe Ma'at, that you may endure long upon the earth.
> Console him who weeps, and oppress not the widow.
> Do not expel a man from the property of his father,
> And do not demote the officials from their positions (45–48).

The advice in this unit is directed to the future ruler alone, although the understanding of Ma'at coheres with Ptahhotep and many of the autobiographical texts. As Lichtheim explains, the sense of "doing" Ma'at remains the same in Merikare: "Truth telling, honest administrators carrying out the laws; justice and benevolence for all."[75] Moreover, this passage highlights an intrinsic link between the actualization of Ma'at and lengthy years: *jr m3'.t w3ḥ.k tp t3* ("Observe Ma'at, *that* you may endure long upon the earth"). We have already cited a similar principle in 121–123, where "every deed committed has its consequence." Such passages do not guarantee a flawless system of causality, but these statements reveal a clear belief in the dangers of destructive behavior and the lasting benefits of Ma'at.

Merikare is most famous for the unambiguous reference to the afterlife as a reward for earthly behavior. While the prospect of present success is one type of incentive (i.e., the connection between Ma'at and lengthy years), the ruler is also promised eternal life for his beneficence and humility:

> Be not confident in length of years,
> For they (the gods) regard a lifetime as but an hour.
> A man will survive after his death,
> His deeds will be set beside him as (his) reward,
> And existence in the beyond is for eternity.
> A fool is he who does what offends them;
> But as for him who reaches them having done no wrong,

---

[75] Lichtheim, *Maat in Egyptian Biographies*, 42.

He will exist there like a god,
Walking proudly like the Lords of eternity (54–57).

This passage exceeds any other we have examined in that it sets forth an otherworldly horizon for the fulfillment of the *Tun-Ergehen-Zusammenhang*. The "deeds" (*zp.w*) of the ruler probably refer to his "misdeeds" (*pace* Tobin), which are literally placed "at his side in piles." As with chapter 5 of Ptahhotep, we find a word play with *ḥʿ.w*, since this term can be translated either as "piles" or "lifetime." This usage of "piles" implies an actual weighing, which brings to mind the depiction found in Spell 125 in the Book of the Dead.

The clear sense of this passage is that the ruler's actions are reviewed to determine if his character merits continued existence.[76] Yet the admonition not to trust in "length of years" is puzzling. Even if Merikare seeks to guarantee ultimate recompense in the hereafter, why would the text undercut the linkage of Maʾat with earthly reward that is made elsewhere in the text? The most likely explanation for these differing assertions is the attempt to create a consistent principle. During periods of competing alliances and shifting territorial claims (like the First Intermediate period), unscrupulous leaders often thrived and had lengthy reigns through ruthless, self-serving policies. As an instructional text, Merikare states that an evil king cannot act with impunity and that moral responsibility (i.e., "doing" Maʾat) is incumbent upon those who hold power. The final judgment scene does not mitigate the primary focus on earthly matters; it merely insures a consistent principle. As McKane explains, "The point of view here is not so much that all injustices will be redressed at death as that there is a relationship between worth and status which nothing can abrogate."[77]

A critical question for our discussion is the possible transfer of this judgment scene to other individuals, or whether this description only applies to the king. While there are numerous parallels between Merikare and other instructions (particularly the praise of Maʾat), this passage concerning eternal life relates to the royal figure alone. The prevailing view during this period was that the average individual did not have the potential to join the realm of the gods in the manner of the ruler, since the king and not the commoner could arrange for proper

---

[76] Assmann, *Death and Salvation*, 74, describes the scene as a life-film that encapsulates the ruler's character and passes before the "knowing" judge's eyes in an hour.
[77] McKane, *Proverbs*, 73.

burial rituals. In the Pyramid Texts of the Old Kingdom, passage is envisioned for the king alone. In Merikare, the mortality of the common person, regardless of whether he is righteous or evil, is explicitly stated: "The man who walked in accordance with Ma'at shall depart, Just as he whose life was pleasure filled will die" (42).[78] It is likely that later readers of Merikare took an expansive view and applied the scene to persons other than the king.[79] Merikare represents an earlier stage than the Coffin Texts (Middle Kingdom) and the Book of the Dead (New Kingdom) in terms of the scope of judgment. In fact, this is one of the earliest descriptions of this type in any text. Regardless of the extent of the application, this passage is somewhat exceptional for an Egyptian Wisdom text in its explicit emphasis on the afterlife.

## 4. New Kingdom Instructions

### 4.1 Instruction of Amenemope

Amenemope is a New Kingdom instruction about which substantial claims have been made. Our discussion has already pointed to the fact that an influential school of thought views Amenemope as a watershed text, a turning point in the wisdom tradition of ancient Egypt, and a reflection of religious and social changes in the larger culture. With regard to its background, this is a *sbȝy.t* from the late Ramesside period.[80] While the only complete copy, Papyrus BM 10,474, can be assigned to the Twenty Fifth or Twenty Sixth Dynasty, most scholars place the original composition at an earlier date. Vernus argues for a setting during the Twentieth Dynasty (twelfth-century B.C.E.), or perhaps the Twenty First.[81] The sage's name (*imn-m-ipt*) is common for this period and well attested in other sources.[82] Agricultural terms and titles in the introduction provide further evidence for this date.[83] The

---

[78] Such a belief resembles many statements on death in Qoheleth (e.g., 2:15).

[79] See Assmann, *Death and Salvation*, 74–77, 383–84, for how the concept was expanded to include others during the Middle Kingdom and beyond.

[80] For the primary text, see Hans O. Lange, *Das Weisheitbuch des Amenemope aus dem Papyrus 10,474 des British Museum herausgeben und erklärt* (Copenhagen: Andr. Fred Høst, 1925).

[81] Vernus, *Sagesses de l'Égypte pharaonique*, 300.

[82] Washington, *Wealth and Poverty*, 14–16, notes the multiple attestations of this name, particularly at Deir el-Medinah.

[83] Vernus, *Sagesses de l'Égypte pharaonique*, 328 n. 13. For a comprehensive review of proposals, see Washington, *Wealth and Poverty*, 11–24.

use of syllabic orthography and numerous Semitic loanwords serve as additional markers, since these were often features of texts from this general period.[84]

The loanwords are often highlighted in scholarly discussions because of the proposed link between Amenemope and the biblical book of Proverbs, particularly Prov 22:17–24:22. While the connection between these two texts seems indisputable, efforts to assert the dependence of Amenemope on the book of Proverbs or a Canaanite source are thoroughly unconvincing.[85] The mere presence of loanwords in no way proves such an argument, since many New Kingdom and Third Intermediate period texts have Semitic roots. In her critical edition of Amenemope, Irene Grumach proposes that both the Egyptian instruction and the book of Proverbs rely on an Egyptian *Vorlage* (referred to in her discussion as "die alte Lehre").[86] Diethard Römheld has vigorously opposed Grumach's thesis about the existence of this older source.[87] The multiple indicators in Proverbs suggest a direct relationship between the two texts, particularly for Prov 22:17–23:11. Israelite sages seem to have adapted material from Amenemope and other Egyptian instructions, tailoring the advice to suit the specific context of Syria-Palestine.[88] In some instances, the advice in Proverbs involves a direct recitation of an Egyptian saying. For present purposes, it is important to note that the details in Amenemope are consistent with an inner-Egyptian tradition of sapiential literature and do not depend on a discourse in Israel that had yet to begin.[89]

---

[84] Washington, *Wealth and Poverty*, 17 n. 21.

[85] A Canaanite *Vorlage* was suggested by W.O.E. Oesterly, "The Teaching of Amen-em-ope and the Old Testament," *ZAW* 45 (1927): 9–24. See the convincing refutation by Ronald J. Williams, "The Alleged Semitic Original of the *Wisdom of Amenemope*," *JEA* 47 (1961): 100–106.

[86] Irene Grumach, *Untersuchungen zur Lebenslehre des Amenope* (MÄSt 23; Munich: Deutscher Kunstverlag, 1972).

[87] Diethard Römheld, *Wege der Weisheit: die Lehren Amenemopes und Proverbien 22,17–24,22* (BZAW 184; Berlin: de Gruyter, 1989), argues for the direct dependence of Proverbs 22:17–23:11 on Amenemope, based on terminological and thematic affinities. The next section of Proverbs (23:12–28) lacks the same close connection to Amenemope. Römheld suggests a different Egyptian *Vorlage* for much of this material, tracing these sayings to a lost text of school miscellanies.

[88] Michael V. Fox, "Two Decades of Research in Egyptian Wisdom Literature," *ZÄS* 107 (1980), 126.

[89] For a recent review of this connection between Amenemope and this section of Proverbs, see Nili Shupak, "The Instruction of Amenemope and Proverbs 22:17–24:22 from the Perspective of Contemporary Research," in *Seeking Out the Wisdom of the Ancients: Essays Offered to Honor Michael V. Fox on the Occasion of His Sixty-Fifth Birthday*

We have discussed the claim that Amenemope represents a shift towards "personal piety" and resignation and away from a consistent framework for retribution (based on Ma'at). In certain respects, this development should not be denied. Amenemope does describe the divine-human relationship in more intimate and detailed terms than previous instructions, and this probably justifies the "piety" label.[90] For example, the conclusion to chapter 7 contains a prayer to the sun deity for health and protection; the inclusion of an efficacious prayer at the end of a maxim is not a feature of Ptahhotep.[91] The discussion of temple practices also reveals a clear interest in religious activities (e.g., 5.20–6.12). Moreover, the text contains numerous references, both direct and indirect, to individual deities, including several key allusions to Thoth.[92] The inclusion of religious language might have functioned in part as a strategic nod to local cultic practices and belief systems in order to popularize this egalitarian instruction.[93]

While a survey of New Kingdom religious developments is well beyond the scope of this discussion, it is productive to consider whether some of the "pietistic" features in Amenemope have an impact on the act-consequence understanding found in this text. An examination of several passages demonstrates that the inclusion of more overtly religious language did not lead to a major shift in terms of a predictable framework for causality, an acknowledgment of divine freedom, and a basic adherence to Egypt's longstanding wisdom tradition. Put simply, Amenemope is not a maverick instruction. The expectations in the prologue ("the guide for well-being," *mtrw n wḏꜣ*, 1.2) and at the end of the instruction ("he will find himself worthy of being a courtier," *gm.f sw m ꜣꜣw smr*, 27.17) demonstrate a correspondence with earlier texts. Moreover, as subsequent analysis will indicate, the passages that supposedly indicate a transformed ethical-theological landscape are not

---

(Winona Lake, Ind.: Eisenbrauns, 2005), 203–20. Shupak argues for a direct relationship between the two texts.

[90] There are examples of a heightened religiosity in Amenemope. Grumach, *Untersuchungen*, 111–12, argues for the reliance of Amenemope on the prayer to Thoth in Pap. Sallier I, 8, 2–7.

[91] See Amenemope 10.12–15. Grumach, *Untersuchungen*, 68–69, notes the contrast between this section of Amenemope and the praise of Ma'at in chapter 5 of Ptahhotep (P 84–98). The inclusion of the prayer indicates a shift from earlier methods of critiquing immorality and greed: "Das Kapitel schließt also wieder mit einer religiösen Note, der auch Schicksals- und Maatgedanke unterstellt sind."

[92] See Vergote, "La Notion de Dieu," 176–79.

[93] McKane, *Proverbs*, 106.

as consequential as some scholars have argued. Ma'at is not replaced in this text by a capricious deity, *p³ nṯr*. Earlier instructions had also recognized "the will of God" as an active force, working in some sort of coordinated relationship with Ma'at. A framework marked by a correlation between virtue and success is characteristic of both early and late instructions, including Amenemope. While Amenemope does not guarantee a completely reliable *Tun-Ergehen-Zusammenhang*, we have yet to find a perfectly consistent framework in any instruction. The deity always plays a role and can alter the seemingly predictable chain of earthly events.

As with earlier instructions, pragmatism and mutual solidarity are important goals in this text. The sage advocates measured speech, the avoidance of greed, and humility before God. Two major topics are used to illustrate these pursuits: a colorful commentary on "the hot-headed man" (*p³ šmm*) and a polemic against corruption.[94] With regard to the "hot-head," Amenemope highlights the dangers of vile speech throughout the instruction (chapters 2, 3, 4, 8, 9, 10, 12, 22). Because of the volatility of this figure, the young charge is told not to fraternize with him:

> For a storm come forth like fire in hay is
> The hot-headed man in his appointed time.
> May you be restrained before him;
> Leave him to himself,
> And God will know how to answer him (5.14–17).[95]

The same motif appears in earlier Wisdom texts: Ptahhotep describes the one who spreads slander as "the hot-bellied one" (*t³ ḥ.t*, P 352), and this type is to be avoided. The word *šmm* occurs in other New Kingdom texts, usually with the article *p³* and/or a possessive pronoun. In Amenemope, the use of the term indicates more than merely a loquacious or impolitic person (although these are critical shortcomings in Egyptian instructions).[96] The hot-head is a lunatic who has lost self-control and is not to be trusted.

---

[94] The translation "hot-headed man" is quite appropriate, since the determinative for *šmm* has a brazier with a flame coming out of it and a bound enemy determinative, indicating its strongly demonic character.

[95] The sense of "answer" in this maxim could be to "take care of" rather than "to punish."

[96] Shupak, *Where Can Wisdom Be Found*, 130, gives a list of New Kingdom citations for this term.

The most famous illustration of the *šmm* in Amenemope is the "parable of the two trees" (chapter 4), where the "truly temperate man" (*grw mȝ*ᶜ) is set in opposition to this "hot-headed" person (6.1–12). The negative type is likened to a lifeless tree in an enclosed area:

> In a moment is its loss of foliage.
> It reaches its end in the carpentry shop;
> It is floated away far from its place,
> Or fire is its funeral pyre (6.3–6).[97]

The *grw mȝ*ᶜ, on the other hand, enjoys pleasant growth: "Its fruit is something sweet, its shade is pleasant, And it reaches its end in a grove" (6.11–12).[98] The parable in Amenemope and the other New Kingdom occurrences of *grw mȝ*ᶜ frequently involve a cultic setting. The same contrast (between the *grw mȝ*ᶜ and the *šmm*) occurs in Pap. Sallier in a famous hymn to Thoth.[99] The thirst of the *grw mȝ*ᶜ is quenched by the god, and this represents the attainment of Wisdom. In addition to these cultic settings, the larger motif of the "silent" figure (*gr*) is popular throughout the Egyptian instructions.[100] Such an individual is one who knows the benefits of measured behavior and accepts the circumstances of his life. According to Vernus, "Le vrai silenceaux, c'est celui qui accepte l'ordre établi et la place que cet ordre lui assigne ce bas monde."[101]

Along with the parable of the two trees, a similar message can be found in chapter 7 of Amenemope: "The boat of the covetous is

---

[97] The religious connotations of this parable are noteworthy, from the initial mention of the temple (*ḥw.t-nṯr*) to the reliance on the Thoth prayer (preserved in Pap. Sallier). Grumach, *Untersuchungen*, 45, argues that this chapter is "eine Art Sammelbegriff für das religiöse Leben...für das Gottesverhältnis."

[98] For alternative translations of this difficult maxim, see Georges Posener, "Le chapitre IV d'Aménémopé," *ŻÄS* 99 (1973): 129–35.

[99] Shupak, *Where Can Wisdom Be Found*, 166–67, demonstrates that the New Kingdom occurrences of *grw mȝ*ᶜ frequently have a religious/cultic connotation. Yet even if the context of chapter 4 in Amenemope is cultic, the contrast between the two figures also applies to other circumstances. Both *grw mȝ*ᶜ and *šmm* have a range of semantic flexibility in Egyptian literature. This broader interpretation is supported by the citation in chapter 7 of Amenemope (10.10–11). The contrast between the *grw mȝ*ᶜ and the greedy individual in this latter passage extends beyond cultic matters, since the *ᶜwn jb* is a conniving figure in any number of situations (see below).

[100] Chapter 24 of Ptahhotep (P 365) and Anii 4.1 are two of the many passages affirming the efficacy of silence. Shupak, *Where Can Wisdom Be Found*, 165, argues that "This human type is the embodiment of all the qualities and traits that are sought by the sage on the social level as well as in the sphere of religion and faith."

[101] Vernus, *Sagesses de l'Égypte pharaonique*, 305.

abandoned (in) the mud, While the skiff of the truly temperate man (sails on)" (10.10–11). A reliable principle of causality is suggested by these lines, and this saying undercuts the argument for the dissolution of this relationship in Amenemope. In this nautical saying, the *grw m$^3$$^c$* is contrasted with a greedy figure (*$^c$wnwtj*), who represents the antithesis of Ma$^3$at in previous texts (e.g., P 298–315 of Ptahhotep).[102] The understanding of proper justice in Amenemope 10.10–11 resembles chapter 5 of Ptahhotep in both content and choice of metaphor ("It is baseness which takes away riches, and wrongdoing has never brought its venture to port.").

With regard to the setting for this instruction, the maxims of Amenemope target a more diverse audience than many of the earlier instructions.[103] According to Vernus, this text presents a set of concerns dominated by "les intérêts et les préoccupations propres à cette petite bourgeoisie de bureaucrates et d'administrateurs subalternes du Nouvel Empire finissant."[104] Although the job description in the prologue is probably embellished, it is noteworthy that the putative author is "The superintendent of produce, who fixes the grain measure, Who sets the grain tax amount for his lord" (1.15–16). This introductory section also describes a host of other scribal functions. As Washington argues, these administrative responsibilities and the sustained polemic against corruption suggest a wide-ranging audience, "the vast sub-elite of the scribal class."[105] During the period in which Amenemope was written, grain shortages, unfair revenue practices (particularly in the redistribution of food supplies), and frequent robberies created a climate of widespread corruption. Amenemope, with its detailed rebuke of dishonest gain, reflects the topsy-turvy circumstances of the late Ramesside era.[106]

As a result of this *Sitz im Leben*, fraudulent behavior receives a great deal of attention in the various maxims. Corrupt practices are repeatedly condemned, often in the service of larger claims about justice. The sage scorns the person who would steal from a crippled man,

---

[102] We have discussed the reference to the greedy having no tomb. Note also Spell 125 of the Book of the Dead, where the deceased declares the he has not been covetous (*jrj $^c$wn jb*). See Shupak, *Where Can Wisdom Be Found*, 107.

[103] The Instruction of Anii also seems tailored to a broader array of officials.

[104] Vernus, *Sagesses de l'Égypte pharaonique*, 304.

[105] Washington, *Wealth and Poverty*, 51.

[106] Washington, *Wealth and Poverty*, 52–83, provides a selection of passages from this period that document corrupt practices. The wealth of evidence from Deir el-Medinah is particularly convincing.

strike an elder, or engage in covetous actions (e.g., 4.4–7). According to Amenemope, the greedy impulse is a violent one that leads a person to act with malice. This theme recurs throughout the text, with chapter 6 offering the longest commentary on theft and corruption. Among the examples cited are tampering with boundary markers and seizing arable land. Both of these offenses carry serious consequences and become paradigmatic for dishonest behavior:

> Do not be covetous (*skn*) for a single cubit of land,
> Nor encroach upon the boundaries of a widow.
> One who transgresses the furrow shortens a lifetime,
> One who seizes (*ꜥg*) it for fields
> And acquires by deceptive attestations,
> Will be lassoed by the might of the Moon (7.14–19).[107]

The "the might of the Moon" refers to Thoth, who watches over all measurements and "lassoes" anyone engaging in deceitful transactions. A correlation between deed and recompense is understood here, since corrupt individuals are held accountable by Thoth. The fate of this crooked person is spelled out later in chapter 6: his own granaries will be plundered (8.6), and his possessions will pass to someone other than his children (8.8).[108] Such an unfortunate turn of events can be avoided through the exercise of restraint. In chapter 5, the sage commands, "Do not take by violence (*ꜥg*) the shares of the temple, Do not be grasping, and you will find abundance" (6.14–15).[109]

Since the greedy impulse is one of the two main themes in this text, Amenemope warns repeatedly against lusting after money. The unbridled pursuit of luxury items is specifically condemned. For example, chapter 16: "What good is one cloaked in fine linen, When he cheats before God?" (18.10–11). A citation from the Mentuhotep stela, which appears at the end of chapter 6, is perhaps the most famous passage in the entire instruction:

---

[107] Egyptian *skn/snk* appears several times in Amenemope (also 14.5; 18.8). According to Shupak, *Where Can Wisdom Be Found*, 109, it means "gluttony" or "avidity," where the object of lust is inanimate. In Amenemope, coveted goods include property and luxury items such as copper (18.8).

[108] A possible inheritance had to be examined by a local official before passing on to the children. If it was found to be fraudulent, property or possessions could be seized.

[109] The term *ꜥg* occurs in several passages criticizing theft (7.17; 18.12; 18.15). Since it is in synonymous parallelism with *ꜣfꜥy* (*ꜣfꜥ*), we can assume that violent appropriation motivated by greed is at issue here.

> Better, then, is poverty in the hand of God
> Than riches in the storehouse;
> Better is bread when the mind is at ease
> Than riches with anxiety (9.5–8).[110]

These admonitions are often followed by a command to be content with one's portion: "Do not exert yourself to seek out excess, your own property is good enough for you" (9.14–15).[111] The assertion that this saying represents an abandonment of Maʾat in exchange for a belief in "arbitrary divine forces regardless of one's good or bad character" cannot be sustained.[112] The point rather is to *affirm* divine justice by promising sustenance for those who seek only what they require and do not use dishonest means to enhance their personal holdings. According to Amenemope, the one who does not strain the limits of his blessings will enjoy self-sufficiency. In chapter 6, the sage declares, "So plough the fields, and you will find whatever you need" (8.17).

In conjunction with the warnings against greed, there is a special concern for the poor in Amenemope. Chapter 13 encourages debt forgiveness with a needy man, and this will lead a righteous creditor to a "path of life" (16.5–8). Perhaps the most revealing statement on this topic occurs in chapter 28: "God loves him who cares for the poor, More than him who respects the wealthy" (26.13–14). As Washington effectively demonstrates, such advocacy is characteristic of other texts from the late Ramesside period.[113] Yet even if this is an admirable and somewhat novel feature of New Kingdom instructions, we cannot glean a liberationist perspective from the content of Amenemope. As multiple passages indicate, this is not a text that advocates class upheaval. Chapter 12 enjoins a servant to respect his master's property (15.9–12); in chapter 27, the pupil is told to be respectful towards an elder (25.21–26.1). Moreover, self-interest plays a role in the call

---

[110] Also 16.11–24. Shupak, *Where Can Wisdom Be Found*, 328–29, notes a pattern in Amenemope, where a famous saying from another text is cited at the end of a maxim without introduction or comment.

[111] This is the alternative translation in Simpson, *The Literature of Ancient Egypt*, 230 n. 26. The Egyptian reads *wḏꜣ n.k ḫrwt.k*. Simpson's primary translation reads, "And your allotment will prosper for you."

[112] Washington, *Wealth and Poverty*, 102, who relies upon the argument of Hellmut Brunner, "Die religiöse Wertung der Armut im alten Ägypten," *Saeculum* 12 (1961), 326.

[113] Washington, *Wealth and Poverty*, 104–7, citing texts of supplications to Amun, who guarded the impoverished classes.

for benevolence. A passage from the Instruction of Anii (Nineteenth Dynasty) offers an illustration:

> As to him who was rich last year,
> He is a vagabond this year;
> Don't be greedy to fill your belly,
> You don't know your end at all.
> Should you come into want,
> Another may do good to you (9.6–8).[114]

According to the content of both Anii and Amenemope, social cohesion will bring long-term benefits to the virtuous individual. Philanthropic acts are beneficial, since the recipient of a kind act might be in a position of power at a future point. In Amenemope, the understanding of relationship and exchange among human beings is often expressed negatively, by describing the cancerous effects of corruption and how it disrupts the justice that should characterize society.

Throughout the maxims of Amenemope, public acts are the primary focus. A person must be honest in his outward, or "official" behavior. If an underling cheats his master, that servant will develop a poor reputation and become permanently unemployed (chapter 12). Only the individual of integrity can prosper. The root $ \underline{d}ȝ $ is significant in this context, since it describes dishonesty in a juridical sense. For New Kingdom texts like Amenemope, it indicates deliberate deception involving one of the following: (1) property theft (e.g., 7.18; 14.9); (2) forgery of accounts (e.g., 16.4); (3) perjury through false oaths (e.g., 7.18; 14.9; 16.1; 20.9).[115] We have discussed the reference to the "deceptive attestations" (ʿnḫ.yw n ḏȝ, 7.18), which are witnessed by Thoth. This is a highly serious offense in Amenemope, and Shupak points out that false speaking is the only act deemed to be "an abomination of God" (13.15–16).[116] The positive figure (grw mȝ ʿ), however, receives a reward: he will be "safe from fear" (10.15). In these passages involving pecuniary matters, there is an assumed correlation between how a person acts and how things will proceed for him. From the perspective of Egyptian and then Israelite sages, prudence and honesty generally bring favorable results.

---

[114] Lichtheim, *AEL*, 2:142.

[115] Shupak, *Where Can Wisdom Be Found*, 94.

[116] Shupak, *Where Can Wisdom Be Found*, 94 n. 53. Significantly, *mt.t* ʿ*d* ("lying word") occurs in antithetic parallelism with *mȝ*ʿ*.t* in Papyrus Insinger (24.17; 32.15). In the biblical book of Proverbs, we have an equivalent term with כזב (see Prov 23:1–3).

The scholarly argument for a shift in the tradition hinges on a few passages in Amenemope. The first is in chapter 21: "Indeed, you cannot know the plans of God; You cannot perceive tomorrow" (22.5–6). For many scholars, such a statement is decisive evidence of a break from tradition, from a belief in predictability to a pietistic, resigned worldview.[117] Yet we have addressed the multiple problems with this thesis. Even if the statement in chapter 21 involves an admission of imperceptibility, such language has multiple antecedents in Egyptian Wisdom literature. In the Teaching for the Vizier Kagemni (preserved with Ptahhotep in Pap. Prisse), the author states, "One does not know what will happen nor what God does when he punishes" (II, 2). A similar saying appears in Ptahhotep: "No one knows what will come to pass when he considers tomorrow" (P 343).[118] The appearance of such language in older instructions demonstrates an early acknowledgement of the unknown in Egypt's wisdom tradition, rather than a later development based on personal piety. The "plans of God" often confound human efforts to understand them, and this is frequently a source of bewilderment and frustration for ancient scribes and sages.

Chapter 20 has generated the most heated arguments about causality in Amenemope. Debate centers on the meaning of lines 21.5–6, with most discussions working from Lichtheim's translation (or a similar one): "Ma'at is a great gift of God, He gives it to whom he wishes." Several scholars follow Brunner in claiming that these lines indicate belief in an arbitrary deity and a break from earlier understandings of causality.[119] As Goedicke argues, however, it is "a priori baffling" that an instruction whose fundamental goal is proper conduct would undermine Ma'at. In addition, "It should be even more perplexing to have such irreverent thoughts in the context of a discourse on proper conduct during judicial proceedings."[120] Goedicke proposes a different reading of the Egyptian phrase *jr m3ꜥ f3 ꜥ3 n nṯr / dj.f sw n mr.f*. Since it is in an indirect genitive construction, the *nṯr* in 21.6 cannot be the

---

[117] Brunner, "Der freie Wille Gottes," 110–11, explains the implications of these lines in Amenemope. He argues that Amenemope signifies a transformation from a "utilitarische Standesethik" to a religious perspective. Brunner further claims, "Auch die Maat, die das Fundament der älteren Weisheit ausmacht, gehört einem religiösen Weltbild an." Cf. Assmann, "State and Religion in the New Kingdom," 78; Steiert, *Die Weisheit Israels*, 33.

[118] Fox, "World Order and Ma'at," 41, cites these two passages to make the same basic point.

[119] See, for example, Grumach, *Untersuchungen*, 137–38.

[120] Goedicke, "The Teaching of Amenemope, Chapter XX," 100.

subject of *dj.f* without an accompanying relative form. He understands *m³ʿ* to be a misspelling of *m³ʿtj* ("righteous, just one," based on 20.22) and takes *f³* as a participle.[121] Moreover, the phrase *n mr.f* should be translated "voluntarily."[122] Simpson adopts these changes in his recent translation of Amenemope: "As for the just man who bears the great- ness of God, He will render himself as he wishes."[123] If this reading is correct, the subject matter relates entirely to judicial procedures for questioning and how the virtuous man will conduct himself. The assumption of a pioneering theological shift in chapter 20 would then rest on an inaccurate translation. Even if Goedicke's translation is suspect, an overarching theological proposition (and a "sea-change" from the earlier understanding) cannot necessarily be inferred from the judicial language in these verses, as Lichtheim has explained.[124]

## 5. *Conclusions*

Based on our analysis of the act-consequence relationship in Egyptian Wisdom literature, several conclusions can be made. First, Brunner's original hypothesis must be rejected for a more nuanced perspective. The shaping of a predictable social realm is a persistent goal in the instructions, including Amenemope. Although pietistic language became a more integral component of sapiential discourse during the New King- dom, this development did not fundamentally alter the larger purpose of Egypt's instructional literature. Throughout the centuries, various sages sought to present a logical framework in which the virtuous life was rewarded and the unlawful person received appropriate punishment. As astute observers of behavioral dynamics and social realities, these authors recognized that a mechanistic framework for causality does not exist. They would have agreed with Gerhard von Rad's statement on divine incalculability: "between the putting into practice of the most

---

[121] A weakness in Goedicke's argument here is that there is no person determinative for his *m³ʿtj* reading.

[122] Goedicke, "The Teaching of Amenemope, Chapter XX," 102. He explains the translation "voluntarily" as antithetic to extracting the truth through "beating" (*knkn*) in 21.8.

[123] Simpson, *The Literature of Ancient Egypt*, 238.

[124] Lichtheim's translation is a more accurate rendering of the Egyptian. This is not a major theological claim, however, but a statement on public testimony. Lichtheim, *Maat in Egyptian Autobiographies*, 100, argues, "Thus the Maat saying need be no more than the observation that not everyone is willing or able to judge fairly and act honestly."

reliable wisdom and that which then actually takes place, there lies a great unknown."[125] Yet the admission of uncertainty does not nullify the enterprise of seeking justice. We must remember that the Egyptian *sbȝy.t* is comprised of hortatory material, not abstract philosophy. The instructions do not reveal a metaphysical order or primitive moral dogma. Like the book of Proverbs and Ben Sira, the goal (often stated) is to shape behavioral patterns for young pupils, including future officials and potentially corrupt administrators.

Second, the Egyptian instructions utilize a host of devices and motifs to describe appropriate behavioral norms, including language about God. The frequent occurrence of the singular *nṯr* in the instructions has led to a variety of theories, such as whether this represents a monotheizing principle, henotheism, and if the inclusion of more polytheistic language is a nod to local cults. Yet certain attempts to clarify this monotheistic/polytheistic question have obscured the larger point of these references in the instructions: to explicate the divine impact on human affairs. Egyptian instructions are anthropocentric and implement deity-language to shape conduct. The earthly sphere, the realm of social interactions, remains the fundamental point of orientation, and this is confirmed by the content of the maxims. Amenemope provides a clear illustration, where a deity is invoked in reference to a specific social problem: "Very painful in the sight of Re is a young man who reproaches an elder" (25.21–26.1). The invocation of Re in this case has a specific pedagogical function, as the sage seeks to explain why a young charge should respect his elders and develop restraint. In many instances where *pȝ nṯr* appears, the use of the impersonal term generally indicates a focus on the earthly realm (at least for this type of literature).[126]

Third, the relationship between Ma'at and the deity is a dialectical one, and the former concept did not recede in favor of a more arbitrary perspective. While the tradition in Egypt did not remain static, there was no crisis precipitated by the abandonment of Ma'at. This concept and the ethical principles it represents continue to appear in later instructions.[127] The decision to privilege one model (indirect causation, the need

---

[125] Gerhard von Rad, *Wisdom in Israel* (trans. J.D. Martin; London/Harrisburg, Pa.: SCM Press Ltd./Trinity Press International, 1972), 101.

[126] An earthly focus and a *carpe diem* mentality can also be found in many of the Harpers' Songs.

[127] See Lichtheim, *Maat in Egyptian Autobiographies*, 101.

to actualize Maʾat) over the other (divine agency) largely depended on the topic at hand and the teaching strategy of the particular sage. For example, Ptahhotep claims that the gift of property derives from God (chapter 22), only to state a few maxims later that a person can gain honor through his own persuasive speech (chapter 25). As subsequent chapters will seek to demonstrate, this tension is intrinsic to ancient instructional literature. The idea of divine control over human events and a more automatic system coexist in most sapiential texts.

Fourth, the Egyptian instructions and the use of Maʾat in these texts relate to the public sphere. This concept is often associated directly with the king and the state: there are numerous references to Maʾat serving or reflecting the king/pharaonic system.[128] Both the instructions and the autobiographies also link Maʾat with social solidarity, as Assmann has shown. The person who exhibits forthrightness in the public realm, whose actions and speech exemplify solidarity, reciprocity, and retribution, "does" Maʾat. Within the specific context of the Egyptian instructions, Maʾat is less a cosmic principle than a practical goal incumbent upon every individual who aspires to success.

Fifth, a critical (and frequently overlooked) feature of the Egyptian instructions is the paucity of references to the afterlife. For a society with a highly evolved belief in otherworldly matters, the prospect of eternal reward would have offered a neat *Tun-Ergehen-Zusammenhang*. Yet with the exception of Merikare (addressed exclusively to the king) and a few scattered allusions in other texts, this feature is conspicuously absent from passages dealing with causality. We have discussed the possible double meaning in chapter 5 of Ptahhotep. There are also references in Amenemope: "How fortunate is he who reaches the West, When he is safe in the hand of God" (24.19–20). Yet these examples are exceptions to the predominantly earthly focus of the instructions, where the righteous individual is promised a variety of present rewards. Rarely do the sages dangle the prospect of eternal existence, and this feature requires further investigation.[129] This earthly focus of the instructions is particularly important for our study, because it demonstrates the

---

[128] This is amply demonstrated in Lichtheim, *Maat in Egyptian Biographies*.

[129] Note the assessment of Erik Hornung, "Lehren über das Jenseits?" in *Studien zu altägyptischen Lebenslehren* (ed. E. Hornung and O. Keel; OBO 28; Fribourg/Göttingen: Universitätsverlag/ Vandenhoeck & Ruprecht, 1979), 218, "Die als *sbꜣy.t* bezeichneten Lebenslehren und die *mḏꜣ.t n.t ḏ.t* genannten Unterweltsbücher oder Jenseitsführer wären dann komplementäre Gattungen der ägyptischen Literatur, von denen die eine Orienterungshilfe im Diesseits, die andere im Jenseits geben soll."

orientation of the tradition and the maxims that influenced Israelite sages. Only later in the Second Temple period would certain Jewish authors turn to the heavenly realm and the possibility of otherworldly retribution.

Finally, it should be apparent from the passages we have considered that a study of act and consequence is a useful way of examining the ethics and theology of the Egyptian instructions. As we proceed with an analysis of Proverbs and later Jewish Wisdom from the Hellenistic period, the Egyptian instructions and the understanding of cause and effect found in these texts provide an important context for the flowering of sapiential literature in Israel. From the association of success with the expression of Ma'at, to the choice of phrasing that implies a proportional response to human behavior, these maxims seek to link a good deed with its reward. While this is a characteristic feature of didactic literature in most cultural contexts, the Egyptian instructions repeatedly emphasize the relationship between human conduct and the consequences of individual behavioral patterns. Even if the instructions do not guarantee an infallible *Tun-Ergehen-Zusammenhang*, there is a palpable effort in these maxims to impress upon the addressee the efficacy of righteous behavior. The person who internalizes the advice will "find himself worthy of being a courtier" (Amenemope 27.17).

CHAPTER TWO

ACT AND CONSEQUENCE IN THE BOOK OF PROVERBS

1. *Introduction*

Any study on the transitions of Israelite Wisdom must account for the book of Proverbs. Without considering the date, social setting, and outlook found in this collection, it is difficult to determine the nature of any subsequent developments. Since it reflects an established ancient Near Eastern tradition, contains practical advice for young pupils, and offers a largely consistent act-consequence presentation, Proverbs seems to represent "standard" sapiential thought. According to many of the sayings in this collection, righteousness brings manifold benefits, and wickedness leads to misery. Illustrations of this mentality can be found in both the discourses of Proverbs 1–9 and the shorter sayings of chapters 10–30. A person who develops the "fear of the Lord," who commits to uprightness and self-improvement, can expect "riches and honor and life" (Prov 22:4). In contrast, "The iniquities of the wicked ensnare them, and they are caught in the toils of their sin" (Prov 5:22). Such statements and the principle underlying them led Koch to speak of an automatic framework, a "built-in and inherent connection between an action and its consequences."[1] This understanding of causality is particularly important for our study, since later Jewish sages reacted to the optimistic perspective found in Proverbs.

Yet this collection does not represent completely reflexive thinking. The compilers of the book present a reliable framework for earthly events, but they also acknowledge the diversity of human experience. Proverbs does not give a thoroughly consistent presentation, conclusions differ from saying to saying, and there is considerable variation across the various subunits. For example, observations on the wicked in one section can be contradicted to suit the exigencies of a different

---

[1] Klaus Koch, "Is There a Doctrine of Retribution in the Old Testament?" trans. T.H. Trapp, in *Theodicy in the Old Testament* (ed. J.L. Crenshaw; IRT 4; Philadelphia: Fortress Press, 1983), 59; originally published as "Gibt es ein Vergeltungsdogma im Alten Testament?" *ZTK* 52 (1955): 1–42.

rhetorical moment.[2] A few proverbs admit that an immoral person can ascend to a position of authority (28:12, 28), but other maxims claim that the unrighteous will not enjoy material success (13:25). It is too easily forgotten that this is a *collection* of sayings, and absolute uniformity is never a stated goal.[3] Not only do we find varied assumptions about life, including an acknowledgment of potential prosperity for the wicked, but divine freedom complicates efforts to offer a reliable system for human behavior and its outcomes. From the affirmation of God's power in 21:30 ("No wisdom, no understanding, no counsel, can avail against the Lord") to the "words of Agur" in 30:1–14, the sages counterbalance statements about the benefits of righteousness with an admission of uncertainty. Because "the Lord directs the steps" (16:9) of all persons, there are limits of individual control over events, and a "veil of resignation" (von Rad) lies over all human knowledge, action, and efforts to construct a purposeful reality. The affirmation of consistency in an uncertain universe is the great paradox of Wisdom literature.

Our task in this chapter is to explicate the act-consequence relationship in the book of Proverbs and to contextualize the sages' views on this issue of virtue-reward and vice-punishment. The setting and date for this collection are certainly relevant for such an inquiry: with a better understanding of when these observations were gathered and the social status of the addressee(s), the larger themes in Proverbs are more easily understood. We can also begin to locate a trajectory for Israel's wisdom tradition and the theological assumptions behind some of the later shifts. This discussion will lead to three important conclusions. First, efforts to locate a comprehensive "world-order" in Proverbs miss the practical nature of the collection, whose addressee often appears to be an impressionable pupil. In crafting their message to such individuals, the editors attempt to instill what had become familiar virtues in sapiential circles: measured public behavior (e.g., discretion, restraint when speaking), proper attitudes towards superiors, fidelity in marriage, care and respect for the poor, and an honest approach to financial matters. As with the Egyptian texts, a pupil's response to

---

[2] Elizabeth Huwiler, "Control of Reality in Israelite Wisdom" (Ph.D. diss., Duke University, 1988), 73–74, points to the uneven presentation of wealth and poverty issues in Proverbs.

[3] It is not certain that the final editors intended this collection to be read as a seamless whole, representing a unified teaching. Since there are disparities and contradictions between various sayings, perhaps consistency mattered less than rhetorical flourish.

these requirements determines success or failure. This is the "order" Proverbs seeks to create. The nexus of deed and result is a function of the motivational nature of the material rather than a naive theology based on "world order." Through a combination of fear and the promise of reward, Proverbs seeks to shape human behavior. Along similar lines, language about God generally has a pedagogical function. Like the Egyptian *sb³y.t*, this is a manual for daily life, and references to the deity and the natural world are introduced in relation to human affairs and outcomes. In addressing the divine role in Proverbs, we will take up the "Yahwistic" redaction theory and its implications for our study of causality. There are variations on this hypothesis, but the basic idea is that the book of Proverbs was supplemented by references to the deity and that such a development coincided with the growth of Israelite religion. The hypothesis of a progression in the book's development based on the insertion of God-language into an originally "secular" instruction has major problems and should not be used to chart the editorial process for this compilation.

Finally, one of the most significant and overlooked features of Proverbs is the lack of explicit interest in human mortality. While the belief in Sheol is certainly recognized (1:12; 15:11, 24; 23:14; 27:20), death did not preoccupy the compilers of Proverbs as it would later sages of the Second Temple period. This feature should occasion little surprise, since ancient Near Eastern instructions often focus on a person's earthly behavior and attitude as opposed to his eventual fate.[4] In this collection, no incipient belief in immortality can be found. This is consistent with most biblical authors, who do not allow for a blessed afterlife, but only for the shadows of Sheol.[5] Yet the fact that Proverbs does not speculate about the possibility of otherworldly retribution is significant, since Qoheleth and Ben Sira have lengthy, even obsessive discussions about death and the possibility of an afterlife.[6] The book of Proverbs actually looks at "death" in ethical terms, as the opposite

---

[4] Even in instructional texts from Egypt, where we might expect a mixture of earthly and otherworldly concerns, there are surprisingly few references to the afterlife.

[5] Bruce Vawter, "Intimations of Immortality and the Old Testament," *JBL* 91 (1972): 158–71. The first unambiguous reference to eschatological expectation for the individual can be found in Dan 12:1–3, although Qoheleth and Ben Sira acknowledge an ongoing discussion on the possibility of immortality. There are also some references in later psalms that might demonstrate a belief in the individual soul surviving after death (e.g., Ps 73:24).

[6] For example, Qoh 2:12–26; 3:16–22; 9:1–10; Sir 40:1–2; 41:1–4. The issue of death in Qoheleth and Ben Sira will be treated at length in chapters 3 and 4.

of living in accordance with Wisdom. The observation in Prov 1:32 is representative: "For waywardness kills the simple, and the complacency of fools destroys them." This is a statement on the perils of foolishness and the belief that some individuals have already perished as a result of their decision not to pursue Wisdom. Their death can accurately be described as "qualitative." Proverbs largely avoids the topic of physical death and does not indicate a serious concern over the idea of one universal fate for all persons, regardless of character. Such a distinction between Proverbs and later instructions allows us to locate a transition among certain sages and groups during the Hellenistic period. Various factors, such as the influence of Greek philosophy, the spread of apocalyptic ideas (as evidenced by texts like *1 Enoch*), and changing political dynamics, had an impact on instructional literature. A debate began to swirl regarding death, immortality, and the viability of earlier perspectives. Ben Sira acknowledges death as the ultimate equalizer but adopts the resignation of earlier sages, while Qoheleth laments the fact that all perceived gains are nullified by death. 4QInstruction, with its eschatological expectation and vivid judgment scenes, provides additional evidence that a major reevaluation occurred. This thematic contrast suggests an earlier time frame for the compilation of Proverbs, including chapters 1–9.[7] It is unlikely that the sages responsible for this collection would be silent in the midst of a major reconfiguration of sapiential ideas, especially a discussion that considered the possibility of eternal life for the righteous individual. The rest of this chapter will address the content of Proverbs, with an eye towards the differences between this traditional instruction and its successors, particularly in relation to retribution and death.

---

[7] The book of Job belongs in this discussion of act and consequence, and it presents special difficulties. The date for Job is debated, but a postexilic date is likely. The archaic Hebrew in the poetic dialogues could just as easily be a stylistic device as a preexilic marker. In addition, much of the content of Job reacts to the logic espoused in Proverbs, if not to the actual instruction. The final form of the book probably dates from the early postexilic period, when a number of core theological issues were being debated. See Avi Hurvitz, "The Date of the Prose Tale of Job Linguistically Reconsidered," *HTR* 67 (1974): 17–34.

## 2. *Structure of Proverbs*

The structure of the book of Proverbs has bearing on our study of act and consequence. The selection and arrangement of sayings reveal favorite topics, ethical priorities, and the diverse use of literary forms. As James Crenshaw explains, Proverbs takes the shape of an anthology of Israelite Wisdom; it is a collection that clearly underwent a complex editing process.[8] Scholars have located a series of subunits, an extended introduction (chapters 1–9), and a different order and at times content in LXX. MT-Proverbs is organized under six superscriptions (1:1; 10:1; 22:17; 24:23; 25:1; 30:1; 31:1), and as the following table indicates, most of these headings attribute authorship of subsequent material to a specific figure or group (Solomon, "the wise," etc.):

> 1:1–7—"The proverbs of Solomon" (prologue)
> 1:8–9:18—Instructions on Wisdom
> 10:1–22:16—"The proverbs of Solomon"
> 22:17–24:22—"The words of the wise"
> 24:23–34—"These also are the sayings of the wise"
> 25:1–29:27—"These are other proverbs of Solomon that the officials of King Hezekiah of Judah copied."
> 30:1–14—"The words of Agur"
> 30:15–33—Numerical sayings
> 31:1–9—"The words of King Lemuel"
> 31:10–31—Hymn on the "capable wife" (acrostic)

With its lengthy speeches and more unified structure, the first major unit of the book (Prov 1:8–9:18) is distinctive in form and to a certain extent character from the sayings that follow. Proverbs 10–31 consists of subunits or "collections" of individual sayings. In these groupings, the two-line saying is the most common form. This type can be an explicit command-prohibition, or a simple declarative statement on life and

---

[8] James L. Crenshaw, "Proverbs, Book of," *ABD* 5:513–15, posits a chronological order for the development of this book: (1) a collection of family teachings (10:1–22:6); (2) sayings with a much broader application (25:1–29:27); (3) more "professional" instruction that duplicates sayings found in Egyptian texts (22:17–24:22) and another body of material that integrates Egyptian concepts and imagery (1:1–9:18). Miscellaneous collections in 24:23–34 and 30:15–33 could have preceded the professional instructions, and the "words of Agur" (30:1–14) and the instruction of Lemuel's mother (31:1–9) were probably added after all of the preceding collections took shape.

human behavior.[9] Numerical sayings, the so-called "better-than" sayings, riddles, and poems also appear in the later sections of Proverbs.

There is often no apparent link between contiguous verses in chapters 10–30, particularly in 10:1–22:16 and 25:1–29:27, which for the most part consist of two-line sayings written in poetical parallelism. Certain proverbs in these units constitute a discrete thought-unit, unrelated to the previous verse in terms of subject matter. For example, some of the sayings of Proverbs 15 have a random quality and are grouped together based on catchwords related to the human body.[10] In addition, references to divine agency are scattered throughout Proverbs 10–31. Sayings that highlight God's power can be found in subunits that also emphasize human freedom.[11] Despite this variation, Proverbs 10–31 is not merely a hodgepodge of subunits, since central themes and phrases appear frequently (e.g., "fear of the Lord," Wisdom vs. folly), and many proverbs are repeated or slightly modified elsewhere in the text.[12] In

---

[9] The distinction between the declarative statement (*Aussage*) and the admonition (*Mahnung*) is frequently noted. The latter type, often expressed in the negative (vetitive), is common in Egyptian instructions, particularly Amenemope. It is well documented that Prov 22:17–24:22 relies on the content of Amenemope and this particular form. Johannes Hempel, *Die althebräische Literatur und ihr hellenistisch-jüdisches Nachleben* (Wildpark-Potsdam: Akademische Verlagsgesellschaft Athenaion, 1930), 175, explains that most of 22:17–24:22 consists of negative admonitions, a far greater proportion than other sections of the book. Aside from stylistic choice, the implications of the distinction (*Aussage* vs. *Mahnung*) are unclear. Some scholars have claimed that the didactic tone of the admonition implies a different (perhaps a school) setting than the more general statements in Proverbs. More recent discussions dismiss such an artificial division, since the declarative statement can also serve a hortatory function. For a review of the debate, see R.N. Whybray, *The Book of Proverbs: A Survey of Modern Study* (HBI 1; Leiden: Brill, 1995), 42–49.

[10] Most of these proverbs are antithetic in style. Multiple topics are addressed (the hot-tempered individual, Sheol, folly), with two "better-than" sayings (vv. 16–17), and scattered references to God (vv. 3, 8–9, 11, 16, 25–26, 29, 33). References to the tongue, mouth, and lips in vv. 1–8, emphasizing the importance of cautious speech, have apparently influenced this arrangement.

[11] In Prov 21:2, the Lord weighs the human heart to test for righteousness; a few verses later, the reader is told that "The violence of the wicked will sweep them away, because they refuse to do what is just" (v. 7). This latter statement implies a more automatic chain of events, free of direct intervention from God. There are also clusters of "Yahweh sayings" (e.g., 16:1–9). See below for further discussion.

[12] Prov 10:1: "A wise child makes a glad father, but a foolish child is a mother's grief." Compare with 15:20: "A wise child makes a glad father, but the foolish despise their mothers." Instances of repetition could be the result of editors bringing together originally separate collections with similar material or an effort by the compilers to emphasize the same points repeatedly. Otto Plöger, *Sprüche Salomos (Proverbia)* (BKAT 17; Neukirchen-Vluyn: Neukirchener Verlag, 1984), argues that the various sections of shorter sayings were originally separate collections, and he includes an additional

addition, many of the sayings can be broken down into logical units, proverbial clusters that relate to a specific theme or idea.[13] The book is largely consistent in presenting ethical norms for the well-ordered life, so that the shorter sayings are not islands, but components of a larger effort to instill a specific set of virtues.[14] Although this collection is not fully consistent in terms of thematic content, one can make certain conclusions about the conservative outlook in this text and the central characteristics of various subunits (see below).

## 2.1 Structure of Proverbs 1–9

The lengthy units of Proverbs 1–9 have a more cohesive structure and clear pedagogical intent than the rest of the collection.[15] Using the familiar framework of advice from a father to his son, Proverbs 1–9 lauds the benefits of seeking Wisdom and the danger of straying from her path. In addition, the author(s) presents a sustained and vivid contrast between Lady Wisdom and the "Strange Woman" (אשה זרה). The decision to follow one figure or the other is a momentous one for the addressee, with far-reaching repercussions for his life and well-being. Most scholars divide these chapters into a series of ten "discourses," each with its own introduction and call to heed the subsequent advice (e.g., 1:8). The discourses are interspersed with passages that praise Wisdom.[16] Kayatz and McKane have argued that these speeches in Proverbs 1–9 resemble the form of the Egyptian instructions, particularly the

---

division between chapters 10:1–15:33 and 16:1–22:16. Proverbs 10–15 is written almost exclusively in antithetic parallelism.

[13] See Knut Martin Heim, *Like Grapes of Gold Set in Silver: An Interpretation of Proverbial Clusters in Proverbs 10:1–22:16* (BZAW 23; Berlin: de Gruyter, 2001).

[14] As an illustration, the command to be "slow to anger" appears repeatedly in Proverbs: 14:29; 15:18; 16:32; 19:11; this individual is the antithesis of the dreaded "hothead" (22:24).

[15] Prov 22:17–24:22 also contains sustained discussion on particular topics (e.g., the polemic against drunkenness in 23:29–35), as do some of the poetic sections at the end of the text, such as the hymn on the "capable wife" in 31:10–31.

[16] See R.N. Whybray, *The Composition of the Book of Proverbs* (JSOTSup 168; Sheffield: JSOT Press, 1994), 11–61. Whybray posits "wisdom additions" that link the father's instruction with Wisdom (e.g., 4:5–9) and a set of "Yahweh additions." Crenshaw, "Proverbs," 515, also divides the text into ten discourses: 1:8–19; 2:1–22; 3:1–12; 3:21–35; 4:1–9; 4:10–19; 4:20–27; 5:1–23; 6:20–35; 7:1–27. Michael V. Fox, *Proverbs 1–9* (AB 18A; New York: Doubleday, 2000), 44–46, calls the ten passages "lectures," since they are presented as moral instruction from a father to his son. Like Whybray, Fox cites "interludes" that offer reflections on Wisdom: 1:20–33; 3:13–20; 6:1–19; 8:1–36; 9:1–18.

prologue of each unit.[17] With regard to the number of authors and editors for this section, this is impossible to determine. Repetitive elements can be indicators of a composite text, but instructional literature often returns to the same themes and motifs for didactic purposes.[18] As for the structural relationship with the book as a whole, the content of Proverbs 1–9 (particularly the discourses) is an appropriate introduction to the entire collection. These warnings echo much of the advice in the shorter sayings. Scholars frequently suggest that this material was added along with the poem of 31:10–31 to form an *inclusio* around the shorter sayings.[19]

## 2.2    Structure of LXX-Proverbs

The ordering of Proverbs in the Greek translation, and in many instances the content, are different from MT, particularly in chapters 24–31. The divergence is considerable in this part of the collection, as the following chart demonstrates:

> *LXX-Proverbs (based on MT versification)*
> 1:1–24:22
> 30:1–14—"The words of Agur" (part one)
> 24:23–34—"These also are by the wise"
> 30:15–33—"The words of Agur" (part two)
> 31:1–9—"The words of Lemuel" (part one)
> 25–29
> 31:10–31—"The words of Lemuel" (part two)

In addition to the larger structural differences shown above, LXX-Proverbs lacks certain verses or entire sections found in MT (e.g., 20:14–19), presents sayings in an altered manner, and in several places seems

---

[17] Christa Kayatz, *Studien zu Proverbien 1–9: eine form- und motivgeschichtliche Untersuchung unter Einbeziehung ägyptischen Vergleichsmaterials* (WMANT 22; Neukirchen-Vluyn: Neukirchener Verlag, 1966). Her linkage of Lady Wisdom and Maʾat is more controversial (see below). Cf. William McKane, *Proverbs* (OTL; Philadelphia: Westminster, 1970), 6–10, 51–182, for a discussion of Proverbs 1–9 and foreign instructions.

[18] Fox, *Proverbs 1–9*, 322, claims that most of the ten instructions come from one author, while the interludes are composite, "midrashic commentaries" on the lectures.

[19] Chapters 1–9 and 31:10–31 contain references to "fear of the Lord" (1:7; 31:30). In addition, both sections are concerned with two contrasting female figures. See Claudia Camp, *Wisdom and the Feminine in the Book of Proverbs* (BLS 11; Decatur, Ga.: Almond Press, 1985); Christine R. Yoder, *Wisdom as a Woman of Substance: A Socioeconomic Reading of Proverbs 1–9 and 31:10–31* (BZAW 304; Berlin: de Gruyter, 2001), 2.

to add substantially to the content of the Hebrew text.[20] Scholars are divided over the reasons for these differences and the implications. Gillis Gerleman and William McKane argue that the text before the Greek translator was basically equivalent to MT, and therefore LXX-Proverbs is the product of a "free" translator. In contrast, Emmanuel Tov understands the content and order to reflect a different *Vorlage*.[21] Since there is repetition and variation *within* MT for many of the sayings, one cannot immediately assume that the differences between MT-Proverbs and LXX are the result of a translator with a clear theological agenda and a sense of latitude about his efforts. In the many cases where one component of the Greek translator's rendering does not fit the saying in MT-Proverbs, a textual variant is the most likely explanation. This has been argued convincingly by Michael Fox.[22] Yet it is certain that LXX adapted and in certain places changed the Hebrew text, regardless of *Vorlage*. If we are not dealing with a variant for a specific saying, the possible reasons for the divergence from MT are varied. In a number of proverbs, the subtleties of sapiential literature do not carry over to another language, and the translator was doing the best he could in transferring from Hebrew to Greek. Moreover, the vocabulary and syntax of MT-Proverbs can be quite difficult and ambiguous; at several points, the Greek translator did not comprehend the gist of a saying or felt he needed to alter it slightly.[23] In certain instances, the translator

---

[20] There are also numerous hexaplaric doublets in LXX-Proverbs.

[21] Gillis Gerleman, "The Septuagint Proverbs as a Hellenistic Document," *OTS* 8 (1950): 15–27; idem, *Studies in the Septuagint, III, Proverbs* (Lund: Gleerup, 1956); cf. McKane, *Proverbs*, 33–35. Emmanuel Tov, "Recensional Differences between the Masoretic Text and the Septuagint of Proverbs," in *Of Scribes and Scrolls: Studies on the Hebrew Bible, Intertestamental Judaism, and Christian Origins Presented to John Strugnell* (ed. H.W. Attridge et al.; Lanham, Md.: University Press of America, 1990), 43–52, claims that not every variant in LXX can be ascribed to the translator's whims. His argument for "recensionally different" editions in Proverbs 15–16 necessitates a different *Vorlage*, as do the respective structures of Proverbs 17, 20, and 31.

[22] Michael V. Fox, "LXX-Proverbs as a Text-Critical Resource," *Text* 22 (2005): 95–128, offers a healthy dose of caution when making assumptions about the Greek translator's process and mindset. According to Fox, this individual usually tries to understand and render the proverb as he perceives it. As a result, "We need not default to the MT whenever a 'translation technique' can be invoked to explain the difference" (p. 97). Fox catalogues a number of instances in which textual variation explains why a certain component in the Greek verse does not seem to fit properly.

[23] Fox, "LXX-Proverbs as a Text-Critical Resource," 102, provides examples of this type, including Prov 18:9. MT reads as follows: גַּם מִתְרַפֶּה בִמְלַאכְתּוֹ אָח הוּא לְבַעַל מַשְׁחִית ("One who is slack in work is close kin to a vandal"). The Greek translator added a negative particle to render the following saying: ὁ μὴ ἰώμενος ἑαυτὸν ἐν τοῖς ἔργοις αὐτοῦ ἀδελφός ἐστιν τοῦ λυμαινομένου ἑαυτόν ("He who does not heal himself by his

chose to nuance or smooth out a proverb, and in other places he seems to have added language for moral or theological emphasis.[24]

In assessing the variants, scholars have studied the Greek version from a text-critical perspective, as a translation of a very complex Wisdom text. Yet LXX-Proverbs should also be examined in its own right, as an instructional document dating from the Hellenistic period. Whether these differences can be attributed to the influence of Greek culture and/or an effort to affirm Jewish ideas in a fluid context is a topic of disagreement and well beyond the scope of this discussion.[25] For present purposes, it is important to look at how retribution and death are addressed in LXX-Proverbs and whether there is a discernible development when compared with MT. In a later section, we will consider possible thematic changes in LXX-Proverbs related to this topic. Specifically, is there is a greater preoccupation in LXX-Proverbs with the contrast between two types (the righteous and the wicked) and the eventual fates of these categories?

### 3. Date

Pinpointing a date for Proverbs is an extremely difficult task. The collection has few historical markers and was compiled by many editors over a lengthy period. Distinct subunits probably had a separate editorial development before being combined into this larger anthology.

---

labors is the brother of the one who harms himself"). "Healing" oneself through work could have seemed odd to the translator, and he might have been working from the form מתרפא (or perhaps reading the III-*hê* verb as a III-*ʾālep*). This complex example demonstrates the need for measured assumptions when assigning a particular motivation to the translator.

[24] For this last category ("moral emphasis"), one example is Prov 13:2. MT reads מפרי פי־איש יאכל טוב ונפש בגדים חמס ("From the fruit of their words good persons eat good things, but the desire of the treacherous is for wrongdoing"). LXX contains a "moralizing expansion" of this verse (McKane, *Proverbs*, 46): ἀπὸ καρπῶν δικαιοσύνης φάγεται ἀγαθός ψυχαὶ δὲ παρανόμων ὀλοῦνται ἄωροι. The reference to the destruction of the wicked ("the souls of the lawless will be destroyed prematurely") has no basis in the Hebrew for this verse. See the section on death in Proverbs for further discussion.

[25] Gerleman, *Studies in the Septuagint*, 28–35, attempts to demonstrate the influence of Greek thought and speech patterns in LXX-Proverbs. Johann Cook, *The Septuagint of Proverbs: Jewish and/or Hellenistic Proverbs?* (VTSup 69; Leiden: Brill, 1997) argues for a conservative Jewish outlook in LXX-Proverbs. Cook also claims that the translator has been influenced by an apocalyptic understanding of retribution and therefore presents a heightened dualism.

The timeless nature of many of the sayings adds to the problem of dating. Scholars have pursued three primary methods for examining this issue and trying to locate the collection: mining the sayings for contextual clues, studying the key references in the headings (e.g., the "men of Hezekiah," Solomon), and evaluating the type of Hebrew used throughout the book. Proposals have ranged widely for every section, from the reign of Solomon to the late Hellenistic period. All efforts to date Proverbs are complicated by the fact that the process of gathering sayings was ongoing in Israel's wisdom tradition. The editors undoubtedly supplemented existing clusters with additional material. Moreover, many if not most of the individual sayings had an oral history, *and* there is often no apparent relationship between contiguous verses in Proverbs 10–30. In many cases, there is simply no way to know when a proverb might have been added. Chapters 1–9 have a more deliberate flow and unified message than the groupings of shorter sayings, and these speeches could have been written in a somewhat different (perhaps later) context, although even this is debated. With such uncertainty surrounding the writing and compilation process, we can only offer tentative conclusions on a date for the final form of the Hebrew text or any of the subsections.

The position taken here is a common one, that the book of Proverbs was gathered and shaped by scribal sages after the exile, but well before Qoheleth and Ben Sira.[26] The suggestion of a Second Temple date for the final editing of the text does not mean that the bulk of the sayings were coined during this later period; a number of individual proverbs and probably entire units circulated prior to the exile. Many statements in chapters 10–30 reflect real-life conditions under a king, and this would seem to indicate a preexilic date.[27] For example, the advice in chapters 28–29 implies a genuine dynamic between a ruler and his subjects. Prov 29:14 states, "If a king judges the poor with equity, his throne will be established forever."[28] The ruler is a figure to be respected and carefully dealt with: "A servant who deals wisely has the king's favor, but his wrath falls on one who acts shamefully"

---

[26] Ben Sira (ca. 190 B.C.E.) clearly has knowledge of the content in Proverbs. Qoheleth provides an alternative perspective and in part reflects a reaction to Proverbs.

[27] Whether this material indicates a royal court setting is a related question (see below).

[28] Other sayings that mention royal power include Prov 14:35; 16:10, 12–15; 17:7; 19:12; 20:2, 26, 28; 24:21; 25:5–6, 15; 28:2–3, 15–16; 29:4, 12, 26; 30:29–31.

(14:35). There are also references to the king in 22:17–24:22, and this section probably originated during a period of cultural exchange with Egypt.[29] All of these sayings naturally fit the preexilic period, when the Israelite monarchy was a viable institution.

Two specific kings are mentioned in the headings, and the historical reliability of these references is a major question. Few scholars today would accept Solomonic authorship (Prov 1:1; 10:1; 25:1) for any of the material in the collection. The authors of Proverbs do not indicate a concern with the early fortunes of the Davidic empire. This factor does not preclude an origin during Solomon's reign, since royal scribes could have crafted and collected sayings with a broad appeal. Moreover, ancient instructions are frequently lacking in historical detail. Yet the assumption of a Solomonic enlightenment, an era of prosperity, innovation, and *belles lettres* that could have produced a text like Proverbs, is undermined by the lack of archaeological evidence for a fully realized empire in Judah during this period. Jerusalem and its environs were underdeveloped in relation to the northern kingdom of Israel.[30] The association of Solomon with Wisdom seems to belong to legend rather than to history, as evidenced by the numerous Second Temple texts ascribed to this famous king.[31] Even if some of the sayings date to this early period in Judah's history, the traditional view of Solomon as a great patron and codifier of Wisdom literature is no longer tenable.

In contrast, the "men of Hezekiah" ascription in 25:1 is possibly accurate, since this is such an oddly specific reference, and Hezekiah (715–687 B.C.E.) is not otherwise associated with sapiential activity.[32] As some of the language in Proverbs assumes kingship to be a present reality, at least a portion of the sayings must date from preexilic monarchs like Hezekiah. This statement implies scribal activity during Hezekiah's reign for the collecting and cataloguing of sayings. The fact that the proverbs are not attributed directly to the "men" (pre-

---

[29] Richard J. Clifford, *Proverbs* (OTL; Louisville: Westminster John Knox Press, 1999), 6.

[30] See Israel Finkelstein and Neil A. Silberman, *The Bible Unearthed: Archaeology's New Vision of Ancient Israel and the Origin of its Sacred Texts* (New York: The Free Press, 2001), 128–45.

[31] The Song of Songs, Psalm 72, the Odes of Solomon, the Psalms of Solomon, the Testament of Solomon, and the Wisdom of Solomon. Qoheleth takes on the persona of Solomon.

[32] The mention of the "men of Hezekiah" appears to be an incidental remark, which supports the argument that the statement is historically accurate. Solomon is the king emphasized in 25:1 and in the other headings.

sumably a group of officials) indicates a process of gathering material and making it accessible to segments of the population. According to this interpretation, the cataloguing of sayings was part of the royal bureaucracy. When considering the possible reasons for the flowering of Wisdom literature under Hezekiah, perhaps the influx of citizenry from the defunct northern kingdom led to an increased literacy rate and a greater exposure to and interest in the instructional genre.[33] It is reasonable to assume that Hezekiah's administration had respect for an international tradition associated with the earliest and most famous southern king and with Egypt, and they wished to further the sapiential enterprise in Judah.[34] Yet even if this is an accurate assessment of Prov 25:1, this one heading is not a reliable basis for dating the entire collection.[35]

The Hebrew used in Proverbs is varied and difficult to assess, especially since the material spans several centuries, and individual sayings frequently had an oral history. In addition, occurrences of older forms might be an archaizing device or an antiquated proverb that was incorporated into a later collection. Conversely, sayings indicative of Late Biblical Hebrew could have been added to existing subunits at a later point. In support of a Persian period date, Washington cites several terms used throughout the text (not just in chapters 1–9) that reflect the use of Late Biblical Hebrew, such as פְּנִינִים ("corals or "pearls"). He also catalogues a list of Aramaisms.[36] Yet as Washington admits, Aramaisms are not always a reliable basis for dating biblical books, and

---

[33] According to William M. Schniedewind, *How the Bible Became a Book* (Cambridge: Cambridge University Press, 2004), 67, the eighth-century marked a transitional period for centralization and population growth in the southern kingdom. This is reflected in the pottery remains from Jerusalem. There are specific examples of royal power associated with Hezekiah, such as the *lmlk* seals.

[34] Clifford, *Proverbs*, 3–4, suggests that the "men of Hezekiah" had all or part of the "proverbs of Solomon" in 10:1–22:16.

[35] Mark Carasik, "Who Were the 'Men of Hezekiah' (Proverbs XXV 1)?," *VT* 44 (1994): 289–300, doubts the reliability of Prov 25:1 and considers it to be an exegetical link between Solomon and Hezekiah, based on linguistic and thematic similarities in the Deuteronomistic accounts of these two kings. Cf. Harold C. Washington, *Wealth and Poverty in the Instruction of Amenemope and the Hebrew Proverbs* (SBLDS 142; Atlanta: Scholars Press, 1994), 115 n. 17.

[36] Washington, *Wealth and Poverty*, 116–22, catalogues the linguistic evidence. He argues that פְּנִינִים (Prov 3:15; 8:11; 20:15; 31:10) has no Semitic derivation and appears to be a late usage. Similarly, the form כֶּתֶר ("crown," 14:18) only has a parallel in Esther (1:11; 2:17; 6:8). Washington cites a few additional cases of Late Biblical Hebrew, but the examples are inconclusive for chapters 10–30. As for Aramaisms, an unmistakable cluster can be found in the "the words of King Lemuel" (31:1–9).

his Late Biblical Hebrew examples are not conclusive enough to settle the issue.[37] In addition, the distribution of Aramaisms is always not smooth in Proverbs; there are more frequent occurrences in chapters 1–9, 22:17–24:22, and 31.[38] While further analysis is needed in this area, the Hebrew used in the shorter sayings does not seem to allow for a postexilic argument based on linguistic evidence alone. Even if the Persian period is the most likely possibility, the case is not yet closed.

A stronger argument for a later date can be made for Proverbs 1–9 and 31. These sections frame the rest of the book, and it is plausible that editors added this material to a preexisting collection(s). We have already discussed the hypothesis that the instructional speeches at the beginning function as an introduction to the shorter sayings, and this supports such a proposed chronology. Among the various proposals, the Persian period is the most popular. In a sociological study of these chapters, Christl Maier claims that the polemic against the "Strange Woman" (אשה זרה) in Proverbs 1–9 represents a critique against exogamy in the manner of Ezra (10:6–44) and Nehemiah (13:23–37).[39] She further argues that the son's opponents in Prov 1:10–19 and 2:12–15 are criminals, and these warnings against thugs originated within a "solidarity group" of Jews living under the Persians. Washington makes a similar claim.[40] Claudia Camp locates these speeches early in the Persian period based on the lack of engagement with the Torah in the manner of Ezra and Nehemiah.[41] While these arguments are quite helpful for understanding the political and social dynamics of the province of Yehud, it is difficult to find any polemic, even an implicit one, against exogamy in Proverbs. A basic problem with this proposal is that the

---

[37] See Avi Hurvitz, "The Chronological Significance of 'Aramaisms' in Biblical Hebrew," *IEJ* 18 (1968): 234–37.

[38] The frequency of Aramaisms in 22:17–24:22 (e.g., מלה /"word" in 23:9) is noteworthy.

[39] Christl Maier, *Die 'fremde Frau' in Proverbien 1–9: Eine exegetische sozialgeschichtliche Studie* (OBO 144; Göttingen: Vandenhoeck & Ruprecht, 1995).

[40] Washington, *Wealth and Poverty*, 156–70, states that the social structure depicted in Proverbs matches well with the ethos of life in the province of Yehud, particularly the warnings about the "Strange Woman." This figure is a threat to the young man's personal stability *and* property rights (i.e., the statement that her "house leads down to death" in Prov 2:18 refers to the ownership of land).

[41] Claudia Camp, *Wisdom and the Feminine in the Book of Proverbs*, 234, places the material earlier in the postexilic period (before Ezra). Yet this issue of Torah engagement is not necessarily consequential for dating the book of Proverbs. Qoheleth, who is clearly writing at a later point during the Second Temple period, does not present a Torah-Wisdom nexus.

temptress described in these chapters is already married. The Strange Woman is seeking to entice a vulnerable lad into illicit sexual relations rather than an unlawful marriage union.[42] In addition, the warnings against gangs could fit any historical period (see below).

Yoder examines the occurrences of late Hebrew forms in these chapters (and 31:10–31) to advance the argument for a later date. Among her examples, the feminine singular construct form יַעֲלַת ("doe," Prov 5:19) only has parallels in Second Temple sources.[43] The preposition בִּית ("between" or "beside," 8:2) is a later replacement for בֵּין. Various Piel forms of הלך appear in 6:11, 28 and 8:20 and seem to be a feature of Late Biblical Hebrew. The Aramaizing וֹת occurs with several feminine nouns in Proverbs 1–9, and this is also suggestive of a postexilic date.[44] The word קִנְיָן ("property," 4:7) is not attested in Old Aramaic, and in the Hebrew Bible this term appears almost exclusively in later passages. Moreover, with the possible exceptions of אֵטוּן ("linen," 7:16) and צוֹפִיה (31:27), there are no Grecisms in Proverbs 1–9 (although this does not prove the argument).[45] Yoder also points to the orthography of these chapters, including the increased occurrence of internal *matres lectionis* points in Proverbs 1–9 and 31:10–31. She catalogues a list of forms like נבורה (Prov 8:14), which are written with *wāw* or *yôd* to mark long-*ū* or long-*ā*, to make the case that these sections of Proverbs resemble a book like Qoheleth more than clearly preexilic works.[46] Finally, the use of אֲנִי as opposed to אָנֹכִי (which does not appear in chapters 1–9) is more common in late texts.

---

[42] Fox, *Proverbs 1–9*, 48–49, notes that Proverbs never raises a concern about the relationships between insiders and foreigners, one of the most pressing issues of the Persian period: "In fact, the social and intellectual concerns of Prov 1–9 evinced in favor of an Achaemenid dating are equally present in Ben Sira, which was written about 190–180 B.C.E."

[43] Yoder, *Wisdom as a Woman of Substance*, 20, cites the additional occurrences of the feminine form in Ezra 2:56 and Neh 7:58.

[44] Yoder, *Wisdom as a Woman of Substance*, 25–26, provides a list of citations.

[45] The former term has been compared to ὀθόνη by multiple scholars. Yet as Yoder, *Wisdom as a Woman of Substance*, 32, demonstrates, Hebrew *ṭêt* does not usually correspond to Greek *theta*, but to *tau*. This is an Egyptian loanword, *jdmy* ("red linen"). On צוֹפִיה, see Al Wolters, "*Ṣôpiyyâ* (Prov 31:27) as Hymnic Participle and Play on *SOPHIA*," *JBL* 104 (1985): 577–87. The problem with Wolters' argument is that צוֹפִיה was not read by LXX translators as a word-play on the Greek term for Wisdom.

[46] Yoder, *Wisdom as a Woman of Substance*, 35–37, attempts to document that the use of *plene* forms is more conservative than what one finds in the Dead Sea Scrolls, but far more frequent than many of the preexilic texts in the Hebrew Bible.

Although much of this evidence is persuasive, particularly the indicators of Late Biblical Hebrew in Proverbs 1–9, neither the thematic issues cited above nor these linguistic examples conclusively settle the argument for a Persian period date. Fox attempts to situate the text on different grounds, arguing that the chapters on the universality of Wisdom (e.g., Proverbs 8) reflect a more "intellectually cosmopolitan" era than the Persian period.[47] Yet even as he argues that the description of this figure in relation to God might indicate an awareness of Greek thought, Fox is not completely convinced of this influence. Perhaps there is another means of dating this material. One possible argument for placing the final form of the text earlier in the postexilic period rests on the lack of interest in death and its implications in the manner of instructional texts like Qoheleth and Ben Sira (both Hellenistic). The discourses in Proverbs reveal no awareness of a later debate on death and the afterlife, and this factor might serve as an important historical marker (see below). In assessing all of the evidence, Clifford offers a cautious and reasonable proposal: "perhaps the best course is to suppose that Proverbs was edited in the same general movement as much of Israel's other sacred literature in the early Second Temple period, that is, in the period from the sixth to the fourth centuries B.C.E."[48]

## 4. *Social Setting*

A better understanding of the *Sitz im Leben* for Proverbs clarifies the largely optimistic perspective in this collection; such an inquiry also provides an important context for later reactions among Second Temple sages. As with the issue of dating the book, proposals on this topic have ranged broadly. Certain commentators have argued that these sayings were compiled and disseminated in some type of educational

---

[47] Fox, *Proverbs 1–9*, 49.

[48] Clifford, *Proverbs*, 6. We also mentioned the possibility of a Yahwistic redaction. Specifically, did a group of postexilic editors modify a largely secular, royal instruction by peppering the text with Yahweh-references and additional sayings about divine authority? Perhaps the development of Israelite religion prompted later editors to infuse a traditional set of sayings with God-language. This possibility often prompts scholars to date the book in stages, based on the insertion of theological language into the various subunits. This hypothesis has major flaws and is not necessarily a useful means of charting the book's development (see below).

context.[49] The teaching of instructional literature could have taken place in the royal court, among lower officials and citizens, or a combination of the two. Another possibility is that the "son" language in Proverbs 1–9 indicates a family origin for some or all of the material in the text (e.g., 4:1–5:23). Perhaps familial instruction remained the norm for most citizens, and formal training centers only developed after the exile. Other scholars claim that Proverbs, or at least the bulk of it, had a popular origin as a collection of "folk" sayings among the poorer classes.[50] Even if the material was subsequently compiled by literate scribes, many commentators argue that the sayings in Proverbs 10–29 have the character of common advice that circulated orally as an idyllic vision for village life.

Before considering these hypotheses in greater detail, it is profitable to make a few general observations on the social setting for Proverbs. While not every saying has to reflect the social status of author and addressee, it is reasonable to assume that the compilers of Proverbs wished to speak directly to the concerns of the individuals receiving this advice. As a result, we can conclude that these sayings target a swath of established citizens in an agrarian economy, many of whom had mercantile interests. The editors of Proverbs use a variety of stylistic devices and motifs to depict real-life situations for such an audience. These are not revolutionary exhortations, nor do they reflect turbulent times. Cultic, national, and covenantal concerns are not part of the discussion. Composed during periods of relative stability, the sayings in this collection promote straightforward behavior and mutual solidarity. The editors seek to preserve existing social hierarchies, while giving some attention to those on the margins. By following the prescribed "path," an individual can expect wealth and contentment. These expectations point to a group of scribal sages who held at least some status and power in Israelite society and wanted to preserve the current system. Many of these characteristics mirror the content and outlook of the Egyptian texts we examined in the previous chapter; Proverbs is clearly part of a larger ancient Near Eastern tradition of sapiential discourse.

---

[49] See Hans-Jurgen Hermisson, *Studien zur israelitischen Spruchweisheit* (WMANT 28; Neukirchen-Vluyn: Neukirchener Verlag, 1968).

[50] See, for example, Claus Westermann, "Weisheit im Sprichwort," in *Schalom: Studien zu Glaube und Geschichte Israels, Alfred Jepsen zum 70. Geburtstag* (Stuttgart: Calwer Verlag, 1971), 73–85; idem, *Roots of Wisdom: The Oldest Proverbs of Israel and Other Peoples* (trans. J.D. Charles; Louisville: Westminster John Knox, 1995).

In light of the sayings about behavior around the king, the ascriptions to Solomon and Hezekiah, and the adages dealing with the monarch's responsibilities, the "royal court" is a plausible setting for Proverbs and the source for many of the sayings. Scholarly discussions about a "royal" setting frequently involve lofty assumptions about the Israelite monarchy prior to the exile. Belief in a Solomonic enlightenment has played an influential role in this hypothesis. This designation, however, need not imply a setting of great opulence or an empire with a vast bureaucracy. "Royal court" can be used to refer simply to the king's orbit and control, meaning the provenance of upper-class administrators and literate officials, as opposed to a more common ("folk") origin.[51] Royal matters come up frequently in Proverbs 10–29, and much of the advice in chapters 28–29 is directed specifically to the king.[52] It is probable that Israelite administrators of various stripes took part in the collection and propagation of sayings. The references in Prov 22:17 and 24:23 suggest a class of "wise men" with access to the king.[53] How this process played out (i.e., the relative proximity of sages to the monarch) is uncertain. In support of this hypothesis, Proverbs is often linked to various royal descriptions in the Deuteronomistic history. Even if Dtr's account of early administrations cannot be read as a precise history of events, preexilic kings surely employed scribal functionaries and literate officials like the ones described in 1 and 2 Kings.[54] A full description of the various job responsibilities is not possible, based on the extant sources. In addition, the relationship between "scribes" and "sages" is far from clear, and one must avoid automatically associating the two titles. Scribes did not necessarily have an interest in Wisdom

---

[51] Such a label does not force the interpreter to accept Dtr's account of Solomon or any other monarch at face value.

[52] An upper-class milieu is implied in several other places, where the addressee is a landowner or person controlling the financial well being of others (e.g., the ראש משביר in 11:26 who distributes grain; the mention of slaveholding in 29:21). See Fox, *Proverbs 1–9*, 9. For a summary of scholarly discussion on the royal court hypothesis, see Whybray, *The Book of Proverbs: A Survey of Modern Study*, 18–22. The main proponent for this royal setting is Hermisson. He argues that a school connected to the royal court produced most of the sayings.

[53] William McKane, *Prophets and Wise Men* (SBT 44; London: SCM Press, 1965). Note also Isa 19:11–12; 29:14; Jer 18:18; Sir 38:24.

[54] The various administrative titles could be an accurate representation of the preexilic bureaucracy. The "royal officials of Judah" (אנשי יהודה עבדי המלך) in 1 Kgs 1:9 presumably include scribes, as does the list of administrators under Solomon (1 Kgs 4:1–19, which mentions a "recorder" and "scribe"). Similarly, there are various officials associated with Hezekiah (2 Kgs 18:18, 37).

literature, nor is there evidence that learning proverbs was compulsory for royal officials. Nevertheless, there are biblical passages that suggest a relationship between scribes and sages, such as Jer 8:8.[55]

Moshe Weinfeld has famously argued that Deuteronomy comes from a class of "scribal-sages" in Jerusalem.[56] He identifies compelling overlaps between Deuteronomy and Proverbs, including sapiential terminology in the Deuteronomic legislation. In addition, the accessibility of Wisdom in Proverbs is parallel to the availability of the new constitution in Deuteronomy for all interested persons (Deut 30:11–14; cf. Prov 8:1–3). Yet if this group of "scribal-sages" populated the court and authored the legal reforms in Deuteronomy, why are they not listed as royal confidantes in the law of the king? The levitical priests are a check on the monarch in Deut 17:14–20 rather than a class of scribal-sages. Even with this type of difficulty, Weinfeld is undoubtedly correct that the cast of official scribes included some of the same individuals who gathered popular sayings and cultivated appreciation for this literature. In a related argument, Fox argues convincingly that "learned clerks" (royal and provincial administrators) became the "membrane through which principles, sayings, and coinages, folk and otherwise, were filtered."[57] These individuals sifted through the treasury of available sayings, oral and written, and developed a largely coherent vision for society and the virtuous life.

Perhaps Israel and Judah had established training programs in which these "learned clerks" gained knowledge of various scribal tasks and exposure to the international wisdom tradition. This is impossible to prove with certainty until much later in the Second Temple period.[58]

---

[55] Jer 8:8 associates being "wise" (חכם) with a group of "scribes" (ספרים). Despite this evidence, we cannot assume that all "scribes" were considered to be "sages." Significantly, there are no חכמים mentioned in Dtr (or elsewhere in the Hebrew Bible) as a class of advisors to the king (but see Jer 18:18). According to R.N. Whybray, "The Sage in the Israelite Royal Court," in *The Sage in Israel and the Ancient Near East* (ed. J.G. Gammie and L.G. Perdue; Winona Lake, Ind.: Eisenbrauns, 1990), 134, the belief that the wise figures in Isa 19:12 are royal advisors is "purely inferential." The prophet's language makes it likely, however: "Where now are your sages (חכמיך)? Let them tell you and make known what the Lord of hosts has planned against Egypt."

[56] Moshe Weinfeld, *Deuteronomy and the Deuteronomic School* (Oxford: Clarendon Press, 1972).

[57] Fox, *Proverbs 1–9*, 11.

[58] Fox, *Proverbs 1–9*, 32–34. James Crenshaw, *Education in Ancient Israel: Across the Deadening Silence* (ABRL; New York: Doubleday, 1998), 88–89, explains that Jerusalem has yielded little inscriptional evidence in this regard. On the international scene, Egyptian instructions like Amenemope link administrative competency with the acquisition of

The question of schools in Israel is complex, especially since the book of Proverbs never mentions the existence of learning centers. We find no distinct references to schools in Israel prior to Ben Sira's mention of a בית מדרש ("house of instruction," 51:23), so all arguments to substantiate their existence must be based on incidental remarks, extrabiblical evidence, and logical deduction. The Chronicler mentions scribal guilds within a family unit (1 Chr 2:55), and there is a reference to King Jehoshaphat's officials teaching in the cities of Judah (2 Chr 17:7–9). Both passages could represent educational practices during the Second Temple period and a fictional attribution to an earlier age. Although the Chronicler's descriptions might reflect postexilic practices, there are compelling reasons for positing the existence of schools as early as the era of the monarchy. In any royal bureaucratic system, the need for administrative consistency is self-evident. Even moderate urbanization would have necessitated a degree of uniformity with regard to bureaucratic structures; institutions cannot be developed solely on the basis of familial instruction. We can reasonably conclude that royal and priestly authorities set up institutions or at least organized programs for the mastery of scribal and cultic tasks (and Hebrew).[59] According to the archaeological analysis of D.W. Jamieson-Drake, the eighth-century is the most likely point for the emergence of such efforts, which would have probably been centralized in Jerusalem.[60] The "men of Hezekiah" ascription and the references to a class of חכמים (Prov 1:6; 22:17) could be related to these schools in some way, though the root חכם does not always have a technical meaning. It usually refers to basic skills and knowledge.

---

wisdom. Young pupils made numerous copies of instructional texts, and there is strong evidence for schools in ancient Egypt. See David M. Carr, *Writing on the Tablet of the Heart: Origins of Scripture and Literature* (Oxford: Oxford University Press, 2005), 65–77. Non-priestly leaders in Israel might have instituted similar training programs, linking Wisdom and scribal success (e.g., Jer 8:8). It is through scribal circles, perhaps close to the Israelite king, that Amenemope and the international wisdom tradition became known in the first place. This link with Egypt *increases* rather than decreases the likelihood of schools in Israel. For a comprehensive study on the possibility of schools, with particular attention to the archaeological evidence, see André Lemaire, *Les écoles et la formation de la Bible dans l'ancien Israël* (Göttingen: Vandenhoeck & Ruprecht, 1981).

[59] Carr, *Writing on the Tablet of the Heart*, 119. A number of preexilic texts indicate a group of trained elites whose goal is to use literacy to "*help* enculturate, shape the behavior, and otherwise mentally separate an educated upper class from their non-educated peers."

[60] D.W. Jamieson-Drake, *Scribes and Schools in Monarchic Judah* (SWBA 9; Sheffield: Almond Press, 1991).

Even if educational opportunities existed for scribal trainees to learn the wisdom tradition along with other administrative matters, many proverbs in the collection have a pithy quality that would have appealed across all socioeconomic categories. The sharing of memorable maxims was not confined to the upper-class members of Israelite society.[61] Several sayings illustrate the point. For example, "Better to meet a she-bear robbed of its cubs than to confront a fool immersed in folly" (17:12). Or "Train children in the right way, and when old, they will not stray" (22:6). Such observations have no markers of royal provenance and probably circulated far and wide in the region. Proverbs of this type probably had an extensive oral history before being included in the collection that survived. We have mentioned the hypothesis that the bulk of this advice originated in a village or "folk" setting and that the book's content largely reflects such a milieu. The final form of the text does not read as a manual for aspiring officials, and proponents of this "folk" hypothesis caution against linking popular sayings with the king's court. Maxims that express concern for the poor and an interest in communal life are often cited. A communitarian perspective is reflected in statements like 19:22: "What is desirable in a person is loyalty, and it is better to be poor than a liar." In light of such proverbs, this hypothesis has merit: a number of sayings in the book seem to lack the specific characteristics of a more elite background. For example, the proverbs relating to marriage have a classless quality and could have originated among diverse sectors of Israelite society (e.g., 12:4; 27:15–16).

While it is an important addition to this debate, the argument for a "folk" origin for many of the sayings and units in the book operates with some vague assumptions. This hypothesis corrects the understanding of Proverbs as merely an upper-class collection, but the language of family or farming does not necessarily indicate a more popular origin for the

---

[61] Recent estimates indicate a low literacy rate during the First Temple period, as little as 5 percent of the population. In terms of content and mindset, R.N. Whybray, *Wealth and Poverty in the Book of Proverbs* (JSOTSup 99; Sheffield: JSOT Press, 1990), 68–69, likens Proverbs to the sayings of preliterate peoples in Africa. Cf. Friedemann W. Golka, *The Leopard's Spots: Biblical and African Wisdom in Proverbs* (Edinburgh: T&T Clark 1993). See the trenchant critique of this comparison in Michael V. Fox, "The Social Location of the Book of Proverbs," in *Texts, Temples, and Traditions: A Tribute to Menahem Haran* (ed. Michael V. Fox et al.: Winona Lake, Ind.: Eisenbrauns, 1996), 234. With regard to the topic of money, Whybray, *Wealth and Poverty in the Book of Proverbs*, 23–61, cites an acute awareness of poverty issues and a cautious perspective on pecuniary matters in Proverbs. He argues that such an outlook could not have come from royal advisers.

text as a whole or for a particular saying. Agricultural metaphors often appear in proverbs and other forms of literature that originated in an urban setting.[62] In addition to their plain-sense meaning, statements about false weights and measures (16:11; 20:10; 20:23), tampering with boundary markers (22:28; 23:10), and the benefits of tilling the land versus engaging in "worthless pursuits" (12:11), can function as general warnings about proper behavior. These offenses have a symbolic value that could apply to any number of situations. Moreover, the descriptions about how to navigate among the power elements of society (e.g., 16:13; 25:15) cannot be the exclusive product of "folk" observers looking in from the outside. The cogency of the reflections and the antecedent Egyptian advice about courtly matters point to a scribal origin for such sayings.[63] In all likelihood, trained scribes (the "learned clerks") gathered from diverse sources, including both foreign instructions and popular sayings from across the socioeconomic spectrum, in an effort to compile an effective, accessible, and colorful collection.[64] The timeless nature of Proverbs is a tribute to the resourceful editors who sifted through available material. This conclusion is critical to our study of retribution and causality: the book was pieced together by established individuals who wished to create and encourage a reliable ethical model and a largely consistent *Tun-Ergehen-Zusammenhang*. The editors' belief in the possibility of present justice and the need to maintain the status quo are indicators of their entrenched social position.

With regard to the presumed addressee, the reference to בני ("my son") in 1:10 and the didactic language of chapters 1–9 suggest an audience of impressionable adolescents and young adults. This is general moral instruction with the express purpose of steering pupils down the proper "path," or way of life. The "son" in Proverbs, who is

---

[62] Fox, "The Social Location of the Book of Proverbs," 233, argues that even an educated, urban sage like Ben Sira could employ diverse metaphors to make a point. He further explains that several sayings in Proverbs "speak from within" the agricultural world (e.g., 11:26; 14:4) and probably derive from a rural setting.

[63] Advice on how to conduct oneself at court is a standard topic in sapiential discourse (e.g., chapters 2–4 of Ptahhotep). As previously stated, the book of Proverbs addresses such matters in detail, revealing an affinity for Egyptian motifs and an interest in scribal/royal affairs. In addition, Fox, *Proverbs 1–9*, 9, points to the interest in goldsmithery (17:3; 27:21), fine jewelry (25:11–12), and messengers (e.g., 10:26) in this book, all indicators of a more urban setting.

[64] Fox, "The Social Location of the Book of Proverbs," 236: "Everything we have was channelled to the court and through it; the flow cannot be supposed to move in the other direction."

clearly at a formative stage in his life, is told to beware of wickedness and heed the public cry of Wisdom (1:20). By accepting her call with diligence and humility, he can "understand the fear of the Lord and find the knowledge of God" (2:5). Success and lengthy days await him if he is upright (3:2), but straying from the correct path will lead him into the clutches of the "Strange Woman" and ultimately "the depths of Sheol" (9:18). Children should trust in God, Wisdom, and their parents to avoid such a disastrous fate. How literally we are to take this father-son paradigm in Proverbs 1–9 is an open question. This motif was common in the wisdom tradition throughout the ancient Near East: fathers regularly instructed their "sons," teaching them the family trade and in some instances how to read and write. Many Egyptian and Babylonian instructions describe children learning proverbs and other skills under the tutelage of their fathers. Some of these texts appear to use "son" figuratively to refer to a pupil or apprentice, so that the designation is a generic one.[65] The book of Proverbs has a similar mixture, with many sayings focusing on the parent-child relationship and its fundamental importance.[66] For example, Prov 4:3–4 should be taken at face value:

> When I was a son with my father,
> tender, and my mother's favorite,
> he taught me, and said to me,
> "Let your heart hold fast my words;
> keep my commandments, and live."

---

[65] A family model is present in many instructions and often explicitly stated. For example, Amenemope addresses the maxims to his "youngest son" (ẓ kt.f n mswf, 2.13). The Instruction of Anii is for the benefit of his son Khonshotep, who is a scribe like his father (9.13). The specificity of these ascriptions suggests that they are historically reliable. Scribal successors, whether relatives of a senior sage or not, often had to undergo a period of apprenticeship or "liminality," during which they received instruction about their duties and how to act in accordance with Wisdom. See Leo G. Perdue, "Liminality as a Social Setting for Wisdom Instructions," *ZAW* 93 (1981): 114–26, who includes a discussion of Ahiqar training his nephew Nadin in a family setting.

[66] The parental role is highlighted at the beginning of the two major units in Proverbs (1:8; 10:1). The administering of corporal punishment (Prov 13:24; 22:15; 23:13–14; 29:15) and steering children from adulterous/deceitful inclinations (6:20–35) are two primary responsibilities. Camp, *Wisdom and the Feminine in the Book of Proverbs*, 251–52, understands the family emphasis to be a postexilic feature that took "complete precedence" over any extra-familial (especially diplomatic) language in the sayings. Yet the familial emphasis could have been equally present in preexilic versions of the text. These two models can be found side-by-side in most Egyptian instructions.

It is clear that responsible parenting has tangible benefits for the dutiful child: the father guarantees lengthy days in 3:2 and prudence in 5:2. Children must heed their parents, whose "commandment is a lamp and the teaching a light, and the reproofs of discipline are the way of life" (6:23).

Yet these proverbs were also intended for public consumption, to be disseminated and shared beyond individual family units. The father-son framework functions as a base model in the book, but such language could also apply to another relative, scribal trainee, or aspiring court official. The "learned clerks" responsible for Proverbs mixed and matched to suit a variety of settings, and it can be assumed that the tradition was often imparted to individuals who had no kinship tie to a particular instructor. For example, Prov 5:12–14:

> And you say, "Oh, how I hated discipline,
> and my heart despised reproof!
> I did not listen to the voice of my teachers
> or incline my ear to my instructors.
> Now I am at the point of utter ruin in the public assembly."

This language does not necessarily demonstrate the existence of full-fledged schools, but it does imply that officials taught proverbs to pupils who were not their children and used the effective threat of public humiliation on adolescent boys. Such statements in the collection suggest both private and public teaching in ancient Israel; the material in this book could not have functioned exclusively as a manual for Israelite homes. For our purposes, whether extra-familial exposure to the tradition occurred in a scribal apprenticeship system, an official school in Jerusalem, or on a somewhat *ad hoc* basis among "learned clerks" is less important than the fact that a group of literate citizens in ancient Israel wished to propagate a particular kind of worldview and did so through public teaching.

In considering the *Sitz im Leben* of Proverbs, we have taken the position that a group of postexilic scribes ultimately compiled the collection, drawing on local and international sources to offer a consistent principle of justice. These redactors used images beyond their own experience to make compelling observations and appeal to a large segment of the populace. Their vision of a harmonious society functions as a unifying thread in the text. As Fox explains, "This is the ideal that the author-redactors of Proverbs-the king's men-*want* us to derive. It is a deliberate and programmatic construal of reality."[67] The compilers of Proverbs endorse the same basic goals as their Egyptian predecessors and remain consistent with the international wisdom tradition up to this point. This collection seeks a society free of corruption in which everyone knows their place, and people rely on one another to protect mutual interests and preserve existing hierarchies. It is a worldview in which obedience to God and virtuous behavior (intertwined in the tradition) bring positive results. Those who earnestly seek Wisdom will find her and thereby attain happiness in the earthly realm. The programmatic language might not always reflect reality, as the editors of Proverbs maintain an upbeat assessment of human possibility in order to motivate the recipients of this advice. The precise language used to articulate this understanding requires further attention, particularly the relationship between divine agency and human initiative.

### 5. Divine Agency and the Yahwistic Redaction Theory

We have mentioned the claim of McKane and others that a postexilic redactor(s) added God-language to a previously secular instruction in Proverbs.[68] This hypothesis is quite relevant to our study, since it raises the possibility of an earlier layer of material in which the deity does not play the same dominant role in determining human outcomes. In his commentary on Proverbs, McKane isolates chapters 1–9, 22:17–24:22, and 31:1–9 as part of an international "Instruction" genre. He argues that these sections are dependent on Egyptian literature and originated during an earlier period (possibly Solomonic) than the shorter clusters in 10:1–22:16. With regard to the latter set of sayings, he posits a progression from a secular, "old school" Wisdom that is concerned with the individual (Class A), to a community-oriented group of proverbs (Class B), and finally God-language indicating Yahwistic piety (Class C). According to McKane, the late preexilic sages responsible for Class C were coming to terms with Yahwism and beginning a process that would culminate in Ben Sira's complete identification of Wisdom

---

[67] Fox, "The Social Location of the Book of Proverbs," 238.

[68] Cf. Joseph Blenkinsopp, *Wisdom and Law in the Old Testament* (Oxford: Oxford University Press, 1995), 26; Whybray, *Composition of the Book of Proverbs*, 157–65, argues that sections of Proverbs were reconfigured to suit a more explicit theological agenda.

and Torah.[69] Blenkinsopp describes a similar sequence, arguing that a "prudential, religiously neutral" set of sayings received a Yahwistic "baptism."[70] Fox has advanced the most cogent argument for this development: he outlines "Egyptian," "Yahwistic," and "theological" stages in the composition of Proverbs.[71] According to Fox, these stages are overlapping and do not represent a strict chronological progression. The middle category signifies a "limited reworking" and an attempt to link the God-concept with normative Israelite religion.[72] Under the rubric of "Yahwistic" sayings, God stands independent of earthly events, yet firmly and ultimately in control of human destiny (e.g., Prov 21:30).[73] Finally, the "theological" stage includes much of the material in Proverbs 1–9, in which personified Wisdom serves as an intermediary between God and humanity.

This type of textual development is possible and might apply to certain sayings, but there are also major problems with the thesis. On the one hand, theological variation between proverbs might represent a shift from educational wisdom to a distinctly Yahwistic stage. McKane points to 13:14 and 14:27 as a paradigmatic example:

(13:14) תורת חכם מקור חיים לסור ממקשי מות
(14:27) יראת יהוה מקור חיים לסור ממקשי מות

The teaching of the wise is a fountain of life, so that one may avoid the snares of death (13:14).
The fear of the Lord is a fountain of life, so that one may avoid the snares of death (14:27).

According to McKane, this example represents an excellent illustration of this transition: "The discipline of piety is substituted for educational discipline and Yahweh takes the place formerly occupied by the wisdom teacher."[74] Yet even if we allow that such changes occurred at several points in the collection, it is problematic to assume a linear progression from a religiously neutral discourse to pietism, particularly if such an argument is used to chart the overall development of the

---

[69] McKane, *Proverbs*, 19.

[70] Blenkinsopp, *Wisdom and Law*, 26.

[71] Michael V. Fox, "Aspects of Religion in the Book of Proverbs," *HUCA* 39 (1968), 57.

[72] Fox, "Aspects of Religion," 67, acknowledges that the specifics of Israelite tradition (history, covenant, and cult) are missing in the "Yahwistic" phase.

[73] The "fear of the Lord" belongs in this category.

[74] McKane, *Proverbs*, 18.

book. As the previous chapter demonstrated, the Egyptian analogy is flawed on this point. The wisdom tradition in Egypt did not undergo the type of complete transformation that is frequently assumed by modern scholarship. The deity stands in Ptahhotep as a powerful force in determining human events. Egyptian instructions both early and late reflect a complex relationship between God ($p^3$ $n\underline{t}r$) and Ma'at, rather than a progression from an automatic framework to a divinely controlled system of causality. Amenemope has a more pietistic tone (and more overtly religious content) than its sapiential predecessors, but early instructions like Ptahhotep also acknowledge the power of God to shape human affairs.

It is doubtful that a version of Proverbs ever existed that contained little or no mention of divine agency. Divine freedom and a self-regulating system are twin features of this collection, and they operate in a complicated dialectical relationship. Statements of a prosaic nature do not necessarily indicate a passive deity, and they certainly do not reflect a "secular" understanding of the created order. As Huwiler argues, "Although it is clear that some sayings claim a connection between act and consequence without mentioning God, it needs to be examined whether this necessarily means that they presuppose divine inactivity."[75] Even with a seemingly clear-cut case like 13:14 and 14:27, we could have an example of *variation* rather than *substitution*.[76] Sayings about God's power can be found throughout the collection, even in units that supposedly consist of preexilic, traditional advice.[77] Although

---

[75] Huwiler, "Control of Reality," 68–69. Whybray, *The Composition of the Book of Proverbs*, 59, argues that in chapters 1–9, Yahweh or Wisdom is mentioned as a source of authority, but not both simultaneously. He suggests "Yahweh additions" in passages like 2:5–8 and 3:26. Significantly, Whybray rules out a *systematic* redaction for chapters 1–9, even if the text was altered or supplemented with God-language in a few places. Most of the non-Yahweh sayings were left intact, creating a kind of interplay in this section.

[76] Frederick Wilson, "Sacred and Profane? The Yahwistic Redaction of Proverbs Reconsidered," in *The Listening Heart: Essays in Wisdom and the Psalms in Honor of Roland E. Murphy, O. Carm.* (JSOTSup 58; Sheffield: JSOT Press, 1987), 323.

[77] Lennart Boström, *The God of the Sages: the Portrayal of God in the Book of Proverbs* (CBOTS 29; Stockholm: Almqvist and Wiksell International, 1990), 109–12, cites chapters 25–29 and the references to the deity in one of the more "secular" sections of the book. Even if the God-sayings are less frequent, divine agency is integral to the message of this unit (e.g., 25:21–22). Katharine J. Dell, *The Book of Proverbs in Social and Theological Context* (Cambridge: Cambridge University Press, 2006), 90–124, catalogues every reference to God in Proverbs. She argues that the "religious and the less religious" existed side by side in the earliest versions of subunits and in the oral tradition of sharing sayings. Heim, *Like Grapes of Gold Set in Silver*, demonstrates the

it is possible that a later hand inserted God-proverbs in several places to supplement the pragmatic advice (especially as the religious tradition developed after the exile), there was never a pietistic moment in which the compilers of Proverbs moved from the predictable, God-as-midwife framework, to a more arbitrary, "Yahwistic" worldview.[78]

Additional examples demonstrate this tension in Proverbs. On the one hand, Koch's understanding of causality in Proverbs works well for many of the sayings. According to 11:3, "The integrity of the upright guides them, but the crookedness of the treacherous destroys them." Here and in other proverbs of this type, Koch assumes that God has set up a system that functions automatically. Elsewhere in the text, however, God intervenes as *the* limiting force. This pattern has a retributive element, with the deity functioning to "bring back" an individual's deed upon them: "And will he not repay humanity according to their deeds (והשיב לאדם כפעלו)?" (Prov 24:12, translation mine). Similar logic can be found in 25:22. For one who deals kindly with an enemy, the same can be expected in return: "the Lord will reward/repay you (ויהוה ישלם לך)." A third, more ambiguous set of sayings contains passive formulations, so that an event simply happens to a person with no explicit reference to the agent (e.g., "Be assured, the wicked will not go unpunished," 11:21). Such observations affirm the idea of a predictable and just society, where a person's character determines his or her fate. Nevertheless, these sayings do not signify an impersonal system, since God often seems to function as an implicit force. This is the so-called "divine passive." The use of a passive verbal form does not necessarily indicate a passive deity.[79]

---

importance of Yahweh sayings in the various proverbial clusters. He concludes that "the often assumed 'secular' background of many sayings, including notions of theological 'reinterpretation', should finally be put to rest" (p. 316).

[78] Jerry Gladson, "Retributive Paradoxes in Proverbs 10–29," (Ph.D. diss., Vanderbilt University, 1975), 225, argues that the God-language in Proverbs represents a "non-polemical, didactic concern for human limitation," as opposed to an editorial layer.

[79] Boström, *God of the Sages*, 114, estimates that 90 percent of the statements in Proverbs contain no direct references to God. Yet even in supposedly non-theological sayings like 10:24 ("What the wicked dread will come upon them, but the desire of the righteous will be granted [יתן]"), God is quite possibly the responsible agent for determining outcomes. McKane, *Proverbs*, 426, assumes that the Lord does the granting in 10:24b. Another example can be found in 11:31: "If the righteous are repaid on earth, how much more the wicked and the sinner!" The same verbal form of 25:22 occurs in 11:31, but in the Pual stem (ישׁלם). According to Koch, "Is There a Doctrine of Retribution," 61, Prov 11:31 represents an automatic process for each individual based on his or her actions (his "schicksalwirkende Tatsphäre"). God must

The relationship between the book of Proverbs and the larger religious scene has bearing on this question of a Yahwistic redaction, in order to consider the presuppositions of Israelite sages. Although the compilers of this collection express no outward interest in the national destiny of Israel or the cultic institutions of the day, their piety might still be influencing their linguistic constructs and understanding of authority. Prov 21:30 is one possible example: "No wisdom, no understanding, no counsel, can avail against the Lord." Does this language signify an implicit devotion to Yahwism and to at least some of the legal material found in the final form of the biblical texts? H.D. Preuss rejects any connection in this regard, claiming that there is nothing distinctively Yahwistic about Proverbs, including the statements on divine agency and human limitation. According to this reading, Proverbs is part of an international genre and completely foreign to the rest of the biblical corpus.[80] In contrast, Roland Murphy posits a connection between the worldview of the sages and covenantal Yahwism. He understands there to be a genuine compatibility between the Wisdom literature and the rest of the Hebrew Bible.[81] In his expansive discussions on this topic, von Rad takes a similar approach.[82] John Collins examines the relationship between the natural theology of the Wisdom literature and incidents of special revelation in other biblical genres. According to Collins, the two function on different levels: "Even when the sages

---

be the controlling agent, however, since the same verb is used of the deity's retributive action in 16:7. Even in the absence of clear-cut juridical language, God can still be associated with passive formulations like 11:31.

[80] H.D. Preuss, "Das Gottesbild der alteren Weisheit Israels," in *Studies in the Religion of Ancient Israel* (VTSup 23; Leiden: Brill, 1972), 117–45. Cf. Herbert N. Schneidau, *Sacred Discontent* (Berkeley: University of California Press, 1976).

[81] Roland E. Murphy, "Wisdom and Yahwism," in *No Famine in the Land: Studies in Honor of John L. McKenzie* (ed. J.A. Flanagan and A.W. Robinson; Missoula, Mo.: Scholars Press, 1975), 119, opposes efforts to construct a biblical theology that dismiss Proverbs as a "pagan" intrusion into the canon. According to Murphy, the ethical responsibilities highlighted in Proverbs are consistent with the Pentateuch and the Prophets: "In short, the formation of responsible character, over and beyond the goals of the decalogue, form the heart of wisdom teaching, and this was seen as responsible Yahwism."

[82] Gerhard von Rad, *Wisdom in Israel* (trans. J.D. Martin; London/Harrisburg, Pa.: SCM Press/Trinity Press International, 1972), 307, argues that the goal outlined in Proverbs consists of determining what is virtuous in any given situation and adopting the right attitude: "In her wisdom Israel created an intellectual sphere in which it was possible to discuss both the multiplicity of trivial, daily occurrences as well as basic theological principles. This wisdom is, therefore, at all events to be regarded as a form of Yahwism, although—as a result of the unusual nature of the tasks involved—an unusual form and, in the theological structure of its statements, very different from the other ways in which Yahwism reveals itself."

speak of Yahweh, they speak of him in language derived from universal human experience."[83] Unlike Ben Sira and the Wisdom of Solomon, which "nationalize" Wisdom at certain points, Proverbs offers more general observations based on daily occurrences. Such a focus differs from the special revelation described in the Pentateuch and the Prophets. Yet there is a noteworthy connection, even if incidental, since the narrative and prophetic texts contain statements on human weakness and divine providence that are similar to what appears in Proverbs. The biblical writers often found common ground, even if they utilized different genres and theological constructs.[84]

Although rigid in his analysis, Preuss is correct that many (but not all) of the sayings in Proverbs could just as easily be found in an Egyptian instruction, with *p³ nṯr* ("the god") substituted for Yahweh. Unlike Preuss, however, we argue that interchangeability with a foreign instruction does not render Proverbs hostile or even alien to the historical credos and prophetic oracles found in the Hebrew Bible. The similarities with antecedent material from neighboring cultures like Egypt indicate that the compilers of Proverbs operated under an established tradition of providing colorful reflections on the particularities of life and the necessary traits, including pietism, that lead to success. This sapiential worldview is not unique to Israelite religion as much as we are able to comprehend it, but the outlook and content of Proverbs are in many respects complementary to other types of biblical literature. This interchangeability is the crux of the debate and the factor that Preuss and other scholars have been unable to accept. The issue centers on whether one believes that insights into common human experience by means of an established genre (the instruction) are a useful supplement to other forms of biblical literature that emphasize special revelation, the unique intervention of Yahweh in Israelite history. For the final

---

[83] John J. Collins, "The Biblical Precedent for Natural Theology," in *Encounters with Biblical Theology* (Minneapolis: Fortress Press, 2005), 97; originally published in *JAAR* 45 (March 1977): 35–67.

[84] John J. Collins, "Proverbial Wisdom and the Yahwist Vision," in *Encounters with Biblical Theology* (Minneapolis: Fortress Press, 2005), 113; originally published in *Semeia* 17 (1980): 1–17, argues that the logic of the "limiting" proverbs corresponds to what we find in certain prophetic passages. For example, the admission of mystery in Prov 21:30 correlates with Isa 44:25. There are also passages in the Historical Books and the Prophets that express caution about the perspective of the sages. See James L. Crenshaw, "Method in Determining Wisdom Influence upon 'Historical Literature,'" *JBL* 88 (1969), 134.

redactors of the Hebrew Bible, the similarity of Proverbs with foreign instructions, even in terms of God-language, does not seem to have been the major concern that it is for modern interpreters.[85] The sayings in this book had an important role in ancient Israelite society, before and after the exile. The fact that the final form of the Hebrew Bible places more of an emphasis on special revelation does not prove that sapiential discourse had a marginal status among ancient purveyors of Israelite religion, nor does it indicate that many sayings in this collection are necessarily pre-Yahwistic.

### 6. *Proverbs, World Order, and Social Solidarity*

Since a number of proverbs in this collection suggest a neat pattern of cause and effect, many scholars have understood Proverbs to be expressive of a "world-order" that is built into the universe.[86] According to this hypothesis, Israelite sages borrowed heavily from Egypt's wisdom tradition, including Maʾat, in describing a self-regulating universe. The world-order hypothesis implies a determinism in Proverbs, or at least in parts of this collection, that functions independently from God. This order marks a consistency in the world, a "natural force like gravity, that automatically and indifferently links consequence to deed."[87] Since certain sayings suggest regularity in earthly events and a deity whose involvement in human affairs is inconstant and/or remote, such a reading is understandable. In isolated passages, the act-consequence

---

[85] As Collins, "The Biblical Precedent for Natural Theology," 94, argues, "The fact that the limiting power may be known by names other than Yahweh in other religious traditions does not detract from the religious value of the concept." The universal aspects of Proverbs are nevertheless striking, particularly if the collection was assembled after the exile, when religious identity had become a more pressing issue. See J. Coert Rylaarsdam, *Revelation in Jewish Wisdom Literature* (Chicago: University of Chicago Press, 1946), 26.

[86] Discussions of a "world order" understanding in Proverbs include Hartmut Gese, *Lehre and Wirklichkeit in der alten Weisheit: Studien zu den Sprüchen Salomos und zu dem Buche Hiob* (Tübingen: Mohr, 1958); Hans H. Schmid, *Wesen und Geschichte der Weisheit: eine Untersuchung zur altorientalischen Weisheitsliteratur* (BZAW 101; Berlin: Töpelmann, 1966); idem, *Gerechtigkeit als Weltordnung* (BHT 40; Tübingen: Mohr, 1968); Ernst Würthwein, "Egyptian Wisdom and the Old Testament," in *Studies in Ancient Israelite Wisdom* (trans. B.W. Kovacs; ed. J.L. Crenshaw; New York: KTAV, 1976), 113–34. Koch does not use the terminology of "order," but his argument in "Is There a Doctrine of Retribution in the Old Testament?" amounts to a similar perspective.

[87] Michael V. Fox, "World Order and Maʿat: A Crooked Parallel," *JANES* 23 (1995), 41, describes the theory but does not subscribe to it.

relationship is expressed in absolute, impersonal terms: "Whoever digs a pit will fall into it, and a stone will come back on the one who starts it rolling" (26:27). Here and in similar sayings, the system in place seems to produce just results automatically. In the opening chapters of the book, the sapiential author points to a logical universe set in motion by a responsible and omniscient deity: "The Lord by wisdom founded the earth; by understanding he established the heavens" (3:19). Indeed, Proverbs 1–9 conveys careful planning by God, who had an important helper in Lady Wisdom (8:22–31).

The world-order hypothesis is a problematic scholarly construct, however, since it oversimplifies ancient instructions *and* imposes modern theological concepts on a collection that is not systematic. This is especially true when one considers the consequences of human behavior as addressed in Proverbs. As Murphy explains of this diverse collection and the world-order hypothesis, "accepted regularities are not the same as an 'order' that is envisioned as operative in the reality of everyday experience and as the goal of the wisdom enterprise."[88] Although many sayings affirm consistency in the outcomes of certain behavioral patterns, we cannot derive a mechanistic principle from this diverse collection. Statements such as "Those who are attentive to a matter will prosper" (16:20), or "The evil are ensnared by the transgression of their lips" (12:13), are not presented as universally true. These are merely assertions of predictability, which we would expect in instructional texts from any number of cultural contexts. The worldview presented by the sages responsible for Proverbs is certainly optimistic, and their larger purpose is to demonstrate the tangible benefits of righteousness. Yet the pursuit of righteousness and goal of consistency do not constitute a world order: it is customary, even required, for didactic texts to offer specified norms for human conduct and then guarantee success for conformity to those norms.[89] With their interest in maintaining social structures and fostering dutiful behavior among new charges, the edi-

---

[88] Roland E. Murphy, *The Tree of Life: An Exploration of Biblical Wisdom Literature* (3d ed.; Grand Rapids: Eerdmans, 1990), 116. While his thinking on this issue has varied, this statement above seems to be Murphy's definitive thesis about Proverbs and "world order."

[89] Fox, "World Order and Ma'at," 40, argues that Wisdom literature, in addition to other prophetic, legal, and historical texts, believes in a "constructed order," which simply means the formation of an orderly society. This constructed order is often *the* stated goal in Proverbs.

tors of Proverbs had a stake in promoting a reliable act-consequence relationship.

Even if Proverbs forecasts good news for the virtuous individual, this work does not reflect the perspective of naive simpletons whose rigid determinism ignores social injustice and the inequalities of life under the sun. While conservative in their outlook, these sages are not identical to Job's friends, who refuse to acknowledge the vagaries of human experience.[90] Numerous sayings in Proverbs admit that the righteous might suffer: "Do no violence to the place where the righteous live; for though they fall seven times, they will rise again" (24:15–16). Moreover, the sages understand the possibility of the wicked prospering and having dominion over the helpless for a time (e.g., 28:12, 28; 29:16). Their basic optimism is therefore mitigated by admissions of the way the world actually works. Proverbs also promises a variety of outcomes, as opposed to one consequence, for specific behavioral patterns. The wicked in particular are associated with a variety of destinies: lack of material necessities, alienation from God, criticism from peers, internal anxiety, and fleeting prosperity.[91] Even with this acknowledgment of diversity, the sages promise a nexus of deed and result. They appear to affirm the idea of what Boström and others call a "character-consequence" relationship. A prevailing message in Proverbs is that both the righteous and the wicked will *eventually* get what they deserve.[92]

The world-order hypothesis also rests on a questionable understanding of Ma'at in Egyptian literature and its relationship to Israel's wisdom tradition. According to the argument, the compliers of Proverbs borrowed heavily from Egyptian instructions, utilizing this famous concept to offer an Israelite version of how the universe operates in a fair and systematic manner. Gese became one of the first advocates

---

[90] For example, Eliphaz: "Think now, who that was innocent ever perished? Or where were the upright cut off?" (4:7). Bildad claims that Job's children deserve their fate: "If your children sinned against him, he delivered them into the power of their transgression" (8:4). On the statements in Proverbs that seem to reflect this logic (e.g., 12:21), see Boström, *God of the Sages*, 122.

[91] Huwiler, "Control of Reality," 74.

[92] Huwiler, "Control of Reality," 65–66, argues that the multiplicity of potential outcomes for human behavior casts doubt on the "character-consequence" paradigm, since there is so little consistency in the relationship between deed and result. Yet this variation is precisely the point of the "character-consequence" argument as the present writer understands it. Wickedness can lead to a variety of outcomes, but the sinner still receives appropriate punishment. While the consequences of individual actions might vary widely, the sages are committed to the idea that sinful behavior is ultimately futile and righteousness profitable. See Boström, *God of the Sages*, 108.

for this type of development: he posited a world-order framework in Proverbs 10–29 parallel to (but not necessarily based on) Ma'at.[93] He also cited expressions that contrast with the prevailing international tradition as he understood it; these "israelitische Sondergut" focus on divine freedom, the independence of Yahweh from the world order.[94] Schmid goes further than Gese, suggesting a direct relationship between Ma'at and the understanding of causality in Proverbs. He points to Hebrew צדק/צדקה as the designated term for this world-order, so that the person who exhibits "righteousness" conforms to the universe as established by God.[95] While demonstrating some important similarities between Egyptian and Israelite instructions in terms of language about the deity, Schmid's overall project has not been accepted as tenable.[96] Another relevant study is that of Christa Kayatz, who provides textual examples (Egyptian and Israelite) of divine "I-speeches" and different types of sapiential discourse.[97] Kayatz argues that the longer speeches of Proverbs 1–9 are preexilic, written during a period of relative stability and cultural interchange with Egypt (probably the Solomonic period), and that the description of Lady Wisdom in chapter 8 corresponds to the goddess Ma'at. According to Kayatz, Ma'at does not correlate precisely with Lady Wisdom, especially since the figure in Proverbs 8 is not a goddess. The editors of Proverbs adapted Ma'at to Israelite conceptions of divine Wisdom in order to present a rational understanding of the created order.[98]

---

[93] Gese, *Lehre und Wirklichkeit in der alten Weisheit*, 31, hedges on the direct influence of Ma'at on Proverbs, claiming that Israelite sages could have developed a similar concept independently. Yet he affirms the same type of world-order thinking in Egyptian and Israelite instructions.

[94] Gese, *Lehre und Wirklichkeit in der alten Weisheit*, 45–50, citing such sayings as Prov 16:1, 9; 20:24; 21:31; 25:2. According to this reading of Proverbs, Yahweh has the sovereign power (defined in terms of "grace") to intercede at any moment.

[95] Schmid, *Gerechtigkeit als Weltordnung*, 158, cites Prov 11:4–6; 11:18–19; 12:28; 13:6; 14:34; 16:8, 31; 21:21.

[96] See the critiques of Roland E. Murphy, "Wisdom Theses," in *Wisdom and Knowledge: Essays in Honour of Joseph Papin* (ed. J. Armenti; 2 vols.; Villanova: Villanova University Press, 1976), 2:197; Fox, "World Order and Ma'at," 39.

[97] Kayatz, *Studien zu Proverbien 1–9*, 89–93, demonstrates form-critical similarities between divine and royal "I-speeches" and the discourses of Proverbs 1–9. The authors of Proverbs 1–9 appear to have known the basic format of these Egyptian speeches (or similar types) and adopted several key features.

[98] Kayatz, *Studien zu Proverbien 1–9*, 119, 138. On the problems with this thesis, see Fox, "World Order and Ma'at," 44–47. Ma'at never makes a speech analogous to the one in Proverbs 8. Both Kayatz and Fox also discuss the possible connection between

Discussion of a possible connection between Wisdom/causality in Proverbs and Maʾat/causality in the Egyptian instructions can be sharpened by dispensing with the world-order framework in favor of a comparative inquiry based on similar understandings of social solidarity. Recent commentators on ancient Near Eastern Wisdom have made this interpretive move. In particular, Assmann's definition of Maʾat as "kommunikative Solidarität/Reziprozität" is an important corrective for understanding how this concept works in Egyptian texts and the nature of its influence. The "justice" that the instructions speak of is a connective justice, which relates more to respect among business associates, neighbors, and family members, than to an impersonal order. Israelite sages clearly admired this aspect of Egypt's wisdom tradition, including the concern for honest public speaking, the elimination of corruption, and care for the marginalized. These features are the very essence of Maʾat in the *sbꜣy.t*. While the redactors of Proverbs do not replicate the complex Egyptian concept in their collection, the concern for public justice is a noteworthy parallel between Proverbs and its Egyptian antecedents.[99] This is a more accurate starting point for Egyptian-Israelite comparative study in reference to Proverbs than the world-order hypothesis.[100] The social orientation is increasingly recognized by biblical scholars as integral to the act-consequence understanding in the collection, a feature shared with the Egyptian instructions. Keller argues that the social sphere is the focal point for a just principle: "Im gesellschaftlichen Leben *ist es nämlich so*, daß der 'Gerechte' Erfolg hat, ja es muß so sein, und das nicht aufgrund irgendeiner Weltordnung, sondern als Folge richtiger Handhabung der gesellschaftlichen Spielregeln."[101] Keller demonstrates the "transactional" nature of the sages' outlook and their interest in a person's public behavior. Economic vocabulary clarifies the principle in Proverbs: "The *wage* of the

---

Wisdom and the Isis aretalogies; these later speeches are a more plausible source for Proverbs 8.

[99] Fox, "World Order and Maʿat," 48: "The Israelites (or their Canaanite predecessors) could draw on Egyptian Wisdom-not necessarily aware of its origins-without importing the entirety of the genre or even its most basic axioms."

[100] The similarities in word choice, particularly expressions involving the "heart" (e.g., Prov 17:3) and "listening" (21:28), and the language relating to justice demonstrate that Israelite sages were aware of these traditions in Egypt.

[101] Carl-A. Keller, "Zum sogenannten Vergeltungsglauben im Proverbienbuch," in *Beiträge zur alttestamentlichen Theologie: Festschrift für Walther Zimmerli zum 70. Geburtstag* (ed. H. Donner and R. Hanart; Göttingen: Vandenhoeck & Ruprecht, 1977), 225.

righteous leads to life, the *gain* of the wicked to sin" (10:16).[102] Similarly,
Bernd Janowski argues that Koch's framework is too rigid for what one
finds in this collection. Citing a list of noteworthy passages in Proverbs
(11:25–27; 21:13; 22:9; 24:24), he argues, "Sie beruhen alle auf der
Grundannahme, daß der Zusammenhang von Tun und Ergehen sich
nicht von selbst, also gleichsam 'automatisch' einstellt, sondern eine
Funktion des Füreinander- bzw. des Gegeneinander-Handelns ist."[103]
Finally, Boström is attentive to the social solidarity aspect. Many of the
statements in Proverbs reflect simple observations and truisms about
life, rather than a highly developed world-order principle. According to
Boström, Proverbs contains idiomatic expressions, often hyperbolized
for dramatic effect, and these seek to instill a set of values into impressionable pupils.[104]

### 7. The Didactic Process in Proverbs

Such readings are accurate: Proverbs functions as a pedagogical resource
for appropriate human conduct and mutual solidarity, particularly for
individuals transitioning to adulthood and scribal responsibilities. The
larger goal of the collection, often stated, is to shape behavior through
encouragement, intimidation, and simple observation of the human
situation. Such an emphasis is most apparent in chapters 1–9, where
the son receives stern warnings that the only "path" (דרך) to happiness
and success proceeds through Wisdom. All other roads lead to wickedness and destruction. In this presentation, the sages present an ethical
dualism that is foundational to the collection. An exploration of this
didactic process and its earthly focus provides a useful framework from
which to evaluate later instructions from the Hellenistic period.

This understanding of the book might seem to be an oversimplification, since many of the sayings are general reflections and not hortatory
in nature. A number of statements in Proverbs are retrospective and
presented as hard-nosed facts about human existence. For example, the
claim that "The poor are disliked even by their neighbors, but the rich

---

[102] Even the deity becomes a participant in the process as the agent who "repays/
rewards" (שׁלם, 25:22).

[103] Bernd Janowski, "Die Tat kehrt zum Täter zurück: Offene Fragen im Umkreis
des 'Tun-Ergehen-Zusammenhangs,'" *ZTK* 91 (1994), 265.

[104] Boström, *God of the Sages*, 125–26.

have many friends" (14:20) is a common-sense assertion. This verse functions as a commentary on behavioral patterns, a general statement on life as the sages have witnessed and experienced it. The observation that the rich have obsequious "friends" is frequent in sapiential texts from many contexts. Yet even if this is not an explicit command, such a truism has a larger purpose for the teaching enterprise of Proverbs. It explains to the addressee an aspect of life under the sun, with the underlying message that a careful person should pay attention to the dynamics of human relationships if he is to succeed.[105] If the advice is overly optimistic about the benefits of righteousness, the book of Proverbs also supplies useful perspectives on the complex web of inter-personal relationships. As they gathered the sayings for this collection, the editors combined hortatory material with pragmatic observations. Some statements function to teach the addressee about the way the world functions, and other sayings have the identifiable aim of shaping behavior through admonishment and/or encouragement.[106] Sayings like this one about rich and poor individuals (14:20) occur in a collection where the purpose is stated from the outset: "For learning about wisdom and instruction" (1:2). One should be observant about human behavior *and* practice "fear of the Lord."

Nowhere is this didactic intent more apparent than the first chapter of the collection, as the young charge is warned about the perils of falling in with recalcitrant youth:

> My child, if sinners entice you, do not consent.
> If they say, "Come with us, let us lie in wait for blood;
> let us wantonly ambush the innocent;
> like Sheol let us swallow them alive and whole,
> like those who go down to the Pit.

---

[105] John J. Collins, *Jewish Wisdom in the Hellenistic Age* (OTL; Louisville: Westminster John Knox Press, 1997), 10, explains the mindset of Proverbs in this regard: "The pragmatic tone of many of the proverbs provides a refreshing realism that measures actions by their effects rather than the intentions of their agents." In addition, James L. Crenshaw, *Old Testament Wisdom: An Introduction* (rev. and enl. ed.; Louisville: Westminster John Knox Press, 1998), 56, argues that even the simple observations have a didactic quality, since "every single recognition of 'the way things are' signaled a step toward mastering the universe."

[106] Murphy, "Wisdom Theses," 192–93, distinguishes between a proverb that merely registers an experience, with no explicit hope for improvement in the future, and a didactic saying that can serve as the basis for further growth. According to this basic distinction, he classifies most of the sayings in Proverbs as didactic.

We shall find all kinds of costly things;
we shall fill our houses with booty.
Throw in your lot among us; we will all have one purse"—
my child, do not walk in their way, keep your foot from their paths;
for their feet run to evil,
and they hurry to shed blood.
For in vain is the net baited while the bird is looking on;
yet they lie in wait-to kill themselves!
and set an ambush-for their own lives!
Such are the ways of all who are greedy for gain;
it takes away the life of its possessors (1:10–19).[107]

This memorable passage attempts to frighten young people at a critical stage in their development. The addressee in chapter 1 is encouraged to follow the correct "path" or "way," avoid the wrong one, and heed the call of Wisdom (her address follows this section in 1:20–33). With regard to the background for 1:10–19, we must consider carefully who the "sinners" (חטאים) in v. 10 represent. Fox maintains that they are hard-core felons and not just occasional transgressors.[108] In contrast, Carol Newsom claims that these individuals are the lad's contemporaries, so that the description in 1:10–19 attempts to contrast patriarchal authority, including financial control over the purse strings, with the enticement of quick monetary gain in the company of one's peers.[109] Newsom's reading is the more convincing one, since rebellious teenagers are a threat to any adolescent boy and his parents, especially if the lure of easy profit becomes part of the equation.

Such a distinction (hardened thug vs. rebellious peer) is actually meaningless to the logic of 1:10–19: the fictitious gang members represent the seductive and wholly evil "other." Their precise background is far less important than the threat they pose to the son and the lesson being imparted. The gang members probably are peers, since they would have the best chance of successfully appealing to the lad's baser

---

[107] Similar warnings against destructive individuals can be found in 2:12–15; 3:31–32; 6:1–19.

[108] Fox, *Proverbs 1–9*, 85, 93, calls attention to the hyperbolic language and dangers of seductive speech in this section, both recurrent features in Proverbs.

[109] Carol A. Newsom, "Woman and the Discourse of Patriarchal Wisdom: A Study of Proverbs 1–9," in *Gender and Difference in Ancient Israel* (ed. P.L. Day; Minneapolis: Fortress Press, 1989), 145, points to the horizontal relationship of the young man's peers (i.e., the same financial footing), as opposed to the father's financial control in a hierarchical structure. According to Newsom, "What lurks beneath the surface is generational chasm, the division of power between older and younger men in a patriarchal society."

instincts. In this and other passages, the sages of Proverbs repeatedly emphasize the dangers of seductive speech.[110] Like the wily seductress portrayed elsewhere in the discourses of Proverbs 1–9 (2:16–19; 5:3–14, 19–20; 6:24–35; 7:1–27), these boys are bad characters who epitomize waywardness. According to the ethical dualism of the larger collection (and the discourses in particular), *any* individual who strays from Wisdom's path becomes a contemptible being. He or she joins the legions of fools whose careless neglect has caused them to forfeit their soul in the pursuit of selfish and ill-gotten rewards (1:19; 28:10).[111] Dishonest persons who employ seductive speech are not to be trusted, no matter how enticing their promises. This type of advice is regularly presented to the addressee in hyperbolic terms, as a black and white contrast between a life committed to virtue and the threat of utter ruin.[112] Examples include the dichotomy between the good and evil "way," the counterbalance between Lady Wisdom and the "Strange Woman" in Proverbs 1–9, the repeated contrast between the wise person and the fool, and the difference between following a wicked gang or righteous Wisdom.

Such language underscores the moralizing thrust of the collection, particularly in chapters 1–9. In his illuminating discussion of these chapters, Raymond van Leeuwen argues that the central purpose of the discourses is protreptic: to convert the "untutored" (פֶּתִי) individual into a discerning, virtuous adult, before he goes astray.[113] A person "enters" (e.g., 4:14) one adult path or the other, and the various warnings aim

---

[110] Jean-Noël Aletti, "Séduction et parole en Proverbes I–IX," *VT* 27 (1977): 129–44, demonstrates the ironic parallels between the gang members' seductive invitation and the words of Wisdom in Proverbs 1–9.

[111] Interestingly, the father never clarifies how the son's involvement in the gang will lead to the loss of his life. Fox, *Proverbs 1–9*, 351, discusses the temptations included in these chapters and the lack of specificity regarding promised retribution. The father promises many wonderful things in exchange for righteous behavior, and his most memorable lines relate to perils in the world. Fox explains the goal: "The supple and multifaceted rhetoric of the wisdom teacher seeks to fortify the youngster's soul against its own fierce passions." If the instruction succeeds, the boy can thrive as a virtuous adult.

[112] Plöger, *Sprüche Salomos*, 15, argues that 1:10–19 represents an extreme circumstance, which cannot be transferred to other situations. Yet this depiction would certainly apply to young people in dangerous areas and to any number of situations encountered during adolescence. Moreover, Proverbs frequently presents choices in such a stark manner, as a choice between life and death.

[113] Raymond C. van Leeuwen, "Liminality and Worldview in Proverbs 1–9," *Semeia* 50 (1990), 113; cf. Perdue, "Liminality as a Social Setting for Wisdom Instructions," 114–26, who advocates an alternative version of the world-order hypothesis.

to steer adolescents into Wisdom's house. Using the anthropological models of Victor Turner, van Leeuwen discusses the "liminal transitions" of young individuals to a better social status and sense of self. Proverbs has a concern with proper boundaries in the journey towards adulthood, such that "Good behavior consists of staying on prescribed paths, evil actions are trespasses over forbidden limina."[114] Boström adopts a somewhat similar interpretation of Proverbs 1–9. The blunt presentation of two paths, two basic alternatives, can be attributed to the pedagogical framework in the collection. These absolute statements serve a hortatory function, as the sages promote traditional points of view.[115]

If Proverbs warns repeatedly that wickedness leads to misery and righteousness is profitable, we find surprisingly few descriptions of how these results are adjudicated. The book contains almost no references to retributive processes. The addressee is told that violence takes away the life of its possessor (1:19) and that "Righteousness guards one whose way is upright" (13:6). Precisely how this occurs is never fully described. The sages seem less interested in the juridical process for an unrighteous person than in shaping human behavior before the conduct occurs. The reason for this tendency again relates to pedagogy. The sages use an admonitory style and the threat of punishment in order to emphasize the *choice* between two lifestyles as opposed to the *processes* that lead to certain outcomes.[116] Rewards (long life, wealth, happiness, progeny) and punishments (premature death, financial ruin, misery) are mentioned repeatedly, but not processes. The Lord is often the controlling agent (15:25), and in other instances we get passive formulations (10:24), but the manner in which justice will be meted out is not usually specified.[117] Boström attributes this vagueness to two motivating factors: (1) it allows the sages to be flexible about outcomes and more attuned to real-life circumstances; (2) general statements about the righteous and the wicked serve a didactic function as the sages impart their traditional advice.[118] In other words, Proverbs seeks to avert disaster before it strikes. To use a contemporary illustration, the discourses in Proverbs 1–9 can be

---

[114] Van Leeuwen, "Liminality and Worldview," 126–27.
[115] Boström, *God of the Sages*, 119–20.
[116] Boström, *God of the Sages*, 112.
[117] Nor is divine mercy part of the act-consequence discussion in Proverbs; statements like the one in 28:13 are an exception.
[118] Boström, *God of the Sages*, 119.

compared to parental pleadings for level headedness on the Thursday before the high school prom, rather than the administering of punishment following any weekend infraction.

This emphasis on the choice between two lifestyles leads to an anthropocentric perspective in the sayings. As with the Egyptian instructions, the world of human interactions and transactions remains the point of orientation in Proverbs. Even the cosmic scene of Wisdom "playing" before Yahweh in chapter 8 is part of a larger unit in which humanity is called to a virtuous life in exchange for earthly rewards (e.g., 8:21). The sayings in this text seek to foster internalization of an approach to life and a series of behavioral qualities that will lead to a harmonious society. Personal success is guaranteed for all who exhibit "fear of the Lord." When the deity is mentioned as an active force, the depiction usually relates to human conduct and Yahweh's ability to respond to it. As divine agency and human initiative work out their complex relationship in Proverbs, the sages do not waver in guaranteeing earthly success to the person who develops a specific set of behavioral traits, to the one who understands that the "fear of the Lord is the beginning of wisdom."

## 8. *Death in Proverbs*

Death is treated briefly and without sustained interest in Proverbs, and the compilers of this collection evince no belief in the possibility of eternal reward. The book is consistent with the larger religious tradition in ancient Israel, so that death is a universal phenomenon, something that cannot be avoided. The implications of human mortality are not treated as a topic worthy of further exploration, and in this respect the collection differs from later instructional texts during the Hellenistic period. In fact, Proverbs frequently speaks of "life" and "death" in ethical terms, rather than dealing with human finitude. There is the famous question of Agur in Prov 30:4: "Who has ascended to heaven and come down?" Yet this first question in a rhetorical series functions as a statement on the inaccessibility of the heavenly realm for humanity and the awesomeness of divine majesty (cf. Job 38–42; Isa 40:12–31). It does not seem to represent an inquiry about the possibility of eternal existence for the righteous soul. For the most part, the compilers of Proverbs ignore the fact that their theological understanding has all individuals proceeding to the same fate, with no alternative destiny for the righteous. Speculation about the heavenly realm is not part of the equation in this collection: the focus is firmly fixed on present circumstances.

At least one scholar has argued otherwise: Mitchell Dahood posits a belief in immortality for the righteous individual in Proverbs, focusing his discussion on 12:28. The MT of this verse reads as follows: בְּאֹרַח־צְדָקָה חַיִּים וְדֶרֶךְ נְתִיבָה אַל־מָוֶת. Following the commentary of Franz Delitzsch, Dahood maintains that אַל represents an "emotionally charged negative," comparable to אַל־טַל in 2 Sam 1:21.[119] He provides Ugaritic examples that correspond with this use of the negative, citing a famous passage that contains *ḥym* and *blmt* in parallelism.[120] This understanding has influenced the NRSV translation of Prov 12:28: "In the path of righteousness there is life, in walking its path there is no death." Such a reading necessitates an infinitive construct in the second half of the verse that should be pointed וּדְרֹךְ ("and in walking").[121] In assessing the meaning of 12:28, Dahood concludes that the Canaanite parallels (on both linguistic and religious grounds) suggest a belief in immortality: "biblical חַיִּים and אַל־מָוֶת preserved a denotation similar to the Ugaritic meaning, but purified by Israelite monotheism and religious outlook."[122]

Despite a clever argument and intriguing linguistic overlaps, Dahood's conclusion is thoroughly at odds with the understanding of death in Proverbs. Even if correct in his translation of this verse, which seems

---

[119] Mitchell Dahood, "Immortality in Proverbs 12, 28," *Bib* 41 (1960), 176–81, citing Franz Delitzsch, *Das Salomonisches Sprüchbuch: Biblischer Commentar über das AT* (Leipzig: Brunnen-Verlag, 1873), 207. Delitzsch claimed that the אַל־טַל in 2 Sam 1:21 is equivalent to אַל יְהִי טַל. He translated Prov 12:28 as "Auf dem Pfad der Gerechtigkeit ist Leben, Und das Wandeln ihres Steiges ist Unsterblichkeit."

[120] Dahood, "Immortality in Proverbs 12, 28," 178. The passage from the Ugaritic texts is from the Keret legend, KTU 1.16 I 14–15: *bḥyk abn nšmḥ blmtk ngln* ("'In your life, our father, we rejoice, in your not dying we celebrate," translation mine). Another example is KTU 1.17 VI 25–38. In this passage, Aqhat dismisses Anat's offer of immortality as fanciful, claiming that it is the lot of all human beings to die: "the death of all I shall die, and I shall surely die." Translation is from Nicolas Wyatt, *Religious Texts from Ugarit* (2d ed.; London: Sheffield, 2002). Such an acknowledgment of human mortality correlates with the understanding of death in the Hebrew Bible. See Vawter, "Intimations of Immortality," 164–65.

[121] The lack of a *mappîq* in נְתִיבָה: is also problematic (i.e., "her path"). Dahood, "Immortality in Proverbs 12, 28," 179, points out that some manuscripts do contain the form נְתִיבָה.

[122] Dahood, "Immortality in Proverbs 12, 28," 181. Dahood also cites Prov 14:32, which he interprets as the just man finding solace in his death (see below for a discussion of this verse and the Greek translation of it).

to be the case ("no death"), Prov 12:28 should not be interpreted as a *statement on immortality*. "Death" in Proverbs, even when invoked as the opposite of life, is used in ethical terms. Waywardness is equivalent to death, and walking in Wisdom's path constitutes life.[123] This type of language seeks to delineate proper boundaries and the futility of wickedness; such an ethical dualism is presented most clearly in Proverbs 1–9, where "life" and "death" are used in a hortatory sense. For example, Wisdom's call is equated with "life" in Prov 8:35–36:

> For whoever finds me finds life and obtains favor from the Lord;
> but those who miss me injure themselves; all who hate me love death.

This statement is a call to seek Wisdom and thereby obtain the Lord's favor. Such a commitment will then lead to earthly fulfillment. The language in these verses has nothing to do with the possibility of otherworldly retribution. As van Leeuwen observes of the distinction between life and death in Proverbs, "The right, the wise road is *already* 'life' (2:8–9, 20; 3:23; 4:11, 18, etc.). Conversely the road of the wicked is *already* dark and pregnant with death (1:15,16,19; 2:19; 4:19)."[124]

No passage in Proverbs can be read as reflective of a belief in human immortality, and the topic of physical death is of little interest to these editors. Eschatological hope or any noticeable preoccupation with the possibility of an afterlife is absent, and this echoes the content of the Egyptian instructions. The world of social interactions remains the focal point, as the sayings describe the virtuous life and the present benefits of seeking Wisdom. Unlike certain psalms, which do contain speculation on this topic, Proverbs focuses on present circumstances and the immediate consequences of individual actions.[125] In the descriptions of chapter 1 (esp. 1:32–33), the sages juxtapose a meaningful life in accordance with Wisdom (= life) and a wicked/foolish path (= death). Grasping the "tree of life" (Wisdom) leads to righteous behavior and contentment in this world, rather than the possibility of immortality.[126]

---

[123] Vawter, "Intimations of Immortality," 169, explains the mindset in the book of Proverbs: "In whatever guise, death is never the fruit of righteousness."

[124] Van Leeuwen, "Liminality and Worldview," 114.

[125] For example, Pss 39:4–6; 49:10–15; 89:47–48; 90:3–6, 9–10; 103:13–16; 144:3–4; 146:3–4. See Shannon Burkes, *God, Self, and Death: The Shape of Religious Transformation in the Second Temple Period* (JSJSup 79; Leiden: Brill, 2003), 30–31.

[126] Burkes, *God, Self, and Death*, 32, provides a list of similar passages: Prov 8:35–36; 10:16–17; 11:4, 30; 12:28; 14:27; 15:24; 16:22; 21:16. She also discusses necromancy and possible cults of the dead in ancient Israel.

When the sages use death language, it often describes a lack of moral character, the antithesis of "fear of the Lord."[127] A statement such as Prov 15:24, "For the wise man's path of life leads upward, in order to avoid Sheol beneath," addresses present responsibilities and potential benefits, rather than the threat of eternal punishment for the transgressor of Wisdom. The person who internalizes "fear of the Lord" can expect a multitude of rewards, but he or she will meet the same fate as the fool. The sages of Proverbs do not respond negatively to this fundamental aspect of their act-consequence paradigm, particularly the idea of one universal fate.

This perspective on death is a critical and overlooked aspect of Proverbs, as Crenshaw explains:

> Naturally, the sages reckoned with death as a real factor, but the book of Proverbs never utters so much as a sigh over the prospect of natural death. The lack of any anxious lament over the universal decree, "You must die," becomes all the more astonishing when we consider the fact that these wise men and women entertained no hope of life beyond the grave.[128]

While Crenshaw is certainly correct that the absence of "anxious lament" is surprising from a modern sensibility, it is nevertheless characteristic of sapiential discourse in Proverbs and its antecedents. Death did not preoccupy the Egyptian sages who had influence over the Israelite editors who compiled the book of Proverbs, nor was the ultimate fate of the individual soul a source of explicit concern among earlier biblical writers.[129] The fact that Proverbs does not address the ephemeral nature of human existence allows us to locate a trajectory in the development of Israelite Wisdom and a Second Temple debate in which the editors of Proverbs did not participate. Qoheleth and Ben Sira have a more developed framework in terms of their approach to human mortality, and even if a traditional sage like Ben Sira affirms many of the assumptions in Proverbs, he is engaging in a later discussion with different parameters.

---

[127] John J. Collins, "The Root of Immortality: Death in the Context of Jewish Wisdom," *HTR* 71 (1978), 180, explains it as a "qualitative" understanding in Proverbs: "It is clearly in this qualitative sense that humanity can choose between life and death."

[128] Crenshaw, *Old Testament Wisdom*, 66.

[129] On the latter point, see Shannon Burkes, *Death in Qoheleth and the Egyptian Biographies of the Late Period* (SBLDS 170; Atlanta: Society of Biblical Literature, 1999), 10–34.

## 8.1   *Retribution and Death in LXX-Proverbs*

This distinction between Proverbs and Hellenistic instructions might also be apparent when comparing MT with LXX-Proverbs, since the latter accentuates the contrast between the wicked and the righteous, and the Greek translator includes more references to natural death. The significance of the variants is currently a matter of dispute in Septuagint studies. We have mentioned that Fox does not understand the Greek translator to be engaging in excessively liberal translations for theological purposes: "LXX-Prov is primarily a *translation,* one aiming at a faithful representation of the Hebrew, and it is best understood in terms of that goal."[130] Yet there are significant variants, which Fox and others have catalogued, and virtually all scholars agree that LXX-Proverbs adds language for moral/theological emphasis in several places. There is a marked discrepancy in 13:2, where MT reads מפרי פי־איש יאכל טוב ונפש בגדים חמס ("From the fruit of their words good persons eat good things, but the desire of the treacherous is for wrongdoing"). The Greek translator offers a radically different version of this verse: ἀπὸ καρπῶν δικαιοσύνης φάγεται ἀγαθός ψυχαὶ δὲ παρανόμων ὀλοῦνται ἄωροι. The reference to the premature demise of the wicked ("the souls of the lawless will be destroyed prematurely") has no basis in MT. Another example occurs in 13:23:

> רב־אכל ניר ראשים ויש נספה בלא משפט
> The field of the poor may yield much food, but it is swept away through injustice.

> δίκαιοι ποιήσουσιν ἐν πλούτῳ ἔτη πολλά ἄδικοι δὲ ἀπολοῦνται συντόμως
> The righteous will be wealthy for many years, but the unrighteous will be quickly destroyed.

MT for this verse is difficult, but the saying clearly promises nourishment for the poor and a lack of sustenance when injustice is present. The Greek translator might be ignoring the Hebrew, working from a different *Vorlage,* or perhaps engaging in a moralizing shift that emphasizes the premature death of the unrighteous. Gerleman has pointed to the translator's tendency to alter the content of a saying so that it reflects antithetic rather than synonymous parallelism, especially since this literary practice became more common during the Hellenistic

---

[130] Fox, *Proverbs 1–9,* 361.

age.[131] Statements on the death of the wicked certainly appear in MT
(e.g., 11:19), but it is significant that the Greek translator changed an
unrelated verse to deal directly with this topic.

A similar variant can be found in 29:13:

רָשׁ וְאִישׁ תְּכָכִים נִפְגָּשׁוּ מֵאִיר־עֵינֵי שְׁנֵיהֶם יהוה
The poor and the oppressor have this in common: the Lord gives light
to the eyes of both.

δανιστοῦ καὶ χρεοφειλέτου ἀλλήλοις συνελθόντων ἐπισκοπὴν ποιεῖται
ἀμφοτέρων ὁ κύριος
A moneylender and a debtor gather together: the Lord makes a visitation for both.[132]

Divine agency is emphasized in both versions, but LXX adds ἐπισκοπὴν
as the object of the Lord's action (with negative subjects), giving the
saying a more judgment-oriented slant. Finally, in Prov 11:7 MT refers
to the lack of hope among the wicked, while LXX mentions the perspective of the righteous:

בְּמוֹת אָדָם רָשָׁע תֹּאבַד תִּקְוָה
וְתוֹחֶלֶת אוֹנִים אָבָדָה
When the wicked die, their hope perishes,
and the expectation of the godless comes to nothing.

τελευτήσαντος ἀνδρὸς δικαίου οὐκ ὄλλυται ἐλπίς
τὸ δὲ καύχημα τῶν ἀσεβῶν ὄλλυται
When a righteous person dies his hope does not perish;
but the boast of the impious perishes.[133]

Whether this is an unequivocal affirmation of the afterlife remains
uncertain, but it is a significant moralizing shift that relates to human
mortality. This is a highly disputed verse.[134]

---

[131] Gerleman, *Studies in the Septuagint*, 18–25.

[132] The language here in LXX (ἐπισκοπὴν ποιεῖται ἀμφοτέρων ὁ κύριος) seems to
have an eschatological connotation.

[133] Johann Cook, "Apocalyptic Terminology in the Septuagint of Proverbs," *JNSL*
25 (1999), 252, cites this passage as evidence for a major shift in LXX-Proverbs.

[134] Clifford, *Proverbs*, 120, argues that a later scribe added רָשָׁע (i.e., the verse originally referred to all of humanity). Perhaps the LXX translator resolved the difficulties with this verse by creating an antithesis between the just and the wicked. Fox,
"LXX-Proverbs as a Text-Critical Resource," 116, argues that the translator had
וְתֹהֶלֶת (= καύχημα) before him, especially since תּוֹחֶלֶת would have worked perfectly
for his treatment of the verse (the Greek translator "would have used it if he had
it"). Fox makes an important point: "A verse can be both interpretive *and* based on
a variant" (p. 108). There is also the case of Prov 14:32, where the Hebrew reads
בְּרָעָתוֹ יִדָּחֶה רָשָׁע וְחֹסֶה בְמוֹתוֹ צַדִּיק ("The wicked are overthrown in their evildoing, but

The variants in Proverbs 1–9 are also intriguing. We find an expansive addition in 1:22, where the Greek translator portrays the dualism of the Hebrew even more starkly than the parent-text.[135] While Cook overstates the "religious" explication of the LXX version in several places, he identifies a heightened contrast between two ways of life in the Greek translation. Cook is careful to distinguish LXX-Proverbs (and Ben Sira) from clearly apocalyptic works, but he asserts the translator's tendency to accentuate dualistic elements from the Hebrew text and add some of his own. Such changes include an added emphasis on death in the context of the fate of the righteous/wicked and whether a person's reputation survives after death.[136] For example, the section we have cited in Proverbs 1 has an interesting variant in v. 12b, as the young thugs are plotting: "let us remove (ἄρωμεν) his remembrance from the earth."[137] The permanence of a good name is also a prominent feature in Ben Sira, and the Greek translator of Proverbs is alluding to this common motif.[138] All of these variants require more systematic study, as the translation technique found in LXX-Proverbs continues to receive a great deal of attention in modern scholarly discussions. It should not be surprising that some of the elements we find in later instructions of the Hellenistic period (e.g., focus on a good name, death) are more prominent in LXX-Proverbs than MT.

---

the righteous find a refuge in their death," translation mine). LXX conveys the saying as follows: ἐν κακίᾳ αὐτοῦ ἀπωσθήσεται ἀσεβής ὁ δὲ πεποιθὼς τῇ ἑαυτοῦ ὁσιότητι δίκαιος ("The wicked are overthrown in their evildoing, but the righteous find a refuge in their integrity"). The translator is following בְּתֻמּוֹ (or בְּתֻמָּתוֹ), and therefore we have a case of metathesis with the Hebrew במותו, which is certainly not part of a statement on the afterlife. Syriac agrees with the Greek reading for this verse. Hebrew במותו is probably not original, since חסה is usually followed by the preposition ב and the source of faith (Fox, "LXX-Proverbs as a Text-Critical Resource," 109). LXX (and Syriac) might have included a reference to the afterlife if they had one before them, but their text was different from MT.

[135] See Cook, *The Septuagint of Proverbs*, 85–87, for a discussion of the variants. There is no reference to "becoming ungodly" (ἀσεβεῖς γενόμενοι) in MT for 1:22.

[136] Cook, *The Septuagint of Proverbs*, 177, addresses the addition of language involving the "righteous" (δίκαιος) and the fate that befalls them in passages like Prov 6:17. Also see the discussion of 1:28 (p. 92). Cook argues that the whole of Proverbs 1 in LXX is aimed at the contrast between good and evil. This is also the case in MT, but LXX-Proverbs seems to add language to sharpen the dichotomy.

[137] MT for this verse reads "like those who go down to the Pit."

[138] Cook believes that many if not most of these additions are the work of a Jewish and not a later Christian translator. Fox, *Proverbs 1–9*, 369, views this variant as dependent on the language in Ps 34 [33]:17b.

## 9. *Conclusions*

In Proverbs, "death" is used qualitatively to describe behavior that is beyond the appropriate boundaries for human conduct. The compilers of this collection do not wrestle with the topic of human mortality in the manner of later sapiential writers. The important point here is that the content of MT-Proverbs precedes a pivotal transition during the Second Temple period regarding death and the act-consequence relationship. The specific factors that led to this transition in the wisdom tradition and the nature of the changes will occupy the rest of this study. For example, the sage Qoheleth represents a significant shift in his treatment of death and its implications. His reflections indicate the beginnings of a profound debate and reassessment of causality, retribution, and the possibility of an afterlife. We now turn to the penetrating observations found in the book of Qoheleth.

# CHAPTER THREE

# WISDOM IN TRANSITION:
# THE BOOK OF ECCLESIASTES

## 1. *Introduction*

The book of Ecclesiastes (or Qoheleth), a classic among ancient Wisdom texts and throughout all of world literature, has received a great deal of attention in the last few decades.[1] Commentaries, major monographs, and entire symposia have taken up these memorable reflections, prompting a reevaluation of the book's meaning, historical context, and the possible influences on its author(s).[2] The reasons for the resurgent interest are varied. An increased scholarly engagement with the sapiential literature of the ancient Near East is a significant factor. As commentators have examined the larger corpus of ancient instructions, it has become increasingly important to determine the period in which Qoheleth had his career, the nature of his perspective, and the factors that shaped his thought. Global tragedy has also led readers to this incisive commentary on human existence. Qoheleth's existential probing is strangely accessible to the modern interpreter, and the uncertainties of recent years have made this an appealing book to examine. As Frank Crüsemann explains, "Unlike any other book of the Bible, we can read him without intermediaries and think we understand

---

[1] Following most commentators, this study will use the Hebrew title "Qoheleth" in reference to this book *and* the author responsible for its content.

[2] For example, Thomas Krüger, *Qoheleth* (trans. O.C. Dean; Hermeneia; Minneapolis: Fortress Press, 2004); Michael V. Fox, *A Time to Tear Down and a Time to Build Up: A Rereading of Ecclesiastes* (Grand Rapids: Eerdmans, 1999); Antoon Schoors, ed., *Qohelet in the Context of Wisdom* (BETL 136; Leuven: Leuven University Press/Peeters, 1998); Ludger Schwienhorst-Schönberger, ed., *Das Buch Kohelet: Studien zur Struktur, Geschichte, Rezeption und Theologie* (BZAW 254; Berlin: de Gruyter, 1997); C.L. Seow, *Ecclesiastes* (AB 18C; New York: Doubleday, 1997); Ludger Schwienhorst-Schönberger, *'Nicht im Menschen Gründet das Glück' (Koh 2,24): Kohelet im Spannungsfeld jüdischer Weisheit und hellenistischer Philosophie* (HBS 2; Freiburg: Herder, 1994); Roland E. Murphy, *Ecclesiastes* (WBC 23A; Dallas: Word Books, 1992); James L. Crenshaw, *Ecclesiastes* (OTL; Philadelphia: Westminster Press, 1987).

him."³ And just as this sapiential author reaches a profound rhetorical moment in the book, Qoheleth undermines the statement by contradicting it. He cites the benefits of Wisdom at one point (2:13), only to bemoan the limitations of his intelligence a few verses later (2:19). This is an overtly paradoxical text, with many incongruous declarations about life, death, and the search for knowledge. The enigma of Qoheleth is another reason for its appeal, as the reader is presented with a fascinating array of contradictory assertions.

The book of Qoheleth is often classified as "crisis literature," a caustic commentary on the absurdity of life and the inadequacy of traditional assumptions as found in the book of Proverbs. For example, James Crenshaw posits the complete absence of an act-consequence nexus and a striking disparity between this author's conclusions and those of his predecessors: "Qohelet discerns no moral order at all. Humans cannot know God's disposition. This argument strikes at the foundation of the sages' universe."⁴ Many statements in the text support such an interpretation, including 2:11:

> Then I considered all that my hands had done and the toil I had spent in doing it, and again, all was vanity and a chasing after wind, and there was nothing to be gained under the sun.

For Qoheleth, life's ledger sheets do not balance, and this perspective places him in somewhat of a protest mode against earlier sages.⁵ When we consider the preoccupation with death in this text, this author's break with the tradition becomes even more apparent. According to Shannon Burkes, Qoheleth understands human mortality to be "the chief flaw

---

³ Frank Crüsemann, "The Unchangeable World: The 'Crisis of Wisdom' in Koheleth," in *God of the Lowly: Socio-Historical Interpretations of the Bible* (trans. M.J. O'Connell; ed. W. Schottroff and W. Stegemann; Marynoll: Orbis Books, 1984), 57.

⁴ Crenshaw, *Ecclesiastes*, 23; cf., Hartmut Gese, "The Crisis of Wisdom in Koheleth," trans. L.L. Grabbe, in *Theodicy in the Old Testament* (ed. J.L. Crenshaw; IRT 4; Philadelphia: Fortress Press, 1983), 143; originally published as "Die Krisis der Weisheit bei Koheleth," in *Les Sagesses du Proche-Orient Ancien, Colloque de Strasbourg, 17–19 mai 1962* (Paris: Presses Universitaires de France, 1963), 139–51. Gese notes the nature of Qoheleth's perspective: "One's personal situation almost never corresponds to one's conduct in life and therefore bears little relation to it. The righteous meet what the unrighteous would meet, and vice versa (8:14)."

⁵ As the previous chapters have demonstrated, Qoheleth does not represent a complete reversal of earlier Wisdom, since neither the book of Proverbs nor antecedent texts from Egypt and Mesopotamia promise an infallible *Tun-Ergehen-Zusammenhang*. Earlier sages had acknowledged the ultimate authority of the deity and the diversity of human experiences, even as they affirmed a character-consequence paradigm.

that embraces and subsumes all other problems in the world."[6] Death is the immutable climax in the human experience, and it nullifies all perceived gains (e.g., 1:11; 2:16; 6:1–6; 9:5, 10). Qoheleth dismisses any possibility of an afterlife (3:16–22; 9:2–9), and this makes him hard-pressed to promote a consistent relationship between a person's deeds and the appropriate outcome. An ominous cloud looms over the human situation and by extension the Wisdom enterprise, since the end of one's earthly existence signifies their ultimate demise, no matter how righteous they have become. This is one of the primary reasons why the author turns to the refrain הבל הבלים (usually translated "vanity of vanities"). The term הבל, which appears 38 times in the text, reflects the author's belief in the futile and transitory nature of life under the sun.[7] When using the frequent refrain הכל הבל ורעות רוח ("all is vanity and a chasing after wind,"), Qoheleth points to a contrast between God's eternal status and humanity's complete inability to transcend earthly existence. Thomas Bolin has recently argued that the connotation of רוח in the refrain describes the eternal "spirit" of God that humanity can long for but never attain (e.g., 3:11), rather than a more generic statement on "chasing after wind." Therefore the phrase should be

---

[6] Shannon Burkes, *Death in Qoheleth and Egyptian Biographies of the Late Period* (SBLDS 170; Atlanta: Society of Biblical Literature, 1999), 2; cf. Seow, *Ecclesiastes*, 55–56.

[7] Deciding on an appropriate rendering for this term is difficult, because הבל does not translate easily into English, and Qoheleth uses it in a variety of contexts. The usual offering "vanity" does not fit many occurrences in the text. The literal meaning of הבל is "vapor" or "breath" (of wind: see Isa 57:13), but this can be abstracted to "nothingness" or "transitoriness" (Krüger, *Qoheleth*, 42). The term can also be used as a derogatory epithet for "idols." LXX uses the negative ματαιότης ("worthlessness," "futility"). Michael V. Fox, *Qohelet and His Contradictions* (JSOTSup 71; Sheffield: Almond Press, 1989), 29–51, offers the translation "absurdity," linking Qoheleth's understanding of human existence to Camus's *The Myth of Sisyphus*: "The essence of the absurd is a disparity between two phenomena that are supposed to be joined by a link of harmony or causality but are actually disjunct or even conflicting" (p. 31). Qoheleth's obvious frustration with unfairness and inconsistency, particularly in relation to death, lends credence to this interpretation. In certain passages, neither "vanity" nor "futility" captures the accurate sense of הבל. For example, "There is הבל that takes place on earth, that there are righteous people who are treated according to the conduct of the wicked" (8:14). According to Fox, "absurd" is the best translation in such verses, since הבל seems to represent "not merely the absence of meaning, but an active violation of meaningfulness" (p. 34). There is also a temporal aspect for certain passages in the book. According to Burkes, *Death in Qoheleth*, 48, the transience of life represents the "overriding theme, the chief absurdity, that rivets the author's attention." A few examples demonstrate the point. In 3:19, which describes the relationship between humans and animals, and in 11:10, where the brevity of youth is addressed, הבל clearly has a temporal meaning.

translated, "All is mortal (i.e., 'fleeting'), but strives for immortality."[8] Bolin's interpretation is not necessarily venturesome, since death is the predominant concern in Qoheleth's discussion (see below).

In this chapter, we will examine the act-consequence relationship, or lack thereof, in Qoheleth, and the probable context for this author's preoccupation with human mortality. Even if earlier Egyptian and Israelite instructions had acknowledged a degree of helplessness in the face of divine freedom, endemic corruption, and inevitable death, the author of this book is more exasperated by the absence of חשבון ("sum" or "accounting," 7:27) than his predecessors.[9] Qoheleth considers frequent injustice to be normative for the society he inhabits and for all other settings (e.g., 5:8), and he does not allow the possibility of an afterlife to rectify any imbalances. Along with Job, this book is rightly classified as a postexilic corrective to earlier instructions amid the changing political and social dynamics of the Second Temple period. This contextual issue is perhaps the most critical one for our study, and it raises a number of questions. If we read Qoheleth as a response to an outmoded or inaccurate sapiential discourse, why did it take the tradition so long to reach such a pivotal breaking point, and what specifically led to a markedly different assessment than what appears in Proverbs?[10] Earlier writers in Israelite history had also witnessed calamitous political events, including hostile invasions by the Assyrians and Babylonians. This created a climate in which basic questions about divine justice and human identity could be addressed, particularly among some of the major prophetic figures.[11] Why did the

---

[8] Thomas Bolin, "Rivalry and Resignation: Girard and Qoheleth on the Divine-Human Relationship," *Bib* 86 (2005): 245–59, examines the understanding of death and human limitation in Qoheleth, utilizing René Girard's concept of "mimetic rivalry." Bolin disputes the usual interpretation of רעות רוח as "chasing after wind." He argues that רוח is used several times in the text (3:19; 11:5; 12:7) to refer to the "animating principle of humanity that is given by God at birth and taken back by God at death" (p. 249).

[9] For example, Amenemope is attuned to economic corruption and the finality of death, and Proverbs allows that the righteous might suffer and the wicked prosper for a time, but the concern with these topics is not as acute as what appears in Qoheleth.

[10] Elizabeth Huwiler, "Control of Reality in Israelite Wisdom" (Ph.D. diss., Duke University, 1988), 70.

[11] Such questions were taken up in Ezek 18 and Jer 31:29–30, which reflect a greater emphasis on individual justice and God's retributive action in relation to a person's deeds. On the relationship between communal and individual identity in ancient Israel, see Joel S. Kaminsky, *Corporate Responsibility in the Hebrew Bible* (JSOTSup 196; Sheffield: Sheffield Academic Press, 1995).

wisdom tradition respond so late to inconsistencies in previous constructs, and what prompted the fascination with human mortality and
its implications? Qoheleth is not the first Jewish sage to discover that
life can be unfair or that death comes to everyone, but he addresses
these matters in a more direct way than the editors of Proverbs. Even
if certain commentators have oversimplified the outlook in the earlier
collection, Qoheleth's ideas about retribution and the possibility for
consistent outcomes represent a clear departure. This discussion will
point to the early Hellenistic period, the era of the Ptolemies, as a time
of reevaluation and reconfiguration within the Jewish wisdom tradition and the most likely setting for this book. Such a proposed date
finds support from linguistic and thematic evidence in Qoheleth and
in other documents from this period. Within this cultural environment,
Qoheleth undertakes a personal experiment "to seek and to search out
by wisdom all that is done under heaven" (1:13), and this leads to a
distinctive understanding of causality. Whether outside influences led
to this break with tradition and overriding concern with mortality (i.e.,
the presence of foreign ideas in Qoheleth) is an important possibility.
In considering the context for the book, the issue of authorial integrity
is also relevant, including the possibility of "orthodox glosses" and the
disputed relationship between the epilogue (12:9–14) and the main
body of text (the "words of Qoheleth" in 1:3–12:7).

In certain respects, the content of Qoheleth represents a crisis
response to earlier Wisdom, but it also signifies a forceful contribution
to a nascent debate on retribution and the afterlife. Many suggestions,
including innovative propositions about individual salvation, challenged
the wisdom tradition during Qoheleth's career and in later periods.
In the wake of shifting political dynamics and revolutionary models,
various authors began to employ apocalyptic terminology as well as
concepts borrowed from philosophical systems. Passages like Dan
12:2–3, *1 En.* 22 and 104, *Jub.* 23:31, 2 Macc 7, and examples from
the corpus of the Dead Sea Scrolls (including 4QInstruction) demonstrate a transformed religious landscape and a new set of proposals
that included eschatological judgment, a belief in eternal life, and in
some cases communion with heavenly angels.[12] The wisdom tradition
was not removed from these changing perspectives. The authors of Ben

---

[12] For a detailed study of these and other important passages related to death and
the afterlife, see George W.E. Nickelsburg, *Resurrection, Immortality, and Eternal Life in
Intertestamental Judaism and Early Christianity: Expanded Edition* (HTS 56; Cambridge:

Sira and the Wisdom of Solomon demonstrate a palpable interest in the issue of retribution and more than a passing familiarity with some of the new models (though they respond to the proposals in different ways).[13] While most of the texts listed above were subsequent to his efforts, the content of his discussion leaves little doubt that the author of Qoheleth was participating in an important reevaluation of death and human possibility. This text diverges from the book of Proverbs on multiple levels, but one of the major differences is a shift from a limited to an obsessive engagement with human mortality. Proverbs largely looks at death in ethical terms, as the opposite of a life lived in accordance with Wisdom. In contrast, Qoheleth conducts his experiment in a different context than earlier Israelite sages, and his discussion reveals an awareness of some of the ideas that had emerged (e.g., 3:16–22). The sage's warnings on death and causality are not simply the work of an independent thinker willing to challenge a simplistic tradition. This text appears to be one of the opening volleys in a major theological discussion within sapiential circles and throughout the world of Second Temple Judaism. The book of Qoheleth belongs at the heart of any discussion on the transitions of ancient Israelite Wisdom, because its author is aware of a new dynamic in the tradition: fulfilling the act-consequence relationship through eschatological means.

## 2. Genre

Qoheleth should be located within the larger rubric of ancient Near Eastern instructional literature, although the book has a distinctive style and set of literary conventions. Like Proverbs, this text is written with humanity as the focal point; Qoheleth reflects on earthly possibilities and events, even as he acknowledges the power of God and finality of death. The book includes many didactic elements, such as the miscellaneous proverbs in chapter 10 that are a staple of the wisdom tradition. The author differs from earlier sages, however, because he insists on verifying things for himself. The impetus for undertaking this project is explicitly stated: Qoheleth wants "to seek and to search out by wisdom all that

---

Harvard University Press, 2006); Émile Puech, *La Croyance des Esséniens en la Vie Future: Immortalité, Résurrection, Vie Éternelle?* (2 vols.; Paris: Gabalda, 1993).

[13] For example, Sir. 15:11–20; 33:10–15; 40:1–2; Wis. 1:12–2:24. These passages will be taken up in subsequent chapters.

is done under heaven" (1:13). The discussion that follows reads as the personal experiment of a critical thinker who conveys a unique set of conclusions. While many sapiential conventions are present, this is a free-flowing autobiographical treatise on inconsistency and death in the human experience. In this pursuit, the dominant literary tactic seems to be what Crenshaw calls "reflection arising from personal observation."[14] In 8:14–15, for example, Qoheleth commends enjoying life to the fullest, while at the same time offering personal experiences or observations (in this case personally witnessing the mistreatment of the righteous and the elevation of the wicked) that brought him to such a belief.[15] Since this is not a formal instruction and because Qoheleth contains autobiographical information (whether historically accurate or not) and many other stylistic devices, the precise literary form is a difficult issue to settle. Commentators have tried to classify Qoheleth according to a specific literary genre, including examples from the Egyptian and Hellenistic context.[16] This is a difficult case to make, since Qoheleth favors an array of forms in his complex and often circular style. These forms include traditional sayings, admonitions in the imperative (e.g., 7:14a), and longer didactic poems (12:2–7).[17] Contrary to the argument of a few scholars, this text does not function specifically as a diatribe or royal testament, even with the polemical language and lengthy royal

---

[14] Crenshaw, *Ecclesiastes*, 28.

[15] Qoheleth also states in this unit (8:10–15) that the wicked do not prosper and that they live an abbreviated life (vv. 12b–13). Yet this is probably a later insertion, perhaps added by the second epilogist who wrote 12:13–14 (see below).

[16] The style of certain passages is similar to the literary form of Egyptian works, including instructional texts, the Harpers' Songs, and the late autobiographies. Fox, *Qohelet and His Contradictions*, 312–13, cites Egyptian and Mesopotamian texts containing a third-person frame narrative that encloses a main portion of first-person text. Usually the material at the beginning and end praises the attributed author as a person of distinction and sagacity. In addition, the "royal" section in 1:12–2:26 resembles the form and content of Merikare, although Qoheleth moves on to other literary types in subsequent sections. The numerous "heart" expressions in Egyptian literature parallel a few passages in Qoheleth (1:16; 2:1; 3:17, 18), and the idea of a personal debate taking place within one individual is similar to the Dispute Between a Man and His *Ba*. It is probable that Qoheleth had an awareness of the literary conventions used in other instructions and perhaps a direct familiarity with certain foreign texts. He was clearly part of an international tradition. See below for further discussion.

[17] Qoheleth contains traditional sapiential material, including admonitions. The book contains longer admonitory speeches such as one finds in Proverbs 1–9 (e.g., Qoh 4:17–5:6; 9:7–10; 11:1–12:7). See Diethelm Michel, *Qohelet* (EdF 258; Darmstadt: Wissenschaftliche Buchgesellschaft, 1988), 30–31. J.A. Loader, *Polar Structures in the Book of Qohelet* (BZAW 152; Berlin: de Gruyter, 1979), 18–28, classifies Qoheleth according to different forms (*Gattungen*).

section in 1:12–2:26.[18] Qoheleth defies simple categorization: there
are no definitive markers of external literary genres (Greek, Egyptian,
or otherwise), and the author's direct dependence on specific texts or
philosophical schools is very difficult to prove (see below). It is reasonable to assume that Qoheleth possessed a wide-ranging knowledge of
the wisdom tradition, some familiarity with external material, and the
ability to assimilate a variety of forms into a disputatious and highly
convincing work. He did not utilize just one literary genre to make his
presentation on the fleeting nature of human existence.

### 3. *Structure and Literary Integrity*

When examining the penetrating statements in Qoheleth, the structure
of this enigmatic text and whether the entire book can be traced to
one author are pertinent issues. Certain verses seem to conflict with the
overall message (e.g., 3:17) and can probably be classified as secondary.
In assessing this topic, scholarly discussion has generally focused on a
few central questions: whether there is an intentional order to the *textus
receptus*, the literary integrity of the book, including the possibility of
"orthodox" glosses, and the frequent suggestion that Qoheleth introduces traditional observations in order to refute them.[19] The relationship between the epilogue (12:9–14) and the rest of the book is also
significant for any discussion of this sort. It is often suggested that an
"orthodox" epilogist attempted to mitigate the "words of Qoheleth"
by inserting language at the end and in a few scattered places, thereby
making the work a more acceptable contribution to a conservative wisdom tradition. If there are editorial additions and the epilogist sought

---

[18] See the discussion in Krüger, *Qoheleth*, 12–14; Martin Hengel, *Judaism and Hellenism: Studies in Their Encounter in Palestine During the Early Hellenistic Period* (2 vols.; Philadelphia: Fortress Press, 1974), 1:115, 2:77 n. 52. Rainer Braun, *Kohelet und die frühhellenistiche Popularphilosophie* (BZAW 130; Berlin: de Gruyter, 1973), 36, 165, cites the diatribe as a dominant form for the text, based on third-century Hellenistic models (Bion of Borysthenes, which does not survive, and Teles of Megara). Christoph Uehlinger, "Qohelet im Horizont mesopotamischer, levantischer und ägyptischer Weisheitliteratur der perischen und hellenistischen Zeit," in *Das Buch Kohelet: Studien zur Struktur, Geschichte, Rezeption und Theologie* (ed. L. Schwienhorst-Schönberger; BZAW 254; Berlin: de Gruyter, 1997), 203–34, claims that the content of Qoheleth has the markings of a symposium, since there are so many generic conventions in the book.

[19] See Crenshaw, *Ecclesiastes*, 34. Hans-Wilhelm Hertzberg, *Der Prediger* (2d ed.; KAT XVII.4; Gütersloh: Mohn, 1963), 30, identifies a series of "Zwar-aber-Aussage" in Qoheleth (i.e., the sage cites a common belief and then refutes it).

to weaken the perspective of the original author, some of the apparent contradictions in Qoheleth can be more easily explained. All of these issues require brief attention if one is to assess the larger thrust of the book and its contribution to the postexilic discussion.

There is no consensus on the structure of Qoheleth, and proposals are almost as numerous as commentators who have written on the topic. A basic division can be made between those who think there is an identifiable and logical pattern to the text and others who are inclined to view Qoheleth as a loose cluster of sentences.[20] Some scholars, particularly Zimmerli, have cultivated a middle position on this question.[21] A notable argument in the "intentional" category is the schema presented by A.D.G. Wright in a series of articles.[22] Wright divides the book into two major sections, 1:12–6:9 and 6:10–11:6 (followed by a final poem in 11:7–12:8), and he points to a tightly organized series of individual units demarcated by refrains. He claims that Qoheleth has 222 verses, with a precise middle point at 6:9–10. The term הבל occurs 37 times, which is equivalent to the number of verses for each section of the book (since $3 \times 37 = 111$). While his careful study of the placement of refrains (1968) is quite useful, the larger numerological proposal requires some manipulation in order for the figures to come out right.[23] Wright is certainly correct that there are *inclusios* in Qoheleth, and several units have a chiastic structure. In addition, the recurrence of phrases can indicate a logical division between individual units, especially since refrains are often followed by a *non sequitur*.[24]

---

[20] For a review of the scholarly discussion, see Ludger Schwienhorst-Schönberger, "Kohelet: Stand und Perspectiven der Forschung," in *Das Buch Kohelet: Studien zur Struktur, Geschichte, Rezeption und Theologie* (ed. L. Schwienhorst-Schönberger; BZAW 254; Berlin: de Gruyter, 1997), 7–14; Murphy, *Ecclesiastes*, xxxv–xli.

[21] Walther Zimmerli, "Das Buch Qohelet-Traktat oder Sentenzensammlung?" *VT* 24 (1974), 230, reasons that the book is "kein Traktat mit klar erkennbaren Aufriss und einem einzigen, bestimmbaren Thema. Es ist aber zugleich mehr als ein Lose Sentenzensammlung, obwohl der Sammlungscharakter an einzelnen nicht zu übersehen ist."

[22] A.D.G. Wright, "The Riddle of the Sphinx: The Structure of the Book of Qoheleth," *CBQ* 30 (1968): 331–334; idem, "The Riddle of the Sphinx Revisited: Numerical Patterns in the Book of Qoheleth," *CBQ* 42 (1980): 35–51; idem, "Additional Numerical Patterns in Qoheleth," *CBQ* 45 (1983): 32–43.

[23] See Crenshaw, *Ecclesiastes*, 40–41, for a critique of the proposal. Wright has to leave off verses in chapter 1 and at the end of the book to balance his numerological schema.

[24] Wright, "The Riddle of the Sphinx," 320–22, catalogues a series of units in 1:12–6:9 that each end with "vanity and a chasing after wind" (הבל ורעות רוח): 1:14, 17 (רעיון רוח); 2:11, 17, 26; 4:4, 6 (no הבל), 16 (רעיון רוח); 6:9. In terms of a chiastic

Even with the frequency of contradictory assertions found in the text, Qoheleth's argumentation often follows a clear structural pattern. A suggested division of units is offered below, following the middle position (Zimmerli's) that Qoheleth is neither a tightly organized treatise nor a random collection of sentences. This text contains a series of timeless and lucid reflections on the transitory nature of human existence, and there seems to be an organizational pattern that relates to this central theme. Within individuals units, there are logical breaking points based on repetitive phrasing and clear topical shifts. This possible structure most closely follows Crenshaw's commentary and the outline of E. Podechard in his magisterial commentary on the book.[25] Significant additions and departures from these respective outlines are listed in italics:

> 1:1—Superscription
> 1:2–3—Motto on the transitory nature of human existence
> 1:4–11—Cycles of life, where everything is forgotten and "there is nothing new under the sun"
> 1:12–2:26—Qoheleth's royal experiment
> *1:12–2:10—Description of the experiment*
> *2:11–26—Conclusions on the futile and transitory nature of human existence*
> 3:1–22—Divine control over all events in the cosmos
> 4:1–16—Inequalities in life[26]
> *4:1—Opening statement on oppression*
> *4:2–3—Advantage of the dead and unborn over the living*
> *4:4–6—Toil and envy*
> *4:7–12—Benefits of companionship*
> *4:13–16—Young rulers and foolish kings*
> 4:17–5:6—The danger of religious vows
> 5:7–6:9—Wealth and poverty issues and the fleeting benefits of toil

---

structure, Norbert Lohfink, *Qoheleth* (trans. S. McEvenue; Continental; Minneapolis: Fortress Press, 2003), 8, posits a "religious critique" (4:17–5:6) at the "center of a palistrophic structure that informs the text as a whole." Lohfink claims his proposed structure is at home in Semitic rhetorical practice, but it also "satisfies a Greek sensibility." Also note Loader, *Polar Structures in the Book of Qohelet*, who posits a series of structural polarities in the text, based on Qoheleth's conviction that everything is ultimately הבל. Cf. Nate Kamano, *Cosmology and Character: Qoheleth's Pedagogy from a Rhetorical-Critical Perspective* (BZAW 312; Berlin: de Gruyter, 2002), who finds a number of convincing *inclusios*.

[25] Crenshaw, *Ecclesiastes*, 48; E. Podechard, *L'Ecclésiaste* (EtB; Paris: Gabalda, 1912).

[26] Crenshaw, *Ecclesiastes*, 48, puts 4:1–3 with what goes before and then divides the rest of the chapter as follows: 4:4–6, 7–12, 13–16. The material in 4:17–5:8 constitutes a different unit.

5:7–8—*Oppression by ruling elites*[27]
5:9–11—*Advantages of the common folk over the wealthy*
5:12–16—*Personal holdings and the finality of death*
5:17–19—*Enjoyment as the only possible solution*
6:1–6—*Transitory nature of life and leaving one's possessions*
6:7–9—*Miscellaneous sayings*
6:10–8:17—Discussion and critique of conventional Wisdom[28]
   6:10–12—Limits of human life
   7:1–14—Miscellaneous proverbs
   7:15–22—Moderation
   7:23–29—Qoheleth seeks an "accounting"
   8:1–9—Relations with rulers
   8:10–15—Righteous and wicked individuals
   8:16–17—God's plan is unknowable/call to pleasure
9:1–10—The shadow of death
9:11–12—Unpredictability
9:13–18—Wasted Wisdom
10:1–20—Miscellaneous sayings
11:1–6—Benevolence and prudence
11:7–12:7—Youth and old age
12:8—Motto (*inclusio*)
12:9–14—Epilogue(s)

This outline and others like it remain tentative: there are other valid ways of grouping the text, particularly in some of the transitional units that demarcate adjoining sections (e.g., 6:10–12). Wright has critiqued structural proposals of this type, calling them scholarly inventions "with no evidence offered aside from the critic's assurance that he sees a sequence of thought."[29] This is an unfair characterization of many careful attempts to outline a difficult text. It is not modern scholarly efforts, but *Qoheleth's* reasoning that is often circular and contradictory. The book bears the imprint of an author who observes life in all of its ambiguity and reflects aloud on the inconsistencies he finds. His discussion, which reads like the journal of a probative thinker, stands as a swirling, insightful commentary on God and the human experience.[30] Nevertheless, we can point to a certain progression in the

---

[27] Crenshaw, *Ecclesiastes*, 48, places these verses with the previous unit, but the subject matter relates more closely to the subsequent discussion of power and economic inequality.
[28] Krüger, *Qoheleth*, 6, divides the text in this way. Crenshaw, *Ecclesiastes*, 48, labels 6:10–12 a "transitional unit."
[29] Wright, "The Riddle of the Sphinx," 317.
[30] Fox calls the sage's efforts a process of both "tearing down" and "building up."

structure offered above, culminating in the author's vivid description of death. The book begins with a reflection on the cyclical nature of the universe (1:4–11), moves to a description of the royal experiment (1:12–2:26), and then proceeds to a consideration of uncertainty and inequality in human society (chapters 4–8). Then the sage concludes by addressing death (9:1–10; 11:7–12:7). Just as all rivers "flow" (הלכים, 1:7) into the sea, so it is that "all people go to their eternal home" (כי־הלך האדם אל־בית עולמו, 12:5, translation mine). The active participles of הלך at the beginning (1:7) and end (12:5) of the main portion of text form an *inclusio* and underscore the author's conviction that every individual experiences an ongoing journey to the grave. The entire book can therefore be read as a pilgrimage from the cycles and vicissitudes of life to the inexorable climax in the human experience. Qoheleth is emphatic about one universal fate for all living persons and structures his text to emphasize such a core belief.

### 3.1    *Epilogue to Qoheleth*

As we assess the structure and literary integrity of Qoheleth, the epilogue (12:9–14) is an important issue to consider. Since 1:2 and 12:8 form an *inclusio*, the language that follows in 12:9–14 seems to represent a secondary frame to the "words of Qoheleth" in 1:3–12:7. This final section is further set off because of the third-person reference to קהלת/"the Teacher" (along with the superscription in 1:1) and the marked differences in thematic content. The text reads as follows:

> 9 Besides being wise, the Teacher also taught the people knowledge, weighing and studying and arranging many proverbs. 10 The Teacher sought to find pleasing words, and he wrote words of truth plainly. 11 The sayings of the wise are like goads, and like nails firmly fixed are the collected sayings that are given by one shepherd. 12 Of anything beyond these, my child, beware. Of making many books there is no end, and much study is a weariness of the flesh. 13 The end of the matter; all has been heard. Fear God, and keep his commandments; for that is the whole duty of everyone. 14 For God will bring every deed into judgment, including every secret thing, whether good or evil.

The way in which these concluding verses are interpreted dictates one's analysis of the entire book and the history of its transmission. Many have argued that the conclusion functions as a critique of earlier assertions on the nature of human existence in the main portion of text. Another possibility is that the final section of the book actually complements what goes before it or at least does not contradict it. Some scholars have argued that the entire text comes from one author, with no apparent contradiction between epilogue and preceding statements. Yet another reading understands the conclusion to represent the authentic feelings of a sage who wrote the main portion of text under a satirical guise. In evaluating these arguments, it becomes apparent that any proposal depends on whether the commentator reads 12:13–14 as a corrective to the main text of Qoheleth or a fitting capstone.

In terms of organization, vv. 9–11 constitute the first unit. The message here is that Qoheleth was a wise sage who participated in an admirable wisdom tradition. These verses are an *apologia* for the primary content in the book as well as the entire sapiential enterprise (e.g., the reference to "arranging many proverbs" in v. 9). Language echoing the book of Proverbs appears in this section, terms such as מְשָׁלִים ("proverbs," v. 9), חֲכָמִים ("wise ones," "sages," v. 11), and verbs indicating the process of instruction.[31] This conclusion in vv. 9–11 has parallels elsewhere in the international wisdom tradition, as many Egyptian instructions contain a laudatory third-person summation that serves to authenticate a particular sage's literary work and career (e.g., Anii). There are also examples of this type of description in both Ahiqar and Ben Sira.[32] With regard to the latter half of the epilogue (12:12–14), here we find a thematic divergence from 12:9–11 and the main body of text. These statements are conspicuously at odds with earlier declarations in 1:3–12:7, where the primary author emphasizes the finitude and randomness of human existence, never mentions the commandments as a source of authority, and seems unconvinced by the efficacy of "deeds" to accomplish favor with God. In addition, the main author of this book ("Qoheleth") is largely uninterested in the obligations of Yahwistic piety (other than a brief section on vows and

---

[31] For a review of the technical sense of the language in these verses and the possibility of a school context, see Jean-Marie Auwers, "Problèmes d'interprétation de l'épilogue de Qohèlèt," in *Qohelet in the Context of Wisdom* (ed. A. Schoors; BETL 136; Leuven: Leuven University Press/Peeters, 1998), 267–82. On the relationship between Qoh 12:9–14 and the book of Proverbs, see Gerald T. Sheppard, "The Epilogue to Qoheleth as Theological Commentary," *CBQ* 39 (1977): 182–89.

[32] Ahiqar is referred to in the third-person as a gifted scribe (1–4). In addition, the parallels between Qoh 12:9–14 and Sir 50:27–29 are compelling, including the similar usage of the root חנה. Both units contain a third-person summary followed by a parenetic conclusion that implores the reader to take the message to heart. See Krüger, *Qoheleth*, 209.

the command to fear the Lord), and he avoids the language of judgment in the context of covenant.[33]

Scholars have approached the apparent discrepancy between vv. 9–11
and 12–14 and its relationship with the rest of the book in several ways.
One possibility advanced by Lauha is that two epilogists added language
at the end of Qoh 1:2–12:8, in vv. 9–11 and vv. 12–14 respectively.
According to his argument, the repetition of יתר in 12:12 and the use
of בני suggest a discrete unit in vv. 12–14, as does the more covenantal
tone of the latter set of verses.[34] Hertzberg posits three epilogists in this
section: vv. 9–11 praise Qoheleth, v. 12 undercuts the main text and
the previous two verses, while vv. 13–14 align the whole book more
closely to Israel's sacred history.[35] This is a logical understanding of
the seemingly composite ending. Others have argued for a basic unity
to this section, while acknowledging that the epilogue is distinct from
the main body of text. Murphy asks, "Is it not possible that there is
only one epilogist, who is *not* criticizing Qoheleth, but in fact praising
the book, while at the same time giving it an interpretation that is
more in line with Sirach?"[36] Following a similar approach, Sheppard
has demonstrated an ideological kinship between the epilogist(s) who
wrote Qoh 12:9–14 and the perspective found in Ben Sira.[37] He argues
that vv. 9–10 are followed by a proverb (v. 11) and then a statement in
v. 12 that a certain collection of "proto-canonical" instructions (which

---

[33] Fox, *A Time to Tear Down*, 229, calls 4:17–5:6 an example of conventional wisdom.
Although he undermines certain assumptions common to his tradition, "Qohelet never
abandons moral and religious principles or repudiates the principle of divine justice." As
part of his affirmation of the tradition, the sage includes the call to "fear God" in the
main portion of text (e.g., 5:6). Most Wisdom writers invoked this concept, however,
and it cannot necessarily be used to propose a single author for the entire book. An
epilogist could have chosen to use it in 12:14 precisely because he found the phrase
earlier in the text. See Gerald H. Wilson, "The Intent and Significance of Qohelet
12:9–14," *JBL* 103 (1984), 178. Like many commentators, this discussion will argue
that the judgment language in a few select passages (most notably 3:17 and 11:9) is
secondary (see below).

[34] Aarre Lauha, *Kohelet* (BKAT 19; Neukirchen-Vluyn: Neukirchener Verlag, 1978),
221–22; cf. Kurt Galling, "Der Prediger," in *Die Fünf Megilloth* (2d ed.; HAT 18;
Tübingen: Mohr, 1969), 124–25; Michel, *Qohelet*, 116.

[35] Hertzberg, *Der Prediger*, 219–21.

[36] Murphy, *Ecclesiastes*, 128.

[37] Gerald T. Sheppard, *Wisdom as a Hermeneutical Construct* (BZAW 180; Berlin: de
Gruyter, 1980), 127, argues, "In sum, only Sirach has exactly the same ideology as
Qoh. 12:13–14, a perspective not expressed in the body of Qoheleth itself. It is, therefore, probable that the redactor of Qoh. 12:13–14 either knew of the book of Sirach
or shared fully in a similar, pervasive estimate of sacred wisdom."

include the books of Proverbs and Qoheleth) are sufficient to explain the goal of instructional literature.[38] The last two verses then reveal a perspective and use of language that are strikingly similar to Ben Sira, including the later sage's allegiance to the Torah.[39]

Two commentators, Fox and Krüger, have defended the epilogue as part of the original creative work of the first author. In his recent commentary, Krüger argues that the person responsible for the entire book takes on the persona of "Qoheleth the preacher" to offer an analysis of human existence. Then in the epilogue, the author who created the persona qualifies some of his earlier statements. Krüger explains the underlying goal of this literary strategy:

> By appearing in the role of the "editor" behind his protagonist "Qohe-leth," the author creates distance between himself and "Qoheleth." *In* this distance he *reinforces* the "words of Qoheleth" by stylizing "Qohe-leth" as a type of a "critical wise man" (vv. 9–10). At the same time, however, he also *relativizes* them by classifying them in the realm of wise "words" and "writings," and he shows their possibilities and their limits (vv. 11–12).[40]

Fox's argument on this issue follows a similar line of reasoning. He claims that the author responsible for the motto (1:2; 12:8) and the epilogue creates a fictional persona in 1:3–12:7.[41] Fox looks at other instructional texts and concludes that the decision to adopt "the ancient convention of presenting the teacher's words through a retrospective frame" derives from the efforts of this first author.[42] Therefore, the entire text comes from one source. The mindset of this author in

---

[38] Sheppard, "The Epilogue to Qoheleth," 188; Wilson, "Intent and Significance of Qohelet 12:9–14," 179. The mention of "these" (המה) in the verse refers to a body of sapiential literature that is apparently sufficient for the recipient of this advice.

[39] Sheppard, *Wisdom as a Hermeneutical Construct*, 126, posits a connection between Qoh 12:13–14 and both Sir 17:6–15 and 43:37. All of these passages relate to the revelation of secret works and the meting out of rewards according to divine justice. Wilson, "The Intent and Significance of Qohelet 12:9–14," 190, favors a link with Proverbs 1–9 based on the similar appropriation of Deuteronomic themes and the connection between Qoh 12:9–14 and Prov 1:2–7. Yet the affinities with Ben Sira are more convincing because of the similarities in language and the probable chronology of these texts (Proverbs 1–9 probably dates from the Persian period). It is not an either-or proposition, however, and the reference to "these" in Qoh 12:12 might include the book of Proverbs, at least the version known to the epilogist at the time of writing.

[40] Krüger, *Qoheleth*, 215.

[41] Michael V. Fox, "Frame Narrative and Composition in the Book of Qohelet," *HUCA* 48 (1977): 83–106.

[42] Fox, *Qohelet and His Contradictions*, 315.

relation to his literary persona is "protective rather than polemical," for "the author does not undermine the persona's ethos or subvert his teachings."[43] Because of the lack of conflict, Fox does not consider his theory about the epilogue to be of great consequence.

In a recent study, Martin Shields argues that an orthodox epilogist is critiquing sages like Qoheleth and the pessimistic outlook found in their works.[44] This epilogist is reacting to the author responsible for the "words of Qoheleth," and in this pursuit he emphasizes the commandments and the certainty of divine judgment (12:13–14). The "human wisdom" that one finds in the main text is intrinsically flawed, from the perspective of this epilogist. The concluding section is the feature of the book that coheres with the rest of biblical literature, and these declarations mitigate some of the skeptical passages earlier in the book. Shields is convinced that the epilogue constitutes the only acceptable perspective in the text, and the book is placed in the canon to highlight the epilogist's warning against the dangers associated with the wisdom tradition. In other words, the primary author's failed experiment only serves to highlight the superiority of the epilogist's piety: "If Qoheleth's message is that there is no sense to be found in the world, the epilogist's message is that sense can only be found in fearing God and keeping his commandments."[45] Such a reading of the book is problematic, because it understates the primary sage's devotion to "fear of the Lord" and the wisdom tradition (at least his version of it) and the brilliance of his reflections.

The most radical proposal can be found in a recent discussion by Carolyn Sharp.[46] Like Fox and Krüger, Sharp argues that one individual wrote the entire book, including 12:9–14. Yet she departs from these scholars with the helpful claim that the "words of Qoheleth" differ considerably from 12:13–14. Sharp maintains that 1:3–12:7 represents the ironic literary device of a pious author who in the epilogue reverses the jaded outlook of the fictional "Qoheleth." According to her proposed schema, the "words of Qoheleth" constitute a dour, hopeless,

---

[43] Fox, *Qohelet and His Contradictions*, 315.

[44] Martin A. Shields, *The End of Wisdom: A Reappraisal of the Canonical Function of Ecclesiastes* (Winona Lake, Ind.: Eisenbrauns, 2006).

[45] Shields, *The End of Wisdom*, 109.

[46] Carolyn J. Sharp, "Ironic Representation, Authorial Voice, and Meaning in Qohelet," *BI* 12 (2004): 37–68.

and ultimately satirical perspective. Even the seemingly positive passages (e.g., 9:7–10) fit this pattern:

> "Qohelet's" rhetorical grasping for joy is a desperate, unconvincing paraenesis that serves only to highlight how distanced his (constructed) reality is from the desired fruits of his lifelong search for wisdom.... We believe what "Qohelet" says only at our peril.[47]

Therefore, 12:9–10 do not offer serious praise, but stand as a backhanded commentary on the inadequacy of the book's primary discussion. The reference to "the making of many books" (v. 12) reflects a critique of sapiential efforts (like "Qoheleth's") that are laughable in relation to 12:13–14. The entire text then functions as a "unified ironic corpus": "The rhetoric of the book drives toward the goal of rendering the command to fear God and obey God's commandments impervious to further irony."[48] This "ironist" believes that the people of the covenant can be united in solidarity around core principles (the commandments) found in other biblical books.[49]

Reading the text in this way enables the interpreter to locate Qoheleth more closely with some of the biblical books that emphasize covenant fidelity, even as it has an emasculating effect on an important voice in the Hebrew Bible. Moreover, this interpretation neutralizes the sage's incisive commentary on the inadequacy of earlier act-consequence understandings in Proverbs. While correct that the differences between the epilogue and the "words of Qoheleth" are profound, the theory of a single "ironist" falters on several points. First, this interpretive move fails to consider the lack of explicit relationship between the Torah (at least the available version of it) and Wisdom in the earlier sapiential books. A rapprochement between the two is not evident in Proverbs or in the main text of Qoheleth; this transformation would only take place in the book of Ben Sira (and implicitly in Qoh 12:13–14). In addition, Sharp does not deal with the many examples of laudatory third-person epilogues in ancient Near Eastern instructions and the tradition of pessimistic literature, particularly in Egypt.[50] Perhaps most

---

[47] Sharp, "Ironic Representation," 59.
[48] Sharp, "Ironic Representation," 63.
[49] Sharp, "Ironic Representation," 67.
[50] We have discussed the third-person frame narrative in such instructions as Ptahhotep, Kagemni, and Ankhsheshonqy. The Dispute Between a Man and His *Ba* shares a number of similarities with Qoheleth, even if the latter is not directly dependent on the Egyptian text as a model. Many Egyptian texts, particularly the late

glaringly, interpretations that elevate the epilogue and critique the main body of text minimize the brilliant, diverse reflections of the author responsible for the "words of Qoheleth." Viewing this text as the work of a critical thinker amid a changing Second Temple landscape does not represent a misguided reading. The individual responsible for these observations stakes a memorable position in an evolving postexilic culture that had begun to grapple more fully with a pastiche of new influences, including innovative suggestions about immortality. Qoheleth bristles at God's complete control over the cosmos, and this forces him to write in a conflicted and at times helpless tone. This book represents a thinker who sees the stark realities of the human situation and bravely comments on them. By likening the penetrating observations found in this text to a "well-drawn villain serving as foil in a film or novel," Sharp understates the positive passages (e.g., 9:7–9) in Qoheleth and the daring lucidity of the more pessimistic conclusions.[51] Robert Gordis comments on the power of Qoheleth's probative style and willingness to describe all aspects of existence: "Whoever has dreamt great dreams in his youth and seen the vision flee, or has loved and lost, or has beaten barehanded at the fortress of injustice and come back bleeding and broken, has passed Koheleth's door."[52]

The epilogue is probably a two-stage redaction: vv. 9–11 praise the author "Qoheleth" as a thinker of some distinction. Hengel suggests that the author of 12:9–11 might have been a personal disciple of Qoheleth, and this is a possibility.[53] Then the last three verses (12:12–14) constitute a second redaction. These are the work of an orthodox glossator who presents a radically disjunctive perspective from 1:3–12:7 and 12:9–11, with the exception of a few scattered verses that are probably insertions. The first verse (12:12) of the second redaction belittles the process of writing too many instructions and could even be a swipe at the content of the "words of Qoheleth." Then this second epilogist mentions the

---

autobiographies, reveal despondency over death that parallels Qoheleth. See Burkes, *Death in Ecclesiastes*, 171–208.

[51] Sharp, "Ironic Representation," 64.

[52] Robert Gordis, *Koheleth-The Man and His World* (TS 19; New York: Bloch Publishing Company, 1955), 3.

[53] Hengel, *Judaism and Hellenism*, 1:127. Significantly, this first epilogist refers to Qoheleth as a חכם ("sage" or "wise one") in v. 9, which probably has a professional connotation. The same holds true for 8:17, since החכם could refer to a debate-partner. See Crenshaw, *Ecclesiastes*, 34–36.

importance of keeping the divine commandments (vv. 13–14).[54] The same editor who wrote 12:12–14 could also have written insertions in 3:17, 8:5, 12b–13 and 11:9b, all of which mention a judgment similar to the language of 12:14.[55] Such passages are at odds with the larger discussion in Qoheleth, where human experience occurs under the shadow of an unknowable, mercurial deity (e.g., 3:14). It is true that the main body of text advocates "fearing" God (3:14; 4:17; 5:6), and this author presents a limited view of human agency and humble acknowledgment of divine majesty. Yet this is different from believing in a deity who expects conformity to a set of legal prescriptions and rewards accordingly. This consistent *Tun-Ergehen-Zusammenhang* is the perspective we find with the second epilogist and in the insertions. The presentation in the main portion of text advocates enjoyment of the fleeting moments in life, precisely because there will be no lasting benefits meted out to the righteous on account of good works (i.e., no judgment of the type promised in 12:13–14).[56] The passages in the text that are "corrections" to such a viewpoint (e.g., 8:12b–13: contrast with the dominant perspective in v. 14) might represent an attempt to make this text more palatable to observant Jews during the Hellenistic period, perhaps at a time when the authoritative status of the book was being questioned. One final point on this second epilogist: the nature of God's judgment in these final verses is a difficult issue to determine, since 12:14 concludes the book without further comment. Yet there is good reason to believe that eschatological judgment is implied by this final verse (similarly 11:9b). We will address this topic in our discussion of the "human spirit" in Qoheleth.

---

[54] Hertzberg might be correct that v. 12 comes from a different hand than vv. 13–14, and therefore we have three epilogists at the end of the book. Nevertheless, it is easier to understand v. 12 as a complaint about the instructional process and a warning against taking "the words of Qoheleth" too seriously.

[55] Numerous commentators argue that 11:9b derives from the second epilogist. The language in this verse (ודע כי על־כל־אלה יביאך האלהים במשפט) is strikingly similar to the MT of 12:14 (identical usage of בוא + משפט—this also appears in Job 14:3). For a full list of scholars who subscribe to this belief, see Armin Lange, "In Diskussion mit Dem Tempel: Zur Auseinandersetzung zwischen Kohelet und weisheitlichen Kreisen am Jerusalemer Tempel," in *Qohelet in the Context of Wisdom* (ed. A. Schoors; BETL 136; Leuven: Leuven University Press/Peeters, 1998), 120 n. 19. Note in particular the argument of Walther Zimmerli, *Das Buch des Predigers Salomo* (3d ed.; ATD 16; Göttingen: Vandenhoeck & Ruprecht, 1980), 238–40.

[56] Murphy, *Ecclesiastes*, 126, notes the irony of including מעשה in 12:14, since it is used throughout the main body of text to indicate the inscrutability of the "work" of God (7:13; 8:17; 11:5; cf. 3:11).

With regard to the actual "words of Qoheleth" in 1:3–12:7, these reflections in all likelihood derive from one sage during the Second Temple period, perhaps at the end of his career and life. The author's paradoxical style leaves the reader puzzled at times, but this feature reveals a tendency to reflect openly on the aspects of human existence the author finds frustrating, rather than to a complex series of insertions. In some cases, Qoheleth seems to refer to the position of a detractor (Hertzberg's "Zwar-aber-Aussage"), and he also cites familiar positions within sapiential circles. The relevant question then becomes why and in what precise setting the sage delivered this set of forceful utterances. When Qoheleth is placed in the correct historical context, the nature of his discussion becomes more apparent, as does the important debate in which he participated.

### 4. *Historical Setting and Possible Influences on Qoheleth*

Determining Qoheleth's historical setting is very difficult and has remained a controversial topic in the study of the book. Like many ancient instructions, the book is devoid of allusions to specific events or figures, and one must therefore mine the text for linguistic and contextual clues that correlate with a particular period.[57] This is a formidable task, since many of the issues raised by the sage are common themes in the wisdom tradition. Such matters as familial relations (9:9), the pitfalls of greed (5:9–13), and the need to fear God (5:7) transcend any specific era. Ancient Near Eastern sages in a variety of contexts had been addressing these topics for centuries. Despite the lack of historical references, several factors narrow down the possible time frame for Qoheleth's career. On the linguistic level, the vocabulary and grammar used in the text are indicative of Late Biblical Hebrew. The presence of two Persian loanwords (*pardēs* in 2:5; *pitgām* in 8:11) and other grammatical markers (e.g., the use of *šin* as a relative form) seem to preclude a setting prior to the exile. Since the inclusion of such late terminology and forms cannot precede the Achaemenid period and because fragments from the text have been found in Cave IV at Qumran (providing a *terminus ad quem*), the date for the "words of Qoheleth" must be some point between the fifth and second-century

---

[57] The allusion to Solomon (1:1) is a literary device: few scholars working on the book today would make the case for authorship during the period of the monarchy.

B.C.E.[58] There are additional indicators of this later date in terms of subject matter, particularly the depiction of a fluid mercantile economy and a more complex discussion of human mortality and its implications. The latter feature is nowhere to be found in the book of Proverbs. This section will argue that a contextual reading of the overriding theme of the book, death, along with other significant markers, particularly economic ones, point to the Ptolemaic period (as late as 200 B.C.E.) as the most likely setting for Qoheleth, when certain issues became more prominent in sapiential discourse.

Based on the author's preoccupation with financial matters and the number of Aramaisms in the book, a few scholars have posited a Persian period date for Qoheleth. The most comprehensive case for this setting can be found in the recent commentary of C.L. Seow, who reads Qoheleth against the backdrop of an expanding economy and an elaborate network of provinces under the Achaemenids.[59] Such an economic climate led to an upstart middle class and a more complex tax structure. The increased use of coinage further democratized the distribution of wealth, allowing a broader cross-section of citizens opportunities for economic advancement. Seow contends that Qoheleth is addressing the system of royal grants under the Persians in 5:17–6:2 and similar passages.[60] The sage finds such policies to be a travesty, particularly when they involve the usurpation of property rights from a hard-working individual. Seow also relies on linguistic evidence, particularly commercial terms, to substantiate his argument. He points specifically to the legal usage of שׁלט (along with the nouns שׁלּיט and שׁלטון) in Qoheleth (2:19; 5:18; 6:2; 7:19; 8:8–9). According to Seow, these terms are not used in a technical, "proprietary" sense after the fourth-century B.C.E.[61] Qoheleth employs this vocabulary in a distinctively vernacular Hebrew, "with its large number of Aramaisms and whatever jargons and dialectical elements one may find in the marketplace."[62] According to Seow, such features, coupled with the

---

[58] The Dead Sea Scrolls manuscript is 4QQoh^a (4Q109), which preserves portions of chapters 5–7.

[59] Seow, *Ecclesiastes*, 21–36.

[60] Seow, *Ecclesiastes*, 23–28.

[61] C.L. Seow, "Linguistic Evidence and the Dating of Qoheleth," *JBL* 115 (1996), 653–54, points specifically to the use of this root in the context of land ownership. Seow claims that a *šallîṭ* is a "wealthy land baron" with far-reaching property rights.

[62] Seow, *Ecclesiastes*, 20–23, argues that חלק ("portion" or "lot"), טחנה ("mill," 12:4), and חשׁבון ("sum" or "reckoning," 7:27) are Aramaisms that relate to the socioeconomic context of the Persian period.

absence of Grecisms in the text, point to the Persian period. The target
audience consisted of a new class of citizenry who had begun to experience changing economic realities and the potential for financial gain
under more accommodating foreign rule.[63] Other scholars have made
a similar case, although conclusions on the presumed audience for the
work differ. Many have posited a more elite setting for the book.[64]

Seow's terminological study of Imperial Aramaic documents offers
a helpful assessment of this important period, but the argument for
placing Qoheleth during the Persian era is inconclusive. Several factors
complicate the proposal. First, the contention that the sage remains
deeply concerned with economic matters is quite accurate, but such
a preoccupation could just as easily fit a later context. The scenarios
described in the Zeno papyri from the Ptolemaic period and the account
of the Tobiads in Josephus (*Ant.* 12.154–234) reveal a class structure
and an administrative hierarchy that correlate with the references in
Qoheleth.[65] Ptolemaic territories had a network of officials, many of
them wealthy and some of them quite corrupt, and Qoheleth's critique
of dishonest administrators might apply to this subsequent period. With
regard to linguistic evidence, the lack of Grecisms does not necessarily
point to an origin during the Persian period. The book of Daniel dates
from the second-century B.C.E., and even in this later work only a few
terms reflect a Greek origin.[66] In addition, it might not be the case that

---

[63] Seow, *Ecclesiastes*, 28, maintains that Qoheleth's audience consisted of commoners
facing the daily risks of ordinary workers (e.g., 10:1 and the reference to dead flies in
a perfumer's ointment).

[64] James Kugel, "Qohelet and Money," *CBQ* 51 (1989), 46, dates the book during
the Persian period. Like Seow, he cites the lack of Grecisms and clear evidence of
Hellenistic thought and the absence of any overt biblical citations in the book. This
earlier era provides the "proper mix of economic stability and linguistic chaos to have
generated this particular work" (p. 49). In contrast to Seow, Kugel claims that Qoheleth directs his message to a group of "financial high rollers" capable of amassing vast
sums of wealth and property, individuals who are unconcerned with small loans and
petty transactions (2:8; 5:12–13; 11:1). Kugel's argument for a wealthier audience has
much to commend it, since the author of Qoheleth speaks from the vantage point of
a property holder with a considerable amount of income and power. The proverb
about "dead flies" is part of a collection of sayings, and its content could apply to
many socioeconomic groups and any number of situations.

[65] See Victor Tcherikover, *Hellenistic Civilization and the Jews* (Philadelphia: Jewish Publication Society, 1959; repr., Peabody: Hendrickson Publishers, 1999), 60, 126–51.

[66] John J. Collins, *Daniel* (Hermeneia; Minneapolis: Fortress Press, 1993), 20. There
are only three undisputed examples of Greek vocabulary in the book of Daniel, and all
of these terms are used in reference to musical instruments (κίθαρις, ψαλτήριον, and
συμφωνία). This shows that a small number of Grecisms in a Second Temple Hebrew

שׁלט ceases to have a "proprietary" meaning after the fourth-century B.C.E.[67] Dominic Rudman has objected to this claim, based on several late passages containing the root.[68] Rudman also cites a verse from Ben Sira and an extant bill of sale in Syriac that support a "proprietary" meaning of שׁלט well into the Ptolemaic era and beyond.[69] Without this argument based on שׁלט, there is nothing specific about the Persian period that forces one to place the book during this time frame, and there are compelling reasons for a later date.

Based on a number of factors, the book is better situated during the period of Ptolemaic rule in Palestine (ca. 319–200 B.C.E.). Several scholars have pointed to the sage's interest in or even dependence on the ideas being put forth by the various schools of Greek philosophy during this period, and this is a possibility (see below). In addressing this question, one must also consider sociopolitical markers in Qoheleth that point to the third-century B.C.E. as the more likely setting. This approach has marked many efforts to place the text historically, despite the limited extracanonical evidence from this era. Hengel posits a Ptolemaic date based on contextual clues, arguing that the harsh and impersonal bureaucracy described in Qoheleth and the link with Egyptian thought and culture (e.g., the royal testament section) make the most sense during this period.[70] Similarly, Krüger maintains that the royal depictions in 1:12–2:26 refer to local potentates from Judea, figures like the high priests or one of the Tobiads. He also states that 10:5–7 is addressing a new class of landowners whom Qoheleth (himself a representative of the established aristocracy) finds repugnant.[71] Other

---

text does not prove (or disprove) a Hellenistic date. Such a principle also applies to the Dead Sea Scrolls, which date from the later period.

[67] To substantiate his argument, Seow relies on the study of Douglas M. Gropp, "The Origin and Development of the Aramaic *Šallîṭ* Clause," *JNES* 52 (1993): 31–36.

[68] Dominic Rudman, "A Note on the Dating of Ecclesiastes," *CBQ* 61 (1999), 50. Rudman argues that the use of the root in Dan 2:38 might have a proprietary connotation, since the king has control over all animals. God gives Nebuchadnezzar ownership over all livestock in the world.

[69] Rudman, "A Note on the Dating of Ecclesiastes," 51, discussing Sir 9:13: "Keep far from a man with the power (שׁלט) to kill, and you will not be worried by the fear of death." Rudman contends that this is a technical usage, since the man in power has a legal right to inflict the death penalty. He also cites an extant Syriac bill of sale from 243 C.E. (P. Dura 28) that includes a technical usage of שׁלט. See Jonathan A. Goldstein, "The Syriac Bill of Sale from Dura-Europos," *JNES* 25 (1966), 11–12.

[70] Hengel, *Judaism and Hellenism*, 1:115–16.

[71] Krüger, *Qoheleth*, 20.

scholars have linked 5:7–8 to the elaborate system of royal landholdings
and taxation that the Ptolemies instituted.[72]

The question then becomes whether there is enough correlative data
from external sources to support a third-century date for Qoheleth,
based on this type of argument. While the extant textual, archaeological, and numismatic evidence does not offer a complete portrait of the
situation facing upper-class citizens in the region, the arguments of
Hengel, Krüger, Schwienhorst-Schönberger, and other scholars have
merit. Many of the sage's reflections are pertinent to the entrepreneur-
ial ethos of the Ptolemaic period, particularly in relation to property
rights, rapid financial loss/gain, and corruption. A bustling economic
culture is described in the Zeno correspondence, which dates from the
middle of the third-century (261–229 B.C.E.). Appollonius, who served
as *dioketes* (the individual in charge of civil administration and finance
throughout the empire) under Ptolemy II Philadelphus (282–246),
had a subordinate named Zeno who spent time traveling in Palestine
(260–258) in order to fulfill a number of imperial duties. While in the
Galilee region, Zeno toured an estate under the direct control of the
*dioketes*.[73] The extant papyri from this correspondence indicate that
property could be granted to a well-connected official (Zeno actually
managed one of Appollonius' estates), but such holdings reverted to
the crown if the individual died or left his post for some reason.[74] The
land could also be taken arbitrarily, and this is a plausible background
for the hypothetical situation in Qoh 6:1–2.[75] In addition to property
rights, Qoheleth rails against structures that lead to corruption. The
complex system of officials described by Zeno might be the target of
Qoh 5:7:

---

[72] See Crüsemann, "The Unchangeable World," 63; Schwienhorst-Schönberger,
'Nicht im Menschen Gründet das Glück', 139–41, argues that these verses are a satirical
commentary on the uncertainty of property holdings during this period and the long
arm of the ruler in Alexandria.

[73] See Günther Hölbl, *A History of the Ptolemaic Empire* (trans. T. Saavedra; New
York: Routledge, 2001), 58–61. He discusses the cleruchy settlements of soldiers in
Transjordan, which led to increased Hellenistic influence in terms of civic organization
and agricultural advancements.

[74] This follows a longstanding tradition in Egypt of property being the ultimate
possession of the king.

[75] Tcherikover, *Hellenistic Civilization and the Jews*, 69, discusses the unscrupulous policies that frequently characterized this period. The text of Qoheleth seems to reflect the
usurpation of property: "There is an evil that I have seen under the sun, and it lies
heavy upon humankind: those to whom God gives wealth, possessions, and honor, so
that they lack nothing of all that they desire, yet God does not enable them to enjoy
these things, but a stranger enjoys them. This is vanity; it is a grievous ill" (6:1–2).

If you see in a province the oppression of the poor and the violation of justice and right, do not be amazed at the matter; for the high official is watched by a higher, and there are yet higher ones over them.[76]

Material evidence from sites in Palestine also illuminates the cultural circumstances of Qoheleth's probable era. Archaeological efforts have revealed a Ptolemaic influence along some of the port cities and inland commercial routes that would have served as logical points of interest for a foreign power.[77] Monument remains and extant coins at various sites demonstrate construction projects as well as active commerce.[78] The extent of the foreign impact in the interior regions is more difficult to assess. It is certain that large pockets of land (e.g., in the northern highlands) were sparsely populated and unaffected by colonial interests arising from Alexandria. In certain locales, Greek settlements developed within close proximity to older cities, and these new towns often became trading centers and hubs of foreign influence.[79] A slave trade flourished under the system set up by the Ptolemies, and this enhanced agricultural efficiency. Such a system might be the background for the reference in Qoh 2:7: "I bought male and female slaves, and had slaves who were born in my house." Even if much of the population experienced little or no lifestyle change under the ruling powers from Alexandria, the situation for a slave-owning aristocrat like "Qoheleth" would have been different. The bulk of his autobiographical information might be overstated or even fictional, but it probably relates to existing class structures and some of the complex decisions facing the elite. As a land baron, "Qoheleth" would have interacted with foreign officials, perhaps finagled for more land and a better tax situation, and reaped the benefits of his property holdings.[80] Certain passages seem to have a Hellenistic coloring (e.g., 2:4–9), and they reflect both an agrarian perspective (including more efficient irrigation systems) and an effort

---

[76] Hölbl, *History of the Ptolemaic Empire*, 59, describes the network of officials under the Ptolemies. Kugel, "Qohelet and Money," 36–38, argues persuasively that נבה in Qoh 5:7 should be translated as "payment taker."

[77] Andrea M. Berlin, "Between Large Forces: Palestine in the Hellenistic Period," *BA* 60 (1997): 2–51.

[78] Berlin, "Between Large Forces," 6. Gaza became a more developed region under the Ptolemies, as did Mareshah. There are also the *yhd* jars, which indicate an active trading policy by the Ptolemaic administration for such goods as oil, wine, and wheat, together with an elaborate tax structure.

[79] C. Robert Harrison, "Hellenization in Syria-Palestine: the Case of Judea in the Third Century BCE," *BA* 57 (1994): 98–108.

[80] Berlin, "Between Large Forces," 9.

at maximizing profit.[81] Qoheleth looks at life as an accountant, always concerned with gaining a יתרון ("profit"), and this fits the culture of the Ptolemaic period.

Another parallel linking Qoheleth to this later period is the book of Ben Sira (ca. 190 B.C.E.). Caution is always in order when positing a contextual link between two instructions. Qoheleth addresses issues related to money that can be found in many antecedent texts, both Israelite and foreign. For example, swift financial loss and the need for obsequious behavior around the wealthy and powerful are addressed in instructions from many distinct historical periods. John Collins notes the difficulty of distinguishing between "the traditional verities of wisdom literature and remarks that are aimed at specific abuses."[82] Nevertheless, the parallels between Qoheleth and Ben Sira suggest more than a common application of standard motifs. Shared themes such as anxiety over money, public decorum, the dangers of commerce, and especially the issue of death, cannot be mere coincidence. The cumulative effect of the evidence suggests that Qoheleth and Ben Sira had their careers during the same general period, even if they were not necessarily contemporaries.[83] It is true that the two sages hold divergent perspectives on key issues: Ben Sira's equating the Torah and Wisdom is one of the many differences. Yet both figures seem to address the same economic climate. When coupled with their mutual interest in human mortality and its implications, the content of these texts points to a similar setting and date. Ben Sira can be dated with relative precision (based on the

---

[81] See C. Robert Harrison, "Qoheleth in Social-Historical Perspective," (Ph.D. diss., Duke University, 1991), 198.

[82] John J. Collins, *Jewish Wisdom in the Hellenistic Age* (OTL; Louisville: Westminster John Knox Press, 1997), 29.

[83] For example, note the similarities with regard to the following topics: the advantage of the wealthy man over the commoner (Qoh 9:13–16; cf. Sir 13:3–13, 20–23); the fluidity of the financial climate in terms of rapid financial gain/loss (Qoh 2:21; 5:12–13; 10:5–7; cf. Sir 18:25–26; 26:28); anxiety over money and lack of satisfaction with what a wealthy person has attained (Qoh 5:9; cf. Sir 31:1–11); concern with public decorum, particularly in the presence of officials (Qoh 10:20; cf. Sir 31:12–32:13, which mentions appropriate behavior at banquet halls); the call for benevolence (Qoh 11:1–2; cf. Sir 35:14–20). In addition, Ben Sira endorses the acquisition of wealth if a person can remain blameless in such a pursuit (31:8–11), but he considers this to be a remote possibility (26:28–27:3). For his part, Qoheleth believes in enjoying the fruit of one's toil (2:24–25) and does not oppose having vast sums of money. Such parallels are too numerous to reflect simply the coincidental application of traditional motifs.

grandson's prologue). The book of Qoheleth was probably written during the same general period, perhaps a generation or two earlier.[84]

## 4.1   Hellenistic Influence?

Throughout the ages, Qoheleth's statements on causality, death, and the nature of human existence have fascinated readers. Many commentators have wondered how he developed his rhetorical brilliance and fatalistic attitude, including the extent and nature of any foreign influences. One frequent suggestion is that the author of this text borrowed from Hellenistic thinkers, whose masterful works had begun to reach literate persons in Palestine. Qoheleth has been characterized as the product of a new Hellenistic spirit taking root in the Transjordan and throughout the territories conquered by Alexander the Great. In fact, many scholars argue that the impact of ideas from the Greek world supersedes any connection to other contexts (i.e., Egyptian or Mesopotamian). As a result, Hellenistic sources explain the author's departure from certain assumptions and thematic interests found in Proverbs. Such proposals usually argue that the sage's perspective is dependent on one or more of the Greek philosophical schools. This interpretive move is one of the more consequential aspects of Qoheleth studies. The decision to posit Greek influence of course has great bearing on one's interpretation of the author as an original thinker and the *Zeitgeist* for his book.

Most aspects of Greek thought have surfaced in scholarly discussions of this type, and if every theory proved to be correct, there would be no choice but to categorize Qoheleth as a trained philosopher *par excellence*. Only a few possibilities can receive attention in this discussion. Schwienhorst-Schönberger contends that the book follows specific Greek forms, including the diatribe.[85] Lohfink makes a more general argument that Qoheleth was part of a "new reality" springing out of Hellenistic educational and cultural practices, and he offers a host of textual examples in support of this claim.[86] Based on his study of late

---

[84] Many scholars claim that Ben Sira knew the content of Qoheleth. See Murphy, *Ecclesiastes*, xxii.

[85] Schwienhorst-Schönberger, *'Nicht im Menschen Gründet das Glück'*, 274–332. Cf. Braun, *Kohelet und die frühhellenistiche Popularphilosophie*, 165.

[86] Lohfink, *Qoheleth*, 6–17. Under this rubric he includes Homer, Aeschylus, Sophocles, along with Plato, Aristotle, and other major philosophers. Lohfink argues that the ascension language in 3:19–21 was influenced by popular Greek culture and more specifically by references to the αἰθήρ ("heavenly sphere"), the abode of the gods. The

epitaphs and dramas from the Hellenistic world, Hengel maintains that
a crisis in *Greek* religion replaced earlier concepts of the deity with more
impersonal, "non-committal concepts of fate," and this development
shaped Qoheleth's sense of resignation.[87] Braun's study represents the
most comprehensive case for a connection between Qoheleth and the
Greek world. He argues that Hellenistic culture had an impact on
the sage's thinking and choice of terminology. For example, the autobiographical section in chapters 1–2 is not dependent on royal testaments
from Egypt, but owes its origin to popular Hellenistic philosophy.[88] In
support of this ambitious thesis, Braun catalogues a list of common
themes and phrases shared by Qoheleth and various Greek writers.[89]
With regard to Qoheleth's dependence on specific schools, Stoic and/or
Epicurean philosophy are the two most common proposals. A cyclical
understanding of time (3:1–9, 15) and history (1:4–11) and a sense of
resignation about life are often associated with Stoic thought.[90] Regarding the possibility of Epicurean beliefs, the language cited in support
of such a background includes the following verses: 2:24 ("There is
nothing better for mortals than to eat and drink"); 4:8–9 and the ref-

---

beings that originated in the heavens ascend back to their point of origin. This is in
contrast to all earthly things (p. 67). Cf. Hengel, *Judaism and Hellenism*, 1:124.

[87] Hengel, *Judaism and Hellenism*, 1:115–26. Hengel points to Qoheleth's understanding
of מקרה (comparing it to the Greek concept of μοῖρα), his emphasis on individuality,
rational thought, and the incomprehensibility of the divine plan as clear markers of
Greek influence.

[88] Braun, *Kohelet und die frühhellenistiche Popularphilosophie*, 161–64.

[89] Braun, *Kohelet und die frühhellenistiche Popularphilosophie*, 146–49, provides a line-by-
line survey of the whole text of Qoheleth, alongside a full list of possible influences
from various Greek sources.

[90] Qoheleth's use of מקרה and the expression מי יודע ("who knows") are also cited
in support of a Stoic background. One of the first scholars to makes this case was
Harry Ranston, *The Old Testament Wisdom Books and Their Teaching* (London: Epworth
Press, 1930), 252–55. Ranston argued that the language in 3:2–8 is a citation from a
"stoicizing Jewish sage" who knew the principle of the right time for everything and
the individual's ability to ascertain the most favorable moment for a particular action.
Cf. Joseph Blenkinsopp, "Ecclesiastes 3.1–15: Another Interpretation," *JSOT* 66 (1995):
55–64. Blenkinsopp dates the book under Ptolemy IV Philopator (ca. 221–204) and
argues that the writings of Zeno, Cleanthes, and Chrysippus had become familiar to the
literati in Palestine during this period. In responding to the quoted material in 3:2–8,
Qoheleth has difficulty with the logic of the passage, since humanity can never gain
true insight into God's plans (3:11). John G. Gammie, "Stoicism and Anti-Stoicism in
Qoheleth," *HAR* 9 (1985): 169–87, argues that the sage was familiar with the tenets of
Stoic thought and included a deliberate mixture of items he agreed and disagreed with,
particularly in relation to Stoic views on death and the act-consequence relationship.

erence to the pursuit of pleasure (also 5:17–19; 9:7–10).[91] Qoheleth's determinism ("What has been is what will be," 1:9) is also considered to be a marker of Epicurean (and Stoic) thought.

Although none of these examples offer definitive proof of Qoheleth's dependence on a philosophical school or Greek writer, the suggestion of a Hellenistic coloring in the text should not be dismissed too quickly. In all probability, an educated figure like Qoheleth would have experienced at least a minimal exposure to new ideas penetrating his cultural context, and so the theory of a Hellenistic *Zeitgeist* by Hengel and others is a logical one. Some of the thematic strands in the text, such as the persistent focus on the individual and the details in the royal testament section, support this interpretation, as does the author's use of certain phrases.[92] For example, Braun makes a plausible case with regard to תחת השמש ("under the sun") and its relationship to the Greek equivalent ὑφ' ἡλίῳ or ὑπὸ τον ἥλιον.[93] Yet even if the likelihood of the connection is acknowledged, we should not overstate the impact on Qoheleth. The utilization of specific ideas or authors does not necessitate wholesale assimilation to a new cultural model, and in the case of Qoheleth, the level of borrowing from Greek thought seems to have been selective and largely superficial.[94] This author's discerning eye gave him the ability to adapt material from various sources, and it is likely that many of the penetrating observations and stylistic features in this text stem from the personal experiences and insights of the sage himself.

---

[91] Charles Francis Whitley, *Koheleth: His Language and Thought* (Berlin: de Gruyter, 1979), 165, places Qoheleth very late, during the reign of Antiochus IV Epiphanes, based on the proposed connection with Epicurean ideas.

[92] Michael V. Fox, "Wisdom in Qoheleth," in *In Search of Wisdom: Essays in Memory of John G. Gammie* (ed. L.G. Perdue et al.; Louisville: Westminster/John Knox Press, 1993), 123, argues that Qoheleth's awareness of Greek thought is likely, because he subscribes to "the fundamental tenet of Greek philosophy-the autonomy of individual reason, which is to say, the belief that individuals can and should proceed with their own observations and reasoning powers on a quest for knowledge and that this may lead to discovery of truths previously unknown."

[93] Braun, *Kohelet und die frühhellenistiche Popularphilosophie*, 50, maintains that the use of the term by Demosthenes and Plutarch had an indirect influence on Qoheleth.

[94] On the difficulty with using the phrase "Hellenistic" to describe Greek influence during this period and for a helpful theoretical discussion about questions of this type, see Burkes, *Death in Qoheleth*, 249–55.

4.2   *Other Influences on the Sage*

Qoheleth was also indebted to more longstanding traditions, particularly from Egypt and Mesopotamia, and he was intimately familiar
with Israel's own sapiential heritage. As with the Hellenistic question,
the nature and extent of the influences are difficult to quantify. Loretz
argues that this book has a thoroughly Semitic orientation and owes
its origins to Babylonian antecedents and the internal discourse in
Palestine.[95] Among the Mesopotamian sources suggested by Loretz
and other scholars, the links to the Gilgamesh Epic and the so-called
"Babylonian Theodicy" are the most striking.[96] There are also corollaries
with Ahiqar, portions of which were found at Elephantine.[97] With regard
to possible parallels between Egyptian literature and Qoheleth, Loretz
rejects any possible Egyptian link to the book of Qoheleth. His rigid
position ignores the international character of the ancient Near Eastern
wisdom tradition and previous occurrences of Egyptian and Israelite
interchange in this area. We have mentioned Merikare and the royal
testament section in Qoheleth and the Dispute Between a Man and His
*Ba* because of the many references to death and the command to enjoy
the present. There is also the possible relationship with the so-called
Harpers' Songs, which reflect a *carpe diem* mentality. Stefan Fischer has
explored the songs and their possible ties to Qoheleth, and he cites a
connection between the call for present joy and a set of New Kingdom
"'haretischen' Harfnerlieder" that derived from the earlier Harpers'
Songs.[98] Fischer makes a compelling case that Qoheleth actually knew
one or more of the "heretic" songs, which advocate embracing present
existence as opposed to an uncertain death. His study demonstrates
that the content and order of these popular songs are strikingly similar

----

[95] Oswald Loretz, *Qohelet und der alte Orient: Untersuchungen zu Stil und theologischer Thematik des Buches Qohelet* (Freiburg: Herder, 1964).

[96] Loretz, *Qohelet und der alte Orient*, 116–22. These parallels have also been discussed
at length elsewhere. For a recent review of the discussion regarding Gilgamesh and
Qoheleth, see Uehlinger, "Qohelet im Horizont altorientalischer Weisheitliteratur,"
180–92. Šiduri the alewife's advice to live life to the fullest (Gilg Me iii 2–14) seems
closely related to Qoh 9:7–10 in terms of thematic and linguistic content. Two additional parallels cited by Uehlinger are Qoh 4:12 and its similarity to a proverb in the
Gilgamesh story, along with a possible link between *šāru* ("wind") and הבל.

[97] Seow, *Ecclesiastes*, 62–63, cites the call for moderation and humility in Ahiqar.
See, for example, Ahiqar 147; cf. Qoh 7:15–16.

[98] Stefan Fischer, *Die Aufforderung zur Lebensfreude im Buch Kohelet und seine Rezeption
der ägyptischen Harfnerlieder* (WAS 2; Frankfurt: Peter Lang, 1999); idem, "Qohelet and
'Heretic' Harpers' Songs," *JSOT* 98 (2002): 105–21.

to Qoh. 9:7–10 and the other "joy" passages in the book, even more so than the commonly cited passage from Gilgamesh. This careful argument and the possible link deserve consideration, as this might be the best example of direct Egyptian borrowing in Qoheleth.[99] On the issue of the late (New Kingdom) autobiographies, Burkes demonstrates similarities based on a parallel concern with death and its implications, particularly the manner in which end-of-life issues threaten all that one has attained. Like Qoheleth, these autobiographical texts focus less on the netherworld than on present existence.[100]

The Demotic instructions Papyrus Insinger and the Instruction of Ankhsheshonqy are other possible sources. These later Egyptian works address many topics, including the incomprehensibility of the divine plan, particularly in the context of an act-consequence discussion. In P. Insinger, the addressee is urged to enjoy earthly moments to the fullest extent possible, and the author acknowledges the possibility of unexpected results through a frequent refrain: "The fate and the fortune that come, it is the god who sends them." In her thematic study of these Demotic texts, Lichtheim demonstrates the transcultural sharing of major ideas by the sages of this period.[101] While P. Insinger seems to have more in common with Ben Sira (a relationship we will consider in the next chapter), the author of the Egyptian text shares a belief with Qoheleth in divine freedom and a large degree of human helplessness.[102] The common subject matter does not indicate the direct

---

[99] The "heretic" Harpers' Songs circulated as popular compositions. They are usually attached to tomb drawings, and some of them contain a call to enjoy one's life, dress in white linen, and to celebrate with one's beloved (*nfrw.k*), referring to a spouse. This order is found in the Antef Song (Papyrus Harris 500) and at least one of the other songs accompanying a tomb drawing (TT 359 Inherchau). Such a sequence precisely mirrors the flow of Qoh. 9:7–10. Fischer, *Die Aufforderung zur Lebensfreude im Buch Kohelet*, 172, also cites a song from Thotemheb (TT 194) about the loss of property when one dies. In addition, the call to "follow one's heart" (Eg. *šms jb*) is a common refrain in both Egyptian instructions and the Harpers' Songs (cf. Qoh 5:19; 9:7; 11:9). Finally, these songs question the idea of eternal happiness for a deceased person and emphasize present existence. According to Fischer, they share with Qoheleth a negative view of death. See also Miriam Lichtheim, "The Songs of the Harpers," *JNES* 4 (1945): 178–212; Burkes, *Death in Qoheleth*, 166–67.

[100] Burkes, *Death in Qoheleth*, 171–208.

[101] Miriam Lichtheim, *Late Egyptian Wisdom Literature in the International Context: A Study of Demotic Instructions* (OBO 52; Fribourg/Göttingen: University Press/Vandenhoeck & Ruprecht, 1983), 13–65, 112–96, focuses on the parallels between Ankhsheshonqy, Ahiqar, Qoheleth/Ben Sira, and Greek texts.

[102] P. Insinger also discusses death and the inability to keep what one has spent a lifetime accumulating (18.6; cf. Qoh 2:21; 4:8; 5:12–14). See Lichtheim, *Late Egyptian*

dependence of Qoheleth on either instruction, but it does suggest the Jewish sage's participation in and knowledge of an international wisdom tradition that wrestled with vexing questions like divine agency and pervasive social injustices.

Other scholars have focused on linguistic evidence as a primary means of placing Qoheleth in a specific context. Some commentators opt for a Hellenistic date based on the grammar, vocabulary (including Aramaisms), and the argument for proto-Mishnaic forms. Antoon Schoors has concluded that the book has numerous features of Late Biblical Hebrew, including the following: the exclusive use of אֲנִי (29 times, as opposed to אָנֹכִי); the feminine demonstrative pronoun זֹה; the inclusion of *matres lectiones* that reveals a middle stage between Qumranic and Biblical Hebrew; the employment of the particle שֶׁ as a relative form instead of אֲשֶׁר; the merging of III-*ʾālep* and III-*hê* roots, and many other examples.[103] In his systematic analysis, Schoors demonstrates syntactical parallels between Qoheleth and the Mishnah; these become even more striking when compared with postexilic texts that are indicative of classical Biblical Hebrew.[104] Such linguistic factors suggest a postexilic date, and some of the syntactical features point to a very late setting.

## 5. *Death in Qoheleth*

All of these issues, from the wealth and poverty language in the book and how it relates to economic circumstances during the Ptolemaic era, to the possible influence of Greek ideas, and finally the terminology and syntax indicative of Late Biblical Hebrew, support the late third-century B.C.E. as the most plausible setting for Qoheleth. The cumulative effect of the evidence suggests a date as late as 200 B.C.E.,

---

*Wisdom Literature*, 156–57. While intriguing, these examples reveal general thematic overlaps and a shared fascination with death, rather than any sort of direct relationship.

[103] Antoon Schoors, *The Preacher Sought to Find Pleasing Words: A Study of the Language of Qoheleth* (2 vols.; OLA 41; Leuven: Peeters Press and Department of Oriental Studies, 1992–2004).

[104] Cf. Gordis, *Koheleth*, 59–62; Crenshaw, *Ecclesiastes*, 31, 50; Galling, "Der Prediger," 74–75. Whitley, *Koheleth: His Language and Thought*, 137–39, catalogues several close affinities with the Mishnah and dates the book significantly later than most scholars (150 B.C.E.). Crenshaw, *Ecclesiastes*, 50, also points to "a Hellenistic coloring" with regard to the vocabulary used for rulers and an expression that only appears in postexilic texts (מִי יוֹדֵעַ). See also James Crenshaw, "The Expression *mî yôdēaʿ* in the Hebrew Bible," *VT* 36 (1986): 274–88.

especially when we consider the strong thematic links between Qoheleth and Ben Sira. Qoheleth was probably not written much later than this period, since the author does not seem to be aware of major upheaval during the second-century, events such as the Maccabean revolt or the various Ptolemaic-Seleucid conflicts for control of Palestine. There are no references, even implicit ones, to such events, and the book seems to address a period of relative peace and economic possibility. Yet despite all of these examples, the issue is not settled. The historical setting for Qoheleth is still open for debate. We found strong indicators in the last section of this chapter, but commentators have raised valid objections about the lack of a decisive marker that proves this context beyond a reasonable doubt. Scholars such as Seow and Kugel have argued forcefully for an earlier date based on evidence, primarily related to financial matters, that has been cited by other interpreters in support of a Ptolemaic setting.

There is, however, another relevant feature that points to this later period as the most likely era for the composition of Qoheleth. A contextual reading of the overriding theme of the book, death, seems to provide just the evidence needed to situate Qoheleth during the Hellenistic period and locate the force of his assertions. According to Collins, "Qoheleth shares with Ben Sira a preoccupation with death that is not found in the older wisdom literature, and must reflect in some way the new circumstances of the Hellenistic age."[105] This assessment is correct: Qoheleth has a palpable concern with death and its implications, which he shares with Ben Sira *but not* with the sages who wrote Proverbs. This critical distinction enables us to posit a significant reevaluation of prior assumptions and new proposals on death and the afterlife during the Hellenistic period. When considering Qoheleth's perspective on the topic and vehement denial of some of the innovative suggestions, both the discussion in which he participated and the precise nature of his ethic become more apparent. This author's contemporaries were presenting pioneering ideas about human existence in relation to death, and some of them were positing an otherworldly fulfillment for the act-consequence relationship. Various authors from this general period had begun to think of the reward for virtue in heavenly terms (e.g., *1 Enoch*, 4QInstruction, Daniel, Wisdom of Solomon), and in his work, Qoheleth mounts a vigorous refutation of any and

---

[105] Collins, *Jewish Wisdom*, 14.

all eschatological proposals. His denial of the possibility for a blessed afterlife demonstrates that he had opponents on this issue *and* that the topic had become a focal point for discussion.

In order to substantiate this particular context, we must first review the perspective among earlier Israelite sages and the fact that they do not share Qoheleth's preoccupation. As the previous chapters have indicated, neither the Egyptian instructions nor the book of Proverbs demonstrate a marked interest in this topic. When invoked as the opposite of life, death functions as an ethical category in Proverbs. Straying from the correct path is equivalent to dying, while walking in the way of Wisdom constitutes "life." Within such a framework, stark language is used as a didactic tool, where the addressee is warned about various pitfalls that lead a person away from Wisdom and towards a "qualitative" death. These sapiential editors, particularly the ones responsible for Proverbs 1–9, create a model based on ethical dualism. Wisdom and discipline lead to lengthy days, prosperity, and progeny, while folly and recklessness invite "death," which actually refers to a life apart from Wisdom. There are many textual examples of this mindset: "Keep hold of instruction; do not let her go; guard her, for she is your life" (Prov 4:13). Conversely, those who stray from the correct path unwittingly choose the seductive route of the Strange Woman: "Her feet go down to death; her steps follow the path to Sheol" (Prov 5:5). The same understanding is used in reference to persons who opt for folly over Wisdom. The association of moral turpitude with death is striking:

> The iniquities of the wicked ensnare them,
> and they are caught in the toils of their own sin.
> *They die* for lack of discipline,
> and because of their great folly they are lost (Prov 5:22–23).

In these verses and in similar sayings, the retributive principle seems to be the loss of any meaningful identity in the present world, since the young charge has, by his own agency, strayed from the proper "way."[106] According to this image, the path of the fool is already laden with death, since he rejected "discipline" (מוסר). Any mention of the afterlife or belief in a final separation of the righteous and wicked is markedly absent in such sayings, as is fretting over the finality of death.

---

[106] Note the parallel structure between death (ימות) and being lost (ישגה) in Prov 5:23. Fox, *Proverbs 1–9*, 205, explains that Hebrew אבד, a frequent verb in the book of Proverbs, can mean "to be lost" or "to perish."

For the most part, Proverbs ignores the subject. This is not the case in Qoheleth, where the end of existence regulates almost every topic that comes under consideration. Not only is Qoheleth an empiricist who wants to examine all aspects of life for himself, but he also sees all reality through the dark prism of Sheol. Since it is probable that Israelite sages finalized the book of Proverbs at some point during the Persian period, we can reasonably conclude that Qoheleth's shift in tone and subject matter addresses the shifting circumstances of a later era, probably the period of Ptolemaic rule. The link with Ben Sira in terms of a shared fascination with death allows us to make this assertion with greater confidence.[107]

Unlike the book of Proverbs, Qoheleth's views on death are complex. This topic seems to have no fewer than six major repercussions for this later sage. First, death nullifies every perceived gain in life, whether material or cognitive. Several statements in chapter 2 put the matter starkly: "I hated all my toil in which I had toiled under the sun, seeing that I must leave it to those who come after me" (2:18).[108] Such declarations reveal Qoheleth's acknowledgment of human limitations and his concrete manner of assessing life and accumulation. This author wants an "accounting" regarding the fate of persons and/or property. Since death can strike at any moment and eradicate a lifetime of accumulated knowledge and possessions (5:14), it becomes impossible for Qoheleth to arrive at a consistent principle of causality.

Qoheleth casts this problem in terms of memory, which is the second aspect of his understanding. After a certain period of time, there will be no enduring remembrance of a deceased person among the living:

---

[107] Although not a formal instruction, Job must also be considered in this framework, since the memorable statements in this book reflect many of the same themes as Qoheleth. The incomprehensibility of the divine plan is a recurring topic, and Job is replete with commentary on divine justice and inconsistencies in the act-consequence relationship (e.g., 4:7; 8:2). In one instance, the protagonist considers and rejects the possibility of an afterlife in a passage that could just as easily be found in Qoheleth (Job 14:1–22). Nevertheless, Job does not reveal a sustained engagement with death and causality (but see 9:22–23); human mortality is not the all-consuming topic that it is in Qoheleth (and to a lesser extent Ben Sira). In addition, Job contains an ending that would suit the sages of Proverbs (chapter 42). His property and family are returned to him, so that he can resume his full and lengthy life, leaving his good name and material possessions to those who come after him. The problem of dating Job certainly adds to the difficulty of understanding the place of this text in the larger Second Temple discussion, but this author was aware of the changing modes of discourse.

[108] This issue of a deceased individual having to leave behind his property is a recurrent theme in the book of Qoheleth (e.g., 6:1–3).

"The people of long ago are not remembered, nor will there be any remembrance of people yet to come by those who come after them" (1:11). The times and seasons are cyclical for Qoheleth (1:5–7), and so is the course of human existence across all generations. All that has occurred in the past will occur again in the future, and no one person is of lasting value in the collective consciousness, no matter how wise or successful they have become. According to the perspective in this text, דוֹר הֹלֵךְ וְדוֹר בָּא ("A generation goes, and a generation comes," 1:4), and this eliminates the possibility of the righteous person's reputation surviving for very long after their death. With such an understanding, it naturally follows that this sage would question the traditional belief in an eternal name. This idea of a lasting reputation had become a standard motif in the ancient instructions, from Ptahhotep to Proverbs.[109] Qoheleth does not accept the notion: nothing alleviates the sting of death for him, not even the optimistic belief that one's good deeds will survive through the memory and success of his or her descendants. On the contrary, this author assumes that everything will be forgotten in an unpredictable, selfish, and cyclical world. His categorical rejection of the hopeful statements in other instructions concerning the durability of a good reputation represents another major departure.

Third and most significantly for this sage: there is a universal conclusion to a person's earthly existence. Referring to all of humanity, Qoheleth declares the following:

> All this I laid to heart, examining it all, how the righteous and the wise and their deeds are in the hand of God; whether it is love or hate one does not know. Everything that confronts them is vanity, since the same fate (מִקְרֶה) comes to all, to the righteous and the wicked, to the good and the evil, to the clean and the unclean, to those who sacrifice and those who do not sacrifice. As are the good, so are the sinners; those who swear are like those who shun an oath. This is an evil in all that happens under the sun, that the same fate (מִקְרֶה) comes to everyone. Moreover,

---

[109] The ability to pass on the legacy of a good name to descendants by virtue of one's own conduct and social standing is a common element of many instructions. For example, in Ptahhotep, the son who listens and is respected by his father will endure through his reputation: "He will be remembered in the mouths of the living, both those who are on the earth and those who will be" (P 562–563); cf. Prov 10:7: "The memory of the righteous is a blessing, but the name of the wicked will rot." With his conservative stance on this topic, Ben Sira is clearly in line with the tradition and at odds with Qoheleth: "The days of a good life are numbered, but a good name lasts forever" (41:13).

the hearts of all are full of evil; madness is in their hearts while they live, and after that they go to the dead (9:1–3).

In chapter 9, the sage refutes the idea that certain behavioral patterns contribute to lasting prosperity or a different "fate." This use of מקרה (vv. 2–3) describes death, the ultimate occurrence that "befalls" everyone.[110] Within this framework, all individuals cease to exist, and good people can die prematurely. Human destiny lies "in the hand of God" (ביד האלהים, v. 1), which is a difficult phrase to interpret. Hebrew ביד האלהים could mean that God directly controls the individual actions of human beings *or* that God dictates (or has the *freedom* to dictate) the consequences of those actions.[111] The latter understanding is certainly consistent with the rest of the book and with the ancient Near Eastern sapiential tradition. Diethelm Michel offers another possible interpretation. Qoheleth might be quoting a popular belief on the possibility of ultimate recompense for the righteous, a suggestion he refutes in subsequent verses (e.g., "the same fate comes to all" in v. 2). In support of this view, Michel compares these verses to a passage from the Wisdom of Solomon, where the addressee is told that the "souls of the righteous are *in the hand of God*, and no torment will ever touch them" (3:1). This is an unambiguous reference to immortality, and Michel posits a similar understanding in Qoheleth (though not a direct relationship between the two texts, since the Wisdom of Solomon is much later).[112] Even if Michel's proposal stretches the sense of Qoheleth 9, this chapter does function as a rejection of eternal possibilities for the human spirit. The point here is to emphasize God's control of all events in the cosmos,

---

[110] Peter Machinist, "Fate, *miqreh*, and Reason: Some Reflections on Qohelet and Biblical Thought," in *Solving Riddles and Untying Knots* (ed. Z. Zevit et al.; Winona Lake, Ind.: Eisenbrauns, 1995), 169, notes that in four passages from the Hebrew Bible (Ruth 2:3; 1 Sam 6:9; 20:26; Deut 23:11), מקרה refers to an unexpected occurrence that happens (or "chances") upon a human being. In these examples, divine agency is not specifically mentioned but cannot be ruled out as a factor in these events. The example of Ruth "happening" upon Boaz's field is instructive: "She came and gleaned in the field behind the reapers. As it happened (ויקר מקרה), she came to the part of the field belonging to Boaz" (2:3). In contrast, Qoheleth uses מקרה only in relation to death in the following verses: 2:14–15; 3:19–20; 9:2–3; 9:11. As Machinist explains of the occurrences of the term in Qoheleth, "death becomes, then, the predetermined defining point of an abstract notion: *miqreh* as the pattern of time that each individual lives out" (p. 170). Here in chapter 9, the sage emphasizes the universality of this experience for all types of people.

[111] Krüger, *Qoheleth*, 168.

[112] Diethelm Michel, *Untersuchungen zur Eigenart des Buches Qohelet* (BZAW 183; Berlin: de Gruyter, 1989), 179–80.

including the common "fate" of the righteous and the wicked.[113]
Death comes to everyone in equal measure, and no amount of virtuous behavior can stave off this inevitable event. The possibility of a
glorious afterlife is not taken up as directly as in 3:16–22, but chapter 9
undermines the traditional act-consequence understanding *and* the idea
of ultimate rewards. Qoheleth casts existence in terms of its definitive
conclusion, so that no earthly success is consequential in the wake of
the great equalizer. This logic clearly applies to wise persons: "The wise
have eyes in their head, but fools walk in darkness. Yet I perceived that
the same fate befalls all of them" (2:14). A reward for virtue is never
guaranteed in the book: "In my vain life I have seen everything; there
are righteous people who perish in their righteousness, and there are
wicked people who prolong their life in their evildoing" (7:15). Even if
the righteous enjoy the fruits of their honest labors from time to time,
death cancels every intellectual and material gain.

With such an understanding, Qoheleth naturally encourages individuals to strive for contentment and utilize existing resources to seek
joy. As many commentators have noted, this text is not hopeless about
the potential for human happiness. Qoheleth is not a true skeptic: he
allows for blissful moments, particularly in the earlier periods of a
person's life, and this is the fourth component of his perspective on
death. When the force of the "joy" passages is taken into account, it
becomes inaccurate to call Qoheleth a completely pessimistic thinker.[114]
In 11:9 he declares, "Rejoice, young man, while you are young, and let
your heart cheer you in the days of your youth. Follow the inclination
of your heart and desire of your eyes."[115] Here and in similar passages
(cf. 9:7–10), the sage implores a youthful addressee to enjoy the fleeting
moments of pleasure that life affords, to soak up the simple radiance of

---

[113] Another tricky issue is the background for "love and hate" in v. 1, whether the
agent is God or human beings. Murphy, *Ecclesiastes*, 90, observes that human beings
would know for themselves the substance of their emotions, and so the latter possibility
is unlikely. For Qoheleth, the unclear element is God's decision-making process, and
therefore the verse probably refers to divine love and hate and the individual's inability
to fathom it. The epilogue to Ptahhotep contains a similar saying about God's love
and hate (i.e., approval and disapproval) being obscure (P 545–546).

[114] A helpful counter to overly pessimistic readings of the book is the essay by
Michael V. Fox, "The Inner Structure of Qohelet's Thought," in *Qohelet in the Context
of Wisdom* (ed. A. Schoors; BETL 136; Leuven: Leuven University Press/Peeters,
1998), 225–39.

[115] Following many commentators, we take 11:9b and the language about judgment
to be an orthodox gloss.

youth, since old age, its deleterious effects, and eventually death overtake everyone (12:1–7). This pursuit is even condoned by God as part of every person's "portion" (9:7, 9). It constitutes an important component of Qoheleth's ethic; the counsel to enjoy life relates to his beliefs on the fleeting nature of human existence. He casts his royal experiment as an effort to see "what was good for mortals to do under heaven during the few days of their life" (2:3), and he comes out of this inquiry with the belief that moments of genuine contentment are possible. Mournful passages are certainly present in the text, as Qoheleth takes issue with the optimism of earlier sages and his contemporaries. He rejects what are from his perspective fanciful understandings of reward and punishment. Since his belief system maintains that everyone progresses to a shadowy existence in Sheol, with no distinction between the righteous and the unrighteous, his discussion often reveals a fatalistic outlook. Qoheleth loathes many aspects of life and questions a burdensome existence marked by a lack of "profit." At multiple points, he reaches a crossroads where he wonders if death is preferable to the unjust and unhappy life many individuals are forced to lead.[116] He frets about the transitory aspects of human existence, the injustice and randomness he finds in the earthly realm, but Qoheleth still finds goodness in the world. He recognizes the beauty of a cherished connection between two human beings (e.g., 4:8–10) and concludes that people who accept their allotted "portion" or "reward" (חלק) will *probably* find glimpses of wonder and merriment during their time "under the sun."

While acknowledging joy, Qoheleth finds the uncertainty of life/death to be maddening, and he categorically rejects the possibility of a beatific afterlife. These final two aspects of his perspective on death are interrelated and will occupy the rest of our discussion in this chapter. On

---

[116] There are several passages in which Qoheleth expresses a hatred for life and a belief that death is in fact preferable. The dead have not beheld evil deeds (4:1–3); the day of death is better than the day of birth (7:1); the sage favors the "house of mourning" over the "house of feasting" (7:2). The author even wonders whether stillbirth is preferable to a life in which a person does not enjoy his portion, and he detests the thought of an improper burial (6:1–6). James L. Crenshaw, "The Shadow of Death in Qoheleth," in *Israelite Wisdom: Theological and Literary Essays in Honor of Samuel Terrien* (ed. J.G. Gammie; New York: Scholar's Press, 1979), 205–16, surveys these passages and the apparent contradiction between this more hopeless tone and the sage's call to joy. Crenshaw concludes that even with the "burdensome character of what is done under the sun," Qoheleth still finds value in life. The sage's contradictory style reflects his existential angst over death, and as Crenshaw explains, he moves from "enthusiastic endorsement of life to flirtation with death as rest, from sheer pleasure over light's sweetness to hatred of life under certain circumstances" (p. 211).

the former point, Qoheleth recognizes that God has a universal decree (death) for all living creatures. He finds it exasperating for humanity to be cognizant of this ultimate fate and yet incapable of understanding the machinations of the deity who determines it. God never even speaks in the book, and this silence signifies (among other things) the remoteness and inscrutability of Qoheleth's Creator.[117] There may be a system in place, but human beings, even the wise ones, cannot ascertain how it works. Referring to humanity, Qoheleth explains that God "has put a sense of past and future (העלם) into their minds, yet they cannot find out what God has done from the beginning to the end" (3:11).[118] Humanity can conceive of the permanence that God has made, but can never really know it. The author's own pursuit of knowledge and his personal experiment have made him a very intelligent and reverential man (Qoheleth "fears" God): "I know that whatever God does endures forever; nothing can be added to it, nor anything taken from it; God has done this, so that all should stand in awe before him" (3:14). This awe is met, however, with a marked frustration about the limitations of Wisdom.

As he confronts death and its frustrating ramifications, Qoheleth dismisses any possibility for the survival of the individual soul. In the latter half of chapter 3, he employs a human-beast analogy to explain his beliefs: "For the fate of humans and the fate of animals is the same; as one dies, so dies the other. They all have the same breath, and humans have no advantage over the animals; for all is vanity" (3:19). According to this understanding, nothing of significance occurs after death. Sheol signifies a shadowy existence, a way of referring to what no longer exists and can never be renewed: "for there is no work or thought or knowledge or wisdom in Sheol, to which you are going" (9:10b). Even as his statements in chapters 3 and 9 are unequivocal, they also reveal a longing to correct the transitory nature (הבל) of life. Qoheleth wants to satisfy the desire for a continuation of existence and therefore an ultimate reward. He expresses sorrow, probably at the end of his life, at the inevitable termination of his quest for Wisdom and contentment. For example, "'What happens to the fool will happen to me also; why

---

[117] Even in the pious glosses and the section(s) written by the second epilogist, the earthly sphere is the point of orientation. For Qoheleth, God is a remote figure whose will cannot be known. See Burkes, God, Self, and Death, 37–85, for a helpful discussion of Job and Qoheleth on this point.

[118] Murphy, Ecclesiastes, 39, calls this a "fantastic statement of divine sabotage."

then have I been so very wise?'" (2:15). This is a noteworthy tension
in the sage's thought: Qoheleth is emphatic about a person's inability
to prove the existence of an afterlife, but he also chafes at the implications of this belief. This book seems to long for a hereafter to rectify
the inequalities the sage has witnessed and to preserve some sort of
*Tun-Ergehen-Zusammenhang*. As an empiricist, however, this author only
accepts what can personally be verified. Despite the optimistic suggestions of his contemporaries, Qoheleth cannot maintain any hope for
individual immortality.

### 6. The "Human Spirit" in Qoheleth

In order to explicate the sage's presentation on this topic more fully,
we must consider in greater detail the possible references or allusions
to the afterlife in the book and the manner in which Qoheleth refutes
them. The most important set of verses in this regard is 3:16–22:

> 16 Moreover I saw under the sun that in the place of justice, wickedness
> was there, and in the place of righteousness, wickedness was there as well.
> 17 I said in my heart, God will judge the righteous and the wicked, for
> he has appointed a time for every matter, and for every work. 18 I said
> in my heart with regard to human beings that God is testing them to
> show that they are but animals. 19 For the fate of humans and the fate
> of animals is the same; as one dies, so dies the other. They all have the
> same breath, and humans have no advantage over the animals; for all is
> vanity. 20 All go to one place; all are from the dust, and all turn to dust
> again. 21 Who knows whether the human spirit goes upward and the
> spirit of animals goes downward to the earth? 22 So I saw that there is
> nothing better than that a man should enjoy his work, for that is his lot;
> who can bring him to see what will be after him?

A textual analysis, building on the work of previous commentators,
yields several important conclusions. First, the judgment language in
v. 17 represents an orthodox gloss, perhaps by the epilogist responsible
for 12:12–14. This has been argued by many scholars, including the
study of A.A. Fischer.[119] In his careful evaluation, Fischer rejects the
possibility that this verse is original to Qoheleth. Both v. 17 and v. 18
begin with the same introductory clause (אמרתי אני בלבי), indicating that

---

[119] A.A. Fischer, "Kohelet und die frühe Apokalyptik: eine Auslegung von Koh
3,16–21," in *Qohelet in the Context of Wisdom* (ed. A. Schoors; BETL 136; Leuven: Leuven
University Press/Peeters, 1998), 339–57.

one of the verses is probably an insertion. Qoheleth's careful rhetorical
style would presumably not involve such a close repetition of identical phrasing. Fischer also notes that the rest of this unit relates to the
inevitable fate of humanity and not to divine judgment, which is the
topic of v. 17. The root שפט does not appear in reference to the deity in
other units, and Qoheleth does not generally emphasize God's retributive action in terms of a separation of the righteous and the wicked.
Elsewhere in the text, the sage focuses on the apparent arbitrariness of
events and the absence of an act-consequence relationship (e.g., 7:15;
8:10–14; 9:1–3). These other verses undermine the logic of 3:17.[120]
Such judicial language actually does occur in other instructions of the
Second Temple period with an eschatological intent, and both Qoh
3:17 and 12:13–14 probably indicate this type of meaning.[121] Passages
from 4QInstruction and the Wisdom of Solomon have parallel understandings, including similar choice of terminology. The correlation is
striking on this point, especially the combination of שפט and רשע in
4QInstruction. While we are in no way suggesting a direct relationship
between the two texts, the connection supports an eschatological reading of these insertions by the second epilogist.[122] By inserting v. 17, this
later editor probably sought to undermine the perspective of v. 16 and
reassure the readers of God's participation in a just universe, including the possibility of a blessed afterlife.[123] With his contrary views on

---

[120] Fischer, "Kohelet und die frühe Apokalyptik," 341.

[121] Leo G. Perdue, "Wisdom and Apocalyptic: The Case of Qoheleth," in *Wisdom and Apocalypticism in the Dead Sea Scrolls and in the Biblical Tradition* (ed. F. García Martínez; BETL 168; Leuven: Leuven University Press/Peeters, 2003), 256, argues that an eschatological judgment is affirmed in Qoh 3:17; 11:9; and 12:13–14. These are all secondary to the original sage and reflect the perspective found in some of the later sapiential works.

[122] In the book of Proverbs, such explicit judgment language is not used in reference to the deity's arbitration of human conduct. Even in Ben Sira, we get few references of this type (see Sir 35:15). With its eschatological expectation, 4QInstruction does contain such an understanding. The beginning of this text states, "In heaven He shall pronounce judgment (ישפוט) upon the work of wickedness (רשעה), and all His faithful children shall be favourably accepted by [Him]" (4Q416 1 10).

[123] There is also the issue of שם in v. 17 and whether it should be translated "there," as a reference to Sheol (Schwienhorst-Schönberger, '*Nicht im Menschen Grundet das Glück*', 117), or as a finite verb ("he put"), with God as the subject. If "there" is intended, the context is probably eschatological judgment. Gordis, *Koheleth*, 224, points to the use of שם in Job in relation to death (1:21; 3:17, 19). The possibility of a finite verb at the end of the verse is unlikely, as many commentators have noted. "There" could also be referring to "life under the sun," as Fox, *A Time to Tear Down*, 215, argues. According to this understanding, שם implies some sort of judicial setting.

death, the actual "Qoheleth" would not subscribe to such a viewpoint.[124] Qoh 3:17 cannot be original to the primary author of this text, whose deity is to be feared because of limitless power, and not due to the evenhanded dispensation of justice.[125] According to Fischer, this raises the question "ob Kohelet überhaupt ein richterliches Handeln Gottes in Betracht gezogen hat."[126]

Without v. 17 as part of the original passage, the unit is more coherent. The author witnesses success among the wicked and failure among the righteous and finds the situation to be unacceptable (v. 16). Then he states that God is "testing" or "separating" humanity to demonstrate that their fate is no different than beasts when it comes to ultimate destiny (v. 18). Both humans and other animals are made from the ground and infused with the same breath, and at the end of life they return to their point of origin (vv. 19–20; cf. 12:7). As for the issue Qoheleth raises about whether the "spirit" of human beings "goes upward" into some meaningful and perhaps ongoing state with God (v. 21), the author's position might seem cryptic at first. The reader already knows the answer to this question, however, based on discussion elsewhere in the book. There can be no eternal existence in the sage's framework. With such an inevitable course of events, human beings had best enjoy every earthly moment, because there is nothing else to anticipate (v. 22).

Even if the unit flows more smoothly without v. 17, multiple questions remain, beginning with v. 18. The grammatical issues related to the verbal form לברם are difficult. God is clearly the subject, but it is unclear whether לברם is an infinitive construct or finite verb with an emphatic *lāmed*.[127] Regardless of the interpretation, the correct sense seems to be that God is "testing" or "separating" all persons "to show them that

---

[124] Galling, "Der Prediger," 96–97, recognizes the distinction between the second epilogist and Qoheleth on this point.

[125] With regard to other passages in Qoheleth that imply a divine judgment, 11:9b has already been cited as an editorial insertion. Also note 5:5b: "why should God be angry at your words and destroy the work of your hand?" This verse seems to be the citation of a familiar proverb and not necessarily reflective of the sage's original thought. Qoheleth certainly believes in the power of divine agency, and even if this verse is original to him, a separation of the righteous and the wicked is not at issue here.

[126] Fischer, "Kohelet und die frühe Apokalyptik," 342. He also points out the language in 8:12b–13, which has already been labeled an orthodox gloss.

[127] God is the agent, and ם- is the direct object referring to humans. The לברם form should probably be read as an infinitive construct, with a presumed copula before the verbal form. See Murphy, *Ecclesiastes*, 30 n. 18b; Crenshaw, *Ecclesiastes*, 103. Seow, *Ecclesiastes*, 167, cites Qoh 9:4 for the emphatic *lāmed* reading.

they are but beasts."[128] Fischer tentatively proposes that the "testing"
(לברם) language in this verse derives from the second epilogist (along
with 3:17), so that an orthodox editor was seeking to add two verses
to focus attention on God's judicial involvement in human destiny.[129]
This is an unnecessary emendation, since the verse can be explained
on the basis of Qoheleth's own thought. Galling contends that the verb
should be understood as "separated" and read in a satirical sense.[130]
In the following verse, Qoheleth disputes the notion that humanity
differs from beasts ("humans have no advantage over animals"), so an
ironic reading makes the most sense. According to this passage, God is
"separating" humanity in order to show their lack of distinctiveness in
relation to other living creatures. Qoheleth is "rubbing it in the face"
of his fellow humans by declaring that their ultimate "fate" is no different from that of beasts. As previously mentioned, this use of מקרה
("fate") in Qoheleth seems to describe that which befalls every person
at the end of their life, rather than the more involved Greek concept
of "Fate" (τύχη).[131]

In assessing the subsequent verses, many scholars claim that 3:19–21
are dependent on the creation accounts in Genesis 1–11. Murphy is
representative:

> Qoheleth is expressing himself in terms of Gen 2:7, where God breathes
> the נשמת חיים, "life-breath," and of Ps 104:29–30, where life is dependent
> upon the presence of the רוח, "spirit," of God in living beings.[132]

---

[128] The Hebrew of the latter half of the verse is just as difficult. LXX reads לְרָאוֹת,
taking the Hebrew as an apocopated Hiphil form (καὶ τοῦ δεῖξαι). The final להם
should be taken as dittography and omitted from translation.

[129] Fischer, "Kohelet und die frühe Apokalyptik," 344, although he is less certain
about v. 18.

[130] Galling, "Der Prediger," 97, cites other occurrences of ברר in support of this
understanding: "Da im nachexilischen Schrifttum (1 Chr 7 40 9 22 16 41) mit ברר
die Erwählung zu einem besonderen (heiligen) Dienst gekennzeichnet wird, dürfte
Q. u.E. in der ironischen Aufnahme des Stichwortes seine Polemik bekunden. 18 wird
von 19b her deutlicher beleuchtet."

[131] This usage in relation to death might reflect the changing vocabulary of Wisdom
discourse during the Ptolemaic period, but we should not align the sage's use of this
term too closely with the more elaborate concept of τύχη. For Qoheleth, death is simply
the "occurrence," the "fate" that happens to every living creature.

[132] Murphy, Ecclesiastes, 37. Cf. Antoon Schoors, "Koheleth: A Perspective of Life
After Death?" ETL 61 (1985), 300, who argues that Qoheleth knew both Gen 2:7, 19
(J) and the רוח חיים language in Gen 7:15 (P): "Koheleth has bound these statements
into a lapidary affirmation of the equality of man and beast."

Murphy also claims that the language in Qoh 3:20 should be linked to Gen 3:19, since both verses describe the human body "returning" to the earth.[133] This particular concept can be found in other biblical passages and even among sages of the Second Temple period (Pss 90:3; 104:29; 146:4; Job 10:9; 34:15; Sir 40:11). This argument assumes that Qoheleth knew the primeval history and utilized ideas from these narratives to underscore the finality of death and the creatureliness of humanity. The problem with this interpretation is that the language in Qoh 3:19–20 does not reveal a particularly detailed reading of the creation accounts. It is difficult to determine how closely the sage assimilated his thought to whatever authoritative tradition existed at the time of composition. Based on the prologue to Ben Sira (especially lines 8–9) and other Jewish texts from the Hellenistic period, it is clear that the Torah and the Prophets were attaining an important status. Moreover, some of the material in Genesis was being used in sapiential circles for the first time, particularly in Ben Sira.[134] For his part, Qoheleth employs common terminology and familiar beliefs about death and the human body in 3:16–22. His discussion represents the traditional Israelite view on this topic. Even if he is alluding to Genesis here, which is possible and perhaps probable, vv. 19–20 represent a fairly limited usage of these stories. In terms of language, the terminological parallels do not necessarily indicate dependence.[135] On the thematic level, Qoheleth declares that human beings are creatures whose material essence will return to the dust, but he never mentions a fall or a belief in sin as a catalyst for death in the manner of a later interpreter like Paul (Rom 5:18). In fact, Qoheleth takes great pains to demonstrate the inconsequentiality of sin in terms of death and its timing (e.g., 9:2–4). The sage makes the point about the similar fate of human and beast and then quickly addresses another topic of concern to him: the possibility of eternal life. These two verses (3:19–20) do not constitute a close intertextual reading of either creation account from Genesis.

---

[133] Murphy, *Ecclesiastes*, 37. The parallel usage of שׁוב and עפר suggests a direct relationship, but these are such common words that the connection could also reflect a shared conceptual belief on what happens to the body at death.

[134] Collins, *Jewish Wisdom*, 80–81, observes that the Adam and Eve story is never mentioned in the Hebrew Bible outside of Genesis. Ben Sira is clearly aware of these narratives and refers to them at several points: 15:11–20; 17:1–24; 25:24; 33:10–13.

[135] The author does not use נשׁמת חיים (Gen 2:7) in either verse. The possible connection to Gen 6:7 in light of the parallel occurrence of אדם and בהמה is more convincing.

Our primary question related to this passage is what Qoheleth means by the "spirit" language in 3:21. Is the sage alluding to beliefs in the afterlife, even if he disagrees with them?[136] This appears to be the progression of his thought in 3:16–22. He cites the traditional view that he shares in 3:19–20 and then proceeds to reference what must have been an emergent idea about righteous souls ascending to a blessed afterlife (v. 21). The grammar of Qoh 3:21 is critical here, particularly the form הַעֹלָה, which MT vocalizes as a definite article rather than an interrogative-*hê*. The ancient versions opt for the latter choice, and this is definitely the preferred reading. It is possible that a subsequent editor changed the pointing to accord with later Jewish beliefs on the afterlife (i.e., "the spirit of humanity, *which* goes upward, and the spirit of the beast, which goes downward,"), but this is not grammatically correct, and Qoheleth himself does not subscribe to such a distinction between human and beast.[137] Nevertheless, the sage is alluding to a belief that righteous souls ascend to heaven, presumably without their decomposing physical bodies, which are in fact no longer needed.

It is sometimes argued that 12:7 negates any possibility of reading 3:21 as a reference to immortality. In this final section on death, Qoheleth declares, "and the dust returns to the earth as it was, and the breath returns to God who gave it" (12:7). Although it is probably the case that 12:7 functions as the author's final dismissal of a possible afterlife, there is a logical relationship between these two verses in Qoheleth (3:21 and 12:7). The sage concludes his reflections by claiming that the "breath" (רוּחַ) of a person "returns" (שׁוּב) to God (signifying the end of earthly life), rather than *ascending* (עלה) to some sort of eternal existence.[138] The distinction between עלה and שׁוּב is noteworthy here, particularly in the context of Greek and Jewish references from this period about the ascent of the soul (see below). The end of the book expresses Qoheleth's own belief, as well as the traditional one, while the statement in chapter 3 refers to the ascent of the soul into an eternal state, a proposal that Qoheleth rejects.[139]

---

[136] Qoh 3:19–20 indicates his disbelief in souls ascending. His use of "who knows" is a rhetorical device, and the answer is a negative one.

[137] Fox, *A Time to Tear Down*, 216.

[138] Fox, *Qohelet and His Contradictions*, 197: "This 'taking back' of the life-spirit does not imply an afterlife, but merely the dissolution of the components of the living being."

[139] Qoh 12:7 is consistent with Ps 104:29–30, which describes the return of the body to the earth and the simultaneous reclaiming of the spirit/breath by God. God is being addressed in these verses: "When you hide your face, they are dismayed; when you

Perhaps the belief that Qoheleth alludes to in 3:16–22 can be traced to foreign ideas. Persian religious traditions included a belief in resurrection, but this does not seem to be the reference point for these verses, and many of the relevant descriptions are much later than the early Hellenistic period.[140] The Pahlavi texts date from the sixth to the eleventh-century C.E., which is obviously subsequent to the period we are considering. Yet Anders Hultgård claims that the otherworldly descriptions in these Persian texts preserve much earlier ideas. The main text indicating an otherworldly journey is the *Ardā Wirāz Nāmag*. In this account, the protagonist is given a tour of the heavens by angels, and he sees the upward path of righteous souls. A collection of these souls are found waiting together for the day of their resurrection (6:3–7).[141] Similar understandings can also be found in earlier descriptions from the *Gāthās* (the oldest element in the Avesta).[142] The "straight paths of benefit" (*Yasna* 43:3) refer to proper ritual behavior that should be taught to the community, which in turn leads to eschatological reward. In a related passage, truthful souls reach a bridge that leads to paradise, while deceitful persons are turned away for eternal punishment (*Yasna* 46:11). Hultgård explains that visionary ascents and the journey of the righteous who have died follow the same path, which leads to the presence of the supreme deity.[143] Qoheleth might have known some of these ideas, even if indirectly. The belief in eternal reward for the righteous remained an important aspect of Persian religion for centuries, although the nature of the descriptions in the earlier texts does not cohere with Qoh 3:16–22 as well as the Greek references to "astral immortality."

Descriptions of the ascent of the righteous are found in Greek texts from Qoheleth's probable period, and these frequently involve a belief

---

take away (אסף) their breath (רוחם), they die and return to their dust. When you send forth your spirit, they are created; and you renew the face of the ground."

[140] Patricia A. Robinson, "The Conception of Death in Judaism and in the Hellenistic and Early Roman Period," (Ph.D. diss., The University of Wisconsin-Madison, 1978), discusses Zoroastrian beliefs on the afterlife and argues that the late biblical writers did not adopt these models. See also Anders Hultgård, "Persian Apocalypticism," in *The Encyclopedia of Apocalypticism, Volume 1: The Origins of Apocalypticism in Judaism and Christianity* (ed. J.J. Collins; New York: Continuum, 2000), 39–83.

[141] Hultgård, "Persian Apocalypticism," 60.

[142] Hultgård, "Persian Apocalypticism," 66.

[143] Hultgård, "Persian Apocalypticism," 68.

in astral immortality.[144] There is a reference in Aristophanes' *Peace*, where a slave makes the following statement to Trygaeus: "That means the legend isn't true, that when we die we turn into stars in the sky (ὡς ἀστέρες γιγνόμεθ' ὅταν τις ἀποθάνῃ)" (*Pax* 833).[145] Similarly, Plato's *Timaeus* mentions a correspondence between deceased individuals and the number of stars (44E). The story of Er in the *Republic* (10.614B–621D) has a clear description of the heavenly ascent of the soul. The "bold warrior" Er is killed in battle, and his soul goes forth from his body. After the separation, Er and a large crowd meet a group of judges with a specific routine: "after every judgment they bade the righteous journey to the right and upwards through the heaven...and the unjust to take the road to the left and downward" (*Resp.* 10.614C).[146] Among these two classes, the righteous souls are "clean and pure," whereas the unjust souls are full of "squalor and dust." This body-spirit dichotomy and upward movement of the pure soul has clear affinities with what Qoheleth seems to be referencing. It is useful background for the type of belief that the Jewish sage is apparently refuting in Qoh 3:16–22. Other examples from the Greek world imply a similar understanding. Hengel cites a few passages in Euripides, where the souls of the righteous go up to a heavenly dwelling-place, the αἰθήρ of the gods.[147] Similarly, Greek epitaphs describe the elevation of deceased individuals to live among the stars forever.[148] Some of the language provides a noteworthy parallel to the reference in Qoh 3:16–22, especially the epitaphs from this period that mention the raising up of the wise into the heavenly realm.[149] Such concepts were logical candidates for assimilation into existing belief systems, as Hengel explains: "It was easier for this view to be accepted because of earlier Old Testament ideas that the impersonal breath of life breathed into men by God could be taken back again by

---

[144] For background on this issue, see Franz V.M. Cumont, *After life in Roman Paganism* (New Haven: Yale University Press, 1922); Alan Scott, *Origen and the Life of the Stars: A History of an Idea* (Oxford: Clarendon Press, 1991); N.T. Wright, *The Resurrection of the Son of God: Christian Origins and the Question of God, Volume 3* (Minneapolis: Fortress Press, 2003), 55–60.

[145] Translation is from B.B. Rogers, LCL.

[146] Translation is from R.G. Bury, LCL.

[147] Hengel, *Judaism and Hellenism*, 2:184 n. 134, for a full list of citations. Among the passages are Euripides' *Suppl.* 1140; *El.* 59. Cf. Lohfink, *Qoheleth*, 67, who maintains that the sage knew of this "Platonizing belief in the immortality of the soul," based on the passages from Euripides. He cites *Suppl.* 532, where the beings that originate from the earth return to it, and the heavenly things go upward.

[148] Hengel, *Judaism and Hellenism*, 1:196–98.

[149] Hengel, *Judaism and Hellenism*, 1:197.

him."[150] The development can be explained even more pointedly: the concept of a simple "return" of the divine breath to God at death was transformed, through a combination of internal and external religious influences, to a belief in the immortal ascent of the righteous soul. Qoheleth opposed this move, and his brief reference seems to represent one of the initial salvos in a major reevaluation of ideas about death and the afterlife, both within and outside of sapiential circles.

In addition to evidence from Hellenistic literature, Jewish texts from the Second Temple period attest to a belief in the survival of the soul and the continuation of human existence in the hereafter.[151] Two texts from the apocalyptic genre are relevant here. In the Enochic corpus, composed between the fourth and first-century B.C.E., deceased persons are referred to as "souls of men" (*1 En.* 9:3).[152] In *1 Enoch* 22, Enoch travels in the West with a group of angels, arriving at a great mountain: "Then I saw the spirit of a dead man making suit..." (v. 5). As George Nickelsburg explains, this spirit and others like it are being held in repositories, "escape-proof pits, in which they experience retribution that is consonant with their conduct and circumstances during their lives."[153] The spirits lie in an intermediate state, "until the time of the day of the end of the great judgment that will be exacted from them" (v. 4). In another reference to judgment (*1 En.* 103:4), the righteous are promised eternal reward: "The souls of the pious who have died will come to life, and they will rejoice and be glad; and their spirits will not perish." A body-soul distinction is at work here, according to Nickelsburg: "For this author eschatological blessing and curse will be granted to the soul or spirit and not the body."[154] These righteous souls must descend to Sheol for a specified period until the moment of their final reward.[155] When they do attain immortal status, however, they remain free from all evil and tribulation and "shine like

---

[150] Hengel, *Judaism and Hellenism*, 1:124.

[151] For useful background, see John J. Collins, "The Afterlife in Apocalyptic Literature," in *Judaism in Late Antiquity. Part 4: Death, Life-After-Death, Resurrection and the World-to-Come in the Judaisms of Late Antiquity* (ed. J. Neusner and A.J. Avery-Peck; Leiden: Brill, 2000), 119–38.

[152] Translations of *1 Enoch* are from George W.E. Nickelsburg and James C. VanderKam, *1 Enoch: A New Translation* (Minneapolis: Fortress Press, 2004).

[153] George W.E. Nickelsburg, *1 Enoch 1: A Commentary on the Book of 1 Enoch, Chapters 1–36; 81–108* (Hermeneia; Fortress Press: Minneapolis, 2001), 302.

[154] Nickelsburg, *1 Enoch*, 523.

[155] An explicit description of the ascent of the righteous is not offered in this passage.

the luminaries of heaven" (104:2). There is a similar understanding in Daniel, where the righteous arise to a blessed existence among the stars. A consequential moment occurs when the "sleeping ones" (the deceased) awake (presumably from Sheol), "some to everlasting life, and some to everlasting shame and contempt. Those who are wise will shine like the brightness of the sky, and those who lead many to righteousness, forever and ever" (12:2–3). There is also a relevant passage from *Jubilees* that belongs with this set of verses. Righteous servants are mentioned who "will rise up and see great peace…and rejoice forever and ever with great joy" (23:30). The passage continues in the next verse, "And their bones will rest in the earth, and their spirits will increase joy, and they will know that the Lord is an executor of judgment" (23:31). This description probably implies the post-mortem survival of righteous spirits among the elect, but this reading is disputed.

A final question relates to the distinction Qoheleth makes between animals and humans and why the sage would present the issue as he does. This peculiarity becomes even more vexing in light of the fact that none of the examples cited above distinguish the fate of the human soul from beasts. In his recent commentary, Krüger has demonstrated the same type of comparison in two late psalms, 49 and 73. Both are frequently cited as reflective of a belief in immortality. In Psalm 49, which addresses the finality of death and the identical fate of fools and wise persons (v. 10), the supplicant proclaims, "But God will ransom my soul from the power of Sheol, for he will receive me" (v. 15). At the end of the psalm, the author declares that human beings who die without understanding are "*like beasts* that perish" (v. 20). Similarly, in Ps 73:22, an ignorant human is compared to a "brute beast" (בהמות), *and* this is juxtaposed with the possibility of eternal life for a righteous human (e.g., "and afterward you will receive me with honor," v. 24). As Krüger explains, "If the idea here is not only deliverance from threatening death, the continued existence of a part of human beings beyond death is expressly juxtaposed to the annihilation of animals in death."[156] The link between these psalms and the subject matter of Qoh 3:21 is quite relevant, because it adds yet another indicator that the discussion in Qoheleth 3 and 9 comes in response to beliefs about deliverance for the individual soul. This reevaluation occurred in Wisdom circles, but

---

[156] Krüger, *Qoheleth*, 94. He also mentions Qoh 2:14–16 in this section.

it also transcended literary genres and involved comparisons regarding humans and animals and their respective fates.

All of these textual examples indicate an important discussion on death and the afterlife during the Hellenistic period and a developing belief in the ascent of the soul as a reward for righteous behavior. Even with all of this evidence, Fischer doubts an eschatological/early apocalyptic background for Qoh 3:16–22 (and the refutation of 9:1–10). He argues that the רוח that returns to God can only be the understanding we find in 12:7 and similar passages. Fischer also claims that we should expect a detailed explanation of the fate of the wicked if Qoheleth actually intended for 3:21 to be understood on an eschatological level (see *Jub.* 23:30; *1 Enoch* 22). And regarding many of the possible parallels, Fischer contends, "Aber erstens erfolgt dieser Aufstieg nicht unmittelbar, sondern erst mit der endzeitlichen Auferweckung von den Toten, zweitens bleibt er einem Kreis von Auserwählten vorbehalten."[157] These are valid points, but the statement in Qoh 3:21 is a passing one, a quick reference to an opponent(s) with whom Qoheleth disagreed. Although the sage does not give a full exposition of the assumed fate of the soul, the background for 3:16–22 is almost certainly eschatological. Qoheleth might not offer a detailed explanation of this alternative understanding in any case, because he only wants to accept what can be verified.[158] He raises the topic briefly in chapter 3 and discusses his own beliefs at length elsewhere in the book (e.g., chapters 9, 11–12). On this point, Hengel, Michel, Perdue, and Krüger have had the better of the argument. According to Michel, passages like Qoh 9:6 and 3:21 are polemicizing against the possibility of life after death, and it is fair to assume of 3:16–22 "daß Qohelet hier gegen Leute argumentiert, die eben die Verbindung von חֵלֶק und Jenseitserwartung vollzogen haben, die also erwarten, 'ihren Anteil' erst nach dem Tode von Jahwe zu erhalten."[159] To this logic and the belief that the soul can ascend to God in some sort of immortal state, Qoheleth responds that a person

---

[157] Fischer, "Kohelet und die frühe Apokalyptik," 356.

[158] It is uncommon to give a full rendering of the opponents' position in ancient Wisdom texts. A full explanation would provide undue legitimacy to a contrary position. Ben Sira's repeated use of the negative "Do not say" formula is a useful corollary. Sirach has a number of perspectives to refute, but he does not lend credence to his opponents' ethical propositions by explicating them fully. The same is true of Qoheleth in chapter 3.

[159] Michel, *Untersuchungen*, 121–22. See also the conclusion of Perdue, "Wisdom and Apocalyptic: The Case of Qoheleth," 251.

can only enjoy their brief earthly existence and can never see or know what is to come afterwards (3:22). The only possibilities for humanity lie in the present, "for there is no work or thought or knowledge or wisdom in Sheol, to which you are going" (9:10).

## 7. Conclusions

Qoheleth's preoccupation with death and complete denial of an afterlife reflect his participation in an emergent debate during the Hellenistic period regarding eternal possibilities for the human soul/spirit. The sage moves beyond the qualitative understanding of death found in Proverbs and engages in a rigorous discussion about the implications of human mortality and the absence of a reliable act-consequence relationship. His work is part of an important discussion both within and outside the thought-world of Second Temple sages, as the ultimate fate of the individual began to receive far more attention than in previous works. Qoheleth categorically rejects any possibility for immortality: all living things, both humans and beasts, descend to a shadowy existence. Such a belief was still very popular among Second Temple sages, including the figure of Ben Sira. Sirach takes great pains to defend the traditional understanding of death against new proposals about the afterlife, but he retains a more hopeful and conservative outlook than Qoheleth. We now turn to the presentation of Wisdom and retribution in Ben Sira.

CHAPTER FOUR

# BEN SIRA'S APOLOGETIC RESPONSE

## 1. *Introduction*

The apocryphal book of Ben Sira (Ecclesiasticus), the longest extant instruction from the Second Temple period, is modeled on the book of Proverbs, even as it reflects the circumstances of a later era.[1] In numerous respects, the author of this text makes a vigorous defense of his sapiential predecessors. He points to honesty, prudence, and piety (i.e., "fear of the Lord") as essential requirements for righteous living. Sirach claims that submission to Wisdom and her tutelage will lead to abundant rewards, including a full and prosperous life and an eternal name (Sir 4:11–19; cf. Prov 2:1–11). The combination of shorter sayings and lengthy theological units is also similar to Proverbs. As he affirms this earlier tradition, Ben Sira also responds to a later and more complex landscape for sapiential discourse.[2] In presenting his conservative outlook, he addresses a group of pupils during the Hellenistic period, when a number of critical issues were being debated and recast. These topics include the relationship between divine determinism and free will, the shadow of death in the human experience, and the type of

---

[1] The original title of the instruction is somewhat of a mystery, since no surviving Hebrew MS contains a superscription with this information. The author's full name is found in a subscript of MS B: "Simon son of Jeshua son of Eleazar son of Sira" (51:30; cf. 50:27). In this discussion, "Ben Sira" will be used for the book *and* the author responsible for its content. We will also use "Sirach" to refer to author and text, along with the standard abbreviation (Sir). For the Hebrew text, see Pancratius C. Beentjes, *The Book of Ben Sira in Hebrew* (VTSup 68; Leiden: Brill, 1997). Francesco Vattioni, *Ecclesiastico: Testo ebraico con apparato critico e versioni greca, latina e siraica* (Naples: Istituto Orientale di Napoli, 1968), provides a convenient synopsis of Heb., Gk., Lat., and Syr. Translations are generally from the NRSV, though alternatives will be offered for certain verses. Because of the difficult, fragmentary nature of the primary text, particularly in the various Hebrew MSS, it is often difficult to produce a definitive translation, especially since only 68 percent of the instruction is extant in Hebrew. Unless otherwise noted, proposed retroversions will follow the commentary of M.H. Segal, *Sēper ben-Sîrāʾ haššēlēm* (4th ed.; Jerusalem: Bialik Institute, 1997).

[2] On Ben Sira's nuanced use of Proverbs, see Jeremy Corley, "An Intertextual Study of Proverbs and Ben Sira," in *Intertextual Studies in Ben Sira and Tobit: Essays in Honor of Alexander A. Di Lella, O.F.M.* (ed. J. Corley and V. Skemp; CBQMS 38; Washington, D.C.: Catholic Biblical Association of America, 2005), 155–82.

retribution one could expect. It is no coincidence that both Qoheleth and Ben Sira discuss these issues at length, with the latter sage challenging Qoheleth's subversion of the tradition, especially the denial of a comprehensible (from a human perspective) plan for earthly events.[3] Sirach's exhortations also presume believers using eschatological language to address ultimate questions (e.g., the understanding found in *1 Enoch*). In the wake of new proposals about the possibility of an afterlife, Ben Sira clings to the traditional understanding of Sheol and the act-consequence nexus. While acknowledging unfairness in the earthly sphere and the finality of death, he posits an ultimately consistent *Tun-Ergehen-Zusammenhang*.

In the changing climate for instructional literature, three additional developments seem to separate Ben Sira from earlier sages, and the relative importance of these issues is a matter of significant disagreement among scholars. The features are as follows: (1) the direct identification of Wisdom and Torah; (2) the striking (for a sage) reverence for priestly matters and cultic leaders past and present; (3) the utilization of Greek ideas and sources to explain the relationship between God and the created order. The first issue is groundbreaking for a sapiential text, since previous Israelite instructions had not characterized obedience to the Mosaic legislation as a means of attaining Wisdom.[4] Ben Sira declares, "If you desire wisdom, keep the commandments, and the Lord will lavish her upon you" (1:26). With regard to the cultic references, it is noteworthy for any instructional text to engage this aspect of religious life, and Sirach reveals an openly deferential attitude toward the priesthood. Many commentators have also argued that the sage had exposure to Hellenistic philosophy and incorporated certain insights from the Greek world into his theological reflections.[5] His presentation of opposites in creation (33:7–15) and description of

---

[3] There is good reason to believe that Ben Sira knew the content of Qoheleth, as many scholars have maintained. For example, Thomas Krüger, *Qoheleth* (trans. O.C. Dean; Hermeneia; Minneapolis: Fortress Press, 2004), 19, argues that even if there are no indisputable references to Qoheleth in the book of Ben Sira, the latter sage, in his efforts at defending the tradition, seems to presuppose the commentary found in the earlier text. See below for further discussion.

[4] The Mosaic legislation is associated with being wise in Deut 4:6. Ezra is a "wise" scribe whose mission is the fulfillment of the Torah (e.g., Ezra 7:25–26).

[5] T. Middendorp, *Die Stellung Jesu Ben Siras zwischen Judentum und Hellenismus* (Leiden: Brill, 1973), makes the most comprehensive case for a Greek influence, citing over 100 examples of direct borrowing by the sage.

Wisdom as a universal common law (e.g., Sirach 24), analogous to the Stoic concept of λόγος, are often cited.[6]

Yet as analysis of this book and these topics continues, it should be acknowledged that Ben Sira sits squarely within the ancient Near Eastern wisdom tradition, as this author defends longstanding assumptions found in Proverbs and other instructions. When examining all of the important innovations in Sirach, one should not consider the scattered priestly passages or traces of Hellenistic philosophy to be the backbone of the sage's thought. This is an instructional document, where the primary goal is to instill specific mindsets and behavioral patterns into a youthful addressee(s), and to promote a consistent principle of earthly justice.[7] Innovative elements are of course relevant, particularly if Sirach helps us understand the fabric of social and religious life during this sparsely documented period.[8] Nevertheless, interpretations of selected passages or secondary themes should not obscure the larger enterprise and the sage's efforts at defending traditional Wisdom. This is a manual for "discipline" or "learning" (מוסר/παιδεία), and its author seeks to influence young men negotiating the changing circumstances of a complex era. The urgency of these sayings indicates the sage's

---

[6] David Winston, "Theodicy in Ben Sira and Stoic Philosophy," in *Of Scholars, Savants, and their Texts: Studies in Philosophy and Religious Thought* (ed. R. Link-Salinger; New York: Lang, 1989), 239–50, argues for Stoic influence on Ben Sira. For a negative view, see Sharon Mattila, "Ben Sira and the Stoics: A Reexamination of the Evidence," *JBL* 119 (2000): 473–501.

[7] Sayings in the spirit of Proverbs and repeated admonitions about worldly temptations indicate the sage's conservative focus. Ben Sira urges all young persons to visit a tutor and learn the tradition (6:34–37). Whether he had his own established school or more informal sessions with pupils is an open question.

[8] Based on the reference to Ptolemy VII Euergetes in the grandson's prologue and the approximate length of two generations, the period in which Ben Sira had his career and wrote this instruction (early second-century B.C.E.) is not in dispute. John J. Collins, *Jewish Wisdom in the Hellenistic Age* (OTL; Louisville: Westminster John Knox Press, 1997), 23, argues that Ben Sira is presented as the product of a lengthy career and does not indicate an awareness of the persecutions under Antiochus IV Epiphanes (175–164 B.C.E.). The praise of Simon II (219–196 B.C.E.) in 50:1–21 suggests that Ben Sira and this high priest were at least near contemporaries, although these words could have been written after Simon's death. The precise date in which the instruction was finalized is less important than locating the basic trajectory of the sage's career, which occurred during a period of relative stability, but also at a time when social and religious life was influenced by Hellenism, apocalyptic ideas, and economic expansion under Ptolemaic and then Seleucid rule. For a summary of research on the setting, see Friedrich V. Reiterer, "Review of Recent Research on Ben Sira (1980–1996)" in *The Book of Ben Sira in Modern Research: Proceedings of the First International Ben Sira Conference, 28–31 July 1996, Soesterberg, Netherlands* (BZAW 255; Berlin: de Gruyter, 1997), 23–61; Richard J. Coggins, *Sirach* (GAP; Sheffield: Sheffield Academic Press, 1998).

participation in an important discussion among contemporaries and his efforts to undercut new proposals about causality and the afterlife. Ben Sira presents a belief in the adequate justice of God, the type of conduct appropriate for all individuals, and a conviction that proper results will be adjudicated in the earthly sphere without recourse to some sort of heavenly or eternal reward.

Many commentators have instead taken this instruction to represent a negative reaction to the influence of Hellenism, so that the basic goal is to defend Jewish identity against a new cultural matrix. Martin Hengel claims that Ben Sira reveals a hostile attitude to the "penetration of the Hellenistic style of life and foreign thought-forms into the Jewish upper class." He further argues, "This starting point gives the whole work of Ben Sira an *apologetic-polemical* basis, which to some degree conflicts with his thought and its indebtedness to traditional wisdom."[9] According to this line of reasoning, Sirach's defensiveness relates to both economic issues and epistemology, as he defends the suppositions of Israel's sapiential heritage and its conservative social ethic. In 3:21, the author states, "Do not study what is too marvelous for you, nor search out what is hidden from you" (translation mine). Scholars have often understood this type of language in the book to indicate a bias against the speculative philosophy associated with Greek thought.[10] There are problems with this thesis, however, since Ben Sira understands the need for scribes like himself and other members of society to interact with persons in power and to develop intellectually (e.g., 39:4). Although he exhorts his pupils to proceed cautiously with such pursuits, this sage endorses the learning of new ideas and cultural exchange, and therefore his approach to Hellenism is not apologetic-polemical. Ben Sira did not oppose foreign ideas or even commercial pursuits if these could be combined with "fear of the Lord."[11] The contours of the sage's discussion reveal an entirely different dynamic

---

[9] Martin Hengel, *Judaism and Hellenism: Studies in their Encounter in Palestine during the Early Hellenistic Period* (2 vols.; Philadelphia: Fortress Press, 1974), 1:138; cf. Victor Tcherikover, *Hellenistic Civilization and the Jews* (Philadelphia: Jewish Publication Society, 1959; repr., Peabody: Hendrickson Publishers, 1999), 144.

[10] Rudolph Smend, *Die Weisheit des Jesus Sirach erklärt* (Berlin: Reimer, 1906), 33, argues that the disparaging בני אדם in 3:24 refers to the Greeks. Cf. Patrick W. Skehan and Alexander A. Di Lella, *The Wisdom of Ben Sira* (AB 39; New York: Doubleday, 1987), 160–61.

[11] Collins, *Jewish Wisdom*, 31.

than the one suggested by Hengel: namely, an inner-sapiential debate over certain theological propositions, including sin and death.

This *is* an apologetic work, but rather than Hellenistic opponents, the author of this instruction targets other sages and groups who were actively questioning the viability of the wisdom tradition, especially those with otherworldly proposals. In an important comparative study, Randal Argall has demonstrated an intriguing relationship between the book of Ben Sira and *1 Enoch* on this point.[12] Even if these two texts diverge in terms of genre and outlook, the parallel subject matter cannot be dismissed as mere coincidence. Both Ben Sira and *1 Enoch* give detailed attention to the created order, the origin of sin, and retribution. Each author refers to the Torah, not on the plain-sense level, but with the goal of "getting behind the now obscure text into some deeper, hidden meaning."[13] Ben Sira presents himself as a paragon of knowledge, a wise figure who can help clarify the mysteries of the universe *and* provide a more realistic and pragmatic approach to life's vexing questions than that provided by the speculative outlook in texts like *1 Enoch*.[14] Argall makes a persuasive case that Ben Sira was familiar with the vivid imagery found in the Enochic corpus, particularly the Book of the Watchers. The extent to which he responded directly to these traditions is an important question that will be considered at length in this chapter. While he seems to have known many of the ideas found in *1 Enoch*, his project is much broader than a specific attack on speculative Wisdom.

Ben Sira's larger goal involves convincing pupils that a merciful God will reward virtuous behavior and that old assumptions about causality are still viable. He upholds the traditional viewpoint by depicting some sort of ultimate reckoning for the wicked, especially those who have prospered all of their lives (e.g., 11:26–27). He confronts Qoheleth's reasoning with an impassioned defense of the retributive justice of God, although he recognizes the efficacy of deceitful behavior (i.e., that

---

[12] Randal A. Argall, *1 Enoch and Sirach: A Comparative Literary and Conceptual Analysis of the Themes of Revelation, Creation, and Judgment* (SBLEJL 8; Atlanta: Scholars Press, 1995); cf. Benjamin G. Wright, "Putting the Puzzle Together: Some Suggestions Concerning the Social Location of the Wisdom of Ben Sira," in *Conflicted Boundaries in Wisdom and Apocalypticism* (ed. B.G. Wright and L. Wills; SBLSymS 35; Atlanta: Society of Biblical Literature, 2005), 89–113, who also demonstrates thematic similarities between these two texts.

[13] Argall, *1 Enoch and Sirach*, 95.

[14] Sirach takes aim at the pronounced interest in dreams and visionary accounts found in *1 Enoch* and other texts.

dishonest persons can prosper indefinitely) in a way that the compilers of Proverbs had not. He does not forsake the traditional understanding of Sheol, but Ben Sira places considerably more emphasis than his predecessors on the idea of a "good name" as a lasting reward for righteousness. This promise of an eternal reputation functions as a way of refuting Qoheleth's skeptical outlook (at least in relation to causality) on one side and the emergent belief in immortality on the other (i.e., the understanding in *1 Enoch*). The sage declares that a good name lasts in a way that nothing else can, including the human spirit. His apologetic efforts represent a critical witness to a tradition that was being challenged by pioneering models, which often included eternal possibilities for the human soul. Certain ideas set forth by Ben Sira demonstrate that even a conservative figure could allow his language to be shaped by shifting ideas and new frameworks (e.g., 33:7–15 and the idea of opposites in creation). The rest of this chapter will attempt to explicate the changing climate for sapiential discourse as revealed in the book of Ben Sira and the lengths that this particular author will go to defend traditional assumptions.

## 2. *Genre*

In evaluating this larger issue, it is fruitful to identify the genre of the book and the different forms found in Sirach. This is clearly an instructional document modeled on the book of Proverbs. Like his predecessors, Ben Sira offers both shorter units of sayings and lengthy discourses. Individual proverbs are usually clustered in thematic groupings, such as the section in 22:19–26 on insults and their impact on friendships.[15] Here and elsewhere, the sage combines simple declarative statements (22:20) with admonitions (v. 23). Since the entire instruction comes from one author, with some notable additions to the text, these units are generally longer and more cohesive than the content of Proverbs. There is also greater uniformity with regard to favorite topics, which include proper etiquette, wealth and poverty, and death. The basic proverb (משל) is a staple for Ben Sira, and he includes both numerical proverbs and comparative ("better-than") sayings. A number

---

[15] For a study of Ben Sira's discourses on friendship and this passage in particular, see Jeremy Corley, *Ben Sira's Teaching on Friendship* (BJS 316; Providence: Brown Judaic Studies, 2002), 191–211.

of hymns also appear. The "hymn to Wisdom" in chapter 24 is imitative of Proverbs 8, and there are multiple hymns of praise: 1:1–10; 18:1–14; 39:12–35; 42:15–43:33; 50:22–24; 51:1–12. In addition, there is at least one petitionary prayer (22:27–23:6) that can be traced to the sage, which is a novelty for a Jewish Wisdom text. The critique of the trades (38:24–34a) and praise of the scribe (38:34b–39:11) demonstrate an awareness of earlier sapiential traditions, particularly in Egypt.[16] Finally, the "Praise of the Ancestors" at the end of the book (chapters 44–50) stands as the biggest formal innovation. Ben Sira's recounting of these individuals and their respective careers is a groundbreaking move for an ancient Near Eastern instruction, although we find similar examples in other Jewish texts from this general period and in Hellenistic speeches.[17] Whether the sage models his tribute on the Greek encomium is a matter of debate.[18]

It is reasonable to ask why the sage completes his traditional instruction with retrospective language about Israelite heroes. On one level, Ben Sira includes the Praise of the Ancestors out of respect for the larger religious culture; this is simply a history he wants his students to know. This section also seems to have an important hortatory function, since it illustrates the promise of a good name. These famous figures have achieved an immortal status, and Sirach promises a similar fate to all righteous persons. The guarantee of a lasting name is a fundamental component of this author's ethic and guarantee of an act-consequence nexus. In the introduction to the Praise of the Ancestors (44:1–15), he declares that these commendable figures (אנשי חסד) "made a name for themselves by their valor" (v. 3). Then he turns to the prickly dilemma

---

[16] The Egyptian Instruction of Dua-Khety (ca. 1900 B.C.E.), also known as "The Satire on the Trades," has a description of the superiority of the scribal profession. For a translation of the Egyptian text, see William K. Simpson, *The Literature of Ancient Egypt* (3d ed.; New Haven: Yale University Press, 2003), 431–38.

[17] Collins, *Jewish Wisdom*, 98, notes similar descriptions in 1 Macc 2:51–60; 4 Macc 16:20–23; 18:11–19, and Hebrews 11 (NT).

[18] Thomas R. Lee, *Studies in the Form of Sirach 44–50* (SBLDS 75; Atlanta: Scholars Press, 1986), argues that the Greek encomium provides the basic blueprint for chapters 44–50. Lee claims that this entire section is concerned with the praise of Simon as an appropriate model for Onias III, and therefore chapters 44–50 function as an encomium to Simon. Burton L. Mack, *Wisdom and the Hebrew Epic: Ben Sira's Praise of the Fathers* (CSHJ; Chicago: University of Chicago Press, 1985), sees parallels between this section and the Hellenistic speeches, and he builds a persuasive case that these chapters are "reminiscent of encomiastic tradition and practice" (p. 129). He argues that the priests, prophets, and scribe-sages in this section each represent an office, "whose holder acts as a tradent, that is, one in a series of successions" (p. 47).

of the unheralded righteous. In v. 9, he states, "But of others there is no memory; they have perished as though they had never existed; they have become as though they had never been born, they and their children after them." This surprising admission suggests an inevitable fading from memory of persons whose actions did not lead to widespread acclaim. Such a statement seems to take Ben Sira into the camp of Qoheleth, who believes that everything done by the common person (or even a famous individual) is ultimately forgotten in a cyclical universe (e.g., "The people of long ago are not remembered," Qoh 1:11). Does Sir 44:9 signify a major departure from Ben Sira's adherence to the tradition? Probably not, since the sage appears to correct himself in v. 10, or at least he weakens the force of the previous verse. He states that godly individuals whose acts are not recorded *do* live on through the memory of future generations: their "righteous deeds have *not* been forgotten; their wealth *will remain* with their descendants" (vv. 10–11).[19] The famous ancestors gained national, immortal reputations through their valor and the holding of key offices, but the same can be said on a smaller scale of anyone who develops "fear of the Lord." Regarding such individuals, Sirach declares that "Their bodies are buried in peace, but their name lives on generation after generation" (v. 14). This conclusion is critical to the parenetic value of chapters 44–50 and the book as a whole. Even if the audience for this text had no chance of attaining the eminent status of Simon, Aaron, or Josiah, through good character they could guarantee their children's future and the durability of their reputation (albeit on a smaller scale). If Qoheleth and Job had used clever reasoning to argue that everyone and everything is eventually forgotten, Ben Sira insists on a lasting reputation for all righteous persons.[20]

---

[19] The reference to טובם in v. 11a probably refers to material possessions rather than moral "goodness."

[20] Shannon Burkes, *God, Self, and Death: The Shape of Religious Transformation in the Second Temple Period* ( JSJSup 79; Leiden: Brill, 2003), 115, explains the sage's perspective: "He reveals a deeper consciousness of death's melancholy inevitability than earlier authors, but determinedly develops traditional confrontations with human finitude through the assertions of individual survival via the family and reputation, which now opens out for the first time in a wisdom work to include the same on the national level."

## 2.1 Priestly References in Sirach

Along with the praise of Aaron (45:6–22) and Simon (50:1–24), the other "priestly" references in Ben Sira and their importance for understanding the book's formal content merit attention. This sage has immense respect for religious institutions, particularly the role of cultic leaders in the social structure, and he alludes to biblical verses that elevate priests.[21] His positive appraisal is apparent in several passages, including the discussion of proper sacrifices in 34:21–35:13 and also 7:29–31, which sanctifies the office of priest: "With all your soul fear the Lord, and revere his priests" (v. 29).[22] Such language has an obligatory tone, as the sage draws on what is for him an authoritative tradition: "honor the priest, and give him his portion, as you have been commanded" (v. 31). There is ample precedent in earlier biblical writings for giving to the priest an appropriate allowance, but earlier instructions had not devoted the same level of attention to this issue as Ben Sira does.[23] Along with the moral requirement that the sage clearly endorses, the inclusion of such language probably has a strategic element. As Benjamin Wright and others have argued, Ben Sira was a scribe-sage and a member of the "retainer" class, and therefore he had to cultivate a careful relationship with priests and other dignitaries in order to maintain his status and livelihood.[24] Preexilic sages had operated under a royal patronage system, negotiating a bureaucracy that deferred to the king and his closest advisers as guarantors of the administrative

---

[21] Saul Olyan, "Ben Sira's Relationship to the Priesthood," *HTR* 80 (1987): 261–86, argues that the author's high regard for the priesthood is pivotal to his overall project, especially the language in Sir 7:29–31. Moreover, the model for Ben Sira's understanding is not an exclusive Zadokite understanding or a pan-Levitical framework, but rather a pro-Aaronid "P" viewpoint. Ben Sira's praise of Aaron and avoidance of triumphal Zadokite language support Olyan's thesis.

[22] Olyan, "Ben Sira's Relationship to the Priesthood," 264, highlights the parallel structure in 7:29 between פחד אל and ואת כהניו הקריש.

[23] For the background of this reference, see Exod 29:27; Lev 7:31–34; Deut 18:3.

[24] Benjamin G. Wright, "'Fear the Lord and Honor the Priest': Ben Sira as Defender of the Jerusalem Priesthood," in *The Book of Ben Sira in Modern Research: Proceedings of the First International Ben Sira Conference, 28–31 July 1996, Soesterberg, Netherlands* (BZAW 255; Berlin: de Gruyter, 1997), 195–96, detects a hierarchical perspective in Ben Sira, where the author is part of the "retainer class," consisting of educated "scribe-sages" who served the priestly elite and other powerful individuals (including Greek officials). Wright utilizes the discussion of Richard Horsley and Patrick Tiller, "Ben Sira and the Sociology of the Second Temple" in *Second Temple Studies III: Studies in Politics, Class, and Material Culture* (JSOTSup 340; London: Sheffield Academic Press, 2002), 74–108, to substantiate the argument that Ben Sira allies himself with the Jerusalem priesthood.

hierarchy (e.g., Prov 25:1). In contrast, the career of Ben Sira occurred during the Hellenistic period, when the absence of a monarch altered the bureaucratic system. As a result, cultic leaders, particularly the high priest, had more influence over the scribal profession and the ability of sapiential figures to teach and disseminate their material.

Even if this language reflects Ben Sira's participation in such a system, this is not a priestly book, nor does its content reflect the concerns of an active cultic leader. The sections on priestly matters, while innovative for an instruction, are relatively few in number.[25] These sparse references should not lead us to question the genre of the book or even its primary focus. It is useful to compare *Jubilees*, which deals extensively with levitical concerns, and Ben Sira. The instructional text does not reflect the same type of halakhic engagement with priestly matters.[26] Our sage clearly has regard for the Jerusalem priesthood and the texts that elevate this institution. Yet the forms, language, and ethical concerns in this book correlate with the author's own sapiential milieu.[27] The description in chapter 7 occurs in a lengthy unit on the appropriate response to different categories of people, including parents (7:27–28), priests (vv. 29–31), and disadvantaged persons (vv. 32–35). The next section encourages prudence with a variety of types (8:1–19). As a result, this discussion of priests constitutes just one element in a diverse list. Similarly, in the section on sacrifices, topics such as concern for the poor (34:24–25) and virtuous behavior (35:5) are familiar tropes for Wisdom writers. Ben Sira is a window into an important period, and his deference to religious institutions is an indicator of both his social status as a member of the "retainer class" and his innovative use of Scripture. Yet these disparate passages do not reflect a priestly *Sitz im Leben* for this instructional document.

---

[25] Collins, *Jewish Wisdom*, 37.

[26] *Jubilees* in all probability dates from a later point in the second-century B.C.E. To a certain extent, the exact date depends on whether one finds explicit references to the Maccabean revolt in the text, particularly in chapter 23. See George W.E. Nickelsburg, *Jewish Literature between the Bible and the Mishnah* (2d ed.; Minneapolis: Fortress Press, 2005), 73.

[27] Helge Stadelmann, *Ben Sira als Schriftgelehrter: Eine Untersuchung zum Berufsbild des vor-makkabäischen Sôfēr unter Berücksichtigung seines Verhältnisses zu Priester-, Propheten- und Weisheitslehrertum* (WUNT 2; Tübingen: Mohr, 1981), argues that Ben Sira was actually a priest, since he functioned as both a scribe and educator after the exile (analogous to Ezra). Stadelmann's theory has met with little support (but see Olyan, "Ben Sira's Relationship to the Priesthood," 262–66).

## 3. *Structure and Literary Integrity*

Delineating a structure for Ben Sira is a formidable task. While individual units generally have an internal consistency, the larger instruction has a notebook style. Like many of the texts examined in this study, Sirach can be characterized as "a collection of instructions rather than a tight, coherent, compositional unity."[28] There are noteworthy transitions in the text, such as the hymn to Wisdom in chapter 24 as an obvious midpoint and the Praise of the Ancestors in chapters 44–50 as the concluding section. The first half of the book, 1:1–23:28, has the following divisions: 1:1–4:10; 4:11–6:17; 6:18–14:19; 14:20–23:27; and 24:1–34.[29] Along with these subsections, five passages on Wisdom (1:1–10; 4:11–19; 6:18–37; 14:20–15:10; 24:1–34) seem to punctuate the first part of Ben Sira. With regard to the second half (25:1–51:30), the divisions are as follows: 25:1–33:18; 33:19–39:11; 39:12–43:33; 44:1–50:29; 51:1–30.[30] The entire instruction probably developed over time, as the author accumulated proverbs and added lengthy reflections. In addition, chapters 1–23 contain more traditional proverbs than the latter half of the book. The concluding units have more hymnic (and overtly theological) material, along with the Praise of the Ancestors.[31]

Any attempt at establishing a clear structure is compounded by the difficulty of sorting through the various versions and recensions of Sirach. This is without question the most complex aspect of Ben Sira studies. Only a portion of the Hebrew is extant and spread across multiple manuscripts, and the order of these Geniza fragments differs from

---

[28] Collins, *Jewish Wisdom*, 46. Cf. Alexander Di Lella, "Wisdom of Ben-Sira," *ABD* 6:936.

[29] Di Lella, "Wisdom of Ben Sira," 936, proposes an additional division between 14:20–19:17 and 19:18–23:27.

[30] This is the suggested division in Collins, *Jewish Wisdom*, 45–46, utilizing the proposals in Segal, *Sēper ben-Sîrāʾ haśśālēm*, and Wolfgang Roth, "The Gnomic-Discursive Wisdom of Jesus Ben Sirach," *Semeia* 17 (1980): 35–79. While the notebook style complicates efforts at discerning a structure, in many cases the author provides a clear break before commencing with a new topic (e.g., 33:16–18).

[31] Jack Sanders, *Ben Sira and Demotic Wisdom* (SBLMS 28; Chico, Ca.: Scholars Press, 1983), 62–103, argues that the insertion of hymns towards the end of the book (Sir 39:16–31; 42:15–18; 43:2–8, 22–26) indicates Sirach's awareness of a similar ordering in Phibis (P. Insinger). Sanders builds on the original argument of Paul Humbert, *Recherches sur les sources égyptiennes de la littérature sapientiale d'Israel* (Neuchâtel: Secrétariat de l'Université, 1929).

the Greek versions.[32] In many instances, the Greek and Hebrew disagree in both meaning and content.[33] The medieval manuscripts (A, B, C, D, E, and F) are fragmentary, often suspect, and do not always yield a reliable translation.[34] With certain verses, the only course of action is to construct a retroversion of the Hebrew based on other translations. This understanding of an H[1] text, which is a reconstruction based on G[1] (the grandson's translation), remains a possible way of arriving at the sage's original efforts, although this is ultimately hypothetical and not an actual version of the book.[35] In other cases, the Syriac translation provides the best means of determining the sense of particular proverbs and even entire units. For our purposes, it is noteworthy that many of the G[2] recensions (based on a different Hebrew recension: H[2]) evince a belief in the afterlife. These insertions flatly contradict the main body of text, where the original sage is opposed to the idea of an otherworldly reward for virtuous behavior.[36]

## 3.1    *Prayer for Deliverance in Sirach 36*

Certain units in Ben Sira are viewed by many scholars as later additions, especially sections that appear to be at odds with the sage's outlook and the period in which he had his career. The prayer for deliverance in 36:1–22 (33:1–13a; 36:16b–22 in G[1]) and the concluding poem in 51:13–30 are two important possibilities. The prayer is consequential for this study, since it contains apocalyptic language and a mindset that seems out of place in this instruction. Sirach 36 does not cohere with the more pragmatic tone found elsewhere in the text. The fact that this is a petitionary prayer does not preclude authorship by the original sage, since there is another example of this type in 22:27–23:6. Yet Sir 36:1–22 does not seem to fit the political circumstances of the sage's day.

---

[32] The Hebrew order of 30:25–33:13a and 33:13b–36:16a is inverted in the Greek.

[33] See Benjamin G. Wright, *No Small Difference: Sirach's Relationship to Its Hebrew Parent Text* (SCS 26; Atlanta: Scholars Press, 1989).

[34] Skehan and Di Lella, *The Wisdom of Ben Sira*, 60, also note the ambiguity with possible editorial additions: the Hebrew in a medieval manuscript could be a gloss, retroversion from Syriac or Greek, or possibly a verse from H[2]. It is frequently impossible to determine what one is dealing with for a particular verse.

[35] For an explanation of this terminology, see Skehan and Di Lella, *The Wisdom of Ben Sira*, 55.

[36] The obvious expansion in Sir 2:9c (G[2]) introduces the idea of eternal life: "For his reward is an everlasting gift (δόσις αἰωνία) with joy." See below for further discussion.

The violent plea in v. 12 is difficult to contextualize: "Crush the heads of the hostile rulers who say, 'There is no one but ourselves.'"[37] The "hostile rulers" presumably refer to a Seleucid leader, perhaps Antiochus III (the Great) or Antiochus IV Epiphanes. The latter figure is improbable if this section is original to the sage: it is virtually certain that Ben Sira pursued his career during the reign of Antiochus III, prior to the turbulence of the Maccabean period. Wright has attempted to locate the harsh statements in the prayer during the tenure of Antiochus III, claiming that Ben Sira longed for independence from Ptolemaic and then Seleucid control.[38] He claims that this author admired Simon's ability to work the system, negotiating with foreign rulers like Antiochus for religious freedom and the upkeep of Jerusalem.[39] The high priest's success in bargaining might have given Ben Sira hope for "a kind of *de facto* independence under a passive Seleucid rule."[40] During the years after Simon's death in 196 B.C.E., Wright points to Antiochus's defeat at Magnesia and his subsequent need to pass along a heavier tax burden to Seleucid subjects. After the prosperity and optimism of Simon's career, perhaps burdensome circumstances led Ben Sira to a more desperate, fiery outlook, which included an intense desire for independence: "The tone of the prayer may be the outcome of his disappointment at the way things had developed."[41] The assessment of Simon in 50:1–24 probably comes after the high priest's death, but this argument for nationalistic eschatology in Ben Sira's thought is contrary

---

[37] MS B (v. 10) has ראש פאתי מואב with אויב written in the margin. This is an allusion to Balaam's oracle in Num 24:17, which was utilized extensively during this period.

[38] Benjamin G. Wright, "'Put the Nations in Fear of You': Ben Sira and the Problem of Foreign Rule," *SBLSP* 38 (1999): 77–93, posits a number of veiled criticisms against the ruling powers in Sirach (e.g., 4:15; chapters 10–11).

[39] Simon II undoubtedly played a role in the transition from Ptolemaic to Seleucid rule, as noted in Wright, "'Put the Nations in Fear of You,'" 91. He is also credited with restoring the Temple.

[40] Wright, "'Put the Nations in Fear of You,'" 91. Cf. Skehan and DiLella, *The Wisdom of Ben Sira*, 420, who argue that the poem in chapter 36 matches the spirit of Ben Sira and his "sure faith in the God of Israel and his prophetic hope of relief from pagan oppressors (35:22b–26)."

[41] Wright, "'Put the Nations in Fear of You,'" 92. Cf. Johannes Marböck, "Das Gebet um die Rettung Zions Sir 36,1–22 (G 33,1–13a; 36,16b-22) im Zusammenhang der Geschichtsschau ben Siras," in *Memoria Jerusalem. Freundesgabe Franz Sauer* (ed. J.B. Bauer and J. Marböck; Graz/Jerusalem: Akademische Druck und Verlagsanstalt, 1977), 93–115. Skehan and Di Lella, *The Wisdom of Ben Sira*, 422, argue that the arrogance of Antiochus III is the background for the statement in Sir 36:12b: "'There is no one but ourselves.'"

to the larger spirit of the instruction and historically implausible. It is unlikely that a figure like Antiochus III, who is lauded for his assistance with the rebuilding of Jerusalem and for generally good relations with Jews (especially Simon), would suddenly be the object of such derision in this text.[42] Moreover, if Ben Sira had a transformation that led him to this fervent language about independence and the destruction of the surrounding nations, it would stand to reason that the entire instruction would reflect such a sea-change and not just one passage. Ben Sira had never known an independent Israel, and the instruction (apart from chapter 36) does not indicate explicit hope for such a remote possibility. The sage had his career during colorful times, and he affirms the capability of God to alter the balance of power, but his perspective is not revolutionary.[43] It is far more likely that the prayer was added later in the second-century by an individual(s) who had to endure the reign of Antiochus IV Epiphanes.[44]

Along with the historical issue, the tenor of the prayer seems to conflict with the conservative ethic found throughout the maxims of Ben Sira. Elsewhere in this instruction, the sage urges caution and deftness with persons in authority, and he guarantees success for those willing to work the system with honor (e.g., 31:12–32:13, and the encouragement of collegial interaction with powerful persons). A young charge should respect the system in place and learn to bide his time: "Among the great, do not act as their equal; and when another is speaking, do not babble" (32:9). The request to obliterate a national foe (36:9, 11–12) and the inclusion of a prophecy concerning violent deliverance (36:20–21) do not cohere with the conciliatory advice in other passages. In this book, the primary author does not oppose societal structures, and he certainly does not advocate their dismantling: "Rather, he takes a synchronic view, where the goal of history lies in the establishment of

---

[42] Collins, *Jewish Wisdom*, 110–11, notes the positive assessment of Antiochus III in Josephus (*Ant.* 12.129–153) and the fact that this ruler was contemporaneous with Simon.

[43] Ben Sira does mention "the nations" at several points in this discussion (e.g., 4:15), and in chapter 10 he criticizes the haughtiness of kings, possibly the Ptolemaic and Seleucid rulers of his day (Skehan and Di Lella, *The Wisdom of Ben Sira*, 224–26; cf. Wright, "'Put the Nations in Fear of You,'" 81–82). The assertion that "The Lord overthrows the thrones of rulers, and enthrones the lowly in their place" (10:14) has ample precedent in earlier biblical material, especially the Song of Hannah (1 Sam 2:7–8). It allows readers to recall rulers from the recent and more distant past. See below for a treatment of 35:22–26.

[44] Middendorp, *Die Stellung Jesu Ben Siras*, 132.

certain institutions and offices."[45] While he takes pride in the courage
of Israel's forbears, including victories on the battlefield (46:1–6 and
Joshua; 47:7 and David), such events are firmly anchored in the past for
this sage. Ben Sira retains a belief in the possibility of affecting change
within existing institutions and presents a measured discourse in this
pursuit, as he lauds the benefits of being a scribe and the opportunities
afforded by this profession.

For purposes of the current study, the most important elements in the
prayer are eschatological/apocalyptic terms and perspectives not found
elsewhere in Sirach. For example, there is the petition for "new signs"
and "other wonders" in v. 6, a clear allusion to Exod 7:3, followed by
a call in v. 10 to "Hasten the day/end, and remember the appointed
time (החיש קץ ופקוד מועד)."[46] This language echoes other texts from
this general period that use apocalyptic language and otherworldly
belief systems (e.g., Daniel, *1 Enoch*).[47] The combination of the Divine
Warrior motif with a final "end" is present in both *1 Enoch* and Sir
36:1–22, although the importance of the flood is emphasized only in
the former text (*1 En.* 10:16–11:2; 91:5–9).[48] Those who view the passage as original have to explain the apparent discontinuity between a
prayer characterized by nationalistic eschatology and the rest of Ben
Sira.[49] Argall argues that such eschatological concerns are present as

---

[45] Collins, *Jewish Wisdom*, 111.

[46] G has a third colon, "and your mighty deeds will be proclaimed," while MS B
reads, "Who will ask you, 'What are you doing'?" The former is to be preferred. The
linking of the "end" and the "appointed time" can be traced to Hab 2:3 ("For there
is still a vision for the appointed time; it speaks of the end"). Such a combination also
appears in Daniel, where the context is clearly apocalyptic (10:14; 11:27, 35). See
Collins, *Jewish Wisdom*, 110.

[47] Marböck, "Das Gebet um die Rettung Zions," 107, posits a more limited eschatology in Sirach 36, especially when compared to the use of such terms as קץ in Daniel.
This, too, is part of the equation in the prayer: "Dennoch dürfte die Bitte den Horizont
der Hilfe in einer aktuellen Notlage überschreiten in Richtung eines eschatologischen
Zeichens, als Vorschein eines endgültigen Handels Gottes für sein Volk."

[48] Argall, *1 Enoch and Sirach*, 240. Another parallel is the visitation of the Divine
Warrior upon the wicked. The language in *1 Enoch* refers to punishment for the wicked,
"the great judgment, in which there will be vengeance on all and a consummation
forever" (*1 En.* 25:3; cf. Sir 36:8).

[49] Argall, *1 Enoch and Sirach*, 219, makes a connection between the terminology of
Sir 24:8–12 and chapter 36. He points especially to the dual use of "a resting place"
(ἀνάπαυσις) for Wisdom in Jerusalem (24:7a) and "your resting place" (מכון שבתיך/
τόπον καταπαύματός σου) in 36:13. According to Argall, "While he has not explicitly
mentioned Wisdom in Sirach 36:13, 16–19, the reference to Jerusalem as God's resting place is a subtle reminder of her presence" (p. 219). Yet this prayer in chapter 36
addresses deliverance from hostile forces so that the Lord can dwell securely in Zion.

part of the original work, but the author had a limited view of the type of deliverance that was possible or even desirable. According to this argument, 36:13, 16–19 indicates a respect for those persons leading the people in Jerusalem: "Ben Sira shows a desire for continuity before and after the eschatological battle. The exiles return to Zion and recognize the legitimacy of the status quo.... Zion is vindicated as the locus of Wisdom."[50] Similarly, Marböck understands the language in this section to represent an important element of the sage's thought, particularly the connection between the Zion motif and eschatological prophecy.[51] Yet even restrained eschatology is not part of Ben Sira's pedagogical efforts elsewhere in the text. His goal is to defend the essential goodness of God and the evenhanded dispensation of divine justice *without* recourse to apocalyptic or excessively nationalistic proposals. One could argue that the prayer longs for restoration without any real end-time component, but even on this point the sage seems more inclined to accept the priestly theocratic regime under Seleucid/Ptolemaic rule, rather than presenting a forceful case for the restoration of the Davidic line.[52] Royal messianism and eschatological expectation are not part of the original sage's enterprise.

---

The rest of Sirach does not follow in the same spirit. For example, in the Praise of the Ancestors, the sage does not explicitly long for the restoration of the Davidic line (47:1–11) and seems to favor Aaron.

[50] Argall, *1 Enoch and Sirach*, 218–19.

[51] Johannes Marböck, *Gottes Weisheit unter uns: zur Theologie des Buches Sirach* (HBS 6; Freiburg: Berlin, 1995), 163–64, discusses a variety of biblical texts (e.g., Ps 102:14) and passages in Ben Sira that suggest an eschatological perspective. He argues that Sir 36:1–22 is thoroughly compatible with the Praise of the Ancestors and the rest of the instruction (especially 17:17: "He appointed a ruler for every nation, but Israel is the Lord's own portion"). Marböck sees a plausible link between the reference in 36:12 and Antiochus III (p. 159) and notes the parallel use of Israel and Zion in Sir 24:8,10; cf. 36:13–19 (p. 161). He argues that chapter 36 reflects the sage's theology: "Das Gebet bekräftigt gerade durch die ständige Berufung auf Gottes erwählendes Handeln an Volk und Stadt die schon für das Väterlob festgestellte Idee einer geschichtlichen Kontinuität und die Lebendigkeit des Glaubens an Gottes Handeln auch in der Gegenwart Ben Siras" (p. 165).

[52] Jeremy Corley, "Seeds of Messianism in Hebrew Ben Sira and Greek Sirach," in *The Septuagint and Messianism* (BETL 195; Leuven: Leuven University Press/Peeters, 2006), 301–12, examines all possible references to messianic expectation in both the Hebrew and Greek texts of Ben Sira. Corley notes that both texts allude to Isa 11:10 and a "root" for the Davidic line (47:22), but the Greek translation underscores the messianic intent more forcefully (pp. 304–5). John J. Collins, "Messianism in the Maccabean Period," in *Judaisms and Their Messiahs at the Turn of the Christian Era* (ed. J. Neusner et al.; Cambridge: Cambridge University Press, 1987), 98, argues that only the secondary addition of chapter 51 offers unambiguous support for the restoration of the monarchy: "For Sirach himself the glory of David belongs to the past."

The verses preceding chapter 36, Sir 35(32):22b–26, are pertinent to our discussion, as many commentators have argued that this section sets the table for the content of the prayer. Unlike 36:1–22, this section probably derives from the original sage. Ben Sira's language in 35:22b–26 draws upon the powerful imagery of earlier biblical traditions, with such phrasing as כגבור in v. 22c.[53] This motif of the Lord as Divine Warrior is an allusion to Isa 42:13 and to earlier poetic passages. For Ben Sira, the Lord judges the people and intervenes on behalf of the righteous (vv. 23–25). With regard to the Lord wreaking vengeance "on the nations" (35:23), perhaps the author means a specific oppressor here, so that his actual purpose is a polemic against either the Ptolemies or Seleucids. The use of גוים appears to be a generic one, however, a condemnation of anyone who subverts the will of God. The description of the intervention and judgment of God in this manner is striking for an instruction, but these verses do not necessarily indicate a specific commentary against an external power or even a local group in Palestine. Instead, this unit functions as a general theological statement on the consistency of the act-consequence relationship and the impartiality of God's judgment. The author extols the unbending fairness of a deity who persists "until he repays mortals according to their deeds" (35:24).[54] While the terminological similarities between this unit and the prayer provided a logical insertion point for the addition of 36:1–22, the latter passage has a more nationalistic emphasis. Rather than straining to assimilate the prayer into a more traditional instruction, why not identify the strident language of Sirach 36 with the era of Antiochus IV Epiphanes, along with texts like Daniel? This prayer probably originated under later and more trying circumstances than the period of Sirach's career.[55]

---

[53] Argall, *1 Enoch and Sirach*, 214 n. 510, points to other units in Ben Sira with similar vocabulary.

[54] The Hebrew is עד ישיב לאנוש פעלו. This language guarantees a just God and a predictable universe in the tradition of Proverbs (cf. Prov 12:14; 19:17).

[55] For one of the more comprehensive efforts at proving the secondary status of this passage, see Middendorp, *Die Stellung Jesu Ben Siras*, 125–32, who uses both lexical and thematic evidence. He argues, "Dazu gehört der Wort- und Schriftgebrauch, die eschatologischnationale Prägung des Abschnittes, die Verwandtschaft mit späterer Literatur (Daniel, Kriegsvolle) sowie die verhältnismässig einfache Erklärung, die für eine Einfügung des Gebets an dieser Stelle gefunden werden kann" (p. 125). Gregory Schmidt Goering, "To Whom Has Wisdom's Root Been Revealed?: Ben Sira and the Election of Israel" (Ph.D. Diss, Harvard University, 2006), 220–39, suggests that the sage borrowed the prayer from another source. The inclusion of a "pre-existing petitionary prayer" explains why this chapter does not precisely fit the context of the

### 4. *Historical Setting and Possible Influences on the Sage*

In the preceding sections on genre and structure, we mentioned the date for this instruction and some of the factors that shaped Ben Sira's "ethic of caution."[56] It is virtually certain that this author enjoyed a successful career at the turn of the second-century, during an era of relative stability prior to the Maccabean revolt. Much of what we discussed regarding Qoheleth and the economic background of Ptolemaic Palestine also applies to this later instruction. The Zeno correspondence from the third-century and Josephus' account of the Tobiads suggest a period of bustling commercial activity. Even if the changes did not penetrate completely into Judean society, savvy entrepreneurs *and* scribes who could establish the right connections had much to gain.[57] While the evidence does not necessarily point to a sizeable foreign presence in some of the interior districts, the imperial policies of the Ptolemaic and then Seleucid administrations led to an aggressive tax system throughout the region. All lands technically belonged to the crown, and authorities naturally wanted to collect as much revenue as possible.[58] Many inhabitants of Syria-Palestine enjoyed a degree of autonomy and the opportunity to work the system for financial gain, especially if they formed alliances with the appropriate officials. In such a climate, there is an implicit juggling act required by the exhortations in Ben

---

book. He compares the prayer to Psalm 104 and 108, arguing that the Seleucid figures in Sirach 36 represent the primordial chaos depicted in these psalms and that this section reflects the sage's creation theology. According to Goering, "The purpose of the prayer is to arouse the deity to reestablish his mastery by removing Israel's enemies" (p. 232). The problem with this interpretation is that it still does not explain the disparity between Sirach's measured sapiential discourse elsewhere in the book and the tenor of the prayer. Why would the sage choose to include it?

[56] On the significance of this designation, see Jack Sanders, "Ben Sira's Ethic of Caution," *HUCA* 50 (1979): 73–106.

[57] Horsley and Tiller, "Ben Sira and the Sociology of the Second Temple," 74, state that the details of economic life within individual districts are difficult to verify. They argue that the numismatic and archaeological findings taken by Hengel (*Judaism and Hellenism* 1:23–29) and others to reveal major growth and systemic change have no relevance for the bulk of the population. The *yhd* and *yrślm* jars often cited as evidence of a thriving economy were unearthed along the coastal plain, and the coinage discoveries from this period have occurred primarily in Samaria. Although Horsley and Tiller make a cogent case regarding continuity of life for many agrarian villagers (i.e., no enhanced prospect for commercial success), Ben Sira's descriptions of those actually involved in mercantile practices imply a period of significant growth.

[58] Tcherikover, *Hellenistic Civilization and the Jews*, 67–68, discusses the Zeno papyri and the process of local tax collection in Syria.

Sira. The sage is concerned about his students' ability to participate actively in the larger society while maintaining the requisite "fear of the Lord." Although he warns against complete assimilation to new influences and favors uprightness over the lure of dishonest gain, he is not opposed to cultural participation and in many places lauds the benefits of wealth and political power. Sirach claims that "Riches are good if they are free from sin" (13:24).[59] Withdrawal from the society would not have been an option for his pupils in any case, since their professional obligations required them to interact with the established classes. The possibility of having a successful career is appealing (8:8), although Ben Sira is anxious about unbridled commerce (26:28–27:3) and sycophantic behavior around the elite (13:3–13, 20–23).

We mentioned that the advice in this text targets those pupils most likely to interact with the rich and powerful, the "retainer class" of scribes. Some of the designations used in the book confirm the future role of Ben Sira's pupils as retainers. For example, "Do not slight the discourse of the sages, but busy yourself with their maxims; because from them you will learn discipline and how to serve (להתיצב) princes" (8:8). The use of להתיצב implies a subservient but important role in the presence of powerful persons (שרים/μεγιστάντες). Ben Sira identifies himself as a "scribe" (סופר/γραμματεύς) in 38:24, and his optimistic assessment of the profession suggests a similar future for his pupils. He points to the possibilities for advancement in this field: other occupations do not afford one the opportunity to "attain eminence in the public assembly" or "expound discipline or judgment" (38:33).

Sirach's use of reward and punishment language to address economic issues is a critical component of his presentation. In 29:11 he declares, "Lay up your treasure according to the commandments of the Most High, and it will profit you more than gold." As with many of the earlier instructional texts we have examined (e.g., Anii), the underlying motivation for honest financial dealings is not altruistic, but practical. Straightforward, generous acts will cause goodwill in subsequent

---

[59] Ben Sira cites the benefits of being a member of the more leisured element of society. Not only does the scribe have more time for reflection (38:34b–39:11), but also the company he keeps enables him to enjoy the benefits of wealth, especially at banquets (31:12–32:13). Such an activity is an opportunity for excitement. Oda Wischmeyer, *Die Kultur des Buches Jesus Sirach* (BZNW 77: Berlin: de Gruyter, 1995), 107–8, outlines the relevant passage in Sirach, which is thoroughly Hellenistic in orientation. Young lads should be cautious at their first banquets, but everyone can enjoy themselves.

172 CHAPTER FOUR

transactions, and this will function to keep a person away from poverty. For example, loan arrangements with a neighbor are ultimately beneficial for the lender: "Keep your promise and be honest with him, and on every occasion you will find what you need" (29:3).[60] Ben Sira is also more realistic (or simply more upfront) than Proverbs about the possibility of longstanding financial success through dishonest means. He understands that hucksters can prosper over an extended period, even a lifetime. Such an attitude, especially the reality of corruption, relates to Sirach's economic context. Within the climate of his day, this author insists on some sort of ultimate reckoning for persons who have cheated and not suffered during their lifetime. In chapter 11, he offers a promised reversal:

> Do not say, "What do I need, and what further benefit can be mine?"
> Do not say, "I have enough, and what harm can come to me now?"
> For it is easy for the Lord on the day of death to reward individuals according to their conduct (v. 26).
> In the day of prosperity, adversity is forgotten, and in the day of adversity, prosperity is not remembered (v. 25).
> An hour's misery makes one forget past delights, and at the close of one's life one's deeds are revealed.
> Call no one happy before his death;
> by how he ends a person becomes known (11:23–28).[61]

This passage guarantees a *character*-consequence relationship, a concept that is even more applicable to this later instruction and its context than to earlier texts. Ben Sira argues that the greedy merchant will eventually receive punishment, but this might not occur until the moment of death (11:26). While he states elsewhere in the instruction that "retribution (עכרון) does not delay" (7:16), here in chapter 11 Ben Sira acknowledges unpredictability. Since his students were witnessing corruption in the marketplace, he seeks to promote an ultimate accounting, when every person will be evaluated and sentenced by a just God. A final set of events at death will lead to an eternal reputation for the just person and infamy for the wicked. The exact process for this divine judgment is not

[60] To support this assertion, the sage promotes the idea of an observant deity, who notices all transactions and is merciful or punishing based on a person's behavior (18:13–14). The same is true of Thoth in the Egyptian texts.

[61] Segal argues that the lines in Hebrew were transposed before the writing of G¹. In addition, the Greek translation concludes the unit (v. 28) with καὶ ἐν τέκνοις αὐτοῦ γνωσθήσεται ἀνήρ. MS A reads כי באחריתו ינכר איש and is translated above. See Skehan and Di Lella, *The Wisdom of Ben Sira*, 236–37.

spelled out in detail, and Ben Sira's guarantee is complicated by the fact that he posits no belief in otherworldly retribution. As one way of promoting honesty and "fear of the Lord" instead of unabashed material pursuits, Ben Sira predicts increased anxiety for the one who frets too much about money: "Wakefulness over wealth wastes away one's flesh, and anxiety about it drives away sleep" (31:1; cf. Qoh 5:10–12). This is a difficult case to make: troublesome thoughts and nightmares occur earlier in the sinner's life (and not in every case), and the details of any final "settling of accounts" on a person's deathbed are not thoroughly explained. According to James Crenshaw, "Perhaps we can assume that the multitude of attempts to solve the nagging problem of the delay in retribution indicates that Sirach was never quite happy with any of his solutions."[62] As we continue to sort through the author's views on act and consequence and retribution, the number of illustrations relating to pecuniary matters should not go unnoticed. Corrupt practices elicited a sharp social commentary from the sage, but they also provided an effective vehicle for him to present larger propositions on the consistency of divine justice.

## 4.1   Hellenistic and Other Influences

If the socioeconomic context of pre-Maccabean Palestine has bearing on the content of Ben Sira, the literary sources and philosophical ideas that influenced him are varied and more difficult to assess. The extent of this author's familiarity with the Demotic instructions and his indebtedness to Hellenistic thought are pressing topics in the study of the book and can only receive brief attention here. When addressing this issue, one must consider not just the existence but also the significance of any borrowing. Even if there are traces of Egyptian Wisdom and Greek philosophy, the impact of foreign sources on the sage's larger project should not be overstated. There is little evidence from this period that any of Sirach's contemporaries, within the wisdom tradition or outside of it, wrote in Greek.[63] If certain maxims in the text find parallels in another source, they had perhaps become part of the *Zeitgeist* and should not necessarily be seen as dependent on a particular text. As a

---

[62] James L. Crenshaw, "The Problem of Theodicy in Sirach: On Human Bondage," in *Theodicy of the Old Testament* (ed. J.L. Crenshaw; IRT 4; Philadelphia: Fortress Press, 1983), 131; originally published in *JBL* 94 (1975): 47–64. See below for a more extended treatment of this question in relation to death.

[63] Hengel, *Judaism and Hellenism*, 1:88–92.

literate individual with an interest in pithy maxims, it is probable that
this author would have endorsed well-known sayings by including them
in this collection. We can also assume that at least some of the material Sirach came across during his travels and interchange with other
cultural traditions (51:13) influenced the content of this instruction.[64]
For example, evidence for a direct relationship between Ben Sira and
the poetry of Theognis seems unassailable.[65]

In addition, Sirach's familiarity with Stoic ideas is a possible point
of contact, although a debated one. We have mentioned the study of
Sharon Mattila, who posits a discontinuity between certain Stoic concepts and the content of Ben Sira. Along with the idea of the cosmic
λόγος, which is absent from Sirach, Mattila notes the dichotomy between
the Jewish sage's act-consequence understanding and the lack of such
a framework in Stoic writings. Ben Sira affirms predictability under
the guidance of a fair deity: "The sinner will not escape with plunder,
and the patience of the godly will not be frustrated. He (God) makes
room for every act of mercy; everyone receives in accordance with
one's deeds" (16:13–14).[66] Stoic writings offer no such guarantee, since
individuals are subject to the vicissitudes of fate (ἡ εἱμαρμένη). These
are valid points, but Mattila is too strident in her dismissal of any possible influence in this regard. We do find traces of Stoic thought in Ben
Sira, especially in relation to divine omnipotence. While no reasonable
argument would call Sirach a Stoic text, this author borrows selectively
from ideas and concepts with which he was at least partially familiar.[67]
The Jewish sage wrestles with a central paradox also found in Greek
writings: both Ben Sira and the Stoics hold divine determinism and
human freedom in tension (or contradiction). David Winston and Ursel
Wicke-Reuter have catalogued possible points of contact, particularly
in relation to God's omnipotence and an appropriate time for earthly

---

[64] Middendorp, *Die Stellung Jesu Ben Siras*, 13–24; Sanders, *Ben Sira and Demotic Wisdom*, 28–29.

[65] For example, Sir 6:10: "And there are friends who sit at your table, but they will not stand by you in time of trouble." Cf. Theognis 115–116/643–644: "Many become comrades dear beside the bowl, but few in a grave matter."

[66] Sharon Mattila, "Ben Sira and the Stoics," 478.

[67] Mattila, "Ben Sira and the Stoics," 500, doubts the possibility of Ben Sira's exposure to these ideas in his travels, even in Alexandria. Yet Winston, "Theodicy in Ben Sira and Stoic Philosophy," 240, cites the embassy of Sphaerus to Alexandria on behalf of Cleanthes (Diog. Laert. 7.185) as one indicator of the spread of Stoic thought in the region.

events.[68] Winston argues that for Sirach, this is an area of dependence on Stoic thought, since "The older wisdom literature did not feel this contradiction too keenly."[69] While a "freedom-determinism" dialectic exists in Ben Sira, Stoic texts, and the Demotic instructions, this is not a Greek innovation, but an absolutely critical feature of ancient Near Eastern instructional literature from the earliest periods.[70]

Although the influence of Egyptian literature on Ben Sira is undeniable, his indebtedness to Demotic instructions remains an open question.[71] A few scholars, primarily Humbert and Sanders, have pointed to explicit textual links between the late Egyptian instructions and Ben Sira, which would indicate the Jewish sage's direct dependence on the Demotic texts.[72] While Sanders demonstrates similar subject matter

---

[68] Winston, "Theodicy in Ben Sira," 241–42, cites a possible parallel between the divine determinism of Sir 39:21, 29–30 ("everything has been created for its own purpose") and the Stoic contrast of providence tending to the earthly sphere or sending floods/conflagrations (Origen, *Cels.* 4.64; Philo, *Prov.* 2.31–32). A similar understanding of causality in both the natural and moral realms can be found in P. Insinger 30.1–6. Winston also claims that the call to praise the deity for orchestrating a suitable moment for every deed (Sir 42:15–43:33; 39:33–35) is analogous to the Stoic glorification of God (Epict. 1.16.15.21). Cf. Ursel Wicke-Reuter, *Göttliche Providenz und menschliche Verantwortung bei Ben Sira und in der Frühen Stoa* (BZAW 298; Berlin: de Gruyter, 2000); idem, "Ben Sira und die frühe Stoa. Zum Zusammenhang von Ethik und dem Glauben an eine göttliche Providenz," in *Ben Sira's God: Proceedings of the International Ben Sira Conference-Ushaw College 2001* (ed. R. Egger-Wenzel; BZAW 321; Berlin: de Gruyter, 2002), 268–81, who cites the similar understandings of divine omniscience and the status of evil persons in Ben Sira (as described in 39:12–35 and 16:24–18:14) and the early Stoics.

[69] Winston, "Theodicy in Ben Sira," 243.

[70] As chapters 1–2 of this study have argued, earlier sages struggled with the same issue of divine providence and human freedom/initiative. In Ptahhotep, we find the initial command in the prologue, "Instruct him (the addressee), for no one is born wise" (P 41), counterbalanced by the statement that "evil was fated in the womb" (P 217). Similarly, the book of Proverbs reveals a tension between determinism and the efficacy of good behavior. While "the Lord directs the steps" (16:9), and the "answer of the tongue" (16:1) belong to the deity, human initiative is shown to bring tangible results. The young pupil is given a choice between two paths, and his decision-making is of great consequence. The one who hearkens to the advice of his parents and heeds the call of Wisdom will prosper: "Prize her highly, and she will exalt you; she will honor you *if you embrace her*" (4:8). Winston does point to the absence of fate language in the context of birth in Proverbs, a feature that does occur in Sir 1:14–15.

[71] See the recent analysis of Matthew J. Goff, "Hellenistic Instruction in Palestine and Egypt: Ben Sira and Papyrus Insinger," *JJS* 36 (2005): 147–72.

[72] The parallel use of proverbs about the busy little bee (Sir 11:3; Ins. 25.3) demonstrates Ben Sira's acquaintance with sayings from non-Israelite collections. There are also markedly similar descriptions of how a master should treat slaves (Sir 33:24–28; cf. Ins. 14.4–11), which is probably the most convincing parallel (Sanders, *Ben Sira and Demotic Wisdom*, 95).

and a few of his citations suggest a relationship of some sort, many of the proposed examples are also found in the book of Proverbs and earlier Egyptian instructions. This suggests an unrelated application of traditional sapiential motifs by the respective authors of P. Insinger and Sirach.[73] Even if Sirach knew some of the content of these Demotic texts, which is entirely plausible, neither Ankhsheshonqy nor P. Insinger provided Ben Sira with a base model for his work, any more than a specific Greek text or author.[74] The similarities in terms of theological assumptions are actually more compelling, particularly in relation to act and consequence, death, and the freedom-determinism contrast. Regarding the first issue, Ben Sira states that "A stubborn mind will fare badly in the end, and the one who loves what is good will be driven along by it" (3:26, MS A, translation mine). Monostich sayings in Ankhsheshonqy reflect the same mentality: "He who is patient (lit. 'wide of heart') in a bad situation will not be harmed by it" (14.6).[75] Concerning human mortality, we mentioned the ultimate reckoning that occurs at the moment of death in Ben Sira (e.g., 11:27). Both P. Insinger and Ankhsheshonqy depict a similar event (Ankhsh. 11.21–22; Ins. 19.19–20).[76] Sirach describes a burial and no afterlife for the righteous (38:16; 44:14), and P. Insinger declares that "The end of the godly man is being buried on the mountain with his burial equipment" (Ins. 18.12).[77] On the agency question, even if Ben Sira does not have a specific concept for "fate," he presents a determinism-free will paradox, emphasizing divine sovereignty at certain points (33:12–13), and human responsibility in others passages (15:15). In similar fashion, P. Insinger

---

[73] For example, the encouragement of corporal punishment and harsh discipline (30:1–13) occurs in both Proverbs (13:24; 19:18; 23:13–14; 29:15) and Ahiqar (79–83).

[74] Sanders, *Ben Sira and Demotic Wisdom*, 102, concludes, "Ben Sira has relied on *Phibis* more heavily than on any other foreign literature; and the Egyptian work has provided to him his basic ethical position." We cannot agree with this summary, since the sage's discussion is directed primarily to those within his own tradition, and his ethical positions are consistent with a longstanding discourse in Israel.

[75] Translations of the Demotic texts are from Miriam Lichtheim, *Ancient Egyptian Literature, Volume III: The Late Period* (Berkeley: University of California Press, 1980).

[76] We have also mentioned Aeschylus in the *Agamemnon* (928). Cf. Herodotus *Hist.* 1.32, 1.86 ("Until he is dead, do not yet call a man happy, but only lucky"); Euripides, *Andr.* 100; *Tro.* 509; Sophocles, *Trach.* 1, cited in Miriam Lichtheim, *Late Egyptian Wisdom Literature in the International Context: A Study of Demotic Instructions* (OBO 52; Fribourg/Göttingen: University Press/Vandenhoeck & Ruprecht, 1983), 131 n. 115.

[77] There is a brief reference to the afterlife as a venue for punishing the wicked immediately prior to this verse (Ins. 18.8–11).

has a refrain about "fate" and "fortune" resting in the hands of the deity. Yet a person can also control his destiny in P. Insinger 6.17: "Poverty does not take hold of him who controls himself in purchasing." All of these examples suggest an effort among instructional authors during this period to address some of the most difficult theological issues, including human mortality. It is certain that the tradition of sharing ideas and sayings between Egypt and Palestine continued into the Hellenistic age, and the shifting circumstances of this period had an impact on both Ben Sira and his Egyptian counterparts. The common subject matter in these instructions suggests a lively sapiential discourse that took up major propositions.

### 5. Ben Sira's Pedagogy and Promise of Retribution

If the book of Ben Sira represents an apologetic response to a changing tradition, there is also a constructive component to this instruction. The author dispenses advice on a myriad of topics, and he often revisits favorite themes. It is useful to sketch the specific requirements in the presentation of מוסר/παιδεία, since many of the sage's exhortations relate to his beliefs on death and retribution. From the outset, the essential obligation in this text is "fear of the Lord." According to Josef Haspecker, this concept is the "Grundthema und wichtigstes Bildungsanliegen Sirachs in seiner pädagogischen Schrift."[78] Without the appropriate outlook and conduct associated with it, no pupil can hope to secure a blessed existence. At the beginning of his instruction, immediately after the initial description of Wisdom (1:1–10), Ben Sira describes the necessity and benefits of "fear of the Lord." Reverence must be cultivated and "interiorized" through faithfulness and love of God, and then earthly rewards, including a peaceful conclusion to life, will follow.[79] The sage makes a bold promise from the outset:

> The fear of the Lord is glory and exultation, and gladness and a crown of rejoicing. The fear of the Lord delights the heart, and gives gladness

---

[78] Josef Haspecker, *Gottesfurcht bei Jesus Sirach* (AnBib 30; Rome: Pontifical Biblical Institute, 1967), 198.

[79] Roland E. Murphy, *The Tree of Life: An Exploration of Biblical Wisdom Literature* (3d ed.; Grand Rapids: Eerdmans, 1990), 78–79, cites an "interiorization" of the traditional "fear of the Lord" concept in Ben Sira, based on passages like 2:15: "Those who fear the Lord do not disobey his words, and those who love him keep his ways."

and joy and long life. Those who fear the Lord will have a happy end; on the day of their death they will be blessed (Sir 1:11–13).[80]

This description stands in contrast to the portrait of death elsewhere in the text as a moment for judging the wicked and rendering some sort of painful conclusion to earthly existence (e.g., 11:26–28; 18:24). This promise of ultimate reckoning is an important element in Ben Sira's defense of the *Tun-Ergehen-Zusammenhang*, and it reveals a more nuanced perspective than the book of Proverbs. This author is more observant (or candid) than his predecessors: he acknowledges that friends can turn into enemies (37:2), a righteous person might experience strife (40:8–9), and death comes to everyone (41:1–4). Yet he also persists in affirming the traditional model: "Consider the generations of old and see: has anyone trusted in the Lord and been disappointed? Or has anyone persevered in the fear of the Lord and been forsaken?" (Sir 2:10). Even if a pupil witnesses a righteous person struggling or the wicked prospering, he should remain committed to the virtuous path. Fortunes can change quickly: "for it is easy in the sight of the Lord to make the poor rich suddenly, in an instant" (11:21). If a wicked individual does not receive his comeuppance, Ben Sira promises a settling of accounts at the conclusion of life (e.g., 18:24). Although he does not offer a full description of this final event, such an assurance allows him to affirm a character-consequence relationship and remain faithful to the framework of his predecessors.

Three additional features of Sirach's "fear of the Lord" concept are indicative of his larger outlook and will receive attention throughout the remainder of this chapter. First, Ben Sira cites the commandments (i.e., the Mosaic legislation) as a means of attaining Wisdom (1:26). The precise relationship between Wisdom/"fear of the Lord" and the Torah is a complex question, which will be taken up in a later section.[81] Another important element in Sirach's pedagogy is the need for

---

[80] Cf. Deut 6:2, which also associates lengthy days with obedience.

[81] The "fear of the Lord" and "Wisdom" are basically equivalent in Sirach 1 and throughout the book, though the sage often refers to Wisdom as the prerequisite, the "root" (1:20a) for acquiring "fear of the Lord." Otto Kaiser, "Die Furcht und die Liebe Gottes. Ein Versuch, die Ethik Ben Siras mit der des Apostels Paulus zu vergleichen," in *Ben Sira's God: Proceedings of the International Ben Sira Conference, Durham-Ushaw College 2001* (ed. R. Egger-Wenzel; BZAW 321; Berlin: de Gruyter, 2002), 42, explains the relationship between the two in Sirach 1: "Denn die göttliche Weisheit durchdringt den Kosmos und ist der Quell aller menschlichen Weisheit, die Furcht des Herrn aber ihre Wurzel, Fülle und ihr Kranz."

a tutor. A good teacher (like Ben Sira!) is mandatory for an aspiring scribe: through willingness *and* the right instructor (6:34–37), a person can "attain" Wisdom.[82] Sirach seems to place little trust in a person's ability to be self-taught (*pace* Qoheleth). His young charges must submit fully to the Lord's and by extension their teacher's discipline, and only then can they reap the benefits of their acquiescence. The final issue is agency: specifically, whether Ben Sira believes that the mindset of every individual (obedient vs. wicked) is predestined in the womb (1:14) or results from his or her specific life choices (i.e., the decision to adopt "fear of the Lord"). The sage ascribes ultimate control to God in determining human outcomes; it is divine mercy that guarantees the bestowal of Wisdom (e.g., παρὰ κυρίου in 1:1).[83] Yet at the same time individuals are responsible for their actions. The relationship between divine determinism and human initiative is critical for the sage, although he never fully resolves the tension (see below).

Even if a young pupil demonstrates compliance with Ben Sira's model, the acculturation process is a gradual one. As he articulates his understanding of מוסר/παιδεία, Ben Sira describes the incremental course of being "possessed" by Wisdom. Like Proverbs, this book stipulates a period of liminality before Wisdom can define a person's existence. One must submit to the "fear of the Lord," and then at a later point righteous behavior will become normative. In this process, the sage describes Wisdom's effect on a pupil in 4:17–18. MS A is missing the middle cola for v. 17, and G[1] uses the third-person feminine singular to refer to Wisdom. The speaker here is personified Wisdom:

---

[82] The famous בית מדרש reference (51:23) does not necessarily indicate an established school, but we can infer from this reference the possibility for pupils to avail themselves of a teacher's instruction to learn the tradition and to function as literate members of the society.

[83] Gabriele Boccaccini, *Middle Judaism: Jewish Thought, 300 B.C.E. to 200 C.E.* (Minneapolis: Fortress Press, 1991), 82, explains the fundamental difference between Qoheleth and Ben Sira on this point. For the earlier sage, חכמה is a human faculty, "the cognitive tool used to investigate reality." Qoheleth states that he applied his own "mind" (without referring to the deity) "to seek and to search out *by wisdom* all that is done under heaven" (1:13). For Ben Sira, Wisdom by definition derives from God. From the outset he states, "All wisdom is from the Lord, and with him it remains forever" (1:1). Ben Sira resembles his predecessor, however, in the lofty estimation of his own abilities. Through his perceived acumen and understanding of "fear of the Lord," he can penetrate the mysteries of God and reveal to humanity (i.e., his pupils) what they need to know. In this respect, the sage becomes a conduit for clarifying Wisdom and the will of God (e.g., 6:22–23).

> For at first I will walk with him in disguise and examine him with testing. She (Wisdom) will bring fear and dread upon him and test him with her discipline (G¹), until the point his heart trusts in me, when I will again direct him and reveal to him my secrets (4:17–18, translation mine).[84]

As our earlier discussion indicated, the book of Proverbs describes a similar progression, where the goal is to convert the "untutored" (פֶּתִי) person into a discerning, virtuous adult.[85] The presentation of the two "paths" in Proverbs 1–9 involves a series of "liminal transitions," as a pupil learns the benefits of virtuous behavior, and teachers seek to steer him from the temptations of youth. Similarly, Sirach highlights dangers and possibilities during the liminal stage. At times he uses maternal imagery (mixed with love poetry) rather than stern warnings: "She (Wisdom) will come to meet him (the addressee) like a mother.... He will lean on her and not fall, and he will rely on her and not be put to shame" (15:2a, 4). Ben Sira understands how difficult it can be to negotiate adolescence and early adulthood and wants to dissuade his pupils from recklessness and folly (cf. Prov 1:10–19). His caution on this point can be traced to a larger retributive principle: for those who reject the nurturing Wisdom figure, ruin is their inevitable destiny, even if it does not happen immediately. For the ones who demonstrate the proper willingness, "fear of the Lord" requires commitment and patience.

Ben Sira also depicts the plight of those who do not follow his advice, particularly the public reaction to an individual's waywardness. There is a marked anxiety in this instruction, as the sage warns about disgrace and its repercussions. In his efforts at instilling "fear of the Lord," he relies on a "shame" concept (בשׁת) to illustrate many of his negative images.[86] This author lists an array of occurrences that lead

---

[84] Argall, *1 Enoch and Sirach*, 59, argues that 4:11–19 is an erotically charged section and that ונליתי לו מסתרי in v. 18b reflects angelophany applied to a "Love Story." Here Wisdom meets the young charge and only reveals her true character after the lad has shown that he is worthy. Argall compares this unit in 4:11–19 to the acrostic poem in Sir 51:13–21.

[85] Skehan and Di Lella, *The Wisdom of Ben Sira*, 150, identify this "probationary suffering for the virtuous" with the Deuteronomic motif of God "testing" persons to determine whether they will obey "the commandments of the Lord" (e.g., Judg 2:22–3:6). The liminal process described in Proverbs and other instructions is the more likely antecedent/model for Sirach's descriptions of a "probationary" period of suffering and testing.

[86] This emphasis on shame is not something we find in earlier Egyptian or Israelite instructions. Collins, *Jewish Wisdom*, 34–35, attributes this feature to Sirach's adaptation of the category from Hellenistic culture (the honor-shame dichotomy). Based on

to disrepute, and he expresses concern over foolish decisions that steer a person from the right course and bring ruin upon him and his family (e.g., 4:20–6:4; 10:19–11:6; 41:14–42:14). In all of these illustrations, the primary concern is the public nature of any humiliation. For example, duplicity, whether in speech or action, leads to a bad reputation: "A liar's way leads to disgrace, and his shame is ever with him" (20:26). "Shame" for Sirach is the inverse of a good name: "*for a bad name incurs shame and reproach* (G); so it is with the double-tongued sinner (MS A)" (6:1). In a unit that reveals both paranoia and a patriarchal perspective, 42:9–14 describes the manifold dangers for a father in relation to his daughter and the specific actions that cause shame. In order to safeguard against acts that lead to disrepute, a pupil should be aware of social realities and the human tendency towards base desires (e.g., 18:30–31). This understanding of בשת does not lead to an endorsement of abstemious behavior, however. The sage's ethic is not puritanical, at least in relation to the male addressee.[87] Like Qoheleth, Sirach has a *carpe diem* mentality: "Give, and take, and indulge yourself, because in Hades one cannot look for luxury" (14:16). Sirach does warn that excess can be dangerous if it threatens a person's reputation (e.g., gluttony in the presence of a superior, adultery). Certain types of behavior threaten one's livelihood and possibilities for advancement. A person who can enjoy himself *and* live within the bounds of the tradition is not only acceptable, but this represents the sage's ideal pupil.

The balance for Ben Sira lies between enjoying life and cultivating a good reputation: a person's failure to attend to the latter has dire consequences. "Disgrace" (קלון/ἀτιμία) is by definition a public issue, even when the topic is a seemingly private matter like familial relations. In the example cited above, Sirach frets over how the father and his family will be perceived by the larger society if a daughter goes astray, since the impact of shame is irreparable (42:11). Sirach's ethical dualism is based on a good name-shame polarity ("a bad name incurs shame"), which is more complex than the "two-paths" language

---

the prominence of the concept in Greek writings, this is a reasonable inference. Yet the sage's own conservative outlook also plays a role in this level of anxiety. Claudia Camp, "Understanding a Patriarchy: Women in Second-Century Jerusalem through the Eyes of Ben Sira," in *'Women like This': New Perspectives on Jewish Women in the Greco-Roman World* (ed. A.J. Levine; Atlanta: Scholars Press, 1991), 1–39, outlines the concept in Ben Sira, with particular attention to the sage's views on women.

[87] His stance towards women, especially daughters, is a different matter altogether. See Camp, "Understanding a Patriarchy."

in the book of Proverbs. Some of the Hellenistic literature from this period includes an honor-shame dichotomy, and Ben Sira could have been familiar with this material.[88] Prior to the section on daughters, he offers a lengthy treatise on the topic of shame (41:14–42:8), where most examples relate to the loss of social standing. He cites his fierce opposition to deceitfulness, adultery, bad table manners, idle gossip, and fraudulent business practices, as well as the need to honor one's parents and discipline children. If his stipulations on such matters are not followed, permanent disrepute will be the result. Nowhere is Sirach's "ethic of caution" more apparent than in these discussions about shameful acts, since a pupil's reputation is his only chance at immortality.[89] By avoiding disgraceful behavior and exhibiting proper decorum, a person can achieve a level of refinement and popular support among his peers: "Then you will show your sound training, and will be approved by all" (42:8). In this sense, Sirach's ethics are eudaemonistic. If the addressee can no longer rely on his good name, this will lead to the loss of tangible benefits.

### 6. *Determinism, Free Will, and Theodicy*

As Ben Sira outlines how to develop "fear of the Lord" and avoid shameful acts, he does not fully clarify a person's ability to submit voluntarily to the content of his teachings. The book never explains whether this model and any resultant success are a possibility for all interested pupils. Sirach does not reconcile statements about Wisdom being created "with the faithful in the womb" (1:14), or some humans being cursed by God from the beginning (33:12), with contrary assertions about the ability to control one's destiny through discipline. Declarations like 1:14 suggest a divine decision to imbue a specific group with the correct mindset, such that everything is predetermined, and the wicked have no chance of success. We find a similar mentality in the Dead Sea Scrolls,

---

[88] The references to "honor" are part of this dynamic: "One who is wise among his people will inherit honor (כבוד/τιμή), and his name will live forever" (Sir 37:26). On the honor-shame relationship in the Greek sources, see Halvor Moxnes, "Honor and Shame," *BTB* 23 (1993): 167–76.

[89] Ben Sira also acknowledges "proper shame," which involves humility and the avoidance of loathsome behavior. For example, "Be ashamed of repeating what you hear, and of betraying secrets. Then you will show proper shame, and will find favor with everyone" (42:1).

although the determinism is more fully developed in such eschatological passages as the Treatise on the Two Spirits.[90] Ben Sira's understanding cannot be so thoroughly predestinarian, since he encourages all of his pupils to submit to Wisdom's yoke for their own benefit (6:30). One of the defining characteristics of didactic literature is the power of human initiative to avoid wrongdoing and thereby achieve positive results, and Sirach is no exception. The sage echoes Deut 30:19 with the statement, "If you choose, you can keep the commandments..." (Sir 15:15). In the same unit (15:11–20), he addresses responsibility for sin: "Do not say 'It was the Lord's doing that I fell away'; for he does not do what he hates" (v. 11). Throughout his instruction, this author cites the power of righteous intentions: a pupil can keep his base desires in check *if* he adopts the "fear of the Lord." Ben Sira maintains, or at least wants his readers to believe, that character is destiny. Nevertheless, there are other passages that underscore the omnipotence of God. These units suggest a tighter divine rein over human choice.

In Ben Sira's defense of the wisdom tradition, this dialectic is an important one, as he makes a more complex assessment of free will and determinism than his sapiential predecessors in ancient Israel. The diverse yet contentious statements in this text seem to reflect a discussion among the author's contemporaries about divine agency, the origin of sin, and human mortality. As he considers these issues, Sirach utilizes the early chapters of Genesis and his own reasoning to promote the belief in a transcendent deity *and* the efficacy of righteous behavior. Aspects of Sirach's style confirm a reevaluation and a debate, especially the repeated use of the negative imperative ("do not say"/אל־תאמר).[91] Although more expansive citations of his opponents' perspectives would provide a useful contrast, his swift dismissals are characteristic of Wisdom discourse from this and other periods.[92] In some cases, he seems

---

[90] For example, "Before they (humans) existed, he (God) established their glorious design. And when they have come into being, at their appointed time, they will execute all their works according to his glorious design, without altering anything" (1QS 3:15–16). Translation is from Florentino García Martínez and Eibert J.C. Tigchelaar, *The Dead Sea Scrolls Study Edition* (2 vols.; Leiden: Brill, 1997–98).

[91] The negative formula (*m dd*) is also a common feature of Egyptian instructions, particularly Amenemope and Anii, although it occurs less frequently in the Israelite book of Proverbs.

[92] James Crenshaw, *Defending God: Biblical Responses to the Problem of Evil* (New York: Oxford University Press, 2005), 100, argues that the "do not say" formula and Ben Sira's use of it "gives voice to heterodox opinions while simultaneously asserting their inadequacy. This particular rhetorical device occurs most often in contexts of theodicy,

to take on those with otherworldly belief systems directly, particularly in relation to sin, accountability, and the nature of Wisdom. Among his opponents on these points were those responsible for what existed of the Enochic books (see below). We can glean from Sirach's style an adherence to Israel's wisdom tradition and a fervent opposition to suggestions being propagated by other sages and groups, all in an effort to promote a consistent act-consequence relationship.

When examining his exposition of this topic, it should be remembered that absolute uniformity is never a stated goal. Ben Sira seeks to pass on the wisdom tradition in a relevant and engaging manner, and systematic theology does not seem to be his aim. When he offers a doctrinal pronouncement in one of the more lofty passages, especially one of the hymns, this statement might contradict or at least undermine a proposition made elsewhere in the book. Apparent discrepancies often relate to context: like the Egyptian instructions and Proverbs, Sirach fluctuates between the poles of divine omnipotence and human freedom to suit the particularities of each rhetorical moment. The reader must always consider the point being made in a specific passage, because like most Wisdom writers, Ben Sira tailors his argumentation accordingly.[93] Throughout the book, he tries out different solutions to vexing theological issues and does not attempt to systematize or even revisit many proposals (e.g., 33:7–15 and the opposites in creation). This is an instructional document that seeks to pass on an established tradition, rather than develop a new philosophical approach. Moreover, Ben Sira presents his exhortations on the other side of Job and Qoheleth *and* during a period in which apocalyptic ideas and speculative philosophy had become part of sapiential discourse. For an author who wished to address all of these competing schools of thought, from doubts about the tradition to otherworldly understandings of retribution, it should not be surprising that his discussion has an apologetic tone or that some of his conclusions are contradictory. As the wisdom tradition evolved during the Second Temple period, it became increasingly difficult for anyone to defend the adequate justice of God without the possibility of eternal existence in some sort of heavenly state.

---

which must have been a popular topic in his day." Crenshaw's argument finds support in other units using אל־תאמר to address theodicy: 5:1–8; 11:21–22; 16:16. See Pancratius Beentjes, "Theodicy in the Wisdom of Ben Sira," in *Theodicy in the World of the Bible* (ed. A. Laato, and J.C. de Moor; Leiden: Brill, 2003), 514.

[93] Collins, *Jewish Wisdom*, 83.

Although it would be inaccurate to call Sirach the first Wisdom writer to affirm both an omnipotent deity and individual autonomy, his efforts at negotiating this relationship lead to some creative theological suggestions. Scholars have devoted considerable attention to Sirach's perspective on this issue and the complexity and/or inconsistency of his thought.[94] On one side is the belief in human "inclination" (יצר) or "free choice" (NRSV). In one of the earliest known allusions to the biblical account of Adam, Ben Sira declares that God created the first human (האדם) at the beginning and left him ביד יצרו (15:14).[95] Despite its negative connotation in certain biblical passages (e.g., the "evil inclination" in Gen 6:5; 8:21), יצר for Ben Sira seems to designate an individual's natural disposition.[96] This neutral understanding of the term echoes Deut 30:15–20, although יצר in Sir 15:11–20 has a more universal connotation than the covenantal language of Moses' speech.[97] For Ben Sira יצר denotes each person's ability to make the right choices, or at least avoid the wrong ones.

Yet complete autonomy is not granted in this passage or elsewhere in the book: we might translate ביד יצרו in v. 14 with "in the power of their temperament" rather than "free choice" (NRSV): "It was he who created human kind at the beginning, and he left them in the power of their temperament" (translation mine). In his presentation,

---

[94] Jean Hadot, *Penchant Mauvais et Volonté Libre dans La Sagesse de Ben Sira (L'Ecclésiastique)* (Brussels: University Press, 1970); Gerhard Maier, *Mensch und Freier Wille* (WUNT 12; Tübingen: Mohr, 1971), 24–116; Gian Luigi Prato, *Il Problema della Teodicea in Ben Sira* (AnBib 65; Rome: Pontifical Biblical Institute, 1975); Crenshaw, "The Problem of Theodicy in Sirach," 47–64; Collins, *Jewish Wisdom*, 81–96; James K. Aitken, "Divine Will and Providence," in *Ben Sira's God: Proceedings of the International Ben Sira Conference, Durham-Ushaw College 2001* (ed. R. Egger-Wenzel; BZAW 321; Berlin: de Gruyter, 2002), 282–301; Beentjes, "Theodicy in the Wisdom of Ben Sira," 509–25.

[95] Along with most commentators, we take חותפו ("his snatcher") in MS A to be a later insertion. There is no place in the sage's thought for a demonic spoiler figure. On the demythologizing tendencies throughout the book, see Boccaccini, *Middle Judaism*, 105. With regard to the earliest readings of the fall story, see John J. Collins, "Before the Fall: The Earliest Interpretations of Adam and Eve," in *The Idea of Biblical Interpretation: Essays in Honor of James L. Kugel* (ed. H. Najman and J.H. Newman; JSJSup 83; Leiden: Brill, 2004), 296, who argues that the Book of the Watchers in *1 Enoch* is probably earlier than this passage in Ben Sira, although the Enochic text does not engage as directly with the Adam and Eve narrative (see below).

[96] Collins, *Jewish Wisdom*, 82. Hadot, *Penchant Mauvais et Volonté Libre*, 13, warns against associating the developed rabbinic understanding of יצר too closely with an instruction that is much earlier and less sophisticated on this point.

[97] Beentjes, "Theodicy in the Wisdom of Ben Sira," 514: "Whereas Moses' speech is presented with a kind of historical context, i.e. Israel entering the land, similar vocabulary has been used by Ben Sira to describe a general anthropological situation."

Sirach reserves a space for God to shape earthly events, and so "free choice" is not entirely accurate. This is not so much a doctrine of free will in chapter 15 as an effort to emphasize responsibility for every action (the sage uses חפץ in vv. 15, 16, 17) and to absolve the deity from any role in causing a person to falter (v. 20). Like the complex heart expressions in earlier Egyptian instructions, Sirach emphasizes human culpability in straying from the proper path.[98] A person must take responsibility for his or her actions, even as the deity retains the power to intervene and shape individual inclinations. We have cited a verse from this section that clarifies Ben Sira's treatment of the issue: "Do not say 'It was the Lord's doing that I fell away,' for he does not do what he hates" (Sir 15:11). Along with death and the possibility of immortality, sin and human accountability had become controversial topics, especially in light of apocalyptic thought patterns involving an "appointed time" for retribution and the transferal of responsibility to external agents.

Additional passages note the gift of discernment by God and the resultant human capacity to avert wrongdoing. The clearest statement on this point occurs in Sirach 17:

> Discretion and tongue and eyes, ears and a mind for thinking he gave them. He filled them with knowledge and understanding, and showed them good and evil (17:6–7).

Ben Sira reads Genesis 1–3 from a sapiential perspective here, so that the ability to distinguish good and evil is an essential and God-given attribute. Moral discernment is a positive gift rather than a forbidden fruit (raising the question of whether the original narrative in Genesis 2–3 has an anti-Wisdom bias). There is no mention of the fall of humanity in Ben Sira, and mortality is part of the original plan ("He gave them a fixed number of days," 17:2), rather than a punishment for disobedience. The capacity for wrongdoing does not stem from any primordial sin. An objection could be raised based on the language of

---

[98] Expressions such as *šms-jb* and *ḥrp-jb* are useful corollaries for Sirach's understanding. The person described with *ḥrp-jb* has skill at making the right decisions, particularly in a stressful situation (e.g., Ptahhotep 60–61). With regard to *šms-jb*, we mentioned the idea of following one's conscience in Ptahhotep 186–193. In Ptahhotep, a person with a receptive heart is able to "hear" God and prosper. In a similar fashion, Ben Sira maintains that the individual whose temperament leads to prudent decision-making can internalize "fear of the Lord" and thereby attain success.

Sir 25:24 and the reference to Eve: "From a woman sin had its beginning, and because of her we all die." Like many commentators, we take this allusion to be a later insertion. The verse is consistent with Sirach's sexist attitude throughout the book, but the original sage understands death to be an intrinsic feature of the divine plan for humanity.[99] Based on this and other references, we can assume an effort during this period to interpret the Genesis account of Adam and Eve's encounter with the snake and subsequent "fall" from an immortal state.[100] Ben Sira offers a creative interpretation of Genesis 2–3 by omitting critical details (such as the fall!) and emphasizing human responsibility. This is part of an attempt to align these creation stories more closely with assumptions characteristic of the wisdom tradition.

If certain passages emphasize human initiative, particularly in 15:11–17:24, Ben Sira also uses deterministic language, including his discussion of binary opposites (33:7–15; ch. 36 in G). The sage wrestles with the existence of evil and the omnipotence of God, and his firm belief in the latter forces him to trace all created elements back to their divine source. He states, "Good things and bad, life and death, poverty and wealth, come from the Lord" (11:14). We find a similar understanding in 33:7–15, the famous presentation of the pairs. In assessing the full range of events in the cosmos and how they relate to divine initiative, Ben Sira describes a series of contrasts, including two classes of human beings:

> In the fullness of his knowledge the Lord distinguished them and appointed their different ways. Some he blessed and exalted, and some he made holy and brought near to himself; but some he cursed and brought low, and turned them out of their place (33:11–12).

Ben Sira uses priestly terms here (cf. Num 16:5–7) and alludes to the banishment of the Canaanites (cf. Exod 33:1–3) in order to provide a cosmological principle of symbiotic pairs. The description in 33:7–15 functions both as an affirmation of God's power and an answer to the theodicy question. Human destiny and indeed the whole of creation lie "in the hands of the potter (היוצר), to be molded as he pleases (כרצון)" (Sir 33:13), and everything comes in necessary opposites. The influence

---

[99] Laying the responsibility for sin and death on Eve does not cohere with Sirach's theological framework. See Collins, "Before the Fall," 296–97.

[100] Collins, "Before the Fall," 293–308, surveys the earliest known references to this story, beginning with Sirach 17.

of Stoic ideas is probable here, as evidenced by similar language in a passage attributed to Chrysippus.[101] In both the Greek text and in Ben Sira, evil is needed as a counterbalance to good, and the one helps define and clarify the nature of the other. Since a duality in creation is apparently part of the original plan, this presentation in Sir 11:14 and 33:7–15 would seem to weaken the force of chapter 15 and other passages about individual autonomy.[102] Yet these "pairs" do not appear to be external, independent agents in Ben Sira. When the totality of the book is examined, the sage's dualism is slight.[103]

In support of this interpretation are the monistic statements in 39:12–35. In this hymn of praise, the sage declares, "No one can say, 'What is this?' or 'Why is that?'—for at the appointed time all such questions will be answered" (v. 17). Later in this unit, Ben Sira addresses theodicy directly: "From the beginning good things were created for the good, but for sinners good things and bad" (v. 25). According to this hymn, there is nothing left to chance in the universe, and every created component has a role to play, from salt to clothing (v. 26). Even vicious and seemingly arbitrary elements such as natural disasters reflect the intentionality of God, since these aspects of creation can inflict punishment upon the wicked (v. 29) and therefore serve a useful purpose. For Sirach, "Evil, which for humankind is a concrete and tangible reality, in relation to God immediately loses all consistency; everything is good because it obeys God's project…"[104] According to the promises in 39:12–35, the righteous need not fear unwarranted tragedy (v. 27). Judgments or mere occurrences in life will ultimately mean fair recompense, even if the meaning of an event is unclear at the time. In his hodgepodge of examples, Ben Sira declares that "these

---

[101] Chrysippus is quoted with the following (from Book 4 of his treatise *On Providence*): "There is absolutely nothing more foolish than those who think that there could have been goods without the coexistence of evils. For since goods are opposite to evils, the two must necessarily exist in opposition to each other and supported by a kind of opposed interdependence…. For how could there be perception of justice if there were no injustices?" This is from Gellius, *Noctes Atticae* 7.1.2–4, *SVF* 2.1169, cited in Collins, *Jewish Wisdom*, 85.

[102] Scholars often compare this passage to the deterministic understanding found in the Treatise on the Two Spirits from the Community Rule (esp. 1QS 3:15–16). Maier, *Mensch und freier Wille*, 111, argues that "das dualistische Auseinandertreten von Gerechten und Sündern ist ein Schritt zu radikalerer Fassung der Sünde als des grundsätzlich Gottfeindlichen."

[103] Goering, *To Whom Has Wisdom's Root Been Revealed*, 59–68, provides a nuanced assessment of this passage and its relationship to biblical antecedents.

[104] Boccaccini, *Middle Judaism*, 108–9.

things," which presumably include the many different elements in the universe, "were created for judgment/punishment (לְמִשְׁפָּט)" (v. 29).[105] This type of monistic framework weakens the force of 33:7–15 and the apparent duality in creation. In addition, Sir 39:12–35 implies a different understanding than chapters 15 and 17 in terms of a person's ability to determine the course of events in his or her life.[106] Context is once again relevant: in chapter 39 the sage wants to account for apparent injustice in the natural world and in the human realm, while in the earlier statements he is emphasizing personal responsibility.

When examining these various passages, it is obvious that theodicy and retribution are difficult topics for Ben Sira, as he attempts to affirm both divine control over the cosmos and the benefits of human initiative. Some modern readings of Sir 39:12–35 suggest that this is solely a hymn of praise and not a simultaneous attempt to account for evil.[107] This interpretation does not give due attention to the sage's theological struggles in this passage, however, and his distortion of human experience in order to defend divine justice. Sirach makes the ridiculous assertion that salt turns bad for the wicked and the patently false claim that natural disasters specifically punish sinners (39:29). The basis for such statements is the belief that everything occurs according

---

[105] The text for 39:29 can be reconstructed (based on the Masada fragments) to include נבר[ראו.

[106] Jan Liesen, *Full of Praise: An Exegetical Study of Sir 39, 12–35* (JSJSupp 64; Leiden: Brill, 2000), 258–59, interprets this section in light of Sirach 15 and 17. According to Liesen, the use of מראש ("from the beginning") in 39:25 is consequential, because it looks back to the initial gift of discernment (17:6) at creation: "When Ben Sira states that the distribution of good and evil is not arbitrary but corresponds 'from the beginning' to the moral quality of people, he seems to refer to the creational endowment with the power to choose and the fact that 'whatever a man chooses will be given to him' (15,17ᵇ)" (p. 259).

[107] Liesen, *Full of Praise*, 264, argues that the phrase, "on the day of reckoning (בעת עברה/ἐν καιρῷ συντελείας)," in 39:29c is critical for understanding this passage. According to Liesen, this description of catastrophes *symbolizes* personal retribution for sinners, which might not come until the end of their life (p. 272). Since they are personified as God's agents elsewhere in the book (e.g., 43:13–17b), Liesen claims that natural disasters have the same symbolic function in this passage. Yet even if there is an implicit understanding of pain for the wicked commensurate with the calamities listed in chapter 39, these items are not merely symbolic. Ben Sira seems to be suggesting the actual occurrence of unfortunate events during every individual's lifetime. Bad things are kept in a "storehouse" for punishment (39:30d), and events will unfold according to the plan of the Creator. Although the sage never explains how these aspects of creation will inflict the wicked with greater frequency, this *is* an attempt to address theodicy.

to the rhythms of an inscrutable but purposeful deity.[108] In this respect, the book resembles Qoheleth: "He has made everything suitable for its time... yet they (human beings) cannot find out what God has done from the beginning to the end" (Qoh 3:11). Sirach differs, however, in that he wants to defend the act-consequence relationship against an array of alternative proposals, including Qoheleth's. Ben Sira insists on an appropriate moment for every event under the sun, just as Qoheleth does, but he goes one step further in promising an appropriate outcome for all persons.[109] The righteous might have to endure things that are unfair, but this will only be temporary, and sinners will eventually receive punishment. In a later passage, Ben Sira declares "To all creatures, human and animal, but to sinners seven times more, come death and bloodshed and strife and sword, calamities and famine and ruin and plague" (40:8–9).

On this last point, Qoheleth and Ben Sira part ways. The latter sage is more nuanced in chapter 40 than in 39:12–35 and the so-called "doctrine of the pairs" (where he seems reluctant to admit that anything bad can happen to the righteous), although he never clarifies in either passage precisely how such proportional punishment occurs. Death can only come once to a person, and the sage's own life experiences surely demonstrated to him the arbitrary nature of the other phenomena he lists. Yet one could argue that Sir 40:8–9 ultimately represents a plea to his students rather than an infallible principle. In other words, the sage's purpose is more pedagogical than theological. Ben Sira wants to hold individuals accountable and instill the "fear of the Lord," and absolute consistency is not a primary concern. Beentjes astutely explains that when one examines Sir 40:1–17 in detail, "it gradually becomes clear that it is not Ben Sira's main intention to describe the basic qualities of human life, but to sketch a series of sanctions by which the wicked could be called to order."[110]

---

[108] The suggestion of Stoic influence is a possibility here, since this philosophical system taught the intentionality of the created order. See Collins, *Jewish Wisdom*, 86.

[109] Gerhard von Rad, *Wisdom in Israel* (trans. J.D. Martin; London/Harrisburg, Pa.: SCM Press Ltd./Trinity Press International, 1972), 253.

[110] Beentjes, "Theodicy in the Wisdom of Ben Sira," 520. Certain statements in Sirach illustrate the point. For example, "All bribery and injustice will be blotted out, but good faith will last forever" (40:12, which is missing from MS B, but a few letters have been found in the Masada fragments). Here and elsewhere, the goal is a reliable principle of justice, where the wicked will be called to account in the earthly sphere.

## 7. *Ben Sira and* 1 Enoch

Ben Sira also dwells on these major theological topics so that he can respond to and in some cases dismiss alternative suggestions. Among Sirach's contemporaries during the early portion of the second-century were those responsible for what existed of the Enochic books. When the content of Ben Sira and *1 Enoch* is examined, the parallel consideration of key issues is striking, particularly in relation to sin and the appropriate language for sapiential discourse.[111] In the opening section of *1 Enoch*, the Book of the Watchers (chapters 1–36), the spread of evil in the world is traced to the fallen angels. Based on the tradition also found in Gen 6:1–7 concerning the "sons of God" who descend from heaven and procreate with earthly women, *1 Enoch* describes a rebellion led by the figures Asael and Shemihazah.[112] Unlike the pericope in Genesis, which contains no explicit moral judgment against these heavenly figures, this text understands the Watchers' descent to be a negative event.[113] In *1 Enoch*, the "sons of God" produce offspring whose violent tendencies lead directly to the flood. They make weapons available to the populace and spread harmful knowledge, including forbidden secrets.[114] In an expansion of the initial story (*1 Enoch* 12–16), the Watchers' sexual acts with earthly women cause evil spirits to go forth from their descendants, which in turn threatens the earthly situation: "But now the giants who were begotten by the spirits and flesh—they will call them evil spirits

---

[111] Argall's systematic study (*1 Enoch and Sirach*) has demonstrated the significance of the parallels and the need for close comparative work with these two texts.

[112] The "Nephilim," or "warriors of renown" (Gen 6:4) are the product of these sexual unions.

[113] One could argue that the flood story in Genesis 6 contains an implicit judgment against the Nephilim and their negative influence, since the description of these giants is immediately followed by the declaration that "the wickedness of humankind was great in the earth" (v. 5).

[114] The traditions involving Asael and Shemihazah are a composite account in the Book of the Watchers, as many commentators have noted. In the Shemihazah strand, the main issue is sexual activity with earthly women. This rebellious act transgresses the heavenly boundary that the angels should have observed. The result is violence in the human realm, and as Nickelsburg, *1 Enoch*, 46, explains, "The ontological consequence of this bloodshed is the earth's transformation into a state of impurity that is in need of ritual cleansing (10:20–22)." With regard to the Asael myth, the Watchers reveal privileged secrets that should not leave the heavenly world, such as metallurgy (for jewelry and instruments of war) and other forms of forbidden knowledge (7:1; 8:1–3; 9:6).

on the earth, for their dwelling will be on the earth" (*1 En.* 15:8).[115] As
a result of their encamping in the human realm, the spirits become the
cause of much wrongdoing (15:11–12). With the descriptions of their
egregious influence in *1 Enoch*, the activities of the angelic figures seem
to be paradigmatic. As Collins explains, "In this way the revolt of the
Watchers becomes the ultimate cause of the existence of evil spirits
and, by implication, of human sin."[116] Significantly, there is no statement in the Book of the Watchers about the *total* absence of sin prior
to this chain of calamitous events. Nevertheless a peaceful world has
been tragically defiled as a result of the Watchers' treachery: the revolt
represents a coarsening of the earthly realm. According to Nickelsburg,
"Primordial rebellion is the cause of present evils: occult knowledge,
bloodshed, and sexual misconduct."[117]

The extent to which Ben Sira tailors his presentation of sin and retribution as a response to the mythic accounts in *1 Enoch* is the pressing
question here. While our sage does not give credence to the explanation for evil in the Book of the Watchers by directly refuting it, there
are several indicators that Ben Sira knew these Enochic traditions. We
mentioned the passage in Sirach 15 and the careful refusal to accept the
outsourcing of responsibility for evil/sin to any external force, especially
God. Even if *1 Enoch* 1–36 does not implicate God, it places the blame
for sin in the heavenly realm, on the shoulders of the rebellious angels.
We can speculate that the target for Sir 15:11 ("Do not say 'It was the
Lord's doing that I fell away'") includes this mythic tradition of the
Watchers and Sirach's rejection of it. Whereas human transgression
is linked directly with Asael in *1 En.* 10:8 ("And over him write all the
sins"), Ben Sira associates responsibility for waywardness with each
individual and the choices he or she makes; this author has no place
for a demonic spoiler figure.[118] He does refer to the "host of the height

---

[115] Nickelsburg, *1 Enoch*, 41, explains the nature of the Watchers' rebellion: "the sin
of the watchers consisted in their violation of the absolute distinction between spirit
and flesh and their defilement of their holiness."

[116] John J. Collins, "The Origin of Evil in Apocalyptic Literature," in *Seers, Sibyls
and Sages in Hellenistic-Roman Judaism* (Leiden: Brill, 1997), 290; originally published in
*Congress Volume: Paris* (ed. J.A. Emerton; Leiden: Brill, 1995), 25–38.

[117] George W.E. Nickelsburg, *Jewish Literature between the Bible and the Mishnah* (2d ed.;
Minneapolis: Fortress Press, 2005), 49.

[118] In *1 En* 8:1–2, Asael stirs up the populace through a variety of destructive tactics.
Nickelsburg, *1 Enoch*, 222, understands the command in 10:8 to signify either a tomb
epitaph or a "bill of indictment" that can be used at the final judgment to hold this
figure accountable for his atrocities.

of heaven" being under the divine power (Sir 17:32) and therefore accountable to God (cf. *1 En.* 18:14). Argall explains the relationship between the two realms in Sirach as follows: "both luminaries/angels and humankind are given commands and prohibitions and possess the freedom to do good or evil."[119] There is, however, no mention of angelic behavior as the source or even a major contributor to human sinfulness in Sirach. In fact, Ben Sira demonstrates little interest in the angelic realm, and he remains fiercely opposed to knowledge sprung from dreams and visionary accounts. He finds the language of heavenly mysteries to be suspect and dangerous to the more traditional pursuit of Wisdom (see below).

References to the giants in Sir 16:5–14 and to the figure of Enoch in 44:16 and 49:14 are additional indicators of Sirach's engagement with these traditions; he has an awareness of and some appreciation for Enochic lore.[120] He cites the account of Enoch being "taken up" by God (Sir 44:16; 49:14). The fact that this figure serves as אות דעת לדור ודור ("a sign for the knowledge of future generations," MS B) points to Ben Sirach's acknowledgement of these stories and their popularity. When referring to the revolt of the Watchers that is so pivotal in *1 Enoch*, Sirach also cites the rebellion in a lengthy list of sins (16:5–14), so that the episode loses uniqueness as an explanation for evil: "He did not forgive the ancient giants (לא נשא לנסיכי קדם) who revolted in their might" (v. 7).[121] When examining the content of this verse, it is apparent that Sirach knows the story about the Watchers' petitions for forgiveness, which is described in *1 Enoch*: "And they asked that I write a memorandum of petition for them, that they might have forgiveness," (13:4). This plea is subsequently rejected by God (*1 En* 14:6–7). Two aspects of Sirach's allusion to this story are pertinent to our discussion. First, the sage affirms once again a consistent principle of retribution, such that no element in the creation can escape divine justice, and everything has a role to play. Second, the Watchers' revolt is a self-contained event

[119] Argall, *1 Enoch and Sirach*, 137–38.

[120] Argall, *1 Enoch and Sirach*, 230–31.

[121] Argall, *1 Enoch and Sirach*, 159, sees Sir 16:7 as a projection of evil into the heavens, which does imply a place for angels in the sage's formulations (cf. *1 En.* 17:3; 18:16; 23:4; 33:3; 36:3). According to Argall, this passage in Sirach 16 emphasizes divine justice and the need for all creatures in heaven and on earth to submit to it. In addition, Argall (p. 230) counters the assertion of Skehan and Di Lella, *The Wisdom of Ben Sira*, 270, who have claimed that the absence of the biblical term (נפלים) functions as a "conscious avoidance of the mythological overtones to the Genesis narrative."

summarily dealt with by God in a just and isolated manner; it has no bearing on the disposition of individual persons, who are each evaluated according to their deeds. In this sense, we can infer a critique in Sirach against interpreting the mythic account as anything more than a passing example of God's activity against rebellious creatures, especially since it comes in a litany of events (16:6–14). Understandings of the revolt like the one in the Book of the Watchers deflect human responsibility onto an external agent, and this move has the potential to undermine a "rational theodicy" (Hengel), which is a fundamental goal for Ben Sira. Boccaccini claims that Ben Sira is like the apocalyptic texts because of his belief that evil is fed by human nature, but he differs "when he denies iniquity as an ontological given."[122] For this sage, all elements in the created order should be alert to the possibility of imminent divine judgment and act accordingly.[123] If God held recalcitrant angels accountable for their insolence, Ben Sira warns his audience that they can expect nothing less.

The Epistle of Enoch also takes issue with the understanding of sin in the Book of the Watchers and responds in a manner that is similar to Ben Sira. In contrast to the earlier account in *1 Enoch*, the Epistle places the blame for sin on humanity: "Thus lawlessness was not sent upon the earth; but men created it by themselves, and those who do it will come to a great curse" (*1 En.* 98:4).[124] The commonality between this language and what appears in the "free will" passages in Ben Sira is noteworthy, particularly Sir 15:11–17:24. Both texts support a consistent act-consequence relationship and the need for human accountability under an omniscient deity.[125] There are also later allusions to the revolt. The reference in 2 Pet 2:4 is interesting, because it resembles

---

[122] Boccaccini, *Middle Judaism*, 105.

[123] No one can act with impunity in Ben Sira, and no act goes unnoticed. Referring to adultery, the Creator's awareness of it, and the individual's inability to hide such an action, the sage declares the following about an adulterer: "His fear is confined to human eyes and he does not realize that the eyes of the Lord are ten thousand times brighter than the sun; they look upon every aspect of human behavior and see into hidden corners. Before the universe was created, it was known to him, and so it is since its completion" (23:19–20).

[124] For the textual problems in this verse, see Nickelsburg, *1 Enoch*, 470.

[125] Nickelsburg, *1 Enoch*, 476–77, takes up the possible targets for these remarks in *1 Enoch* and the remarkable thematic parallels between *1 En.* 98:4–8 and Sir 15:11–17:24. He notes that both passages evince an anti-deterministic polemic, but "this language is subordinate to the overarching interest in human responsibility before the bar of divine justice" (p. 477). Ben Sira wants to affirm the positive outcome of good behavior under a just deity and the dangers of ignoring his advice.

Ben Sira's litany of sinful events in chapter 16, including the order.[126] Such passages highlight human responsibility for sin. This emphasis on individual responsibility is especially important for an author like Ben Sira, who does not like to speculate about the heavenly realm. All of these references suggest a reassessment of major issues like human accountability and divine justice, as new ideas about death and the afterlife, the heavenly realm, and theodicy circulated among Jewish authors of this period.

Ben Sira and *1 Enoch* have additional parallels in terms of sin, judgment, and human accountability, but there are also critical differences. With regard to the similarities, both books discuss a revealed knowledge (through the respective agents of Enoch and personified Wisdom) that can clarify the majesty of God and the nature of divine judgment. The figures of Enoch and Wisdom traverse the universe and enjoy special access to the mysteries of creation (e.g., Sir 24:4–6), although Lady Wisdom does not reveal her secrets in the same manner as Enoch (e.g., *1 Enoch* 32).[127] The descriptions in both texts emphasize the power of God, who controls the hosts of heaven and all of humanity (Sir 42:15–21; cf. *1 Enoch* 14). In an effort to defend the fairness of God, Ben Sira and *1 Enoch* leave open the possibility of swift action by the deity to rectify imbalances in the earthly realm (Sir 5:7; 11:21; *1 En.* 97:10).[128] These two texts diverge, however, in describing when and how justice will be administered. For Ben Sira, Sheol is the ultimate destination of all living beings, and there can be no eternal blessing for any individual, regardless of his or her character. This sage has no eschatological expectation of any sort: retribution must occur in the earthly realm, even at the end of life, when both sinners and righteous

---

[126] 2 Pet 2:4 mentions the angelic revolt: "For if God did not spare the angels when they sinned, but cast them into hell and committed them to chains of deepest darkness to be kept until the judgment." This is followed by a reference to an upstanding Lot and his unrighteous neighbors (vv. 6–7). These verses follow the same order and content as Sir 16:7–8. Jude 1:6–7 has an inverted order, but also contains a reference to both the Watchers ("who left their proper dwelling" and now "lie in eternal chains") and the depravity of Sodom and Gomorrah. All of these lists, of which Sirach is one of the earliest examples, involve a litany of sinful events from Israel's past. These events are usually components of a larger statement on divine judgment. The primordial revolt of the Watchers and the Sodom episode remained important elements in the list.

[127] In Ben Sira, the sage dispenses the necessary knowledge to the addressee, the "hidden things," or "roots" of Wisdom (1:6; 42:19). The meaning of proverbs and parables should be uncovered to instill "fear of the Lord" and avoid harsh judgment from God. See Argall, *1 Enoch and Sirach*, 71, 163.

[128] Argall, *1 Enoch and Sirach*, 244.

persons will be dealt with according to their deeds. The only thing that can transcend earthly existence is the reputation of righteous individuals. Since we do not maintain that Sir 36:1–22 is original to the sage, the hope in these verses for national deliverance and an "appointed time" for future restoration almost certainly derives from a later source.

As for *1 Enoch*, a delay in retribution is frequently promoted, an eschatological expectation that is utterly foreign to Ben Sira's framework. The idea of a final judgment is the most consequential aspect of this worldview, with the promise of eternal punishment for the wicked and immortality for the righteous soul in *1 Enoch* (104:2). Many sections in the corpus also look towards the renewal of the creation following the great judgment.[129] Argall explains that Ben Sira's students knew traditions involving the "catastrophic consequences of final judgment," and the sage wants to convince his pupils that such beliefs are at odds with his understanding of the universe.[130] Ben Sira cannot accept many of the assumptions found in this rival corpus. As an illustration, Argall notes the literary device of a Disputation Speech in both texts. A presumed opponent claims that sinners might escape judgment for their actions (Sir 5:4; *1 En.* 103:6).[131] The different responses in Ben Sira and *1 Enoch* relate to the chronological point in which justice will be mediated. For Ben Sira, everything must occur within the course of each individual's life, while Enoch can promise judgment at the end of days. A promised reversal can give the righteous hope if they remain faithful to God and avoid contact with sinners, who face terrible punishment (*1 En* 96:4; 99:10).[132] In accounting for this distinction, the social location of Ben Sira and his pupils has at least something to do with the focus on present possibilities for joy. His students had much to gain by affirming the probability of justice in their immediate context. Prosperity and success were within their reach, and this is why the sage addresses such topics as table manners and respect for social hierarchies. In contrast, the addressees of *1 Enoch* might have needed the promise of their elect status to compensate for a more peripheral

---

[129] Grant Macaskill, *Revealed Wisdom and Inaugurated Eschatology in Ancient Judaism and Early Christianity* (JSJSup 115; Leiden: Brill, 2007), 30–71, provides a useful analysis of the eschatological elements in the Enochic corpus.

[130] Argall, *1 Enoch and Sirach*, 241. For a representative passage, see *1 Enoch* 100.

[131] Argall, *1 Enoch and Sirach*, 242–243.

[132] Macaskill, *Revealed Wisdom and Inaugurated Eschatology*, 55, notes the parenetic function of the eschatological language in passages like the beatitude of *1 En* 99:10.

and uncertain role in the society.[133] The same situation seems to confront the audience for 4QInstruction.[134]

Much of the tension between these two texts can be traced to questions about the appropriate source for Wisdom. Speculation about the heavenly realm and visionary descriptions are dangerous for Ben Sira, who posits a traditional belief in "fear of the Lord," which is reached by rigorous study and discipline (38:24–39:11). The Torah becomes an important component in this pursuit (see below), whereas the Enochic texts do not have the same explicit allegiance.[135] Sirach rejects an interest in dreams and the interpretive possibilities they provide. In warning against this type of practice, the sage declares, "The senseless have vain and false hopes, and dreams give wings to fools. As one who catches at a shadow and pursues the wind, so is anyone who believes in dreams" (34:1–2). While Sirach's opposition is in the spirit of language found in Deuteronomy and Jeremiah (e.g., Deut 13:2–6), he also seems to be targeting actual opponents who placed faith in the content of dreams.[136] As Wright explains, a standard polemic against "divinations" and "omens" is not the real issue here, but rather a contextualized opposition to contemporary beliefs such as one finds in *1 Enoch*.[137] In the Book of the Watchers, the protagonist repeatedly refers to dreams as the necessary precursor to visionary experiences (e.g., *1 En.* 13:8:

---

[133] For a useful summary on the possibility that the Book of the Watchers reflects an actual debate concerning illegitimate marriages, calendrical issues, and the problems with the priestly establishment, see Wright, "Putting the Puzzle Together," 102–8. Patrick Tiller, "The Sociological Context of the Dream Visions of Daniel and Enoch," in *Enoch and Qumran Origins: New Light on a Forgotten Connection* (ed. G. Boccaccini; Grand Rapids: Eerdmans, 2005), 23–26, warns against speaking too forcefully about an Enochic or Danielic "community." Traditions about Enoch accreted over time, and Tiller does not find evidence for a social movement in *1 Enoch* or Daniel. Nevertheless, the popularity of these texts among those responsible for the Dead Sea Scrolls suggests the importance of the Enochic traditions for marginal communities.

[134] For more on the social location for the Enochic corpus and how this relates to Ben Sira, see Nickelsburg, *1 Enoch*, 64–67; Wright, "Putting the Puzzle Together," 91–93. Enoch's commissioning, the Animal Vision, and the Apocalypse of Weeks seem to indicate a critique against the Jerusalem priesthood (Nickelsburg, *1 Enoch*, 67), suggesting more of an outsider status. Whether the Enochic authors were actually priests is an open question and beyond the scope of our discussion.

[135] Nickelsburg, *1 Enoch*, 50. The only explicit reference to the Sinaitic covenant occurs in *1 En* 99:2.

[136] Skehan and Di Lella, *The Wisdom of Ben Sira*, 409, cite the standard prohibitions in various biblical passages (e.g., Deut 18:10–14), claiming that Sirach refers to these earlier traditions in an effort to oppose any speculative inquiry that is "pagan and unworthy of the true Israelite."

[137] Wright, "Putting the Puzzle Together," 101.

"And look, dreams came upon me, and visions fell upon me"). With his earthly focus, Ben Sira opposes the idea of visionary ascents ("fools are sent winging by dreams") and the complex images that accompany such descriptions. For this sage, the content of a dream reflects the fanciful perspective of the individual who offers the interpretation (34:1–8) and not the will of God. Such activity is a distraction from the "fear of the Lord," the Mosaic law, and a person's daily responsibilities. Sirach does allow for the cogency of dreams "sent by intervention from the Most High" (34:6), perhaps as a nod to earlier biblical traditions (including sapiential ones) that emphasize dream interpretations (e.g., the Joseph cycle in Genesis; Job 4:12–21; 33:15).[138] Yet he is suspicious and largely dismissive of this method as a means of accessing God's plan (Sir 3:21–24). The difference between "mantic" wisdom, which interprets future events through the signs found in dreams, and the practical, investigative wisdom of Ben Sira is certainly relevant here.[139] Studying the נסתרות ("hidden things," Sir 3:22) is both distracting and dangerous and a core reason why this sage is suspicious of the ideas found in the Enochic corpus. In assessing this fundamental difference and the thematic overlaps between *1 Enoch* and Ben Sira, Wright concludes that these texts are the product of competing authors/groups who knew each other's work, did not necessarily like each other, and who actively sought to refute their opponents' positions, sometimes with indirect references.[140]

### 8. *Wisdom and Torah in Ben Sira*

There is another feature in this instructional text that relates to our discussion of causality: the explicit identification of the Torah with Wisdom. Sir 1:26 is representative of this move: "If you desire wisdom, keep the commandments, and the Lord will lavish her upon you."[141]

---

[138] Wright, "Putting the Puzzle Together," 102, notes the difficulty for Ben Sira in relation to some of the positive assessments of dreams in the Hebrew Bible.

[139] Visionary experiences are viewed by many of the prophets as suspicious and foreign (Babylonian). See John J. Collins, *Daniel* (Hermeneia; Minneapolis: Fortress Press, 1993), 49–50, for a discussion of mantic wisdom and Ben Sira's opposition to this type of inquiry.

[140] Wright, "Putting the Puzzle Together," 108, who includes a consideration of *Aramaic Levi* in his discussion.

[141] There seems to be a synonymous relationship between the "commandments" (מצות) and the "law" (תורה) in this instruction. For example, Ben Sira calls upon the

Elsewhere the author claims that "The whole of wisdom is fear of the Lord, and in all wisdom there is the fulfillment of the law" (19:20). However this aspect is understood, it is difficult to deny that Sirach's citation of the commandments as a means of acquiring Wisdom is a prominent feature of this instruction and a major departure from Proverbs. Previous Israelite sages had not presented their advice with references and allusions to the Torah, and it is likely that Ben Sira is addressing a later audience with an established legal corpus (i.e., Ezra 7:6).[142] Scholarly discussions have examined this issue at length, and many of the conclusions are conveniently summarized by Schnabel.[143] Since Ben Sira largely follows the conventions of traditional Wisdom discourse, his use of תורה and related terms and the centrality of the commandments for his ethical project are difficult issues.[144] He employs a variety of phrases to refer to the Mosaic legislation and clearly regards this material as authoritative, but he also uses legal terminology in the service of larger comments on the created order (see below). When examining the book as a whole, it becomes apparent that his allegiance to the Torah is a constituent element in a larger sapiential framework.

The relationship between exclusivism and universalism is a useful way of addressing the references on this topic, since Ben Sira reflects on both the unique gift of the Torah and the universal nature of Wisdom, often in the same passage. Referring to God's act of creating all of humanity, Sirach declares that "Discretion and tongue and eyes, ears and a mind for thinking he gave them" (17:6). This assertion is counterbalanced a few verses later by the more exclusive statement in 17:17: "He appointed a ruler for every nation, but Israel is the Lord's own portion." Based on the latter verse, some commentators posit an

---

addressee "to meditate (הגה, removing the *wāw*) at all times on his (the Lord's) commandments" (6:37). In both Josh 1:8 and Ps 1:2, הגה is used in reference to studying "the book of the law," where the product of such effort is insight and prosperity. See Schnabel, *Law and Wisdom*, 34. Smend, *Die Weisheit des Jesus Sirach erklärt*, 61–62, plausibly reads תורת עליון instead of יראת עליון, basing the emendation on Sir 38:34 (διανουμένου [= מתבונן] ἐν νόμῳ ὑψίστου). Whether the use of תורה in Ben Sira always denotes the content of the Mosaic legislation is a relevant question. There is good reason to believe that certain occurrences of the word allow for a more general connotation (e.g., the "law of life" in 17:11).

[142] One can reasonably ask why Qoheleth never refers to the same authoritative source, since his reflections date from the same general period.

[143] Schnabel, *Law and Wisdom*, 10–15.

[144] Schnabel, *Law and Wisdom*, 31–34, discusses the 12 occurrences of this word in Ben Sira.

ethnocentric perspective in the book, with Wisdom as the exclusive property of Israel. In the centerpiece of the instruction in chapter 24, the author quotes God's command to Lady Wisdom: "'Make your dwelling in Jacob, and in Israel receive your inheritance'" (v. 8). In this unit, Wisdom covers the heavens and earth (vv. 4–6), but ultimately takes up residence in a specific geographic locale (vv. 8–12).[145] According to Schnabel, the sage's specificity in this passage is clear and emblematic of the entire instruction: "Universal wisdom came to dwell, in a rather specific manner, in Israel and especially on Zion in the temple. Israel is thus the inheritance of wisdom."[146] Similarly, Hengel argues that "the universalistic attitude expressed in earlier Jewish wisdom tradition is necessarily qualified; wisdom and pious observance are identified, and the possibility of a profane wisdom dissociated from piety is excluded."[147] Such arguments attach an ideology of "only-ness" to the book of Ben Sira: those who submit to the teachings found in the Torah can exhibit the "fear of the Lord," while non-adherents have no hope for a righteous existence or sustained blessings from God. Moreover, there is no need for those who put their trust in the Torah to look outside the tradition for truth, and certainly not for Wisdom.

If the "apologetic-polemical" label for Ben Sira vis-à-vis "Hellenistic liberalism" is inaccurate, then the argument for a rigid dichotomy between "profane wisdom" and Torah-centered "piety" also misses the mark. According to Sirach, adherence to the commandments is certainly the best way of practicing self-control and establishing right relations with God (e.g., 15:1; 32:15), but it is not the only one. His critique is not against Greek thought or other external sources; we have already noted the sage's willingness to borrow from foreign instructions and ideas, both Egyptian and Hellenistic. While hardly a trained philosopher, this author includes an array of non-Israelite ideas in his instruction.[148] Ben Sira endorses diverse learning, claiming that a student with an educated instructor has great potential (6:34–37). In these verses, we should not assume that "every godly discourse" and all "wise proverbs" (6:35) relate exclusively to the Torah. Like a number of ancient Near

---

[145] In *1 Enoch* 42, Wisdom cannot find a place to rest and settles in the heavens.

[146] Schnabel, *Law and Wisdom*, 28; cf. E.P. Sanders, *Paul and Palestinian Judaism* (Philadelphia: Fortress Press, 1977), 331.

[147] Hengel, *Judaism and Hellenism*, 1:138, who believes that the identification in Sirach also influenced later authors.

[148] In his praise of the scribal profession, Ben Sira mentions the learning process that can take place during one's travels (39:4).

Eastern sages, this author concludes the book by declaring that *his
own instruction* (and not the Torah) represents the definitive source for
understanding Wisdom. At the end of the Praise of the Ancestors, Ben
Sira declares the following:

> Happy are those who concern themselves (יהגו) with these things (i.e., the
> content of the preceding instruction), and those who lay them to heart
> will become wise. For if they put them into practice, they will be equal
> to anything, for the fear of the Lord is their path (50:28–29).

This is a standard conclusion to an instructional document and probably the original ending of the book. Significantly, the sage does not
conclude with an appeal to a definitive legal corpus, as the epilogue
to Qoheleth does (12:13).

Additional factors militate against an overly particularistic understanding of Ben Sira, especially one based on the Torah. This author
does not concern himself with the technical meaning of biblical laws,
nor does he allude to anything from Leviticus. As with the book of
Proverbs, Ben Sira's exhortations generally follow the pattern of addressing various concerns through traditional sapiential discourse. Moreover,
the "fear of the Lord" and the Torah are not synonymous for this
author, since he does not explicitly link the two together.[149] Nor does
he devote an entire passage to the meaning and import of the Mosaic
legislation.[150] Although he places great faith in this established legal collection and refers repeatedly to the commandments, his predominant
focus is not a sacrosanct and definitive "book" of laws. An important
verse in 24:23 would seem to suggest otherwise: "All this (referring to
Wisdom) is the book of the covenant of the Most High God, the law
that Moses commanded us as an inheritance for the congregations of
Jacob." Sir 24:23 is relying on language from Deuteronomy (33:4) that
makes no mention of an actual corpus, and Ben Sira does not associate
Wisdom with a "book" elsewhere in his instruction.[151] It is plausible
that this clause in 24:23a has a similar background to a phrase in Bar
4:1, where Wisdom "*is* the book of the commandments of God, the

---

[149] One could possibly understand a parallelism between 32:15a and 16a.
[150] Johann Marböck, *Weisheit im Wandel: Untersuchungen zur Weisheitstheologie bei Ben
Sira* (Bonn: Hanstein, 1971), 85.
[151] He does, however, refer to the content of his own book in the epilogue: "Instruction in understanding and knowledge I have written in this book, Jesus son of Eleazar
son of Sirach of Jerusalem, whose mind poured forth wisdom" (50:27).

law that endures forever."[152] Ben Sira had ample biblical precedent
from which to develop such an explicit allegiance (e.g., Deut 17:18–19
and the law of the king), but he does not emphasize a "book" of laws
in this instruction.

Commentators often point to Sirach as a forerunner of later developments. Since his instruction reflects a transitional period in Jewish
history and refers so frequently to the commandments, such an interpretive approach is understandable. This author employs biblical allusions throughout the work and supports many of the statutes found in
the Mosaic legislation (warnings against adultery, almsgiving, love of
neighbor, giving over a portion to the priests), with a particular interest in the content of Deuteronomy. In addition, the lengthy Praise
of the Ancestors demonstrates a high regard for certain figures from
Israel's past whose actions and character have given them an eternal
reputation. The reference in the grandson's prologue to the "Law and
the Prophets and the other books of our ancestors" contributes to this
association of Ben Sira with the commandments and an emergent
"canon consciousness." Yet there is no idea of an eternal Torah in Ben
Sira; such a concept would truly take root in rabbinic texts.[153] Although
the sage's devotion to his own religious tradition and its sacred texts is
unequivocal, the basic method of discourse in the book of Ben Sira is
identical to ancient Near Eastern instructions of its type.

At the same time, the Torah is vitally important for Ben Sira. While
his approach allows for openness to foreign ideas, it is beyond dispute
that Israel's legal and narrative traditions are essential components of
his presentation. This material represents an invaluable source from
which to construct ethics, and we should not overstate Sirach's flexibility in straying from his own tradition. For example, there is exclusivist
language in his elevation of the scribe: "How different the one who
devotes himself to the study of the law of the Most High!" (38:34).
Similarly, Sirach tells the addressee to find intelligent friends "and let
all your discussion be about the law of the Most High" (9:15). Since
it sets limits on acceptable conduct and speculation about God, the
Torah is an appealing source of authority, as the sage's maxims seek
to regulate communal life through restrictiveness and a commitment
to benevolent acts. The content of the Mosaic legislation would have

---

[152] Otto Rickenbacker, *Weisheitsperikopen bei Ben Sira* (Göttingen: Vandenhoeck &
Ruprecht, 1973), 125–27.
[153] Hadot, *Penchant Mauvais et Volonté Libre*, 82–209.

been especially useful at the time of the Hellenistic reform in Jerusalem, when an array of innovative ideas were circulating. Ben Sira is
not pioneering this association of Wisdom with the commandments
(cf. Deut 4:5–6), but he certainly embraces it as an ethical approach
and a way of merging Torah-piety with sapiential discourse.[154] In this
sense, the commandments serve a useful function within his apologetic
framework.

Sirach's allegiance to the commandments is ultimately a constituent
element in a larger framework: the Torah is encompassed by a more universal Wisdom in Ben Sira, and not vice versa.[155] For Ben Sira, Wisdom
is a gift from God. When given to humanity it becomes "a disposition
of the mind and character, and as such it cannot be equated with any
collection of sayings or laws, although these are indispensable aids in
the quest for wisdom."[156] Wisdom transcends the realm with which
humanity is familiar, so that the "law of life" (Sir 17:11) is larger than
one written corpus (16:24–18:14). In addition, Sirach's broader vision
is characterized by the use of legal terminology to describe the created
order. For example, חק ("statute") denotes the limits of human potential
(often in relation to death) and the order in the universe. Death becomes
the חוק לשאול for all persons (14:12). There is also a "proper time"
or "statute" for all living beings to obey the commands of the creator
(ובחקם לא ימרו פיו, 39:31; cf. Job 38:33). Such language expresses the
sage's belief in a just world, where everything has an appointed time,
including death. In the sense that legal language and the actual commandments signify the intentionality of the divine plan and a means
of providing order (particularly for those who cannot pursue a scribal
education: 19:24), Ben Sira endorses them as a resource for learning
"fear of the Lord."[157] With his many oblique references to biblical
passages, he is clearly speaking to a population familiar with the legal

---

[154] Matthew J. Goff, *Discerning Wisdom: The Sapiential Literature of the Dead Sea
Scrolls* (VTSup 116; Leiden: Brill, 2007), 130–35, addresses the similarities between
4Q185(4QSapiential Work) and Sirach on this point. 4Q185 1–2 ii 10 also refers to
the bestowal of Wisdom by God to Israel.

[155] Winston, "Theodicy in Ben Sira," 240; John J. Collins, "The Biblical Precedent
for Natural Theology," in *Encounters with Biblical Theology* (Minneapolis: Fortress Press,
2005), 101–2; originally published in *JAAR* 45 (March 1977): 35–67.

[156] Collins, *Jewish Wisdom*, 48.

[157] Sir 19:23 warns against a "cleverness (πανουργία/ערמה) that is detestable." For
Ben Sira and the ancient Near Eastern wisdom tradition in general, it is far better to
be a simpleton than to be crafty and deceitful.

material.[158] Adherence to the laws of Moses is part of a larger agenda,
which involves learning the "wisdom of all the ancients" (39:1), and not
just the Torah, in order to defend the tradition against new proposals
about Wisdom, retribution, and the afterlife.[159]

### 9. Death in Sirach and the Possibility of an Afterlife

In this instruction, unlike the book of Proverbs, death is a central issue,
even in mundane observations (e.g., 19:3). Ben Sira devotes an entire
unit to proper mourning rites for an individual (Sir 38:16–23). Along
with the prescribed number of days in the ritual process, he discusses
the fate of every individual who dies: "Do not forget that he has no
hope" (v. 21, translation mine). The reference to "no hope" conveys
the impossibility of eternal existence for all persons.[160] Ben Sira also
employs the same motif as Qoheleth about the "return" of every human
spirit back to the earth. This description had become a common way
of referring to the life cycle: "The Lord created human beings out
of earth, and makes them return to it again" (Sir 17:1; cf. Qoh 3:20;
Gen 2:7; 3:19). The use of שוב in this verse affirms the traditional
conclusion that human beings were never meant to be anything but
mortal. Reiterer explains the mindset in such passages: "Die Scheol
wird zuletzt der Lebensanleitung nicht als Trost, sondern als Faktum
gegenübergestellt."[161] In response to this understanding of death as the
definitive end of existence, we have discussed the fact that the sage
endorses a modified *carpe diem* mentality, one that adheres to "fear of

---

[158] Von Rad, *Wisdom in Israel*, 245: "All that differentiates Sirach from the older
teachers is that he reinterpreted the expression 'fear of God' for an age to which the
will of God spoke from the written Torah. Basically, however, his thoughts about the
correlation between fear of God and wisdom are no different from those of teachers
in earlier centuries."

[159] Whether the omission of Ezra from the sage's list of historical figures has any
bearing on this issue is a relevant question. It is doubtful that Ezra's "legalism" led to
his absence from the concluding section of the book, as some scholars have claimed.
Sirach respects the law and uses exclusive language himself.

[160] With regard to the meaning of תקוה in 38:21, 41:1d, and elsewhere, see Friedrich
V. Reiterer, "Deutung und Wertung des Todes durch Ben Sira," in *Die alttestamentliche
Botschaft als Wegweisung* (ed. J. Zmijewski; Stuttgart: Verlags Katholisches Bibelwerk
GmbH, 1990), 221, who shows that while the word can have a positive connotation in
this book, "wird aber von Sira meist mit dem Lebensende in Zusammenhang gebracht
und weist so auf das damit mitgegebene Ende der Zukunftsperspectiven." Cf. Sir 30:17
and the passing reference to death as "eternal sleep" (נוחת עולם).

[161] Reiterer, "Deutung und Wertung des Todes," 228.

the Lord." Using language reminiscent of Qoheleth, Ben Sira commands, "Give, and take, and indulge yourself, because in Hades one cannot look for luxury. All living beings become old like a garment, for the decree from of old is, 'You must die!'" (14:16–17). This approach does not apply to all persons: for individuals who are despondent or whose faculties have failed them, death becomes a "welcome decree" (41:2).[162] Both Qoheleth and Ben Sira agree that the number of years in which a person can actually enjoy life is brief (Sir. 10:9–11). The same understanding can be found in 4Q185 (4QSapiential Work), another Wisdom text from this general period.[163] According to 4Q185, life should be enjoyed fully; the text does not mention a blessed afterlife for the righteous soul.[164]

Such a mindset indicates a set of beliefs that resembles Qoheleth in a broad sense, although Ben Sira insists on a consistent principle of justice, a permanent name for all righteous persons, and a more peaceful death. Qoheleth had determined that "there is no enduring remembrance of the wise or of fools, seeing that in the days to come all will have been long forgotten. How the wise die just like fools!" (Qoh 2:16; cf. Job 18:17).[165] He was exasperated by the lack of an accounting in his analysis of earthly existence (Qoh 7:25; 9:10), and he did not allow the possibility of virtuous deeds to secure a lasting reputation for anyone. God should be feared and obeyed, but for Qoheleth there could be no *Tun-Ergehen-Zusammenhang* under the shadow of such an indiscriminate fate. In contrast, Ben Sira insists on an enduring reputation (שם עולם) for the righteous: "One who is wise among his people will inherit honor, and his name will live forever" (37:26; cf. 15:6; 39:9–11; 41:11–13; 44:14). Ben Sira rejects Qoheleth's reasoning: the righteous enjoy the benefit of knowing that their name and deeds will endure, and they can therefore die with greater contentment than the wicked. Sirach invokes this idea of a peaceful conclusion to life as a motivation for righteous behavior: "In all you do, remember the end of your life, and then you will never sin" (7:36). Not only does the sage encourage

---

[162] Reiterer, "Deutung und Wertung des Todes," 222. For infirm persons, Ben Sira cites death as a positive occurrence.

[163] Goff, *Discerning Wisdom*, 123, assesses the difficulties in assigning a more definitive date to this text than the second or first-century B.C.E.

[164] 4Q185 portrays the righteous individual as a person with "a happy heart, riches, and honor" (1–2 ii 12), with no mention of an afterlife.

[165] This is probably an exclamatory statement and not a question (*pace* NRSV). Therefore, we take איך as a lament (cf. Isa 14:12).

benevolent activity in this passage, but also he counsels the addressee to beware of a potentially painful experience at the moment of death. Qoheleth does not disagree with a charitable attitude (Qoh 11:1), but he places no hope in a peaceful conclusion to life, especially since the final years of life can be painful and sad (12:1–8).

Since he does not offer post-mortem possibilities for the righteous, it is incumbent upon Ben Sira to distinguish the nature of the death experience for the righteous from that of the wicked. In discussing the "fear of the Lord" and the benefits associated with it, he never fully explains how a distinctively pleasant death will occur for those who have adopted "fear of the Lord." In one of the hymns (14:20–15:10), he tries to clarify this point. In lieu of eschatological reward, Ben Sira opts to link "fear of the Lord" with an eternal reputation, and this presumably provides satisfaction at the last. The sage explains that Wisdom will come to the faithful addressee "like a mother" (15:2). As a result, this individual will be held in esteem among his peers (v. 5), find joy, "and will inherit an everlasting name" (v. 6). The promise of a permanent reputation as the culminating gift in this section is not coincidental; such a statement represents a challenge to those with different ideas about retribution. This is Ben Sira's answer to the apocalyptic under-standing, Qoheleth, and other individuals questioning the traditional view. The consolation for death is not eschatological vindication but the bestowal of an eternal reputation, a name that lasts through the memory of one's children and possibly (if one is truly righteous and holds the right office) throughout the world. For the wicked, this conclu-sion will be markedly different, especially for the resourceful swindler from whom punishment has not yet been exacted: "For it is easy for the Lord on the day of death to reward individuals according to their conduct" (11:26). Any prosperity will be cancelled, since "An hour's misery makes one forget past delights, and at the close of one's life one's deeds are revealed" (11:27).[166] Yet the problems with this last assertion are considerable. It is difficult for the reader to fathom what type of unique calamities will strike the wicked individual on his deathbed. We can infer a period of despair, brought on by the knowledge that his

---

[166] Collins, *Jewish Wisdom*, 78, notes a similar sentiment in the Greek tragedies (e.g., *Oedipus Rex* 1529), where the idea is that anything is possible up to the point of death. Sirach's goal in 11:26–28 and similar units (18:24) is to leave open the possibility of divine judgment/intervention.

reputation will perish along with his physical body.[167] Even with this image, Ben Sira's end-of-life framework is very difficult to defend as a coherent understanding.

Another way Sirach promulgates his traditional perspective is by affirming the concept of a qualitative death for the fool. Such a person may still be physically present, but he has already perished through his foolishness. In the same spirit as Proverbs, Ben Sira commands the addressee to "Weep less bitterly for the dead, for he is at rest; but the life of the fool is worse than death" (Sir 22:11). In a caustic analogy, he discusses the fool in the context of burial rites. Mourning over fools should last "all the days of their lives" (22:12) as opposed to seven days for deceased persons. With this comparison, Sirach is affirming the idea of the discerning individual as a source of vitality. In contrast, the fool has no possibility for redemption: his spirit died when he decided not to adopt "fear of the Lord" as his *modus operandi*. Yet this motif is not nearly as important in Ben Sira as in Proverbs; the idea of a qualitative death only gets passing mention in the verses cited above. Sirach instead focuses on physical death and its implications, topics that do not interest the authors of Proverbs.

Sirach opposes any and all efforts to promote an otherworldly fulfillment for the *Tun-Ergehen-Zusammenhang*, and there is every reason to believe that he had opponents on this issue. We have seen that such a concept of eternal reward is found in *1 Enoch*: this text speaks of a temporary resting place for the dead (the repositories, or "escape-proof pits"), and then at some point the righteous will be brought into an eternal existence and the wicked receive "recompense for their spirits" (*1 En.* 22:10). In a passage from the Epistle of Enoch, the righteous are promised a position in the heavens, where they will "shine like the luminaries of heaven" (104:2).[168] 4QInstruction offers a similar portrait

---

[167] Ben Sira does not ignore the reality of the procreative process among the wicked. He laments the inevitability of offspring from a sinner and urges the addressee not to rejoice in the growth of a wicked family (16:1–2).

[168] Cf. *1 En.* 93:11–14, which describes the mysteries of the universe and Enoch's ability to understand them: "And who is there of all men who is able to look at all the works of heaven?" (v. 11). These verses are imitative of passages like Job 38–39 and Prov 30:1–4, and according to Argall, *1 Enoch and Sirach*, 125, this passage from the Epistle refers to promises made to the righteous: "The rhetorical questions imply that human knowledge of (esoteric) created phenomena is now possible because it was revealed to Enoch and has been imparted to the righteous as an eschatological gift." With regard to Ben Sira, the sage views himself as the one who can lead his pupils to Wisdom, though not the otherworldly type envisaged by Enoch. In Sir 6:22–23, he

of eschatological reward commensurate with earthly behavior. The author of 4QInstruction does not mention physical resurrection (nor do we find such a depiction in *1 Enoch*), but some sort of permanent glory for the "s[ons] of heaven, whose lot is eternal life (חיים עולם)" (4Q418 69 ii 12–13). For Ben Sira, such hopes are hopelessly speculative and promote a misleading understanding of human possibility. He and Qoheleth are identical on this point: "Who will sing praises to the Most High in Hades in place of the living who give thanks? From the dead, as from one who does not exist, thanksgiving has ceased; those who are alive and well sing the Lord's praises" (Sir 17:27–28; cf. Qoh 9:10).

### 9.1    *References to Eternal Life in Sirach*

The *textus receptus* of Ben Sira does contain scattered references to eternal life, including both the G¹ and G² translations, although this belief can-not be traced back to the original sage.[169] With regard to the grandson's translation (G¹), several instances of departure from the Hebrew relate to death and the possibility of judgment, including 7:17b and 48:11b. The first example implies eschatological expectation, with the statement that "the punishment of the ungodly is fire and worms." The Hebrew of MS A does not convey a judgment scene of this type.[170] The grandson's exact beliefs on eschatology are difficult to clarify, especially since he left intact the original sage's traditional language about death. Based on 7:17b, we can perhaps assume a belief in eternal punishment for the wicked and some type of heavenly existence for the righteous.

In the other Greek version (G²), certain additions to the text are eschatological in nature. We mentioned Sir 2:9c: "For his reward is an everlasting gift (δόσις αἰωνία) with joy." There is 19:19, which also

---

emphasizes his essential role as a guide: "For wisdom is not like her name; she is not readily perceived by many. Listen, my child, and accept my judgment; do not reject my counsel." The force of this statement suggests that Ben Sira wants the addressee to adopt his conservative outlook over and against competing perspectives like *1 Enoch*. Moreover, Ben Sira seems to believe he is a special conduit between God and human-ity, embodying a prophetic role (he speaks like a prophet in 24:33). Nickelsburg, *Jewish Literature between the Bible and the Mishnah*, 60, argues that "The place of prophecy has been taken by the scribe's study and interpretation of the ancient writings, especially the Torah."

[169] For background on G², see Skehan and DiLella, *The Wisdom of Ben Sira*, 55–56.

[170] On the use of "fire and worms" in the context of judgment, see Isa 66:24; Jdt 16:17. Instead of the ἀσεβοῦς in G¹, MS A has תקות אנוש ("the expectation of mortals"), which clearly implies a judicial setting. For an interpretation of 48:11b, see below.

describes the fate of the righteous: "The knowledge of the Lord's commandments is life-giving discipline; and those who do what is pleasing
to him enjoy the fruit of the tree of immortality (ἀθανασία)." With
regard to the wicked, one G² expansion refers to a "day of punishment,"
presumably at a final moment that will lead to eternal suffering for these
individuals (12:6c). While the process is not spelled out in detail by the
redactor, we can infer a reckoning analogous to the descriptions in
*1 Enoch*. There is no mention in these G² expansions of bodily resurrection. Additional passages in the Syriac and Old Latin depict a similar
judgment and a final separation of the righteous and wicked.[171]

There is a possible reference to eternal life in a Hebrew text that
can be traced back to the original sage (48:11), where the subject is
Elijah. The recounting of Elijah's career in the Praise of the Ancestors
(48:4–15) includes discussion of the miracle with the "dead child" (Sir
48:5; see 1 Kgs 17:17–24) and the prophet's own avoidance of death
(Sir 48:5, 12a; see 2 Kgs 2:11). This section also contains a fragmentary line (v. 11) that is understood by Émile Puech to signify belief in a
limited resurrection.[172] The translation of the Greek (G¹) reads "Happy
are those who saw you and were adorned with your love! For we also
shall surely live" (NRSV). With regard to the extant Hebrew for this
verse, the beginning of MS B is אשר ראך ומת.[173] After reviewing earlier
proposals, Puech reads 48:11b as follows: כ]י [חתן ח]יי[ם] [וי]ה[יה. Based
on this reconstruction, Puech's translation of the entire verse would
then be, "Happy is the one who sees you before dying, for you give life,
and he lives (or comes back to life again)." According to this reading,

---

[171] Skehan and Di Lella, *The Wisdom of Ben Sira*, 86, cite references to "eternal life"
in the Syriac translation. In 1:12b, the "fear of the Lord" brings with it "eternal life,"
and the addressee is promised an inheritance with the angels (1:24). Cf. 1:20; 3:1b;
48:11b. In addition, the Old Latin has multiple references to immortality (e.g., 18:22b).
See Conleth Kearns, "Ecclesisasticus, or the Wisdom of Jesus the Son of Sirach," in
*A New Catholic Commentary on Holy Scripture* (ed. R.C. Fuller; London: Thomas Nelson
Publishers, 1969), 549, who discusses the eschatology of the expanded texts, where the
wicked experience divine wrath and the righteous are brought into the "lot" of truth:
"There they will enjoy eternal life, an everlasting reward that brings with it honour
from God and a joy which never ends."

[172] Émile Puech, "Ben Sira 48:11 et la Résurrection," in *Of Scribes and Scrolls: Studies on the Hebrew Bible, Intertestamental Judaism and Christian Origins* (ed. H.W. Attridge
et al.; Lanham, Md.: University Press of America, 1990), 81–91; idem, *La Croyance
des Esséniens en la Vie Future: Immortalité, Résurrection, Vie Éternelle?* (2 vols. Paris: Gabalda,
1993), 1:73–79.

[173] Puech, "Ben Sira 48:11," 84: "Les versions et l'emploi de אשר normalement
au pluriel en hébreu exigeraient un original אשרי ou une vocalisation conséquente
du lexème."

Sir 48:11 clarifies the prophet's eschatological mission to restore the tribes and convert the hearts of the people (v. 10). Puech claims that this verse draws upon the conclusion to Malachi and the description of Elijah's actions prior to "the day of the Lord" (Mal 3:23; cf. Matt 17:11; Luke 1:17). An eschatological role for this prophet is also attested in later rabbinic texts (e.g., *m. Soṭa* 9:15). Yet Puech makes a qualifying statement: "Sans doute, il n'est pas question de résurrection générale, ni celle de tous les justes, mais de juste qui verront le retour d'Elie et sont ainsi assurés de revivre."[174]

At various points, Ben Sira seems to mention traditions that had an authoritative status among his readers, but he himself does not subscribe to the possibility of resurrection for even the most righteous individuals. It is interesting and perhaps indicative of their popularity that Ben Sira refers to the Elijah, Elisha (48:13), and Enoch (44:16; 49:14) ascent stories in the first place. While his reading of 48:11 and 48:13 is innovative, Puech's argument is difficult to reconcile with Ben Sira's explicit statements elsewhere on death in the human experience. Sirach 48 does not posit a belief in resurrection, even for righteous persons like Simon II or the sage himself.[175] With regard to the possibility of limited resurrection among those present with Elijah, even this is difficult to assume from 48:11. Puech makes a speculative reconstruction of a fragmentary verse, and the passage in Malachi that serves as the basis for Sir 48:10 refers to a national day of deliverance and restoration for the righteous in Israel, rather than a belief in the afterlife. Although the sage is assenting briefly to Elijah traditions that his pupils undoubtedly knew, the Hebrew for these verses should not be read as reflective of a limited claim about resurrection. The eschatological import of Sir 48:11 is negligible: this description does not negate the "decree from old" that all human beings must die (14:17).

## 10. *Affirmation of the* Tun-Ergehen-Zusammenhang

As he dispenses advice on a variety of topics, Ben Sira does not simply repeat the principles and theological understanding found in the book

---

[174] Puech, "Ben Sira 48:11," 87.

[175] As Collins, *Jewish Wisdom*, 96, argues, we cannot assume the bestowal of *eternal* life from the Elijah traditions. Perhaps the life conferred by the prophet is only temporary.

of Proverbs. He seeks to make his instruction relevant to a changing tradition, which now included the Torah, while at the same time remaining faithful to Wisdom as he understands it. He promotes the "fear of the Lord" concept to a generation of pupils who had been exposed to a variety of alternative proposals. His promise of a conclusion to life in accordance with one's deeds and an eternal name for the righteous are central ideas in this book. Sirach incorporates these sapiential concepts into his act-consequence understanding. As he assures pupils of the viability of his model, he provides a glimpse of his opponents and the new landscape for sapiential discourse. As Burkes explains, an "undercurrent of disquiet" runs throughout this instruction, indicating an awareness of compelling alternatives: "He argues for his own view with determination, although he admits that the human sense of timing is often different from God's and thus appropriate recompense for good and evil is not always apparent at first, on the individual or the national level."[176]

Even if the divine plan is obscure, Ben Sira insists on the goodwill of God toward those who are virtuous and sure punishment for the wicked. The promise of divine mercy is an important element in this text and not a regular feature of earlier Israelite instructions. Sirach uses the biblical motif of a merciful God to promote a consistent principle: "He makes room for every act of mercy (צדקה); everyone receives in accordance with one's deeds" (16:14). No person should think they can act with impunity, however: "Do not say 'His mercy is great, he will forgive the multitude of my sins,' for both mercy (רחמים) and wrath (אף) are with him, and his anger will rest on sinners" (5:6). The sage warns in this passage that divine wrath can come forth "suddenly" to hold the sinner accountable (v. 7), and if it does not happen in the present, reckoning will surely occur on the "day of calamity" (v. 8). Prato has called this unit in Sir 5:4–8 "un compendio di teodicea," since it contains an objection or boast by the unrighteous person, an answer from the sage, and an exhortation marked by the threat of instant ruin (cf. 1 En. 103:5–6).[177] The language in Sir 5:4–8 includes conceptual and terminological allusions to earlier biblical passages (e.g., Psalm 51), as the sage offers a depiction of God that coheres with the larger Jewish tradition. He presents a benevolent deity as a way of refuting charges

---

[176] Burkes, *God, Self, and Death*, 97.
[177] Prato, *Il Problema della Teodicea*, 367–69.

that his understanding of death and the human experience is too harsh and unforgiving. As Perdue explains, the sage appeals to divine benevolence in order to compensate for a finite existence: "The limitations of human existence (mortality and weakness) are recognized by a merciful God who is sure to forgive those who repent and turn to him."[178] The fact that Ben Sira insists on judgment (or mercy) in the earthly sphere, during each individual's lifetime, is part of his apologetic. He seeks to dismiss any suggestion of a delayed, post-mortem accounting.

Ben Sira also promises descendants (30:4–6), although this cannot compare to the immortality of a good name. We have already encountered this aspect as the focal point of the sage's act-consequence framework. Sirach counters the unverifiable hope for astral immortality and the hard-nosed realism of Qoheleth ("the people of long ago are not remembered") with a hopeful promise that does not stretch the limits of his theological understanding. He repeatedly emphasizes the eternal aspect of a good reputation (15:6; 37:26; 39:9; 41:11–13; 44:8), which is not as prominent a motif in the book of Proverbs (e.g., Prov 10:7). When Sirach states that "The human body is a fleeting thing, but a virtuous name will never be blotted out" (41:11), he is making the assumption that a righteous life automatically yields an eternal reputation. Conversely, the descendants of the unrighteous must suffer the consequences of their ancestor's sin for many generations (41:5). While this is not a pioneering motif for an instructional text, in the book of Ben Sira a good name receives unparalleled attention. Boccaccini explains the distinctiveness of the theme in Sirach:

> It is obvious that the boundaries of individual existence, so uncertain and fleeting, were by then felt to be too narrow for divine retribution to fill. The conservation of one's name is thus affirmed as the truest and most authentic reward for the righteous, better than any riches or even a long and happy life.[179]

## 11. *Conclusions*

With evidence from Qoheleth, the Enochic texts, 4QInstruction and other passages from the Dead Sea Scrolls, and the reflections of Ben

---

[178] Leo G. Perdue, *Wisdom and Creation: The Theology of Wisdom Literature* (Nashville: Abingdon, 1994), 263.

[179] Boccaccini, *Middle Judaism*, 121.

Sira himself, we can point to a widespread reevaluation of the traditional understanding of retribution and causality. Because of repeated references to certain topics, it is reasonable to posit an ongoing reassessment during the period of Ben Sira's career. This process had begun at least as early as Qoheleth's era (late third-century B.C.E.). The intriguing evidence from 4QInstruction gives added support for the "eschatologizing" of Wisdom, at least among certain groups and sages. In attempting to discern the contours of this debate, there is no need to argue (nor is it likely) that Ben Sira had direct knowledge of all or even most of the extant references mentioned above.[180] Although he almost certainly knew parts of *1 Enoch*, as Argall and others have claimed, we can also suppose that Ben Sira is responding to other figures whose instructional collections no longer survive. Established contemporaries were circulating eschatological understandings of act and consequence, including the promise of a heavenly ascent for righteous individuals. The force of Qoheleth and Ben Sira's discussion implies a set of opponents with such belief systems. With the discovery of 4QInstruction, we can point to a document that is reflective of many of the ideas that this Jerusalem sage so vigorously opposed. We now turn to this fragmentary text and its implications for our understanding of Wisdom and retribution during the Second Temple period.

---

[180] As the next chapter will argue, 4QInstruction might have been written after Sirach's career, towards the end of the second-century B.C.E.

# CHAPTER FIVE

# WISDOM IN TRANSITION:
# MYSTERY AND ESCHATOLOGY IN 4QINSTRUCTION

## 1. *Introduction*

The preceding chapters on Qoheleth and Ben Sira have pointed to a reassessment of Jewish Wisdom during the early Hellenistic period, as the type of retribution one could expect and the possibility of an afterlife became debated topics within the tradition. Qoheleth is disturbed by human finitude and his inability to grasp the mysteries of the universe, while Ben Sira affirms a just Creator and the lasting power of a good name. Both sapiential authors are strongly dismissive of the belief in individual immortality, presumably in response to certain contemporaries. Yet the limited number of available texts has constrained a full understanding of otherworldly proposals from this period and the contours of any reevaluation. The Enochic works include a number of innovative ideas, as do Greek references about the ascent of the soul after death. Even with this evidence, further examples have been needed in order to identify the fundamental changes within the wisdom tradition. This is a primary reason why the discovery and publication of 4QInstruction (*Musar le-Mevin*), the longest sapiential text found near the Qumran settlement, marks a watershed moment in the study of Jewish instructions.[1] Scholars now have access to a text from the late second-century B.C.E. (see below) that exhibits a belief in eschatological reward for the righteous and eternal punishment for

---

[1] This text is preserved in 1Q26, 4Q415–418, 423, and there are six (possibly seven) copies. Unless otherwise noted, transcriptions and translations will follow John Strugnell and Daniel J. Harrington, *Qumran Cave 4.XXIV: Sapiential Texts, Part 2. 4QInstruction (Mûsār Lĕ Mēvîn): 4Q415ff. With a re-edition of 1Q26* (DJD 34; Oxford: Clarendon Press, 1999). Strugnell and Harrington's comprehensive edition will hereafter be cited as "*DJD 34.*" In future references, these scholars will be referred to as the "editors" of 4QInstruction, rather than repeating their names for every citation. Another effort at reconstructing this fragmentary text is that of Eibert J.C. Tigchelaar, *To Increase Learning for the Understanding Ones: Reading and Reconstructing the Fragmentary Early Jewish Sapiential Text 4QInstruction* (STDJ 44; Leiden: Brill, 2001). His reading of key phrases will be used in this discussion.

the wicked. The complex understanding of causality and retribution in 4QInstruction is pivotal to our study of a major transition and the focus of this final chapter.

In discussing appropriate behavior and its consequences, 4QInstruction offers a fusion of practical advice and apocalyptic ideas. If the warnings in this text are heeded and the addressee develops the necessary discernment, eternal salvation becomes a possibility. This functions as a way of extending a consistent act-consequence relationship and represents a decisive break from the earthly rewards (lengthy days and an eternal reputation) promised by the compilers of Proverbs and Ben Sira. In multiple passages, the author of 4QInstruction uses otherworldly language to depict his view of the created order and the relationship between God and humanity. Through an innovative use of available constructs, this text offers a startling framework for causality. Wicked individuals face punishment in Sheol, but the righteous addressees are presented with the promise of immortality in some sort of glorious state. With such an understanding, this work represents a changed dynamic within the tradition and a movement beyond longstanding typologies for reward and punishment. 4QInstruction demonstrates the diversity of sapiential discourse during the Hellenistic period: certain references are similar to *1 Enoch*, but radically different from Ben Sira. This text is also a seminal example of later belief systems on the immortality of the righteous soul, found in the Wisdom of Solomon (e.g., 3:1–11) and in subsequent books like *4 Ezra*.[2] The combination of ideas in 4QInstruction forces modern interpreters to refrain from rigidity with modern generic categories (Wisdom and apocalypticism) and to consider the various reasons for innovative ideas during this period. When compared with the other instructions we have examined throughout this study, from Ptahhotep to Ben Sira, 4QInstruction offers a revolutionary *Tun-Ergehen-Zusammenhang*.

---

[2] The parallels between 4QInstruction and some of the language in the New Testament are also noteworthy. Comparative work on 4QInstruction and sapiential/apocalyptic passages in the gospels is in its nascent stages. See Matthew J. Goff, "Discerning Trajectories: 4QInstruction and the Sapiential Background of the Sayings Source Q," *JBL* 124 (2005): 657–73; Grant Macaskill, *Revealed Wisdom and Inaugurated Eschatology in Ancient Judaism and Early Christianity* (JSJSup 115; Leiden: Brill, 2007), 72–195.

## 2. *Structure and Literary Integrity*

Because of its fragmentary condition, the exact structure and overall content of 4QInstruction are uncertain. The unfortunate state of the extant fragments precludes a full understanding of the text's meaning and significance. 4QInstruction contains both admonitory sections and longer discourses on God and the mysteries of creation, but it is very difficult to determine basic organization. In some cases, there is more than one copy of a particular unit, and textual overlaps supplement missing letters or phrases. When all of the available passages are examined, however, the significant gaps in the text are still an interpretive issue. As several scholarly discussions have demonstrated, pivotal phrases are often unclear.[3] As a result, the possibility of determining meaning from structure, especially in terms of corollaries between the more speculative units and admonitory passages, is extremely difficult. Based on what remains of 4QInstruction, the organization of available material resembles the notebook style found in Qoheleth and Ben Sira. The author(s) of this text moves from one theme to another, with little apparent flow between sections.[4] A more complete version might demonstrate a structural intentionality that is now obscured by the fragmentary state, but this is uncertain. Nevertheless, the thematic content of many of the longer fragments is not necessarily random; many individual units have an inner coherence, such as 4Q416 2 iii 15–21 and the discussion of honoring one's parents and balancing religious commitments with the demands of marriage.

In attempting to reconstruct 4QInstruction, several commentators have sought to determine textual overlaps and basic flow, particularly for the larger fragments.[5] Since their efforts are documented in detail elsewhere and not the focus of this study, only a few points are in order. Scholars have identified the opening unit of 4QInstruction, a portion of which appears in 4Q416 1. The wide right-hand margin of this fragment (3.3 cm) indicates a gap before the commencement of writing,

---

[3] Tigchelaar, *To Increase Learning*, 26, notes the difficulty of ascertaining contiguous fragments for this text.

[4] Daniel J. Harrington, *Wisdom Texts from Qumran* (London: Routledge, 1996), 40.

[5] See Tigchelaar, *To Increase Learning*, 28, 161–62, who cites the need for tentative conclusions. Torleif Elgvin, "The Reconstruction of Sapiential Work A," *RevQ* 16 (1995): 559–80, attempts to piece together the larger blocks of material; idem, "An Analysis of 4QInstruction," (Ph.D. diss., Hebrew University of Jerusalem, 1997), 11–35; also *DJD 34*, 17–19.

and there is general consensus that this section marks the beginning of
the work.[6] In terms of subject matter, the unit offers a judgment scene
analogous to the beginning of *1 Enoch* (1:1–9). The statements in the
opening column of 4QInstruction are in the third-person, whereas much
of the text is in the second-person singular. Rather than admonishing
the addressee, the tone of this opening passage is cosmological/escha-
tological. Tigchelaar has undertaken the most comprehensive analysis
of 4Q416 1, and his findings have yielded several conclusions relevant
to our study.[7] With the help of textual overlaps from 4Q418, his tran-
scription and translation convincingly demonstrate the eschatological
orientation of the passage.[8] In this opening scene, God establishes
"luminaries" and "signs" (4Q416 1 7–9) and then evaluates humanity
from afar:

> in heaven He shall pronounce judgment upon the work of wickedness,
> and all His faithful children shall be favourably accepted by [Him its
> end. And they shall be in terror. And all who defiled themselves in it
> (בה), shall cry out. For the heavens shall fear, and the earth too shall be
> shaken (from its place)] The [s]eas and the depths shall be in terror, and
> every spirit of flesh will cry out. But the sons of heaven [shall rejoice in
> the day of] its [judg]ment. And all iniquity shall come to an end, while
> the period of truth will be completed [(4Q 416 1 10–13).[9]

When compared with the other sapiential texts examined in this study,
this is an innovative introduction, which depicts God's regulation of all
elements in the cosmos and the certainty of divine judgment.[10] Within
such a framework, all people will be evaluated according to whether

---

[6] Harrington, *Wisdom Texts*, 41; cf. *DJD 34*, 17.

[7] Eibert J.C. Tigchelaar, "Towards a Reconstruction of the Beginning of 4QIn-
struction (4Q416 Fragment 1 and Parallels)," in *The Wisdom Texts from Qumran and the
Development of Sapiential Thought* (ed. C. Hempel et al.; BETL 159; Leuven: Leuven
University Press/Peeters, 2002), 99–126.

[8] Tigchelaar, "Towards a Reconstruction of the Beginning of 4QInstruction,"
122–25, claims that the text might begin with משכיל (translated as "sage") in the first
line, based on 4Q418 238. With the help of other fragments (4Q418 221 and 222) that
Tigchelaar places at the beginning of the text, he leaves open the possibility that the
sapiential teacher's primary responsibility is set forth from the outset, as an important
precursor to the eschatological scene: "to increase learning for the understanding ones
(להו[ס]יף לקח למבינים). See also Tigchelaar, *To Increase Learning*, 245–46.

[9] The antecedent for בה in line 11 is the "work of wickedness" (עבודת רשעה) in
line 10.

[10] Tigchelaar, "Towards a Reconstruction of the Beginning of 4QInstruction," 126,
notes the shift from the discussion of the luminaries in 4Q416 1 7–9 to divine judgment. The two seem to relate in some way, but any connecting word or short clause
is missing from the fragment.

they have completed their assigned task and remained loyal to God's decrees. In a similar manner, the beginning of *1 Enoch* refers to "righteous chosen who will be present on the day of tribulation" (1:1), and then the author proceeds to depict the deity "coming forth" to assert authority over the heavens and the earth (vv. 4–9). From a structural standpoint, it is noteworthy for a sapiential text to begin with this type of a cosmological scene, including a description of final judgment, as opposed to praising Wisdom (Sirach 1) or laying out the pedagogical goals from an earthly perspective (Prov 1:1–7). In this respect, the opening unit of 4QInstruction represents a seismic shift from more traditional Wisdom books.

The most striking structural aspect of 4QInstruction is the combination of longer discourses like the one cited above with shorter sections of mundane advice. Regarding the more traditional elements, there are warnings on a variety of standard themes. For example, "Do not stuff yourself with food when there is no clothing, And do not drink wine when there is no food. Do not seek after delicacies when you lack bread (לחם)" (4Q416 2 ii 18–20, translation mine).[11] Such mundane advice on the dangers of gluttony could just as easily be found in any of the Wisdom texts considered earlier in this study. In 4QInstruction, however, this type of admonition is interspersed with theological discourses on the addressee's access to divine mysteries. One pivotal passage is 4Q417 1 i (formerly numbered as frg. 2 i), where the young pupil (the מבין) is told to ponder "the wondrous myster[ies of the God of the Awesome Ones" (line 2). This is followed by a call to commit to the speculative content of this teaching for ultimate deliverance as a member of the "spiritual people" (as opposed to the "fleshly spirit"). Proverbs and Ben Sira also combine lengthy speeches with pithy admonitions, but the longer and more theological sections in these traditional texts do not have the same eschatological component. With its otherworldly aspect, such units are critical to the message of 4QInstruction.

As we proceed with an analysis of the language in 4QInstruction and its implications, including the all-important רז נהיה concept (translated in this discussion as the "mystery that is to be") that lies at the heart of this text, it is necessary to ask whether this mixture of theological discourses and mundane advice reflects literary layers or the complex

---

[11] According to the editors (*DJD 34*, 107), the use of לחם might indicate either "bread" (ordinary food) or "meat" (a luxury item). The point is that a person must attend to the basic necessity of clothing before satisfying any appetites.

efforts of a single source. This question forces the interpreter to separate or assimilate the diverse content of this text and justify any structural argument with reference to the modern generic categories of Wisdom and apocalypticism. Torleif Elgvin has posited originally separate strands in 4QInstruction, one (parenetic) dealing with prosaic matters and the other (theological discourses) with divine mysteries and judgment (e.g., 4Q417 1 i).[12] According to his interpretation, the combination of mundane and theological units in 4QInstruction signifies conflation, because the two strands are divergent in both style and orientation. The inclusion of speculative material alongside advice relating to farming, usury, and familial relations makes the most sense if an editorial process is assumed:

> The two layers we can discern in 4QInstruction appeal to different sources of authority. The wisdom admonition (both in the Hebrew Bible and in 4QInstruction) promotes knowledge based on reason.... The discourses of 4QInstruction, in contrast, appeal to the mystery to come, the divine mysteries revealed to the elect circle, as authority.[13]

According to Elgvin, a group with a sectarian consciousness incorporated traditional admonitions into a clearly apocalyptic work. He argues that those who compiled and organized the practical content of 4QInstruction preceded the closed community responsible for many of the Dead Sea Scrolls.

This is a well-constructed argument, and Elgvin highlights the diversity of the extant fragments. Yet the content of 4QInstruction does not seem to reflect different layers, but an effort by one source to associate righteous behavior with access to the heavenly realm and wickedness with eternal punishment. The connection between present ethical responsibilities and final judgment is an important one: whatever the precise meaning of the "mystery that is to be," we can assume that this overarching concept combines earthly requirements for righteous living, a nuanced understanding of divine majesty, *and* eschatological expectation (see below).[14] As with the teaching of Wisdom in earlier

---

[12] Torleif Elgvin, "Wisdom and Apocalypticism in the Early Second Century B.C.E.—The Evidence of 4QInstruction," in *The Dead Sea Scrolls Fifty Years After Their Discovery: Proceedings of the Jerusalem Congress, July 20–25, 1997* (ed. L.H. Schiffman et al.; Jerusalem: Israel Exploration Society/Shrine of the Book, Israel Museum, 2000), 231.

[13] Elgvin, "Wisdom and Apocalypticism," 231.

[14] The phrase רז נהיה appears throughout the text, in both the practical sections and the discourses, thus weakening Elgvin's argument for two sources of authority in 4QInstruction.

instructions, parents are supposed to pass on the content of the mystery
to their children (4Q416 2 iii 18), and those who know it are supposed
to meditate on this concept at all times (4Q417 1 i 6).[15] This synthesis
of the practical and otherworldly leads to a different ethical model, since
eternal reward becomes a possibility for the righteous pupil. Elgvin is
quite right that there are two levels of meaning in 4QInstruction, but
these are complementary and work in the service of a larger project:
to impress upon the addressee the need for uprightness and conformity
to the vision set forth in this text. This vision includes a final judgment
and the possibility of eternal salvation.[16]

### 3. The Promise of Retribution

As the last section indicated, 4QInstruction establishes an eschatological
framework for the evaluation of human conduct, and the text includes
noteworthy phrases and a few units that describe the nature of reward
and punishment for each individual. Of the two categories, the far
more vivid portrait concerns the dreadful fate of the wicked, which
results from their lack of discernment. A complete version of the text
might reveal a more detailed description of what sort of reward is in
store for the righteous, but this is impossible to determine. This pronounced emphasis on the fate of the unfortunate lot might signify an
effort to steer the recipients of this advice into good decision-making;
a useful analogy would be the description of the rebellious thugs in
Prov 1:10–19 and the parenetic function of that unit. There is also
a tendency in many apocalyptic texts to describe wrathful judgment
upon those who belong to the wrong group.[17] Through stark imagery,
4QInstruction conveys the consequences of being part of the non-elect

---

[15] The editors understand the subject of נלה in line 18 to be the parents ("they")
rather than God. See *DJD 34*, 122.

[16] John J. Collins, "The Eschatologizing of Wisdom in the Dead Sea Scrolls," in
*Sapiential Perspectives: Wisdom Literature in Light of the Dead Sea Scrolls. Proceedings of the Sixth
International Symposium of the Orion Center for the Study of the Dead Sea Scrolls and Associated
Literature, 20–22 May, 2001* (ed. J.J. Collins et al.; STDJ 51; Leiden: Brill, 2004), 60–61,
explains that "The mystery does not require that one behave in a way that is counter
to earthly wisdom." Cf. Matthew J. Goff, *The Worldly and Heavenly Wisdom of 4QInstruc-
tion* (STDJ 50; Leiden: Brill, 2003), 15, who argues that Elgvin's two-layer hypothesis
rests on a "rigid notion of generic purity."

[17] John J. Collins, *The Apocalyptic Imagination* (2d ed.; Grand Rapids: Eerdmans,
1998), 7, shows that judgment/destruction of the wicked is a universal feature of this
literature.

class, sometimes referred to in this text as the "fleshly spirit." One of the most important sections in this regard is 4Q418 69 ii, which (along with the opening unit in 4Q416 1) constitutes the major judgment scene in the extant fragments:

> You were fashioned [by the power of G]od, But to the everlasting pit shall your return be. For it shall awaken [to condemn] you[r] sin, [And the creatures of] its dark places [ ] shall cry out against your pleading. And all those who will endure forever, those who investigate the truth, shall rouse themselves to judge y[ou. And then] will all the foolish-minded be destroyed, And the children of iniquity shall not be found anymore, [And a]ll those who hold fast to wickedness shall wither [away. And then,] at the passing of judgement upon you, the foundations of the firmament will cry out, And all the [ ]...will thunder forth [...] (4Q418 69 ii 6–9)[18]

In this description, the author portrays a judgment scene for the wicked and an ultimate cessation of their existence. Those belonging to the "foolish-minded" (אוילי לב) and "children of iniquity" (בני עולה) category will face punishment, presumably in Sheol, which seems to be the reference point for the "dark regions." Such individuals are "destroyed" (ישמד) or disappear: they will "not be found anymore" (לוא ימצא עוד). A few commentators have noted that this passage contains second-person plural forms and distinctive references when compared with the rest of 4QInstruction. Mention of the "foolish-minded" (אוילי לב) occurs only in this passage, and some notable terminology, particularly רז נהיה, is absent.[19] The usual designation for the addressee in this text is the singular term מבין ("understanding one"), rather than the plural nouns that occur in this unit. As a result, it has been suggested that the description comes from another source.[20] Yet this use of plural forms might not be conclusive enough to indicate a different provenance; the tone of this unit and the terminological affinities (e.g., עולה) with the rest of the text suggest that it was part of the original instruction.[21]

---

[18] Tigchelaar, *To Increase Learning*, 210, reads יבשו in line 8 as "they will be ashamed," rather than "they will wither away" (*DJD 34*, 281).

[19] See section 7 for an extended treatment of the phrase רז נהיה.

[20] Tigchelaar, *To Increase Learning*, 217–22, notes the use of second-person plural forms in this passage, as opposed to the frequent use of מבין elsewhere in the text. 4Q418 55 reflects the same tendency.

[21] There might be a terminological link between the warning not to be contaminated "by iniquity" (בעולה) in 4Q417 1 i 23 and this fragment from 4Q418 69 ii, which includes mention of the "children of iniquity" (ובני עולה). Also note the use of לוא and עוד in reference to the punishment of the wicked (4Q418 69 ii 8), a negative phrase that echoes the withholding of insight (called the "vision of Hagu") from the

The eschatological depiction in this fragment coheres with the tenor of other passages in 4QInstruction. If it is indeed original to the text, as seems likely, this judgment scene is a useful indicator of the larger perspective in 4QInstruction, especially since the fate of the wicked is juxtaposed with a discussion of the "truly chosen ones" (בחירי אמת) in 4Q418 69 ii 10–15. Unlike the earlier instructions we have examined in this study, obedience to the ethical norms in 4QInstruction has eternal consequences.

The declaration in 4Q418 69 ii 7 that "all those who endure forever, those who investigate the truth, shall rouse themselves to judge y[ou" (וכול נהיה עולם דורשי אמת יעורו למשפטכ[ם) has led to speculation about the author's belief in resurrection. Elgvin and Puech interpret the phrase as an affirmation of physical resurrection.[22] According to Elgvin, the author of 4QInstruction relies on similar language in *1 Enoch*: "the righteous will arise from his sleep" (91:10). Moreover, Elgvin maintains that this belief conforms to the description of the Essenes in Hippolytus (*Haer.* 27).[23] In a similar assessment, Puech points to parallel evidence from the Hebrew Bible to make the case for 4QInstruction's acknowledgment of resurrection for those who were righteous during their lifetime.[24] This interpretation has been questioned by several scholars, who instead see the phrase in line 7 as a depiction of angels rousing themselves to take part in the final judgment.[25] In support

---

"fleshly spirit" in 4Q417 1 i 17 (ועוד לוא נתן). See below for a more detailed treatment of 4Q417 1 i.

[22] On the question of resurrection in 4QInstruction, see Torleif Elgvin, "Early Essene Eschatology: Judgment and Salvation according to Sapiential Work A," in *Current Research and Technological Development on the Dead Sea Scrolls: Conference on the Texts from the Judean Desert, Jerusalem, 30 April 1995* (ed. D.W. Parry and S.D. Ricks; STDJ 20; Leiden: Brill, 1996), 143–44; Émile Puech, "Les Fragments Eschatologiques de 4QInstruction (4Q416 1 et 4Q418 69 ii, 81–81a, 127)," *RevQ* 22 (2005): 89–119.

[23] Elgvin, "Early Essene Eschatology," 143–44.

[24] Puech, "Les Fragments Eschatologiques," 99. He compares the language of this passage to statements in Job 14:12, Isa 26:19, Dan 12:2, and Ps 17:15. The last three biblical units, according to Puech, indicate a belief in resurrection for the deceased who exhibit righteous behavior. Puech notes the use of עור in the passage from Job: "so mortals lie down and do not rise again; until the heavens are no more, they will not awake or be roused out of their sleep (לא־יערו משנתם)." In addition, Puech claims that the verb דרש does not describe angelic behavior in 4QInstruction or other scrolls, and he posits a parallel between this description in 4Q418 69 ii and the final judgment scene in *1 En.* 27:3.

[25] Tigchelaar, *To Increase Learning*, 211, points to the use of קיץ and עור in the judgment scene of Ps 35:23 and to *1 En.* 100:4, another description of a final judgment; cf. Collins, "The Eschatologizing of Wisdom," 56–57. Goff, *Worldly and Heavenly Wisdom*,

of the latter understanding is the fact that Second Temple descriptions of otherworldly possibilities for the righteous often refer to a spiritual existence of some sort and not necessarily to physical resurrection (Qoh 3:21; *1 En.* 103:4; 104:2, etc.).[26] This scene in 4Q418 69 ii relates to emulating the heavenly host: the righteous individual is made aware of a final judgment in which angels will be involved in the process.[27] The message seems to be that those who aspire to become like the angels should cease with their complaining, since celestial figures have obeyed the statutes of God in perpetuity and not grown weary from such a privilege (line 13).[28] The eternal promise therefore has a pedagogical function, since it encourages the addressee to delight in the divine instruction and to focus attention on righteous conduct.

Other judgment scenes in the text, including the opening fragment of 4QInstruction, describe a similarly conclusive fate for the wicked. Earlier Wisdom texts could only threaten a premature demise and/or a qualitative death. The declaration in the book of Proverbs that "The wise man's path of life leads upward, in order to avoid Sheol below" (15:24) relates to *present possibilities* and the belief that the fool's path is already pregnant with death, even if his physical body is technically functioning (cf. Sir 22:11–12). The apocalyptic imagery of 4QInstruction represents something altogether different. In 4Q416 1, the author predicts that God "will pronounce judgment upon the work of wicked-

---

176–77, cites language in line 4Q418 69 ii 13 about the angels never tiring of the "works of truth." It is far more likely that these are the figures who "rouse themselves" against the "foolish of heart."

[26] John J. Collins, *Apocalypticism in the Dead Sea Scrolls* (London: Routledge, 1997), 110–29, surveys many of the relevant passages and the type of post-mortem existence implied.

[27] Goff, *Worldly and Heavenly Wisdom*, 178, cites the occurrence of צבא ("host") in the opening unit of 4QInstruction (4Q416 1), in what appears to be the role of supporting judges (the Hebrew is fragmentary for these lines). In addition, the Lord appears "with his army" for judgment in *1 En.* 1:4.

[28] This description does not depict the present fellowship with the angels (realized angelology) that occurs in the Hodayot, but a hortatory summons to take good conduct and praise seriously, just as the heavenly hosts have done. With regard to וּבֹנֵי הֹשׁמים[ in lines 12–13, this almost certainly refers to the angels and not to humans or "ange-lomorphic men." This last possibility has been argued by Crispin Fletcher-Louis, *All the Glory of Adam: Liturgical Anthropology in the Dead Sea Scrolls* (STDJ 42; Leiden: Brill, 2002), 120. Florentino García Martínez, "Marginalia on 4QInstruction," *DSD* 13 (2006): 29–37, offers a thorough review of debate over this phrase and demonstrates that this can only be a reference to angels; cf. *DJD 34*, 290. The shift from the second-person to the third-person וּבֹנֵי הֹשׁמים[ clinches the argument. The elect human group (בחירי אמח) is addressed in the second-person and encouraged to model their behavior after the tireless efforts of the "sons of heaven."

ness" (lines 10–11), and the ones who have "defiled themselves" through
such activity will be in a state of agony. Similarly, 4Q418 113 1 refers
to a point when "there comes an end of ini[quity" (עד תום עוֹ֯לֹה).[29] The
idea of a final cessation for one group, based on their earthly conduct,
signifies a major shift within the Jewish wisdom tradition.

With regard to the specific vocabulary related to judgment in this
opening unit and in other passages, קץ ("period") and פקודה ("visitation") do not occur in the previous sapiential books we have examined
with the same connotation as one finds in 4QInstruction. The term
קץ appears in other apocalyptic texts from the second-century, however, and פקודה occurs frequently in the Scrolls with the connotation
of judgment.[30] In 4QInstruction, at a future (eschatological) point, "all
iniquity will come to an end, while the period of truth (קץ האֹמֹת) will be
completed in all periods of eternity (בכל קצי עד)" (4Q416 1 13). There
is a similar statement in the Apocalypse of Weeks (1 En. 91:12) about
the "periodization" of history throughout the ages, and we have already
established corollaries between this opening section of 4QInstruction
and the theophanic scene at the beginning of the Book of the Watchers.[31] Moreover, 4Q417 1 i 7–8 refers to "their punishment (פקודתֹם),
in all ages everlasting, and the punishment of eternity (פקודת עד)."[32]
The point of such language is to convey a final, eschatological moment
in which the wicked will be held responsible and all iniquities will be

---

[29] This fragment has only a few intelligible words, and the editors reconstruct the
next line (2) to refer to "a visitation (פקודת) of pe[ace" (DJD 34, 339). This is apocalyptic terminology.

[30] Florentino García Martínez, "Wisdom at Qumran: Worldly or Heavenly?" in
*Wisdom and Apocalypticism in the Dead Sea Scrolls and in the Biblical Tradition* (ed. F. García
Martínez; BETL 168; Leuven: Leuven University Press/Peeters, 2003), 10. With regard
to קץ, see for example, Dan 8:17, 19; 9:26. The use of קץ in Sirach 36 serves as a
likely indicator of the secondary status of this passage. The term פקודה appears in a
number of the Dead Sea Scrolls, including the Treatise on the Two Spirits (e.g., 1QS
3:13). For the primary text, see Dominique Barthélemy and J.T. Milik, *Qumran Cave 1*
(DJD 1; Oxford: Clarendon Press, 1955). In 4QInstruction, פקודה occurs 16 times, and
it appears 20 times in the other 1Q–11Q texts (Tigchelaar, *To Increase Learning*, 240–41).
In both the Treatise on the Two Spirits and elsewhere in the Scrolls, it usually has
an eschatological connotation. On whether the term indicates a final "visitation" (or
"punishment") or refers to the difficulties encountered during each individual's lifetime,
see Armin Lange, *Weisheit und Prädestination: Weisheitliche Urordnung und Prädestination in
den Textfunden von Qumran* (STDJ 18; Leiden: Brill, 1995), 61. In 4QInstruction, it seems
to describe a final "visitation."

[31] Elgvin, "An Analysis of 4QInstruction," 103.

[32] There is also extant language in 4Q416 4 1, which contains the expression "the
pe[riod of] wrath." For further discussion of this phrase and others like it involving קץ
(in both the Scrolls and Daniel), see Goff, *Worldly and Heavenly Wisdom*, 189–97.

accounted for, the type of "reckoning" that Qoheleth had hoped for but never maintained as a possibility.[33] In utilizing such terms as קץ, the author of 4QInstruction tailors them to suit a creative mixture of sapiential and apocalyptic ideas. For example, this text does not rely on an explicit scheme involving periods like Daniel and the Apocalypse of Weeks.[34] Even if there is an implicit chronological understanding in 4QInstruction, what ultimately matters is the addressee's knowledge and ability to separate himself from iniquity before the final "visitation."[35] The intent here seems to be didactic: the addressee should understand the profound implications of his daily behavior. The author does not stress the imminence of this judgment, but he does emphasize its inevitability. Unlike Ben Sira's vague language about a retributive moment at death, these apocalyptic terms in 4QInstruction convey the threat of a decisive judgment.

Since the telos of the wicked differs from their righteous counterparts in this work, it naturally follows that the concept of Sheol would take on a more consequential meaning than in earlier instructions. 4QInstruction contains references to "the pit" (השחת) (many of them fragmentary), and this designation seems to represent the endpoint for individuals who transgress during their lifetime and belong to the "fleshly spirit" category. The "everlasting pit" in 4Q418 69 ii 6 becomes the destination of the "foolish-minded." There is a similar use of this phrase in the Treatise on the Two Spirits (1QS 4:11–14), which describes "visitation" (פקודה) upon evil persons "for eternal damnation by the scorching wrath of the God of revenges, for permanent terror and shame without end with the humiliation of destruction by the fire of the dark regions."[36] In addition, 4QInstruction has an intriguing allusion to the Korah episode in the book of Numbers, where the apparent intent is

---

[33] Goff, *Worldly and Heavenly Wisdom*, 190, argues that the use of this language in 4QInstruction relates to a final eschatological moment: "By describing judgment as eternal, it is considered to be in a sense effective throughout history, even though it is only implemented at its end."

[34] Goff, *Worldly and Heavenly Wisdom*, 193: "This wisdom text shows no interest in enumerating the periods of history."

[35] Collins, "The Eschatologizing of Wisdom," 53, cites phrases like כל קצי עד as indicative of a chronological scheme similar to the Apocalypse of Weeks, even if this is not directly stated in the text. Like the Apocalypse of Weeks, 4QInstruction "presupposes a similar division of history, and even of 'eternity', into periods."

[36] Translation is from Florentino García Martínez and Eibert J.C. Tigchelaar. *The Dead Sea Scrolls Study Edition* (2 vols.; Leiden: Brill, 1997–98).

to depict the wicked being swallowed up by the earth.[37] In a similar portrait, *1 En.* 10:13–14, describes rebellious angels being led away to the "fiery abyss," to the "prison where they will be confined forever." It is likely that the person(s) responsible for 4QInstruction knew some of these traditions and the ideas associated with an eternal punishment for sinners, particularly the images from *1 Enoch*.[38] For those authors with an apocalyptic understanding of reward and punishment, Sheol was no longer a more neutral term referring to the universal destination of humanity (e.g., Qoh 9:10); it had become the endpoint/punishment for sinners who transgressed during their lifetime. This idea would be developed in much greater (and diverse) detail among later generations of Jewish and Christian authors.[39]

The righteous (the "spiritual people"), on the other hand, do not endure punishment in the "everlasting pit." In 4Q418 126 ii 7–8, the fates of the wicked and the righteous are juxtaposed: "And to shut (the door) (ולסנור) on the wicked, [ ] But to raise up the head of the poor, In glory everlasting and peace eternal (בכבוד עולם ושלום עד)."[40] The occurrence of סנר here is noteworthy: the term is used in the Hodayot

---

[37] The reference to the "judgment of Korah" occurs in 4Q423 5 1, which is an allusion to the story in Num 16:32–33. The original narrative describes the earth "swallowing" (בלע) those associated with this rebellion (v. 32).

[38] The many similarities between the Enochic corpus and 4QInstruction, particularly the apocalyptic language, suggest a common milieu of origin. Elgvin, "An Analysis of 4QInstruction," 169–70, posits the dependence of the Wisdom text on *1 Enoch*. Among his examples for a direct literary relationship is the reference to an "eternal planting" (מטעת עולם), which appears in both 4Q418 81 13 and in *1 Enoch* (10:16; 93:5, 10). Yet this designation also occurs in other scrolls (e.g., 1QH 14:15 and 16:6) and does not necessarily have the same connotation in every text. Whether such terminological affinities indicate direct dependence is a matter of debate. For a more cautious assessment, see Loren Stuckenbruck, "4QInstruction and the Possible Influence of Early Enochic Traditions: An Evaluation," in *The Wisdom Texts from Qumran and the Development of Sapiential Thought* (ed. C. Hempel et al.; BETL 159; Leuven: Leuven University Press/Peeters, 2002), 245–61. According to Stuckenbruck, the commonalities between the two works (and Daniel) do not necessarily suggest a direct relationship, but "a growing body of sources extant from the 2nd century B.C.E. whose ideas were able to cross-fertilise as their distinct forms of apocalyptic wisdom took shape" (p. 261).

[39] For example, note the treatment of eternal punishment in *4 Ezra* (ca. 100 C.E.): "And if it is one of those who have shown scorn and have not kept the way of the Most High, and who have despised his Law, and who have hated those who fear God–such spirits shall not enter into habitations, but shall immediately wander about in torments, ever grieving and sad, in seven ways" (7:79–80). Translation is from Bruce M. Metzger, "The Fourth Book of Ezra," in *The Old Testament Pseudepigrapha Volume 1: Apocalyptic Literature and Testaments* (ed. J.H. Charlesworth; Garden City, NY: Doubleday, 1983).

[40] The editors are uncertain about the width of the lacunae in this fragment, but the general context and message of the Hebrew are clear enough (*DJD 34*, 353).

to describe the "doors of the pit" closing (סגר) upon the wicked (1QH 11:18; cf. 1Q27 1 i 5–6). In contrast, the righteous addressee in 4QInstruction (designated as "poor" in 4Q418 126 ii) stands to inherit eternal life. God creates the universe, and everything happens according to the divine pleasure (רצונו in 4Q418 126 ii 5). Events under God's control include the separation of the righteous and wicked and a unique eschatological blessing for the favored group. Language elsewhere in the text confirms this hopeful perspective: there is a reference to "eternal joy" (שמחת עולם) in 4Q417 2 i 12 in the midst of a discussion concerning "the birth-times of salvation" and "who is to inherit glory and toil" (line 11). In a related section, 4Q418 81 includes language about the addressee's separation from the fleshly spirit. His "lot" has been cast among the "[Go]dly [ones]" (lines 4–5).[41] This is a delayed gift: the author implies that the addressee will receive the same "inheritance" as the angels (lines 12–13), *if* he first spends a lifetime honoring them and committing himself to the content of these teachings. Similarly, in the opening unit of the text (4Q416 1), the promise is extended that "His (God's) faithful children will be favorably accepted by [Him" (line 10), if they develop the requisite discernment (line 15).

Elsewhere in 4QInstruction, the elect category is commanded to glorify God and promised an eternal reward in exchange: "For he has raised up your head out of poverty, And he has seated you with nobles, And he has placed in your power an inheritance of glory" (4Q416 2 iii 11–12, translation mine). The "nobles" (נדיבים) in this passage probably mean the angelic host, with whom the addressee will share fellowship after being evaluated favorably by God.[42] The language is an allusion to Hannah's prayer in 1 Sam 2:8: "He raises up the poor from the dust; he lifts the needy from the ash heap, to make them sit with princes (להושיב עם־נדיבים) and inherit a seat of honor" (cf. Ps. 113:7–8). In contrast to the biblical texts, this designation in 4QInstruction does not appear to indicate an aristocratic class of superiors. The precarious social situation for the pupil would seem to preclude the

---

[41] The line is fragmentary here, but this is the editors' best guess at a reconstruction (*DJD 34*, 300).

[42] Goff, *Worldly and Heavenly Wisdom*, 210–11, has recently made this argument; cf. Benjamin G. Wold, *Women, Men, and Angels: The Qumran Document Musar leMevin and its Allusions to Genesis Creation Traditions* (WUNT 201; Tübingen: Mohr Siebeck, 2005), 155–56. This term is cited in *DJD 34*, 118, but the editors do not specifically address the background for נדיבים.

possibility of such a major economic leap.[43] The individuals addressed in this text have little chance of gaining social equivalence to actual nobles. The language in 1 Sam 2:8 and Ps 113:7–8 became a natural fit for application to the angelic realm in 4QInstruction, since these passages describe God's decision to elevate a struggling group to glorious heights. Other statements in the Scrolls support this interpretation of נדיבים as an allusion to angels.[44] Whether a "realized eschatology" should be inferred from this passage is a related question; this description suggests some type of present election for the addressee, even if this is not a topic of great interest in 4QInstruction.[45] When considering the text as a whole, the addressee's eternal glory will only follow a righteous existence.[46] A person's earthly behavior determines the true reward, and the "inheritance of glory" promised to the righteous will more than compensate for current struggles.

For our examination of causality in these texts, it is interesting that 4QInstruction connects righteous behavior with the bestowal of lengthy days and an eternal reputation. For example, in 4Q416 2 iii 19, longevity is guaranteed for individuals who honor their parents (למען חייכה ואֿרוך ימיכה; cf. Sir 3:6). A full and content life as a reward for virtue is in line with traditional Wisdom. In similar fashion, 4QInstruction offers an eternal name for one who does not embezzle money given by a stranger. Such an honest individual can presumably die in peace: "Then you may lie down with the truth, and when you die your memory will blos[som for ev]er, ואחריתכה will inherit joy" (4Q416 2 iii 7–8).[47] Perhaps ואחריתכה relates to the offspring of the righteous

---

[43] An unexpected windfall does not seem possible for members of this group, and this is not promised elsewhere in the text (see below). It is difficult to reconcile this language with the statement in line 9, which seems to describe sudden material gains. Yet the content of 4Q416 2 iii 11–12 suggests a metaphorical reading for these two lines, especially since the text cited from 4Q418 126 ii 7–8 also uses poverty language to describe the eschatological deliverance of the righteous.

[44] Matthew J. Goff, *Discerning Wisdom: The Sapiential Literature of the Dead Sea Scrolls* (VTSup 116; Leiden: Brill, 2007), 43 n.137, cites another allusion to Hannah's prayer in 4Q427 7 ii 8–9, which includes a reference to fellowship with heavenly beings.

[45] This passage appears to blur the distinction between present status and future glory to a degree. On the differences between the implied delay in 4QInstruction and some of the units involving present glory in the Scrolls, particularly in the Hodayot, see Goff, *Worldly and Heavenly Wisdom*, 212–13.

[46] The addressee can still be "contaminated" by iniquity (4Q417 1 i 23) and faces adversity in his present existence; contrast with the pupil's future glory (4Q417 2 i 10–12).

[47] Translation is from *DSSSE* 2:851.

person, as suggested by parallel sayings in other instructions. The belief
in proud descendants and a lasting reputation are central guarantees
in Ben Sira (e.g., Sir 15:6; 37:26; 39:9; 41:11–13; 44:8). There seems
to be a different connotation in this passage, however. It is possible to
read this term in 4Q416 2 iii 7 as a reference to the afterlife. Elgvin
interprets this line as follows: "and in the end you will inherit joy."[48]
It could also be translated as "your hereafter," so that ואחריתכה refers
to the spiritual state of a righteous individual after judgment.[49] If this
reading is correct, this passage represents another example of the
"eschatologizing" principle that seems to be at work in 4QInstruction.
Old sapiential constructs are transformed by radical understandings
of act and consequence.

All of these fragments in 4QInstruction invite consideration of the
type of existence enjoyed by the righteous in their immortal state. Since
physical resurrection is never cited as a possibility for the elect category,
the "peace eternal" for the addressee presumably involves some sort
of spiritual existence. The allusions to angelic figures by such terms as
נדיבים suggest a shared fellowship of some sort, although 4QInstruc-
tion does not offer a vivid description on the order of *1 En.* 104:2–6.
Another strong indicator of heavenly existence with the angels is the
mention of "eternal joy" in 4Q417 2 i 12. In support of this reading, Goff notes the phonetic similarity between שמחת עולם ("eternal
joy") and שחת עולם ("eternal pit").[50] Elgvin posits astral immortality
in 4QInstruction, an understanding similar to Dan 12:3, *1 Enoch*, and
Wis 3:7.[51] This interpretation is certainly plausible, although the extant
fragments do not contain any specific imagery of this sort. Statements
on the fate of the righteous are indirect and often occur in fragmentary
lines. The available sections of this text do not allow us to clarify the
author's eternal vision with certainty, although it is beyond dispute that
he possessed a belief in individual immortality. The references listed
above imply a state of permanent blessing for the מבין who heeds this

---

[48] Elgvin, "An Analysis of 4QInstruction," 113.
[49] John J. Collins, "The Mysteries of God: Creation and Eschatology in 4QInstruc-
tion and the Wisdom of Solomon," in *Wisdom and Apocalypticism in the Dead Sea Scrolls and
in the Biblical Tradition* (ed. F. García Martínez; BETL 168; Leuven: Leuven University
Press/Peeters, 2003), 294.
[50] Goff, *Discerning Wisdom*, 42 n. 134. The Treatise on the Two Spirits makes the
same distinction (1QS 4:6–14)
[51] Elgvin, "Early Essene Eschatology," 143.

advice: his "holy spirit" (4Q416 2 ii 6) lives on in some way, "in glory everlasting and peace eternal" (4Q418 126 ii 8).

With regard to the adjudication process, we have already cited language in the text that emphasizes divine agency, including the opening section: "in heaven He shall pronounce judgment upon the work of wickedness, and all His faithful children will be favorably accepted by [Him" (4Q416 1 10). God evaluates human conduct in 4QInstruction and decides appropriate recompense, and this is thoroughly consistent with passages in earlier instructions, apocalyptic texts, and language elsewhere in the Scrolls. For example, in the Book of Mysteries (1Q27 1 i 3–4), the wicked will be harshly judged, because they "did not know the mystery that is to be, and the former things they did not consider. Nor did they know what is to come upon them. And they did not save their lives from the mystery that is to be."[52] Goff sees a difference between 4QInstruction and the understanding found in Mysteries and earlier instructions on this issue of divine involvement in the judgment process: "4QInstruction differs from both Mysteries and traditional wisdom in its affirmation of divine agency at judgment."[53] Goff's conclusion on this point is problematic, because it oversimplifies the dynamic in didactic literature between divine agency and more automatic processes. Goff is correct that God decides human outcomes in 4QInstruction, including rewards for the righteous, but this is no different from many statements in earlier instructions, including texts that are completely lacking in eschatological vision. For the sages who compiled Proverbs, the deity can play an active role in judging humanity: "will he (God) not repay a person according to his deeds?" (Prov 24:12; cf. Prov 15:22). Ben Sira also posits an active role for the deity: "For it is easy for the Lord on the day of death to reward individuals according to their conduct" (Sir 11:26). In addition, sayings that mention Wisdom as an arbiter of human conduct (playing a role similar to the mystery in 1Q27 1 i 3–4) or even passive formulations about what happens to a person do not necessarily presume divine *in*activity. Judgment language or the absence of it can merely indicate rhetorical variation as opposed to

---

[52] Translation is from Torleif Elgvin et al., *Qumran Cave 4.XV: Sapiential Texts, Part I* (DJD 20; Oxford: Clarendon Press, 1997), 38.

[53] Goff, *Worldly and Heavenly Wisdom*, 203.

major theological distinctions.[54] On this issue of divine agency and the possibility of direct intervention by God, 4QInstruction is consistent with the wisdom tradition *and* with parallel passages in the Scrolls.

Nevertheless, the depiction of a final judgment and contrasting fates in 4QInstruction resembles the Enochic corpus, Daniel, and other passages from the Dead Sea Scrolls, more than Ben Sira and Proverbs. The eschatological language is indeed noteworthy for an instructional document, as this author provides an otherworldly means of adjudicating the consequences of individual behavior. Its author does not warn the addressee that the eschaton is imminent, but multiple passages indicate the inevitability of a final reckoning and a separation based on each person's conduct. 4QInstruction combines the "ethic of caution" found in Ben Sira and earlier Wisdom texts with a belief in deliverance for the righteous elect. While offering a consistent principle of causality, this work states that imbalances will not be rectified until a much later point.[55] In this respect, 4QInstruction transcends the earthly focus of prior instructions, even as its mundane warnings are anchored in the exigencies of everyday life. As Collins explains of 4QInstruction and the Epistle of Enoch, "All of this literature was an exercise in bricolage, piecing together a new view of the world that drew motifs and ideas from many sources."[56] When examining 4QInstruction, it becomes apparent that many authors during the Second Temple period did not adhere to the literary models of their predecessors or to contemporaries with more traditional ideas. The piecing together of various motifs indicates a fluidity with regard to generic conventions and innovative ideas for retribution. The apocalyptic worldview created the possibility for a consistent *Tun-Ergehen-Zusammenhang.*

---

[54] 4QInstruction does use judicial scenes in a more explicit manner than earlier instructions (e.g., 4Q416 1 10); this type of description is more closely related to the apocalyptic worldview.

[55] Collins, "The Eschatologizing of Wisdom," 60, explains that there is no "interim ethic" in 4QInstruction. The text implies that "One should live one's life *sub specie aeternitatis.* This does not mean that one should neglect this life, but that one should live it properly."

[56] Collins, "The Eschatologizing of Wisdom," 63.

## 4. *Apocalyptic Eschatology in a Wisdom Text*

The last section mentioned that many of the warnings in 4QInstruction are in the same spirit as more traditional instructions.[57] Admonitions in 4QInstruction frequently resemble Proverbs and Ben Sira, although the language in this text suggests a more precarious financial situation for the intended audience.[58] The need to pay back loans quickly is a topic of concern in all of these texts, especially if an individual presents a personal item or property as collateral (4Q416 2 ii 4–6; cf. Prov 6:1–5; 22:26–27).[59] Yet 4QInstruction discusses poverty as a reality for the addressee, whereas the earlier instructions do not assume it. Another instance of commonality is the call to respect one's parents: "Honour thy father in thy poverty, and thy mother in thy low estate. For as God is to a man, so is his own father, and as the Lord is to a person, so his mother" (4Q416 2 iii 15–16).[60] Filial piety is a familiar theme in Proverbs (23:22) and Ben Sira (3:1–16), and statements in 4QInstruction are in line with this emphasis on honoring both parents.[61] Finally, certain

---

[57] In addition, the designation מבין ("O understanding one") is used repeatedly, and this is comparable to the singular addressee of other instructions ("my son"). The use of מבין and the singular imperative do not mean a single addressee. The stylistic convention of directing admonitions to one pupil is a staple of ancient Near Eastern instructions from all periods. The plural מבינים is also used in this text (e.g., 4Q418 221 3).

[58] The frequent statement, "You are poor" (4Q415 6 2; 4Q416 2 ii 20; 4Q416 2 iii 2, 8, 12, 19; 4Q418 177 5), characterizes the addressee's actual economic status.

[59] While fragmentary, these lines in 4QInstruction seem to be addressing the practice of surety (Goff, *Worldly and Heavenly Wisdom*, 140–41). Ben Sira has a somewhat different take on this topic, since he views honest lending as a benevolent act (29:1). This sage is not as anxious about the lending process as the author of 4QInstruction: Sirach 29 evinces a standard wariness about loans, but some of the statements in this unit imply a better economic position for Ben Sira's students than what we find in 4QInstruction (e.g., Sir 29:7–14).

[60] There are several textual problems in this unit. Regarding כאב לאיש כן אביהו in line 16, it should be noted that 4Q418 has כאל. The use of "Father" in reference to the deity would be unusual for a text from this period, but not unattested. The reading would have to be definite ("like the Father"), and this is unlikely. The editors (*DJD 34*, 120–21) argue against basing a reading of אב on *lectio difficilior*. It is probable that אב was written in error, due to the subsequent אביהו. In addition, Strugnell and Harrington's understanding of כאדנים (in the phrase וכאדנים לגבר כן אמו) as a reference to God is convincing, especially since this construction is parallel to כאל.

[61] 4QInstruction affirms the need to respect both parents, including specific language about honoring mothers that is characteristic of Israelite Wisdom. What is distinctive about 4Q416 2 iii is the advice that parents should reveal (נלה) to their children the "mystery that is to be" (line 17). This statement, which implies familial instruction for the central concept in 4QInstruction, raises questions about the setting and manner in which the material was passed along (see below).

warnings reflect the pragmatic tone of earlier instructions, especially in the realm of everyday transactions. For example, "Be an advocate for your own business interests (לֹהִצבֹכֹה)" (4Q417 2 i 12, translation mine). The message of 4QInstruction on this point is that a person should look out for his own welfare in the marketplace, while not taking more than he needs (4Q417 2 i 18).[62]

This mixture of apocalyptic motifs and mundane advice forces the interpreter to wrestle with the modern generic constructs of Wisdom and apocalypticism, particularly the role of social context in a particular author's choice of terminology and ideas. In addressing the relationship between the two categories, Gerhard von Rad famously argued that Wisdom is "the real matrix from which apocalyptic literature originates."[63] This hypothesis has generated a number of scholarly responses, many of them critical of von Rad's basic premise. Collins notes that apocalyptic literature regularly involves angelic mediators, eschatological expectation of a final judgment, and the belief that the world is in a less than perfect state.[64] None of these salient features are characteristic of the biblical instructions, and some of the sages vigorously opposed them. The last chapter pointed to Ben Sira's vehement denial of eternal possibilities for humanity and his rejection of visionary experiences. Scholars looking for corollaries with a text like 4QInstruction have had more success in linking the otherworldly, speculative ideas and terminology found in this text with Daniel and *1 Enoch*.[65]

---

[62] The situation of the addressee is more tenuous here than in Proverbs and Ben Sira, as evidenced by the frequent references to his poverty.

[63] Gerhard von Rad, *Old Testament Theology* (2 vols.; trans. D.M.G. Stalker; Louisville: Westminster John Knox Press, 2001), 2:306. Cf. Lange, *Weisheit und Prädestination*, 301–6, who endorses von Rad's theory and applies it to 4QInstruction and other texts from the Dead Sea Scrolls. He argues that the appeal to revelation, a dualistic worldview, and a rational principle for framing larger questions (a "world order") are part of the sapiential heritage: "In diesem Zusammenfließen von präexistenter Ordnung, kosmischem Dualismus und Offenbarungstheologie sind erste Schritte auf dem Weg zur Apokalyptik getan" (p. 305).

[64] John J. Collins, "Wisdom, Apocalypticism, and Generic Compatibility," in *In Search of Wisdom: Essays in Memory of John G. Gammie* (ed. L.G. Perdue et al.; Louisville: Westminster John Knox Press, 1993), 165–85.

[65] The hypothesis that 4QInstruction serves as evidence for the emergence of "apocalyptic" out of traditional Wisdom has not been accepted by many scholars. Both the milieu of origin and the terminology for such texts as Daniel and *1 Enoch* seem to be the more likely background for much of the content. Elgvin, "Wisdom and Apocalypticism," 239, is closer to the mark in his association of the longer discourses with these apocalyptic works: "One finds frequent references to esoteric wisdom, *raz* and *raz nihyeh*.... Similar to *1 Enoch*, the reception of wisdom is constitutive of salvation

Nevertheless, these two generic categories cannot be neatly divided, especially after one surveys the diverse content of many documents from the Hellenistic period.[66] The combination in 4QInstruction is significant, and it raises important questions about the fluidity between Wisdom and apocalypticism and the possible sociopolitical reasons for bringing together different elements in an instructional document. J.Z. Smith's *Map is Not Territory* is helpful on this point, since he describes apocalypticism as "*wisdom lacking a royal patron.*"[67] Smith does not focus specifically on Jewish Wisdom and the emergence of apocalyptic thought during the Second Temple period; he attempts to locate trajectories in ancient Egyptian texts (from Neferty to the Potter's Oracle) that evince an "apocalyptic" understanding of society and the created order.[68] Moreover, his definition is an oversimplification of the complex relationship between these modern categories of Wisdom and apocalypticism. Yet the statement is useful for distinguishing the conservative advice of Proverbs (royal background) and Ben Sira (dependent on the priestly establishment) from the more "independent" conclusions of 4QInstruction.[69]

Smith also offers the paradigm of a "locative" worldview, where the status quo is affirmed by "scribal elites who had a deep vested interest in restricting mobility and valuing place."[70] This "self-serving ideology" results in the glorification of existing structures and the possibility of present fulfillment (i.e., justice and prosperity) within those structures. Again, this model does not cohere fully with Proverbs and Ben Sira, since the sages responsible for these texts speak out against corruption

---

and life eternal. 4QInstruction shares what has been described as the core of the apocalyptic message: the unmasking of the otherwise unknown secrets of God. The composition has a hortatory character and a clear interest in the afterlife: the elect will attain to their ultimate reward."

[66] George W.E. Nickelsburg, "Wisdom and Apocalypticism in Early Judaism: Some Points for Discussion," in *Conflicted Boundaries in Wisdom and Apocalypticism* (ed. B.G. Wright and L. Wills; SBLSymS 35; Atlanta: Society of Biblical Literature, 2005), 17–39, addresses the parameters of these two categories for many of the texts in this study.

[67] J.Z. Smith, *Map is Not Territory* (Chicago: University of Chicago Press, 1978), 81.

[68] Whether one wants to call the end of Neferty an "apocalyptic" scene is debatable, but it certainly depicts a society in turmoil and a conclusion to present earthly circumstances: "I will show you a land in turmoil. He who was weak of arm is (now) a possessor of might" (54).

[69] By independent, we mean that the author of 4QInstruction does not require support from the royal or priestly authorities, nor does his readership seem to be located in the more established classes (see below).

[70] Smith, *Map is Not Territory*, 293.

and blatant mistreatment of the poor. Smith's "locative" label can nevertheless be useful for differentiating the ideology of 4QInstruction from its more official sapiential counterparts, especially since the editors of Proverbs and then Ben Sira had to rely on establishment circles for income and public support.[71] Traditional beliefs on death and retribution are not necessarily a function of an author's social status, but it is noteworthy that a more established sage like Ben Sira affirms traditional understandings *and* actively seeks to refute speculative new proposals. Speaking to a retainer-class audience, he maintains that justice in the present context is possible. In contrast, the author of 4QInstruction does not promise worldly success to virtuous individuals. He instead constructs an elaborate view of the universe, which the addressee must learn and internalize in order to be delivered from death. This work shares a great deal with the Epistle of Enoch on this point, since the righteous elect in both texts are promised eternal reward irrespective of their social status.[72] The author of 4QInstruction does not condemn the acquisition of wealth in the manner of the Enochic books nor does he oppose existing social structures. Yet he does share with the Epistle a belief in final judgment commensurate with one's behavior, and the implied audience for both texts seems to be a group on the periphery of society. Another helpful corollary on this point is the use of apocalyptic-eschatological language among some of the earliest Christian writers. Claudia Setzer has demonstrated that the appeal to resurrection by figures like Paul and Justin gave marginal communities the strength to adapt to difficult social circumstances and "live in the world as it is."[73] The belief in some form of the afterlife is certainly a theological statement, but the presence of otherworldly language also relates to

---

[71] It is once again appropriate to ask where Qoheleth fits on this spectrum, since he does not appeal to or praise priestly figures. Perhaps this author was economically self-sufficient and therefore somewhat of a "freelance" sage. The persona in the book suggests an individual who enjoyed considerable property holdings. Although he endorses a pragmatic approach to earthly living, the tone of Qoheleth does not indicate that this author was a member of the retainer class.

[72] Benjamin G. Wright, review of Matthew J. Goff, *The Worldly and Heavenly Wisdom of 4QInstruction*, *JBL* 124 (2005), 548–53.

[73] Claudia Setzer, *Resurrection of the Body in Early Judaism and Early Christianity* (Boston: Brill, 2004). She explicates the manner in which "resurrection constructs community" in these texts. Reflecting on Paul's attitude in the Corinthian correspondence, Setzer argues that the apostle's peripheral status as a member of a small sect and his belief in the afterlife are closely related. His reflections on resurrection lead to a certain confidence: "Resisting the economic patronage system in place, he works for himself and takes up

social identity: "it functions as a shorthand for an interlocking web of values, a condensation symbol that helps to construct community."[74] Although physical resurrection is not guaranteed in 4QInstruction, the choice of generic constructs and the assurance of eschatological deliverance relate directly to a marginalized social location for both author and audience.[75]

With this combination of traditional sapiential elements and apocalyptic ideas, we endorse Harrington's categorization of 4QInstruction as a text in which a human sage "presents wisdom in an apocalyptic framework," as opposed to a book in which God or a divine angel reveals "apocalyptic wisdom."[76] Many of the descriptions in this text and some of the terminology (such as "mystery" language) can be described as "apocalyptic." In using "apocalyptic" vis-à-vis 4QInstruction, this designation *need not* refer to "an extreme form of eschatology," or a pure apocalypse.[77] Many ideas in 4QInstruction, especially in the discourses, such as the idea of a final separation of the righteous and the wicked, occur in other books with explicitly apocalyptic interests (e.g., *1 Enoch*). Since we are maintaining that this type of synthesis indicates a major transition within the sapiential tradition, these modern categories will receive attention throughout the remainder of this chapter.

## 5. *Social Setting for 4QInstruction*

The previous section demonstrated the importance of social location for the complex vision of 4QInstruction, a text that originated on the

---

collections for other churches. He promotes different customs in prayer, banquets, legal disputes, and personal conduct, all at odds with the surrounding society" (p. 68).

[74] Setzer, *Resurrection of the Body*, 144.

[75] See below for a more thorough treatment of the social context for 4QInstruction.

[76] Daniel J. Harrington, "Wisdom and Apocalyptic in 4QInstruction and 4 Ezra," in *Wisdom and Apocalypticism in the Dead Sea Scrolls and in the Biblical Tradition* (ed. F. García Martínez; BETL 238; Leuven: Leuven University Press/Peeters, 2003), 355, where he contrasts the understanding in 4QInstruction with *4 Ezra*, his example of a "classic apocalypse."

[77] Daniel J. Harrington, "Two Early Jewish Approaches to Wisdom: Sirach and Qumran Sapiential Work A," *JSP* 16 (1997): 26, distinguishes 4QInstruction from the literary genre apocalypse. For a discussion of the basic genre and its relationship to the Dead Sea Scrolls, see John J. Collins, "Genre, Ideology, and Social Movements in Jewish Apocalypticism," in *Mysteries and Revelations: Apocalyptic Studies since the Uppsala Colloquium* (ed. J.J. Collins and J.H. Charlesworth; Sheffield: Journal for the Study of the Old Testament, 1991), 11–32; idem, *Apocalypticism in the Dead Sea Scrolls*, 1–11.

periphery of the society. Moreover, this entire study has emphasized the importance of context for understanding the sapiential perspective in a particular text, and 4QInstruction is no exception. Proposals on the precise setting for this work have ranged widely. According to the editors of *DJD 34*, this advice functioned as a resource for priestly administrators to train young officials, presumably in some type of "school" setting.[78] Armin Lange has also argued for a priestly background, and he claims that this text derives from a sapiential group affiliated with the Temple. He further states that 4QInstruction signifies the "eschatologizing" of Wisdom and a set of beliefs that is chronologically and typologically similar to the Treatise on the Two Spirits, the Book of Mysteries, and the epilogue to Qoheleth. For 4QInstruction and these other texts, Lange argues that the Torah is vitally important. This sapiential work also shares with this literature an interest in the Temple cult and in responding to the skeptical model found in Job and the primary text of Qoheleth. According to Lange, the author of 4QInstruction moves beyond the "crisis literature" phase (found in Job and Qoheleth) by offering a new world order principle: "Ursprünglich beinhaltete die weisheitliche Urordnung den Tun-Ergehen-Zusammenhang, die Ordnung der Natur, ethische Normen und einen ethischen Dualismus. Diese Vorstellung wird schrittweise transzendiert, eschatologisiert und historisiert."[79] While this discussion of the "eschatologizing" of Wisdom is helpful, some of Lange's other arguments are difficult to support, particularly the suggestion of a Temple context for 4QInstruction.[80]

---

[78] *DJD 34*, 19–22. In a separate statement on this topic, Harrington, "Two Early Jewish Approaches to Wisdom," 37, makes a somewhat different argument (using the former title for this work): "Perhaps Sapiential Work A was intended as a handbook for training leaders within a Jewish movement."

[79] See Lange, *Weishseit und Prädestination*, 190. Also note Armin Lange, "Eschatological Wisdom in Qoheleth and in the Dead Sea Scrolls," in *The Dead Sea Scrolls Fifty Years After Their Discovery: Proceedings of the Jerusalem Conference, July 20–25, 1997* (ed. L.H. Schiffman et al.; Jerusalem: Israel Exploration Society/Shrine of the Book, Israel Museum, 2000), 817–24.

[80] We have already discussed the problems with the "world-order" hypothesis for instructional texts (chapter 2). The author of 4QInstruction does assume divine regulation of the universe from creation onwards and therefore an orderly cosmos. This "world-order" concept is too vague, however, to describe the varied presentation in Second Temple Wisdom books, including 4QInstruction. Moreover, this text does not seem to be correcting Qoheleth or Job, since there are no direct references or even allusions to these sapiential books. In addition, the main text of Qoheleth reflects an awareness of otherworldly understandings like the one found in 4QInstruction (e.g., Qoh 3:16–22). Qoheleth was part of this sapiential debate over eschatological possibili-

Two scholars who have worked extensively on this text, Tigchelaar and Elgvin, have other proposals. Tigchelaar views 4QInstruction as a guide for a general audience and not a specific group. Some of the standard conventions, such as a singular addressee, and the traditional subject matter (marriage, farming, daily transactions) imply a more public setting.[81] In a more recent study, Tigchelaar has modified this hypothesis in light of his argument about the didactic language found in the opening fragment of the text.[82] With regard to Elgvin, his two layer-hypothesis assumes the incorporation of traditional admonitions into the esoteric reflections of a specific community, a group analogous to those responsible for *1 Enoch*.[83] Even if his redaction theory is problematic, Elgvin's argument on the setting has merit. The content of 4QInstruction suggests a group mentality during a relatively peaceful period. As with the apocalyptic vision in the Enochic books, 4QInstruction claims to have the complete and necessary information for understanding the mysteries of the universe. This text offers a dualistic framework in which a group of "spiritual people" has access to the mysteries of creation (4Q417 1 i 16). The emphasis on special election differs from the more general contrast in Proverbs and Ben Sira between those who adopt the "fear of the Lord" and the multitude of fools who do not. In attempting to define the composition of the elect group in 4QInstruction, however loosely confederated it might have been, Elgvin is probably correct that a specifically priestly audience is not the target of this advice.[84] 4QInstruction alludes to the "law of mixed things" (Lev 19:19; Deut 22:9–11) in 4Q418 103 ii 2–9 and utilizes priestly language in key passages (e.g., 4Q418 81 4), but the cult and the Temple do not receive much attention in this text. It

---

ties, not prior to it. Finally, the association of 4QInstruction with some sort of Temple group overstates the cultic (or even national) interests in this sapiential document.

[81] Eibert J.C. Tigchelaar, "The Addressees of 4QInstruction," in *Sapiential, Liturgical, and Poetical Texts from Qumran: Proceedings of the Third Meeting of the International Organization for Qumran Studies, Oslo 1998* (ed. D. Falk et al.; STDJ 35; Leiden: Brill, 2000), 62–75.

[82] Tigchelaar, *To Increase Learning*, 245–46, is more receptive to the possibility of a learning context for some sort of a group.

[83] Torleif Elgvin, "Priestly Sages? The Milieus of Origin of 4QInstruction and 4QMysteries," in *Sapiential Perspectives: Wisdom Literature in Light of the Dead Sea Scrolls, Proceedings of the Sixth International Symposium of the Orion Center for the Study of the Dead Sea Scrolls and Associated Literature, 20–22 May, 2001* (ed. J.J. Collins et al.; STDJ 51; Leiden: Brill, 2004), 78. He understands the priestly language in passages such as 4Q418 81 to be largely symbolic (*pace* Lange) and claims that the author of 4QInstruction was dependent on the Enochic traditions that existed at the time.

[84] Elgvin, "Priestly Sages," 79–83.

is more likely that a specific group (or groups) developed a discourse involving traditional warnings and apocalyptic terminology, and their advice included allusions to biblical laws.[85] All of these elements were encompassed by the esoteric teaching known as the "mystery that is to be." Devotees received the advice, presumably from a senior member of the group (a משכיל), who wished to pass on certain concepts for righteous living.[86] According to the fragmentary content of this text, pupils are to understand the required knowledge in order to develop discipline and guarantee their salvation, because eminent status in the earthly realm is unlikely.

In searching for the specific background for the recipients of this advice, 4QInstruction describes individuals struggling to meet basic living requirements. The pupil is repeatedly designated as poor (e.g., 4Q416 2 ii 20), and these passages seem to refer to economic rather than spiritual poverty. The fact that the scribal position is not elevated and advice about behavior around the elite is nowhere to be found suggest a different social setting than the offerings of wealthier sages. Unlike his established counterparts, the author of 4QInstruction does not advise a youthful scribe or official on how to conduct himself as he rises through the ranks (e.g., Sir 8:8). This is a text that presumes the vagaries of agricultural and family life, including the need to barter and sell in order to live.[87] Goff maintains that the language of 4QInstruction indicates "a range of economic positions," with the intended audience consisting of "commoners" living in a society in which indebtedness was a constant issue.[88] This is a logical conclusion and a plausible description of a nebulous group. For such a context, we can also conjecture that many of the targeted recipients were not fully literate. The fact that the addressee is told to "*gaze* (נבט) upon the mystery that is to be" (4Q416 2 i 5) in order to grasp the secrets of the universe suggests focused study of this concept, perhaps in some type of group setting. Many of the theological passages in 4QInstruction also imply some

---

[85] See below for a treatment of 4QInstruction and its relationship to the group responsible for the undisputed sectarian texts.

[86] 4QInstruction does not use the term תורה, but this work does allude to biblical texts as an authoritative source and employs biblical terminology and legal concepts in its formulations (see below for the discussion of Torah and the mystery).

[87] 4Q418 81 15 links the מבין with manual skill (בחכמת ידים). The specific content related to agricultural matters implies a group of recipients who often face precarious circumstances. Cf. 4Q423 3 2; 4Q423 4 1–2; 4Q423 5 5–6, all of which assume an audience of farmers.

[88] Goff, *Worldly and Heavenly Wisdom*, 148.

sort of visionary experience for both teacher and pupil (see below).[89] The mystery concept and the details behind it could have circulated as a type of oral Wisdom, a visionary blueprint for those who lacked the status of the retainer class.[90]

The composition of this group precludes the traditional promise of money and status, although it is important to note that 4QInstruction refrains from vilifying the acquisition of wealth. The content suggests an audience of minimal to very modest means: in certain passages the addressee struggles at subsistence level (4Q417 2 i 17–19), and in other units minor financial gain remains a possibility (4Q418 81 18–19). For such a class of individuals, many of the standard rewards for "fear of the Lord" (e.g., "riches and honor" in Prov 22:4) are simply unrealistic, and this is of course problematic for a didactic work. It is true that the practical advice about various financial situations, such as how to barter and avoid debt-slavery, provides valuable counsel for the addressee's well being. Yet these admonitions cannot promise an earthly reward for righteousness, since bitter circumstances are too often an intrinsic feature of subsistence living.[91] Within such a framework, monetary gain and the wealthier classes are not criticized. There is language in 4QInstruction encouraging a person who comes into sudden wealth to enjoy his good fortune, although such an occurrence is unlikely.[92] For the poor addressee who suddenly thrives, such an individual should "walk" (התהלך) in his good fortune, while not coveting more than he needs (4Q416 2 iii 8–9). Determining the intent of this line is difficult, especially in relation to the fragment as a whole: "But if ישיבכה to glory, walk (in it)." Wright is convincing in his argument that the subject of ישיבכה is God ("If *He* restores you") and not a group of individuals.[93]

---

[89] Wright, review of Goff, 550.

[90] Matthew J. Goff, "The Mystery of Creation in 4QInstruction," *DSD* 10 (2003), 163, cites the other verbs relating to the mystery, all of which have a similar connotation: "inquire" (דרש), "meditate" (הנה), "examine" (דרך), and "grasp" (לקח).

[91] In 4Q423 3 2, the possibility of a successful harvest season is linked to comprehension of the "mystery that is to be." Yet this is different from the promises extended by more upper-class sages like Ben Sira.

[92] 4QInstruction does not criticize the acquisition of wealth. Unlike the Epistle of Enoch (e.g., *1 En.* 97:8–10), present impoverishment is not an advantageous state that signifies election, but a reality to be accepted. According to this approach, a person whose financial fortunes improve can enjoy the success. When the acquisition of wealth is mentioned, the claim is not made that material goods represent false treasures.

[93] Benjamin G. Wright, "The Categories of Rich and Poor in the Qumran Sapiential Literature," in *Sapiential Perspectives: Wisdom Literature in Light of the Dead Sea Scrolls, Proceedings of the Sixth International Symposium of the Orion Center for the Study of the Dead Sea*

According to this reading, the statement in 4Q416 2 iii 8–9 is an acknowledgment of divine omnipotence, "the familiar wisdom assertion that God is in control of all things."[94]

As a result of this precarious financial situation, 4QInstruction has a more difficult challenge than Ben Sira in convincing its audience that present benefits are a possibility. Another model is needed in order for this advice to qualify as salutary. The vision in 4QInstruction leads to a different set of rewards and an alternative retributive principle. Successful comprehension of the "mystery that is to be" might not bring enhanced social status or wealth, but the faithful individual can assure his salvation as a member of the "spiritual people." The financial advice in this text fits a relatively broad range of low-income occupations, but the tie that binds these disparate addressees is their common election and knowledge of the "mystery that is to be." The speculative passages in this work forge a distinct communal identity through the promise of eternal life. For the faithful pupil, God bestows an incomparable "inheritance of glory." The מבין can have confidence in his ultimate fate even if present circumstances are a struggle. The pupils' status invites an apocalyptic framework; their poverty necessitates something other than a "locative" model for prosperity and justice. The promise of an otherworldly inheritance is a move that the author of 4QInstruction *has* to make, since the harshness of present living eliminates any possibility other than an eschatological framework *or* the denial of a *Tun-Ergehen-Zusammenhang* (Qoheleth).[95]

---

*Scrolls and Associated Literature, 20–22 May, 2001* (ed. J.J. Collins et al.; STDJ 51; Leiden: Brill, 2004), 115, addresses the difficulties with this passage. We mentioned the fact that 4QInstruction does not allow for a financial windfall elsewhere in the text. In addition, 4Q418 9 8 has this construct with the verb in the plural (יושיבוכה), and the editors use this fragment as a basis for translating 4Q416 2 iii 9 as follows: "If (men) restore you to splendor" (*DJD 34*, 113). Yet the verb in 4Q416 2 iii 8–9 seems to have a singular subject (God).

[94] Wright, "The Categories of Rich and Poor," 115–16. This might also be a way of expressing skepticism about what is possible for the addressee's present social context as opposed to the infinite capabilities of God.

[95] The discrepancy between the condemnation of the wealthy in the Epistle of Enoch and the absence of such a polemic in 4QInstruction is an interesting issue. Goff, *Worldly and Heavenly Wisdom*, 151, claims that for the addressee of 4QInstruction, eschatological reward is cast in pecuniary terms, as a unique form of wealth (e.g., נחלת כבוד). Therefore, the addressee's elect status "does not heighten class tension but mitigates it." In other words, the ultimate "inheritance" of 4QInstruction is far more valuable than any material gains. Yet we must also consider why certain Enochic passages are not similarly tolerant of wealthy individuals. Perhaps the distinction between the two

## 6. *Date*

The extant fragments of 4QInstruction are all in Herodian script, but they seem to preserve an earlier text. The editors of *DJD 34* suggest the third or early second-century B.C.E., but they do not specify a more precise date for the work.[96] Lange locates the sapiential document during the Maccabean period.[97] Elgvin's most recent position is to place both literary layers among "pre-Essene circles in the pre-Maccabean period," and therefore contemporaneous with the career of Ben Sira.[98] Difficult circumstances are described for the recipients of this advice, such as oppressive creditors and the need to borrow money, and the extant fragments do not evince an awareness of political upheaval or religious persecution. For Elgvin, this suggests a pre-Maccabean date. These "pre-Essene circles" then passed on their instructional material to subsequent groups, including those responsible for the undisputed sectarian literature of the Dead Sea Scrolls. In his recent studies of 4QInstruction, Goff concurs with much of Elgvin's reasoning, but is cautious about pinpointing a more precise date than some point during the second-century.[99]

The relative chronology of certain texts (including scrolls that appear to be using 4QInstruction as a source) and the development of the apocalyptic genre are important factors for dating this text. It is reasonable to assume that the discourses of 4QInstruction were composed after apocalyptic traditions such as one finds in the Enochic books had been established for a period in the collective consciousness.[100] The shift in the wisdom tradition coincided with the development of the Enoch traditions, and the changes depended on many of the terms and ideas found in apocalyptic texts. 4QInstruction most likely derives

---

perspectives relates to sapiential reserve about cursing the wealthy and vilifying material gain (or the desire for it). As a Wisdom text, 4QInstruction tilts more closely to standard caution on this point. The addressee's "inheritance of glory" does not mean that persons should avoid earthly opportunities for success. In contrast, the Enochic texts are more explicitly and consistently apocalyptic in orientation and have a different agenda in terms of economic distinctions and the elect status of the poorer classes.

[96] *DJD 34*, 21.

[97] Lange, "In Diskussion mit dem Tempel," 113–59. In his discussion of 4QInstruction, Mysteries, and the epilogist for Qoheleth, Lange places the period of composition around the Maccabean revolt, when cultic identity became a major concern in the wake of the Hellenistic reform (pp. 157–58).

[98] Elgvin, "Priestly Sages," 83.

[99] Goff, *Worldly and Heavenly Wisdom*, 230–31; idem, *Discerning Wisdom*, 65–67.

[100] Goff, *Worldly and Heavenly Wisdom*, 230. Cf. Elgvin, "Priestly Sages," 83–87.

from a later period than the Epistle of Enoch (early second-century)
and is probably later than the book of Daniel (ca. 164 B.C.E.).[101]
Elgvin argues convincingly that this text does not seem to struggle
with the realities of the Maccabean revolt. Even if sapiential texts are
often lacking in historical detail, the mundane advice suggests a time
of relative stability. Yet it is more likely that 4QInstruction was written *after* the tumultuous period of the revolt, based on the chronology
we are outlining. The possible date can be narrowed further because
of language in the Hodayot and the Treatise on the Two Spirits (preserved in 1QS). 4QInstruction seems to have been a source for these
two works.[102] Recent discussion has pushed back the probable date for
the origins of the sectarian community at Qumran from the middle of
the second-century to no earlier than the beginning of the first. The
work of Jodi Magness has cast doubt on any remains at Qumran that
date prior to 100 B.C.E.[103] In addition, the references to the Teacher
of Righteousness in the Pesharim and Damascus Document and his
relationship with the "Wicked Priest" can no longer be linked with
confidence to various figures from the second-century.[104]

Based on a chronology for these texts from the corpus of the Dead
Sea Scrolls (and the fact that 4QInstruction would have to precede the
other two), the late second-century B.C.E. is the most likely period of
composition.[105] This setting would place the author of 4QInstruction

---

[101] Whether or not the author of 4QInstruction was directly dependent on the
Epistle is less important than if these ideas had been established long enough for this
text to draw upon them with a casual frequency. The author's use of available terms
and ideas suggests an established apocalyptic tradition.

[102] Elgvin, "Priestly Sages," 84; idem, "An Analysis of 4QInstruction," 160–61.
Tigchelaar, *To Increase Learning*, 199–200, outlines the compelling terminological affinities
between 4QInstruction and the Treatise on the Two Spirits (primarily in 1QS 3:13–18
and 1QS 4:15–26) and in the Hodayot (1QH 5:19, 23, 26, 29).

[103] Jodi Magness, *The Archaeology of Qumran and the Dead Sea Scrolls* (Grand Rapids:
Eerdmans, 2002), 64–65, notes the earlier dependence on the chronology in CD 1:3–11.
Yet the reference to 390 years is not reliable, and Magness also claims that none of
the pottery remains catalogued by Roland de Vaux (*Archaeology and the Dead Sea Scrolls*
[rev. ed.; Oxford: Oxford University Press, 1973]) should be dated to the middle of
the second-century.

[104] See John J. Collins, "The Time of the Teacher: An Old Debate Renewed," in
*Studies in the Hebrew Bible, Qumran, and the Septuagint Presented to Eugene Ulrich* (ed. P.W.
Flint et al.; VTSup 101; Leiden: Brill, 2006), 217–29. The various references to the
Wicked Priest do not necessarily suggest the same individual in every case and can-
not be linked to the second-century with confidence. Definitive conclusions about the
identity of the Teacher and the Wicked Priest are not possible.

[105] It is possible, if not probable, that the Treatise on the Two Spirits circulated
independently of the Community Rule and was later added to it. For the various

a few generations later than the career of Ben Sira. Such a proposal has further justification in light of the reassessment of prior sapiential assumptions taking place during this century. We have already established Ben Sira's opposition to otherworldly proposals and different forms of speculative Wisdom, and now we have an example of such a perspective in 4QInstruction (along with *1 Enoch*). There is of course a related issue with this date and the argument for a relatively fluid audience of recipients: the relationship between 4QInstruction and the undisputed sectarian literature of the Dead Sea Scrolls. We will return to the controversial "sectarian" question at the end of our discussion, after more clearly establishing the didactic process in this teaching and the eschatological vision of its author.

## 7. *The Didactic Process in 4QInstruction*

With the title of his recent study, Tigchelaar cites the larger purpose of 4QInstruction: "*to increase learning for the understanding ones*" (4Q418 221 3). This sapiential work expects the מבין to hone his power of discernment, maintain an awareness of divine omnipotence, and demonstrate behavior that accords with a mindset of reverential awe. Such expectations resemble the content of Ben Sira and Proverbs, but with two major innovations: 4QInstruction incorporates otherworldly expectation into the ethical framework, and rather than Wisdom or "fear of the Lord" as the focal point for the learning process, the "mystery that is to be" becomes the key to enlightened existence. The meaning and purpose of this foundational yet enigmatic concept require a closer analysis.

The phrase רז נהיה consists of the noun רז ("mystery"), followed by a Niphal participle of the verb היה; it is translated and interpreted in various ways by commentators.[106] The term רז appears in the book of Daniel and in *1 Enoch*, where it describes the revelation of divine knowledge and secrets. The use of רז in such texts can signify belief in a future moment of reckoning and/or an interest in describing the secrets of the heavenly realm. The language of Dan 2:28 is representative: "but there is a God in heaven who reveals mysteries (נלא רזין), and

---

positions concerning when the Treatise became an authoritative source for the Dead Sea sect, see Collins, *Apocalypticism in the Dead Sea Scrolls*, 43.

[106] For a full list of occurrences of this phrase in 4QInstruction, see Goff, *Worldly and Heavenly Wisdom*, 30 n.1.

he has disclosed to King Nebuchadnezzar what will happen at the end
of days."[107] Lange associates the phrase רז נהיה with his version of the
world-order hypothesis and translates "das Geheimnis des Werdens."
According to this reading, the concept pertains to the creative work
of God, which is embodied in the Torah. The "mystery of being" is
reminiscent of the established order Lange finds in Proverbs 1–9.[108]
Elgvin posits an apocalyptic background for the "central revelatory
concept" in 4QInstruction and opts for the "mystery to come." The
phrase represents "an apocalyptic reinterpretation of the biblical and
early Jewish concept of the 'Wisdom of God,' which stresses the esoteric
nature of divine revelation."[109] Both of these arguments have merit
and are not mutually exclusive, especially since רז נהיה seems to have
a multivalent function in 4QInstruction. This is a positive concept for
peripheral believers, who utilized both sapiential and apocalyptic ideas.
As the following discussion will argue, the "mystery that is to be" represents both God's creative activity and a reinterpretation of Wisdom
in light of available constructs.[110]

The mystery appears as the necessary object of the pupil's attention,
much the same role that Wisdom plays in earlier instructions.[111] As
evidence of this cause and effect relationship in 4QInstruction, we can
point to the use of result clauses in this and more traditional sapiential
works. Various units indicate the important relationship between success and discernment. For the person who grasps the mystery concept
in 4QInstruction, clarity and tremendous benefits are possible, just as
the faithful pupil in Proverbs achieves success by heeding Wisdom's
call. For example, Prov 2:1–11 includes conditional clauses about the
pupil's need for attentiveness and the resultant success: "if you indeed

---

[107] There are also the Aramaic portions of *1 Enoch* (4QEn$^c$ 5 ii 26–27; cf. 106:19),
where Enoch declares, "I know the mysteries of <the Lord> that the holy ones have
revealed and shown to me."

[108] Lange, *Weisheit und Prädestination*, 40.

[109] Torleif Elgvin, "Wisdom With and Without Apocalyptic," in *Sapiential, Liturgical
and Poetical Texts from Qumran: Proceedings of the Third Meeting of the International Organization
for Qumran Studies, Oslo 1998* (ed. D. Falk et al.; STDJ 35; Leiden: Brill, 2000), 25.

[110] As Goff, *Worldly and Heavenly Wisdom*, 41, notes, it is not necessary to make a choice
between an "apocalyptic" or a "sapiential" understanding of the mystery. Moreover,
this concept should not be seen as a rejection of earlier models or a "crisis response":
"4QInstruction's apocalyptic worldview is more simply understood as a consequence of
the reception of older wisdom in the late Second Temple period in light of perspectives
and traditions common to this era."

[111] Wisdom does not disappear in 4QInstruction: there are references to חכ[מ]ה and
ע[ר]מה in 4Q417 1 i 9, describing God's creation of the universe.

cry out for insight...then you will understand the fear of the Lord and find the knowledge of God" (Prov 2:3–5). A similar pattern appears in 4QInstruction, with the mystery replacing Wisdom as the central object of devotion and study. The addressee must first contemplate the mystery, and "then (ואז) you will know truth and iniquity, wisdom [and foolish]ness" (4Q417 1 i 6–7). The conjunction אם appears 32 times in 4QInstruction (including fragmentary passages), and it often occurs in phrases that seek to guide the addressee in daily situations (borrowing money, familial relations), followed by a statement of the probable consequence. Many conditional statements guarantee discernment for the faithful addressee. An important construction appears in 4Q416 2 iii 14–15: "Study the mystery that is to be, and perceive all the ways of truth, and reflect upon all the roots of iniquity. *Then* (ואז) you will know what is bitter for a man, and what is sweet for a person" (translation mine). According to such conditional statements, the mystery concept in 4QInstruction allows for correct decision-making under present circumstances, and it impresses upon the addressee the certainty of eschatological judgment.[112] Wisdom traverses the universe and is present with God at the beginning of creation in Proverbs (8:22–31) and Ben Sira (24:1–34), but the figure in these books can only mediate earthly rewards for the faithful pupil.[113] In contrast, the מבין of 4QInstruction who understands the mystery stands to inherit an eternal reward.

In terms of temporality, most translations opt for a future sense, including Elgvin and the editors' "mystery that is to come," "le mystère futur" in *DJD 1*, and the "mystery that is to be," which is adopted in Goff's recent studies of 4QInstruction and in the current discussion. The isolated use of the participle in the Dead Sea Scrolls and other texts from this period frequently conveys a future sense ("what will be"),

---

[112] Bilhah Nitzan, "The Ideological and Literary Unity of 4QInstruction and Its Authorship," *DSD* 12 (2005), 265, notes the inclusion of "worldly wisdom" (דרך ארץ) in 4QInstruction, covering such matters as filial piety. The command to study the mystery in 4Q416 2 iii 14 is followed by advice on honoring one's parents. There is also "knowledge of the preordained lot of a man for his own sake," and this is included in longer discourses like 4Q417 1 i. Mystery language appears in both types of material, and Nitzan correctly argues that these diverse sections come from one source.

[113] Elgvin, "Wisdom and Apocalypticism," 237, argues that descriptions of the mystery in 4QInstruction are part of a development in "apocalyptic circles" that reflects a reinterpretation of divine Wisdom, particularly the figure of Proverbs 1–9. In the current discussion, we are not making a claim for a direct imitation of Lady Wisdom in 4QInstruction's presentation, but a reconfiguration of traditional sapiential assumptions by means of an eschatological vision and apocalyptic constructs. It should be noted that in 4Q418 126 ii 5, Wisdom is involved in God's creative process (ומחוכ[מתו]).

although there are also past tense occurrences.[114] One important passage in 4QInstruction uses a tripartite formula to describe the unfolding of events throughout the ages, with the Niphal participle referring to what has happened in the past: "everything that has been made to be in it, to what is currently taking place, and what will take place in it (כול הנהיה בה למה היה ומה יהיה בוֹ)" (4Q418 123 ii 3–4, translation mine).[115] The varied use of the phrase precludes a strictly future understanding for רז נהיה. Based on passages like 4Q418 123 ii 3–4, the concept in 4QInstruction seems to describe God's eternal relationship with the universe, including the capacity for judgment.[116] Two other passages in the Scrolls, one from the Community Rule and the other from the Book of Mysteries, contain the exact phrase and support such a broader definition. We already cited the passage in the Book of Mysteries, where the context of רז נהוה is final judgment. The occurrence in the Community Rule relates to the revelation of divine power.[117]

When assessing רז נהיה in these units, the aspect of temporality emphasized in one's translation cannot capture the heart of this concept, which is God's control of the cosmos. For this reason, we might understand and even translate רז נהיה as the "mystery of that which is made to be," thereby describing God's dominance over all creation, during all periods. Harrington's definition reflects this intricate dynamic in 4QInstruction: "The *raz nihyeh* is a body of teaching concerning the mysteries of the cosmos, the proper behavior of human beings,

---

[114] Torleif Elgvin, "The Mystery to Come: Early Essene Theology of Revelation," in *Qumran Between the Old and New Testaments* (ed. F.H. Cryer and T.L. Thompson; JSOTSup 290; Sheffield: Sheffield Academic Press, 1998), 133. The use of the participle in 1 QS 11:8–9 (קץ נהיה) has a future sense, as do the occurrences in the War Scroll (1:12; 17:5). Also note the future connotation in 1QS 3:15, at the beginning of the Treatise on the Two Spirits: כול הויה ונהייה.

[115] The editors do not venture a guess regarding the reference point for the feminine suffix (בה). Goff, *Worldly and Heavenly Wisdom*, 57–58, lists passages with a more inclusive use of the Niphal participle, so that "the entirety of the chronological scheme" is included.

[116] John J. Collins, "Wisdom Reconsidered, in Light of the Scrolls," *DSD* 4 (1997), 273–74, defines the term along the same lines: "The *raz nihyeh* seems to encompass the entire divine plan, from creation to eschatological judgment."

[117] The phrase רז נהיה occurs in the Community Rule (1 QS 11:3–4): "For from the source of his knowledge he has disclosed his light, and my eyes have observed his wonders, and the light of my heart the רז נהוה" (*DSSSE* 1:97). In the Book of Mysteries (1Q27 1 i 3–4), this term describes the ignorance of the wicked, who will be harshly judged because they "did not know the mystery that is to be, and the former things they did not consider. Nor did they know what is to come upon them. And they did not save their lives from the mystery that is to be."

and eschatology."[118] Building on this understanding (and the language from 4Q418 123 ii 3–4), Nitzan argues that the "'the mystery that is to be' expresses the apocalyptic axiom that 'all that is occurring and shall occur' is preordained by God...and may be discovered, taught, and studied by elected human beings."[119] With such a strong eschatological component in 4QInstruction, the mystery has to remain the central object of focus for the adherents of this advice, since it holds the key to understanding the history of the world, finding success in daily activities, and most importantly, to special election that can deliver one from death.

For the מבין, the mystery must be learned and applied in everyday life, although the exact manner of complying with this concept is not completely clear. The mystery is certainly efficacious: if understood and applied correctly, it leads to beneficial rewards. It is taught by parents (4Q416 2 iii 18) and remains a useful guide for making daily choices in the human realm. For example, a farmer should reflect on this concept in order to receive a plentiful harvest (4Q423 3 2). Yet many of these references do not specify what exactly the farmer is supposed to meditate upon or the specific details of a parent's teaching. In contrast to the statements containing mundane advice, some of the longer discourses reveal more information about the content of the mystery and its eschatological import. Perhaps the most important passage in this regard is 4Q417 1 i (formerly numbered as 2 i), where the author outlines basic requirements:

> [And by day and by night meditate upon the mystery that is to] come, And study (it) continually. And then thou shalt know truth and iniquity, wisdom [and foolish]ness thou shalt [recognize], every ac[t ]in all their ways, Together with their punishment(s) in all ages everlasting, And the punishment of eternity. Then thou shalt discern between the [goo]d and [evil according to their] deeds. For the God of knowledge is the foundation of truth And by/on the mystery that is to come He has laid out its (= truth's) foundation (4Q417 1 i 6–9).[120]

In this unit, the mystery stands as the necessary precursor to discernment. Comprehension of it leads to good decision-making and

---

[118] Daniel J. Harrington, "Mystery," in *Encyclopedia of the Dead Sea Scrolls* (ed. L.H. Schiffman and J.C. VanderKam; New York: Oxford University Press, 2000), 1:590. See below for discussion on whether this signifies an actual written document.

[119] Nitzan, "The Ideological and Literary Unity of 4QInstruction," 262.

[120] On the difficulties with lines 8–9, see *DJD 34*, 158, especially the discussion of יסוד/סוד and the mistaken writing of אישה for אוש.

deliverance at the final judgment. Based on this passage, we might understand the "mystery that is to be" as an overarching pedagogical concept for righteous behavior and salvation. Knowledge of its content gives the addressee a better understanding of the divine plan, moral discernment, and eternal life.

The longer discourses and the diverse occurrences of רז נהיה in this text raise another pertinent question: what is the implied medium for communicating the "mystery that is to be"? 4QInstruction requires the addressee to "meditate" on the mystery, but it does not fully clarify, at least in the extant fragments, how a person accomplishes this task. Since this is an esoteric teaching, perhaps it is appropriate and even intentional that the concept remains "mysterious" to a degree. Harrington has suggested that the mystery represents a specific body of teaching, "an extrabiblical compendium" (and therefore not the Torah) for intended recipients.[121] Possibilities include the Book of Mysteries, with its clear interest in cosmological matters, the Treatise on the Two Spirits in 1QS, or perhaps the "book of Meditation/Hagu," which is mentioned in the Damascus Document and the Rule of the Community.[122] This "book of Hagu" might be synonymous with the "Torah of Moses" or the "book of Torah" highlighted in other scrolls, or to some esoteric document connected with the Qumran community.[123] There is a reference to a "vision of meditation on a book of memorial (לספר זכרון)" in 4Q417 1 i 16, a passage that involves an important contrast between the "spiritual people" and the "fleshly spirit" (see below). There could be a relationship between the "book of Hagu" and the vision referred to in this passage, but this is uncertain. The mystery in 4QInstruction might not refer to a specific corpus of laws or esoteric reflections, even if those responsible for this work made use of a written document(s)

---

[121] Harrington, *Wisdom Texts*, 49. Cf. Ben Zion Wacholder and Martin G. Abegg, *A Preliminary Edition of the Unpublished Dead Sea Scrolls: The Hebrew and Aramaic Texts from Cave Four* (2 vols.; Washington, D.C.: Biblical Archaeology Society, 1992), 2:xiii.

[122] This "book of Meditation/Hagu" is mentioned three times in the Damascus Document (CD 10:6; 13:2; 14:8 [restored]) and in 1QSa 1:7, which reads ההגי. According to Steven D. Fraade, "Hagu, Book of," in *Encyclopedia of the Dead Sea Scrolls* (ed. L.H. Schiffman and J.C.VanderKam; New York: Oxford University Press, 2000), 1:327, Hagu is an object of study and learning in all of these examples.

[123] See Fraade, "Hagu," 1:327, for a review of the options and scholarly references on this topic. Possible candidates include the Temple Scroll, the Rule of the Community, or a text that is no longer extant.

for source material.[124] The verbs that encourage the addressee to focus his attention on the mystery do not necessarily describe a process of studying a written work, despite the enigmatic reference to a "book of memorial" in 4Q417 1 i 16. It is possible that the recipients of this advice found symbolic value in some type of heavenly tablet; other apocalyptic texts from this period contain references to divine revelation by means of a written work.[125] For example, Methuselah receives instruction from his father Enoch in the form of books (*1 En.* 82:1–4), and he is supposed to pass this material along to future generations. Daniel also has vital information in a sealed document (12:4), and there is also the "book of truth" (Dan 10:21).

There could be a mystical component to accessing the mystery. We have mentioned statements in 4QInstruction implying that the mystery has already been "revealed" (נגלה). Subsequent commands to "gaze" upon it perhaps indicate some type of visionary experience. Many commentators are rightfully circumspect about assuming an elaborate set of practices based on brief and uncertain references in the discourses, but we should leave open the possibility that "meditation" on the mystery involved creative forms of ritualistic teaching, including the mystical experiences that can accompany such processes. The "vision of Hagu" perhaps involves a conceptual framework and a set of practices that relate directly to the "mystery that is to be" and somehow encapsulate its content.[126] This interpretation has further justification if the "vision of Hagu" pertains to the angelic realm and the acquisition of knowledge. A comparable passage from *1 Enoch* sheds light on this issue. In the introduction to the Apocalypse of Weeks, the protagonist gains insight through a vision:

---

[124] John J. Collins, *Jewish Wisdom in the Hellenistic Age* (OTL; Louisville: Westminster John Knox Press, 1997), 123, argues that the mystery could be the subject matter to which the various writings suggested by Harrington refer.

[125] This passage alludes to Mal 3:16, as many commentators have noted. Heavenly tablets and books are important in many apocalyptic texts, including Daniel, *Jubilees*, and *1 Enoch*. See Collins, "The Eschatologizing of Wisdom," 54.

[126] Goff, *Discerning Wisdom*, 33, cites commonality between the vision and the "mystery that is to be" in terms of divine judgment. He also points to the fact that the addressee is never told to study or meditate on the vision, although he is repeatedly encouraged to focus on the mystery. Unfortunately, we only get one enigmatic reference to this vision among the extant fragments. Other occurrences of the term might clarify its meaning and link it more closely with the eschatological and ethical background of the "mystery that is to be."

> After this Enoch took up his discourse, saying, "Concerning the sons of righteousness, and concerning the chosen of eternity, and concerning the plant of truth, these things I say to you and I make known to you, my sons, I myself, Enoch. The vision of heaven was shown to me, and from the words of the watchers and holy ones I have learned everything, and in the heavenly tablets I read everything and I understood" (*1 En.* 93:1–2).

According this description, Enoch has a three-fold experience: visions, words from the angels, and access to heavenly tablets. These elements are interrelated and the source of his revelation.[127] The heavenly tablets in this passage are associated with the "vision of heaven" and lead to the protagonist's comprehension of the divine will. In much the same way, the "spiritual people" of 4QInstruction have special knowledge of God's plan for humanity, angels are involved in the maintenance of the universe and the judgment process (e.g., 4Q418 69 ii), and a "book of memorial" is associated with the capacity for discernment and the mysterious "vision of Hagu." It is impossible to determine the author's precise understanding and expectations for such visionary experiences, but the similarities with the Apocalypse of Weeks suggest a mystical element for both the "mystery that is to be" and the "vision of Hagu." This is a significant departure from the earthly focus of earlier instructions and the wisdom tradition's wariness about dreams and otherworldly visions. Speculative inquiry is an integral part of 4QInstruction, related to its eschatological vision.

This concept was also shared through public teaching. The idea of "examining" (דרש) or "grasping" (לקח) the secrets of the universe probably indicates focused attention, by means of "lectures" from an instructor, or dialogue with a neighbor(s). Frequent instruction within individual families is also implied by the text (4Q416 2 iii 18). The occasion and format for such teaching could have been flexible and contiguous with other gatherings (for religious observances?). Such sessions might have involved the introduction of new concepts related to the mystery.[128] Ancient sayings in a variety of contexts became known

---

[127] See Nickelsburg, *1 Enoch 1*, 442, who compares this passage to the tristich formula in *1 En.* 1:2–3 and 81:1–2.

[128] Whether this is called a "school" depends on one's definition of the term and if literacy is seen to be a prerequisite for such a designation. In the interest of avoiding any implied connection between the marginalized setting for 4QInstruction and the official training centers where scribal education occurred, we do not use the term "school" in reference to this text.

through these informal processes. The dissemination of the advice
found in 4QInstruction was probably intermittent. The background for
many of the warnings, particularly the advice on agricultural matters,
the dynamics of family life, and how to negotiate a hostile marketplace, does not imply communal living. We can posit a regular return
to menial occupations and traditional familial structures by those who
shared and reflected upon this material.

While conclusions about the relationship between the "vision of
Hagu" and the "mystery that is to be" must remain tentative, the
speculative language of 4QInstruction raises the issue of revelation
versus empirical epistemology and how this plays out in the text. On
the one hand, the mystery is given to the addressee at several points
in this instruction, including the fragmentary passage in 4Q418 184 2
(with the deity as the subject): "(He) who has revealed into your ear
about (or 'by') the mystery that is to be (אֲ[שֶׁ]ר נלה אוזנכה ברז נהיה)"
(translation mine; cf. 4Q418 123 ii 4).[129] Another passage conveys a
similar understanding of the bestowal of truth and insight: "And as
for you, he has opened up insight for you and given you authority
over his storehouse, and an ephah of truth has been assigned to you"
(4Q418 81 9, translation mine). According to Rofé, 4QInstruction
and other texts from the Dead Sea Scrolls emphasize revelation over
and against a lifetime of accumulated knowledge: "These godly gifts
make human beings equal to angels, not only in terms of status, but
as one sacred community."[130] Instead of the earlier paradigm based on
empirical learning, the pupils of 4QInstruction are privy to the secrets
of the universe because of a special status conferred by the Creator.
This model places no confidence in "gray hair" as "a crown of glory,"
gained by leading an observant and obedient life (Prov 16:31). Elect

---

[129] The phrase ברז נהיה in this line could also be instrumental: "by means of the
mystery that is to be." In addition, the editors read the אשר in this fragment as "*how*
He uncovered…" (*DJD 34*, 408).

[130] Alexander Rofé, "Revealed Wisdom: From the Bible to Qumran," in *Sapiential
Perspectives: Wisdom Literature in Light of the Dead Sea Scrolls, Proceedings of the Sixth International
Symposium of the Orion Center for the Study of the Dead Sea Scrolls and Associated Literature,
20–22 May 2001* (ed. J.J. Collins et al.; STDJ 51; Leiden: Brill, 2004), 2. Rofé seeks to
substantiate a series of late texts in which "Age and experience do not grant wisdom;
it is the spirit emanating from God that instructs men" (p. 6). Among the passages he
cites in support of this shift are Job 32:6–9; 33:13–18; Sus 63; 11QPS[a] 27:1–4. The
chosen ones of God (e.g., 1QS 11:7–9) receive discernment and an eternal promise,
irrespective of their age or status as senior sages: "These two go hand in hand very
well: divine, inspired wisdom and communion with heavenly beings-a choir of angels
and mortals" (p. 3).

individuals are not rewarded because of diligent attention to the tradition, but because God has revealed things to them and included them
in the "lot" of the holy ones.

The presentation is not so simple in 4QInstruction, however. If
certain statements in the text imply a process of selection based on
divine disclosure, others require a course of study and discipline. The
addressee must exercise restraint in his daily activities (e.g., 4Q416 2
ii 18–20) and "gaze upon the mystery" for ongoing enlightenment.[131]
The passages highlighted by Rofé suggest a divine decision to imbue
some individuals with special gifts, and 4QInstruction clearly elevates
the position of the righteous elect. Yet this does not eliminate the
need for studying the mystery or becoming a wiser person. Empirical
epistemology plays an important role in 4QInstruction, particularly in
4Q417 1 i 6–13. According to Werman, "The *Mevin* is instructed to
look at human conduct during every period of world history and at the
rewards and punishments meted out for the past, present and future.
From this a person can deduce which deed is good and which is bad."[132]
We have already cited the conditional constructions in 4QInstruction,
which include the promise of enlightenment for a dedicated pupil. A
person should "meditate upon" (הגה) the mystery and "study (it) con-
tinually" (דורש תמיד): "And then you shall know truth and iniquity"
(4Q417 1 i 6). The mystery contains the "foundation of truth" (4Q417
1 i 8), and the addressee has to seek this source always, considering
the glory of God during all periods. Language in 4QInstruction that
implies a preordained status for a particular group does not negate the
need for a lifetime of learning: "increase in understanding greatly, And
from each of thy teachers get ever more instruction" (4Q418 81 17).
Throughout the text, but especially in this passage from 4Q417 1 i,
the addressee must submit himself to a learning process, because he is

---

[131] Cana Werman, "What is the *Book of Hagu?*" in *Sapiential Perspectives: Wisdom Literature in Light of the Dead Sea Scrolls, Proceedings of the Sixth International Symposium of the
Orion Center for the Study of the Dead Sea Scrolls and Associated Literature, 20–22 May 2001*
(ed. J.J. Collins et al.; STDJ 51; Leiden: Brill, 2004), 125–40, cites the necessity of
ongoing attentiveness.

[132] Werman, "What is the *Book of Hagu?*" 131.

part of a chosen group.[133] A pupil's elect status does not alleviate the need for diligence and the ongoing pursuit of knowledge.

If the "mystery that is to be" represents a conceptual framework for present responsibility and the promise of future glory, something that the faithful pupil is supposed to meditate upon, does it have any relationship with the Torah?[134] Unlike Ben Sira, there is no explicit equation of Wisdom and Torah in 4QInstruction, and the Mosaic legislation is never thematized. Ben Sira repeatedly cites the Torah as an authoritative source and trumpets its importance throughout his discussion. While the author of 4QInstruction also employs the biblical laws as a means of framing communal life, he does not include the same type of praise. In fact, תורה does not even appear in the extant fragments. Nevertheless, the sapiential work does refer to the legal material at various points. Allusions to biblical laws are simply included in specific prohibitions without reference or comment. The book of Numbers figures prominently in these examples.[135] Even with these scattered references in the fragments, some scholars, including Elgvin, have argued that the mystery somehow replaces the Torah: "Different from Sirach 1 and 24, Bar 3:9–4:4, 4Q525 and 11QPsᵃ 154, true wisdom and earthly blessings have their source in (studying) *raz nihyeh*, not in (following) Torah."[136] Elgvin's conclusion on this point is too dismissive of a clear engagement with the Torah in 4QInstruction. The mystery and the Torah are related in a sense: perhaps the Mosaic legislation can more accurately be categorized as an important source for 4QInstruction, albeit without any formal acknowledgement by the author. The legal references and the allusions to the Torah in 4QInstruction are part of a larger ethical and apocalyptic presentation that is encompassed by the

---

[133] As the previous chapter indicated, Ben Sira has a similar tension between election and the need for learning (e.g., Sir 1:14 and 4:11–31)

[134] Lange, "In Diskussion mit dem Tempel," 113–60, has posited a close relationship between the mystery and the Torah.

[135] For example, 4Q 418 81 3 seems to draw on the language of Num 18:20: "He is your portion and inheritance among the sons of Adam." Another allusion to Numbers (15:39) can be found in the fragmentary text of 4Q417 1 i 27: "You shall not go astray afte[r] you[r] heart and /after/ your e[y]es[."

[136] Elgvin, "Wisdom With and Without Apocalyptic," 24.

"mystery that is to be."[137] Read in this way, the Torah is a component of the mystery, but not the center of its content.[138]

### 8. *The "Spiritual People" and the "Fleshly Spirit"*

The available content of 4QInstruction draws a clear distinction between those who have knowledge of and access to the "mystery that is to be" and the unfortunate souls who do not. In the Hebrew Bible, the longstanding assumption had been that all human beings perish, and then their breath returns to God, the source of all the living. 4QInstruction offers a different understanding, since individuals in the elect category receive the promise of otherworldly existence. As a result, the contrast between the two groups in this text is stark and more consequential. One of the most important descriptions of this framework occurs in 4Q417 1 i. Here we find an account of the gifts bestowed to אנוש and the "spiritual people." The status of this category differs markedly from the position of the non-elect group:

| | |
|---:|---:|
| ואתה | 13 |
| מבין רוש פעלתכה בזכרון הש̇לום כי ]בא חֿרֿוֿת ׳חוק{כה} וֿחקוק כול | 14 |
| הפקֿודֿה | |
| כי חרות מחוקק לאל על כול ע̇ן̇ולות] בני שֿוֿת וספר זכרון כתוב לפניו | 15 |
| לשמרי דברו והואה חזון הֿהגוֿ׳ לֿספר זכרון וינחילוֿנֿוֿ לאנוש עם ׳׳ רוח | 16 |
| כֿ׳י̇א | |
| כתבנית קדושים יצרו ועוד לוא נתן הגוֿ׳ לרוח בשר כי לא ידע בין | 17 |
| ]ט̇וֿ]̇ב לרע כמשפט [ר̇]וֿחו̇ vacat [ | 18 |

13 And you,
14 O understanding one, inherit your reward in remembrance of retri[bution when it] comes. For engraved is the ordinance, and ordained is all the punishment.

---

[137] Lange, *Weisheit und Prädestination*, 90, claims that for the author of 4QInstruction, God's work at creation is embodied in the Torah. Based on his reading of 4Q416 2 iii 18–19, which alludes to the fifth commandment, the mystery is directly associated with the Mosaic legislation. With such language in the text, Lange maintains that the central concept of 4QInstruction resembles the understanding of an eternal Torah in later rabbinic literature. For an assessment of Lange's proposal, see Goff, *Worldly and Heavenly Wisdom*, 70–72.

[138] One passage (4Q416 2 ii 8–9) refers to "your statutes" (חוקיכה) and "your mysteries" (וברזיכה) in a parallel structure, but as we saw with Ben Sira, the use of חק does not necessarily refer to the Torah.

15 For engraved is that which has been ordained by God against all the
in[iquities] of the children of Sheth. And written in His presence is
a book of memorial

16 for those who keep His word. And it is the vision of meditation/Hagu
on a book of memorial. And He gave it as an inheritance to אנוש
along with a spiritual people,

17 s[inc]e his/their inclination is in accordance with the image of the
holy ones. But meditation/Hagu has still not been given to the fleshly
spirit, for it knew not the difference between

18 [go]od and evil according to the judgment of its [sp]irit (4Q417 1 i
13–18, translation mine).

When examining the language in this unit, the ethical dualism of
4QInstruction becomes apparent. The contrast between the elect
category, the "spiritual people," and the non-elect class, the "fleshly
spirit," marks the baseline distinction in this work.[139] In certain respects,
the presentation of the two groups in 4QInstruction resembles the
Wisdom-folly contrast in Proverbs (e.g., 2:1–22) and the poem on the
rewards of Wisdom in Sir 4:11–19. All of these sapiential texts refer
to a specific group of righteous individuals with special access to God
and a program of discipline for maintaining their status. 4QInstruction
diverges, however, in its use of the more speculative mystery concept to
differentiate categories of people. The distinction is also more sharply
drawn than the series of antitheses in Proverbs 1–9 or the binary
contrasts in Sirach, especially since 4QInstruction has expanded the
horizon for reward to include some sort of immortal promise. Using
the foundational stories in Genesis to delineate two types, 4QInstruc-
tion makes the case for the superiority of the elect category. The מבין,
if he wishes to remain part of this group, should sequester himself
from the "fleshly spirit," follow the earthly stipulations set forth in this
work, and reflect on both historical and heavenly matters.[140] This course
of action is possible, because God has endowed him with the gift of
discernment (lines 7–18).

---

[139] The elect are also called the "men of good favor" (אנשי רצון) (4Q418 81 10), "His
faithful children" (בני אמתו) (4Q416 1 10), and "the truly chosen ones" (בחירי אמת)
(4Q418 69 ii 10). With regard to the wicked, there is a reference to the "foolish-minded"
(אוילי לב) in 4Q418 69 ii 8. All of these can be seen as variations on the contrast
between the "spiritual people" and the "fleshly spirit."

[140] Nitzan, "The Ideological and Literary Unity of 4QInstruction," 278, cites language in 4QInstruction (4Q418 81 2) that requires the addressee to separate himself:
"Such separation imparts holiness to him for the service of God, like that of the priests
and the holy angels, makes him honored in the present by people and God, and assures
his righteousness and honor under the eschatological judgment of God."

With regard to some of the textual issues in this "vision of Hagu" unit, discussed at length in other studies, we read שלום (line 14) as שָׁלוּם and translate the term as "retribution."[141] The preceding word is taken as the noun "remembrance" (זִכְרוֹן), instead of an infinitive construct. One of the main issues in this section is a final judgment, and both terms fit such a context. The "engraved" language draws on Exod 32:16 and occurs elsewhere in the Dead Sea Scrolls, particularly in the Hodayot. On the disputed בני שית in line 15, one possibility is that the reference is to the patriarch Seth.[142] This reading does not necessarily work, since the figure of Seth is portrayed positively in Genesis and other Second Temple texts, and the clear intent of the lines in 4QInstruction is to describe a wicked class of people.[143] The probable background for this designation is Num 24:17 and mention of the "Shethites" (or "children of Seth") in Balaam's oracle.[144] The בני שית are therefore synonymous with the "fleshly spirit" whose punishment by God is assured but has not yet taken place.[145] Such a judgment against this "fleshly spirit" category is also promised at the very beginning of 4QInstruction (4Q416 1 12).

One's translation of ועוד לוא dictates any interpretation of the phrasing in line 17, particularly אנוש. Wold's recent study understands ועוד לוא to mean "but no more," implying that "the vision of Hagu" was originally given to all of "humanity" (אנוש), and then subsequently taken away from just the "fleshly spirit" category.[146] The more likely sense of ועוד לוא and the one that accords with the thrust of the unit is to read the phrase as "still" (or "not yet"), which conveys a continual withholding of insight from the "fleshly spirit," a resolute denial by God that began at creation.[147]

---

[141] This is a reconstruction by the editors of a poorly preserved line (*DJD 34*, 162). There could be an *'ayin* here instead of a *šin*. Elgvin, "An Analysis of 4QInstruction," 256, suggests העֵ[ט ("stylus"), and this reading has support in the Hodayot (בחרת זכרון in 1QH 9:24). Yet it is difficult to see how "stylus" fits this exact context. Goff, *Worldly and Heavenly Wisdom*, 85–86, offers the reconstruction הֹעֹ[וז ("might").

[142] Lange, *Weisheit und Prädestination*, 87.

[143] For a positive treatment of Seth during this period, see Josephus (*Ant.* 1.68).

[144] A similar use of the designation occurs in CD 7:21, where the issue is punishment for the wicked that has not yet occurred.

[145] Harrington, *Wisdom Texts from Qumran*, 55; Goff, *Worldly and Heavenly Wisdom*, 91.

[146] Wold, *Women, Men, and Angels*, 135–41.

[147] A similar example of this construction with the meaning "not yet" can be found in 2 Chron 20:33: "Yet the high places were not removed: the people had not yet set (ועוד העם לא־הכינו) their hearts upon the God of their ancestors."

The meaning and best translation for אנוש in line 17 have puzzled commentators since the publication of 4QInstruction. The options vary considerably, and one's interpretation has major implications for the understanding of this unit and the entire text. With regard to Wold's proposal that אנוש represents "humanity" in general, the emphasis on special election for a group of persons in 4QInstruction weakens the argument for divine bestowal of a visionary gift to everyone.[148] The ethical dualism of 4QInstruction does not allow for the granting of the "vision of Hagu" to all of humanity. Moreover, this suggestion does not have support elsewhere in 4QInstruction, where the people of "fleshly spirit" are viewed negatively (4Q416 1 12; 4Q418 81 1–2).[149] This use of אנוש might instead refer to the antediluvian Enosh, as suggested by Lange, Brooke, and the editors of *DJD 34*.[150] Yet there are problems with this argument, especially since the figure of Seth is not the background for the earlier reference in this passage, and the offspring of Enosh and Seth are not set off against each other in this manner elsewhere.[151] Moreover, Enosh is not generally used as an isolated example of righteousness; the name occurs in a chain of figures in Sir 49:16 and later literature.[152] Elgvin suggests that אנוש should be understood as a reference to the elect community, and he bases this assessment on the language of 1QS 11:5–6: "when my eyes looked upon what was eternal, insight that was hidden from humanity (אנוש), and knowledge and intelligent design [which were hidden] from the sons of humanity" (translation mine).[153] The use of אנוש in this passage

---

[148] Wold, *Women, Men, and Angels*, 139, claims that lines 15–18 "depict the creation of all humanity in the image of the angels as well as recipients of special revelation (Haguy)."

[149] See Goff, *Discerning Wisdom*, 34 n. 99.

[150] Lange, *Weisheit und Prädestination*, 87; cf. George J. Brooke "Biblical Interpretation in the Wisdom Texts from Qumran," in *The Wisdom Texts from Qumran and the Development of Sapiential Thought* (ed. C. Hempel et al.; BETL 159; Leuven: Leuven University/Peeters, 2002), 165; *DJD 34*, 165.

[151] See John J. Collins, "In the Likeness of the Holy Ones: The Creation of Humankind in a Wisdom Text from Qumran," in *The Provo International Conference on the Dead Sea Scrolls* (ed. D.W. Parry and E. Ulrich; STDJ 30; Leiden: Brill, 1999), 610–12.

[152] See Steven D. Fraade, *Enosh and His Generation: Pre-Israelite Hero and History in Postbiblical Interpretation* (SBLMS 30; Chico, Ca.; Scholars Press, 1984), 27. When Enosh is cited as a "righteous antediluvian," his name usually appears in a list.

[153] Elgvin, "Mystery to Come," 143 n. 78. James C. VanderKam, review of M.J. Goff, *The Worldly and Heavenly Wisdom of 4QInstruction*, CBQ 67 (2005), 118, has recently suggested that אנוש in this pericope refers to the class of righteous individuals (the שמרי דברו in the same line). According to this proposal, אנוש would be another designation in a string of titles to the same elect group. The problem with this

actually refers to a large *non-elect* category from whom secrets are being withheld, the general lot of humanity. As a result, Elgvin's primary evidence for this reading actually undermines the argument for אנוש as an elect community.[154]

Another possibility is that אנוש is a reference to the biblical Adam, especially since this pericope draws on the language and ideas found in Genesis 1–3.[155] In contrasting two classes, the author of 4QInstruction uses the creation narratives to describe the gift of discernment upon the "spiritual people" (i.e., those who know the difference between good and evil). In this effort, 4QInstruction could be lifting up the model of the first human and the intellectual capabilities he received at creation. Since there are similar allusions to this figure both in the Scrolls and in other texts from the Hellenistic period, an allusion to Adam makes sense. As the previous chapter mentioned, Ben Sira refers to the creation of humanity and the gift of discernment by utilizing the Genesis accounts (Sir 17:1–24). In addition, this interpretation of 4Q417 1 i finds justification in the use of אנוש in the Treatise on the Two Spirits to describe God's initial creation and the dominion of humanity over the earth. The language in this passage relies on Genesis: "He created man to rule the world (והואה ברא אנוש לממשלת תבל)" (1QS 3:17). 4QInstruction does not use האדם in the "vision of Hagu" pericope, and this is perplexing, since the form appears in both creation accounts (Gen 1:27; 2:7). Yet the occurrence of אנוש in the Treatise on the Two Spirits (1QS 3:17) in reference to God's creation of humanity indicates flexibility during this period concerning the various terms for the first person. In addition, Collins maintains that the "vision of Hagu" section uses Gen 1:27 to associate the "spiritual people" category with the angelic host.[156] The "inclination" (or "fashioning," יצר) of the "spiritual

---

suggestion is that אנוש and שמרי דברו are clearly distinguished in this passage and separated by עם.

[154] Elgvin, "Mystery to Come," 143 n. 78, provides a list of occurrences for אנוש in 4QInstruction, where it refers to more than one individual and can be used to label offensive sectors of the population (4Q418 55 11; 4Q418 77 3). Elsewhere in the Dead Sea Scrolls, it indicates a plural group, usually "humanity" (e.g., 1QH 9:25).

[155] Collins, "In the Likeness of the Holy Ones," 610–12. Cf. Goff, *Worldly and Heavenly Wisdom*, 96–99.

[156] Collins, "In the Likeness of the Holy Ones," 612–14, understands כתבנית קדושים as a paraphrase of בצלם אלהים (Gen 1:27), and he takes אלהים to be a reference to the angels rather than God. Fletcher-Louis devotes an entire study (*All the Glory of Adam*) to an "angelomorphic anthropology" of Second Temple texts, including the Dead Sea Scrolls. He posits a tendency to confer angelic status on figures and groups, including the "vision of Hagu" pericope from 4QInstruction.

people" is in accordance with a heavenly pattern that relates to the first human.[157] It is significant that various sources, including later rabbinic works, also associate Adam with the angelic realm. For example, the Treatise on the Two Spirits includes a portrait of these interrelated subjects (the righteous elect, Adam, and the angels), where the chosen group receives the "wisdom of the sons of heaven" in order to achieve the "glory of Adam" (1QS 4:22–23). Other texts elevate the first human in a similar manner, including *Jubilees*.[158] 4Instruction seems to be an early example of this interpretive move, even if the distinctions between the righteous and unrighteous categories are not as developed as they are in the Treatise on the Two Spirits.

The author of 4QInstruction utilizes all of this language from Genesis to demarcate two types, the "spiritual people" and the "fleshly spirit." The distinct creation stories in Genesis 1–3 assist him in this pursuit. This is somewhat analogous to Philo, who presents a contrast between the original human of Genesis 1, fashioned as the "heavenly man, being made after the image of God," and the mortal in Genesis 2–3, who lacks the necessary discernment and comes from the earth.[159] The author of 4QInstruction assumes a differentiation of this sort, although he does not unpack the two categories through an elaborate philosophical system, as Philo does. In Genesis 2–3, the male figure is entirely mortal, made from the "dust of the earth" (Gen 2:7), and he is not wise. The "fleshly spirit" of 4QInstruction, with its inability to understand the difference between good and evil, resembles and in a sense represents this figure. On the other side, the righteous addressee is a member of the "spiritual people." Through his access to the "vision of Hagu" and special endowment at creation (כתבנית קדושים), he can hope for the same enlightenment and spiritual fellowship with

---

[157] The translation depends on whether one takes יצרו as a verb or a noun. Harrington reads יְצָרוֹ ("he fashioned him"), with the deity as the subject (cf. Gen 2:7). Yet this term could also signify an affirmation of the elect class's ability to emulate the angels. Therefore the noun "inclination" would be the better translation. The fact that an individual's "inclination" naturally favors the correct approach does not imply a lack of agency, however. The מבין must remain attuned to the mystery, and his eternal blessing is not guaranteed (see below).

[158] Collins, "In the Likeness of the Holy Ones," 616–17, points to later depictions of Adam's formation in the image of the angels (e.g., *Gen R.* 21:5). Cf. Goff, *Worldly and Heavenly Wisdom*, 97, who cites a passage from *Jubilees* in which Adam receives instruction from the angels in the garden (3:15).

[159] Philo famously reads the accounts in Genesis as indicative of a double creation (*Opif* 134–35).

the angels that the first Adam enjoyed.[160] This seems to be an effort at explaining why there are two sets of people in the world; the second creation story had become a useful way of characterizing the sinful group. 4QInstruction is clearly struggling with issues of causality, evil, death, and the role of divine agency, just like Qoheleth, Ben Sira, and the author of the Treatise on the Two Spirits. According to this "vision of Hagu" passage, human beings must be able to reason soundly, and the only persons who can achieve the proper level of discernment are those who belong to the "spiritual people." During the early Hellenistic period, the Genesis creation stories became essential tools for highlighting this duality, and the fact that we find so many allusions to these accounts in other texts demonstrates their central place in the debate and reassessment of core theological issues.

Since the distinction between the "spiritual people" (רוח עם) and the "fleshly spirit" (רוח בשר) is so crucial to 4QInstruction, it is fruitful to explore the meaning of this terminology in greater detail. The "fleshly spirit" in 4Q417 1 i cannot understand the difference between good and evil. Such individuals suffer for their lack of access, especially at the final judgment. At this stage in its usage (i.e., later than most of the biblical writers but earlier than the more developed dichotomy found in Philo and Paul), בשר does not seem to involve a negative evaluation of corporeal existence. In his survey of the term in the Dead Sea Scrolls and subsequent literature, Jörg Frey has demonstrated that בשר in 4QInstruction can denote a class of people who are incapable of understanding the totality of the divine plan.[161] In some passages from the Scrolls, the term seems to have a neutral connotation and needs a modifier, but in other examples, such as 4Q417 1 i 13–18, בשר itself

---

[160] Collins, "In the Likeness of the Holy Ones," 616–17, explains the difference between 4QInstruction and Ben Sira in terms of their respective readings of the Genesis accounts. According to Ben Sira, God created Adam and bestowed the gift of discernment (17:7), but he also left him and the rest of humanity ביד יצרי ("in the power of their temperament," 15:14). For 4QInstruction, the figure who cannot distinguish between good and evil is not the same type whom the Creator fashioned according to the image of the holy ones. These categories constitute two distinct classes, the "fleshly spirit" and the "spiritual people."

[161] Jörg Frey, "Flesh and Spirit in the Palestinian Jewish Sapiential Tradition and in the Qumran Texts: An Inquiry into the Background of Pauline Usage," in *The Wisdom Texts from Qumran and the Development of Sapiential Thought* (ed. C. Hempel et al.; BETL 159; Leuven: Leuven University Press/Peeters, 2002), 379. Frey also notes the use of the term in the Hebrew Bible: בשר can denote human frailty and the transitory nature of earthly existence, but not necessarily an inclination to sin or disobedience (p. 396).

is negative and does not require adjectival emphasis.[162] Language in other texts attests to a similar understanding of "flesh," particularly in the Hodayot and Community Rule. For example, "What, then, is flesh to understand [your mysteries?] How can dust direct its steps?" (1QH 7:24).[163] A passage in the Community Rule refers to the individual who belongs to "evil humanity" (לאדם רשעה) and also "to the assembly of unfaithful flesh" (ולסוד בשר עול)(1QS 11:9); a few lines later there is a stated fear of falling prey to "the sin of the flesh" (בעוון בשר) (11:12). In these examples and in 4Q417 1 i 13–18, the "fleshly spirit" suffers from a fractured relationship with God. Failure is inevitable, since these individuals lack the ability to make the correct choices in life. Their ineptitude leads to a clear separation from the righteous, with devastating consequences. A final punishment is forecast at the very beginning of 4QInstruction: "And every spirit of flesh will be destroyed" (4Q416 1 12).

## 8.1   *Free Will and Determinism in 4QInstruction*

This portrait of two groups in 4QInstruction suggests a deterministic understanding of the created order and human destiny in particular. The text states that the "mystery that is to be" has already been revealed to the addressee (4Q418 123 ii 4), and therefore the process described in the "vision of Hagu" passage is a continuation rather than an initiation, a command for the pupil to use the discriminatory powers bestowed by God. It has been argued that the emphasis on divine revelation and determinism exceeds any other dynamic in this text. Heavenly tablets or books are featured in the Enochic texts (*1 En.* 47:3; 93:2; 108:3; cf. *Jub.* 30:20–22); future events, including judgment, are frequently alluded to in this type of material. Perhaps the "mystery that is to be," the "vision of Hagu," and the "book of memorial" in 4QInstruction contain similar information and imply a rigid determinism. Many recent studies emphasize such a deterministic outlook. Goff

---

[162] Frey, "Flesh and Spirit," 378, points to passages from the War Scroll and the Community Rule that use בשר and require a negative modifier (e.g., בשר עול in 1QM 4:4 and 1QS 11:9; בשר אשמה in 1QM 12:12). A reference in the Hodayot uses the רוח בשר designation in the same way as 4QInstruction, to refer to a group lacking discernment: "[However, what is] the spirit of flesh to understand all of these matters and to have insight in [your wondrous] and great counsel?" (1QH 5:19–20). Translation here is from the *DSSSE*, 1:151.

[163] This passage proceeds to praise God's "spirit," which can transform human beings and bring salvation.

gives particular emphasis to this aspect: "Determinism is a natural expression of 4QInstruction's emphasis on God's dominion throughout history.... God has arranged in advance every deed as part of the divine plan governing reality that is revealed to the addressee."[164] As proof of this mindset, he cites 4Q417 1 i 10–11: "He [ex]pounded for their un[der]standing every d[ee]d So that man could walk in the [inclination] of their/his understanding." Such language on the divine plan in 4QInstruction is perhaps analogous to the content of the Treatise on the Two Spirits. The beginning of this unit describes God's intentions for humanity, where the deterministic aspect is unequivocal:

> From the God of knowledge stems all there is and all there shall be. Before they existed he established their entire design. And when they have come into being, at their appointed time, they will execute all their works according to his glorious design, without altering anything (1QS 3:15–16).[165]

This language from the Treatise on the Two Spirits is similar to the content of 4Q417 1 i 10–11 and other passages from 4QInstruction. Yet even if 4QInstruction mentions an "inheritance" for every person (4Q418 81 20) and uses apocalyptic language to refer to the "period of truth" (4Q416 1 13), this text does not share the more pronounced dualism of the Treatise on the Two Spirits. The contrast between the two categories of people is less developed in 4QInstruction, especially since the "vision of Hagu" passage and other relevant units do not contain a light-darkness contrast. This is a recurrent feature of the Treatise (e.g., 1QS 3:19).

A closer parallel to 4QInstruction in terms of the relationship between determinism and human initiative can be found in some of the constructs used by Ben Sira. In 4Q417 1 i, God reveals the "mystery that is to be" in order to emphasize divine majesty and give elect individuals the necessary power of discernment. Ben Sira, in his discussion of the

---

[164] Goff, *Worldly and Heavenly Wisdom*, 66–67. He tempers this statement with remarks elsewhere: "4QInstruction stresses that the addressee's affinity with the angels is not automatic. It is something he must nurture and develop" (p. 110). Nitzan, "The Ideological and Literary Unity of 4QInstruction," 279, claims that this text is not "a random collection of sapiential instructions, but rather a deliberately composed work, written by a specific author, who adhered to an apocalyptic-deterministic ideology."

[165] *DSSSE*, 1:75.

divine gift of knowledge, offers a similar portrait: "He filled them with knowledge and understanding, and showed them good and evil. He put the fear of him into their hearts to show them the majesty of his works" (Sir 17:7–8). We find the same sequence in 4QInstruction, since the mystery leads to a better awareness of divine omnipotence, and this gift also involves the capacity for enlightened awareness. Because of the use of apocalyptic motifs and "inheritance" language, it can be tempting to overstate the deterministic understanding found in 4QInstruction. The addressee enjoys a favorable status with the deity and the prospect of ultimate deliverance: "And (just as) among all the[ Go]dly [Ones] has He cast thy lot (נורלכה), And has magnified thy glory greatly" (4Q418 81 4–5). Yet this does not signify a preordained status, an infallible guarantee of fellowship with the heavenly host. An intentional ordering of the creation and a special endowment for a particular group are noteworthy features of Ben Sira (e.g., 1:14), and still the righteous pupil possesses the capacity to sin. A person's "inclination" can tilt in the wrong direction if diligence is absent.

4QInstruction does not offer a grand theological scheme based on rigid determinism. One of the most important issues throughout this entire discussion has been the relationship between free will, determinism, and divine agency, and how complex the presentation can be in ancient instructions. The use of predestination language in an instructional text can serve as a pedagogical device designed to motivate pupils. As far back as Ptahhotep, sages made assertions such as "evil was fated in the womb" and "he whom the gods guide is one who cannot err" (P 217–218). This type of statement impresses upon the pupil that he enjoys a special status and should act accordingly. In 4QInstruction, the use of such terms as נורל ("lot") and the inclusion of apocalyptic-deterministic ideas intensify the portrait of a divinely ordered framework for human behavior and outcomes. Other passages, however, mitigate the more deterministic elements. 4QInstruction understands the possibility of wayward behavior and warns the addressee: "Do not be contaminated by evildoing (אל תתנע בעולה), [for everyone who is contaminated] with it shall not be treated as guiltless" (4Q417 1 i 23–24). This admonition comes immediately after the "vision of Hagu" section, suggesting that the addressee's status as a member of the "spiritual people" is not a *fait accompli*. The same is also true to an extent for the Treatise on the Two Spirits: the "sons of light" have the capacity to falter. The Treatise contains language that indicates a degree of human agency and on ongoing struggle within the heart of each individual.[166]

There seems to be a level of psychological dualism at work in 4QInstruction (particularly 4Q417 1 i), so that an internal רוח בשר threatens each person's well being and long-term prospects for success. Even if the "spiritual people" have the ability to discriminate, they also have agency. If they make poor choices, this can lead to separation from the righteous lot.[167] The promised inheritance, the addressee's likeness to the holy ones, and his access to the mysteries of creation: all of these things can be read from a didactic perspective. Pupils must reflect the glory that has been bestowed upon them and seek to live as members of an elect community. If an individual is negligent, he can be "contaminated" by iniquity, just as the one who strays from the "fear of the Lord" can suffer a qualitative death in earlier instructions.[168] In support of this understanding is the fragmentary passage in 4Q423 1 2, which uses the terminology of the Eden story to describe two choices for the addressee. The garden metaphor represents the dilemma of all pupils: "He set you in charge of it to till it and guard it." There is language in this fragment about "[rejecting] the evil and knowing the good" (line 7), and this is similar to the description of two choices in Sirach 17.[169] As Collins explains, this is not realized eschatology, but the presentation of two paths: "the text does not describe a permanent eschatological state, but still envisages the possibility of transgression."[170] As noted throughout this chapter, the consequences of wayward behavior differ

---

[166] We find the same psychological struggle between two forces in the Treatise on the Two Spirits: "Until now the spirits of truth and injustice feud in the heart of man: they walk in wisdom or in folly" (1QS 4:23–24). 4QInstruction does not reflect the cosmic dualism found in the Treatise, as Collins, *Apocalypticism in the Dead Sea Scrolls*, 41, explains. He attributes the mythological aspect of the Treatise to Zoroastrian influence (pp. 43–45).

[167] The importance of social context cannot be forgotten in this examination of dualism. On the relationship between ethical dualism in the wisdom literature and how this can differ in apocalyptic works, see John G. Gammie, "Spatial and Ethical Dualism in Jewish Wisdom and Apocalyptic Literature," *JBL* 93 (1974), 378.

[168] There is mention of a יצר בשר in 4Q416 1 16, and unfortunately the line is fragmentary. Based on the use of בשר throughout 4QInstruction, it seems fair to assume that those who belong to this fleshly category have no chance of a favorable judgment from God.

[169] The inclusion of language about "thorns and thistles" for the unfaithful draws on Gen 3:18.

[170] Collins, *Jewish Wisdom*, 126, responding to Elgvin's argument that this passage indicates a realized eschatology, a current share in the "glory of Adam" (cf. 1QS 4:23).

radically from the other instructions we have examined, but the lack of rigid determinism is consistent with the tradition. Based on his choices, the addressee's inheritance can be forfeited though iniquity, resulting in eternal torment, *or* he can continue to meditate on the mystery and move to "glory everlasting and peace eternal."

### 9. *4QInstruction: A Sectarian Document?*

Our discussion of social location, ethical dualism, and eschatological hope in 4QInstruction brings us to the "sectarian" question.[171] Since seven copies of 4QInstruction have been found near Qumran, all in the same Herodian script as the rulebooks, it must have been a document of some importance during at least a portion of the community's existence. We have established the marginal status for the individuals addressed in this text and the importance of this factor for situating some of the apocalyptic language. The special election of the addressee, especially his access to privileged mysteries, suggests an exclusivist context at least somewhat analogous to the undisputed sectarian documents. Moreover, the "spiritual people" of 4QInstruction are a more clearly defined lot than the general category who heed the call of Wisdom in Proverbs and Ben Sira. The self-definition of this group includes a belief in their special inheritance vis-à-vis the rest of society, and this is also the case for the community described in the rulebooks (e.g., CD 7:5). There are also clear terminological parallels with other statements in the Dead Sea Scrolls, including the Damascus Document. While the occurrences are not numerous, a few of the examples are compelling and perhaps indicative of a common milieu of origin.[172] Although this

---

[171] As with all efforts at classifying ancient documents, preliminary definitions have great bearing on any conclusions, especially what the modern scholar understands "sectarian" to mean. For background on this question, see Jutta M. Jokiranta, "'Sectarianism' of the Qumran 'Sect': Sociological Notes," *RevQ* 78 (December 2001), 223–39; Carol Newsom, "'Sectually Explicit' Literature from Qumran," in *The Hebrew Bible and Its Interpreters* (ed. W.H. Propp et al.; Winona Lake, Ind.: Eisenbrauns, 1990), 167–87.

[172] We have discussed the terminological affinities between 4QInstruction, the Treatise on the Two Spirits, Mysteries, and the Hodayot. There are also parallels with some of the rulebooks, including mystery language. In particular, the phrase "eternal planting" (מטעת עולם) occurs in 4Q418 81 13 and in the Community Rule (1QS 8:5; 11:8; cf. 1QH 14:15; 16:6). Torleif Elgvin, "Admonition Texts from Qumran Cave 4," in *Methods of Investigation of the Dead Sea Scrolls and the Khirbet Qumran Site: Present Realities and Future Prospects* (ed. M.O. Wise et al.; Annals of the New York Academy of Sciences 722; New York: New York Academy of Sciences, 1994), 185, provides a detailed list of common

work presupposes a traditional familial structure that is at odds with the quasi-monastic setting outlined in the Community Rule, this factor does not preclude a sectarian origin, since family life is assumed in the Damascus Document.[173] It is probable that the more open and mixed-gender model described in the Damascus Document developed before the Community Rule; such a framework does not contradict the admonitions of 4QInstruction. Elgvin has suggested that the description of the "camps" in CD 7:6–7 is an appropriate background for understanding 4QInstruction; this stage represents for him a pre-יחד period in the community's existence.[174]

There are several problems with this argument for a sectarian origin, however. 4QInstruction does not presuppose the developed communal structures in the rulebooks, even those found in the Damascus Document.[175] 4QInstruction never mentions a Teacher of Righteousness and does not appeal to the Torah as an authoritative source. This last distinction is perhaps the most significant factor in addressing this issue: while the "mystery that is to be" and the Torah are not mutually exclusive, the discrepancy between the repeated references to the Mosaic legislation in the rulebooks and the lack of a direct appeal in 4QInstruction suggests a non-sectarian origin.[176] The source of authority, the "mystery

---

vocabulary. His examples include the phrase "to walk perfectly" (להתהלך תמים), which occurs in 4Q415 2 i 3 and 4Q417 1 i 12; cf. CD 1:20–21; 8:4–5; 1QS 1:8; 9:19. For further instances of similarity, see Elgvin, "Mystery to Come," 113–50. Lange, *Weisheit und Prädestination*, 121–70, 195–270, also discusses the common terms (primarily in the Treatise and the Hodayot, but also the parallels with CD 2).

[173] John J. Collins, "The Nature and Aims of the Sect Known from the Dead Sea Scrolls," in *Flores Florentino: Dead Sea Scrolls and Other Early Jewish Studies in Honour of Florentino García Martínez* (ed. E.J.C. Tigchelaar; Leiden: Brill, forthcoming), outlines the noteworthy differences between the Damascus Document and the Community Rule. These include the assumption of married life in the former text: divorce is discussed in CD 13:16–17, the instruction of children in 4Q266 9 iii 6, and sexual relations in 4Q267 9 vi 4–5 and 4Q270 7 i 12–13. In contrast, the Community Rule never addresses familial structures in this manner.

[174] Elgvin, "Wisdom and Apocalypticism," 246.

[175] Members must submit to the authority of the מבקר in the Damascus Document (e.g., 13:6–7), and such a figure is not stipulated in 4QInstruction. The organization of communities with a minimum of ten members in CD 13 is much more specific than anything from the fragments of 4QInstruction.

[176] Lawrence H. Schiffman, "Halakhic Elements in the Sapiential Texts from Qumran," in *Sapiential Perspectives: Wisdom Literature in Light of the Dead Sea Scrolls, Proceedings of the Sixth International Symposium of the Orion Center for the Study of the Dead Sea Scrolls and Associated Literature, 20–22 May, 2001* (ed. J.J. Collins et al.; STDJ 51; Leiden: Brill, 2004), 89–100, discusses several instances of disagreement between 4QInstruction and the rulebooks on legal matters. Topics include the details of such observances as marriage vows and the laws concerning mixed species.

that is to be," is markedly different for the author of 4QInstruction. In addition, it seems clear that 4QInstruction targets a broader and more loosely confederated group than the one presumed by the Damascus Document. The addressee of 4QInstruction can pursue his livelihood with autonomy. He can conduct business in the marketplace, trading goods and avoiding usurious situations.[177] There is no common control over the purse strings, as one finds in the rulebooks. The individuals responsible for the undisputed sectarian texts were certainly capable of producing stylistically diverse documents and adhering to the generic conventions of sapiential literature, which usually avoids cultic references and extensive halakhic engagement. Yet the available fragments and likely chronology for 4QInstruction suggest a rather fluid group prior to the formation of the יחד. Because it was copied repeatedly, we can hypothesize that much of 4QInstruction had significant appeal among the community responsible for the explicitly sectarian texts, just as the Enochic books and *Jubilees* did. Part of this appeal can be traced to the combination of admonitory material with eschatological promise, which had become an important interpretive move during this period. The use of apocalyptic constructs to guarantee a consistent *Tun-Ergehen-Zusammenhang* would have assisted this and other marginal communities with their self-understanding, even if those responsible for the undisputed sectarian documents had a more closed community and did not subscribe to every detail of 4QInstruction.

## 10. *4QInstruction and the Wisdom of Solomon*

4QInstruction reflects a larger transition within the wisdom tradition, as the otherworldly horizon for reward and punishment became a permanent part of sapiential discourse. One of the most important examples in this development is the Wisdom of Solomon, which shares a number of features with 4QInstruction, despite its later date and clear

---

[177] According to Catherine M. Murphy, *Wealth in the Dead Sea Scrolls and in the Qumran Community* (Leiden: Brill, 2002), 165, 4QInstruction contains standard *topoi* from instructional literature that contradict the frequent assumption in the rulebooks of a closed economy. Moreover, Goff, *Discerning Wisdom*, 61–62, notes that the references to the elect in the rulebooks do not generally associate this movement with an impoverished group of individuals (*pace* 4QInstruction).

fascination with philosophical terminology and thought.[178] In the so-called "book of eschatology" (Wis 1:1–6:21), the author refers to a group of misguided individuals whose skepticism about the afterlife leads to reckless, hedonistic behavior. In chapter 2, he quotes their perspective, which consists of a belief in the fleeting nature of individual existence, particularly in terms of memory: "For we are born by mere chance, and hereafter we shall be as though we had never been" (Wis 2:2; cf. Qoh 1:11). According to these fools, there is no possibility of an afterlife, since the soul is not immortal (Wis 2:3). The righteous, however, conduct their lives in a virtuous manner and enjoy an altogether different fate: "But the souls of the righteous are in the hand of God, and no torment will ever touch them" (3:1). Their radiance will "shine forth" (3:7), implying a belief in the immortality of the spirit/soul. Humanity is created for "incorruption" (ἀφθαρσία) in Wisdom, an important term for this text (2:23; 6:18, 19). The noun ἀθανασία ("immortality") also appears frequently (3:4; 4:1; 8:13, 17; 15:3).

The author of 4QInstruction was not an Alexandrian Jew influenced by the Platonic notion of the immortal soul, but these two instructional texts share a surprising number of features. Both emphasize the survival of the righteous after death, presumably in a state that does not involve physical resurrection.[179] Eternal life in the Wisdom of Solomon is not automatic: as with 4QInstruction, eschatological reward is contingent upon upright conduct and God's gracious response. In the later text, the gift of immortality depends in large measure on human awareness. Wicked persons in the past have failed, because they "did not know the secret purposes (or 'mysteries') of God, nor hoped for the wages of holiness, nor discerned the prize for blameless souls" (Wis 2:22; cf. 4Q417 1 i 18). The righteous, on the other hand, are located with the "lot among the saints" (Wis 5:5), and this is quite similar to some of the election language in 4QInstruction (e.g., 4Q418 81 5). A radical, neat application of the *Tun-Ergehen-Zusammenhang* occurs in both texts: the righteous enjoy "glory everlasting and peace eternal" in 4QInstruction (4Q418 126 ii 7–8), and in the later sapiential work,

---

[178] The date for the Wisdom of Solomon is debated. David Winston, *The Wisdom of Solomon* (AB 43; New York: Doubleday, 1979), 4, 22–23, locates the text around the turn of the era.

[179] In Wis 3:7–8, it is predicted that the righteous will "run like sparks through the stubble" at the time of their "visitation." Collins, "The Mysteries of God," 293, argues that the language correlates with the use of astral imagery in other texts (both Jewish and Hellenistic) from this period and should not be taken too literally.

"the righteous live forever, and their reward is with the Lord; the Most High takes care of them" (Wis 5:15).[180] There is no concept of Sheol in the Wisdom of Solomon; the wicked simply cease to exist.[181] Nor is there a category of fleshly people in this later book; the distinction in Wisdom of Solomon involves an internal contrast within each individual (4QInstruction also has a psychological level). Both texts utilize mystery concepts to explain access to the Creator and the success of certain persons, and these authors rely on the Genesis stories to construct their respective descriptions of the cosmos.[182] In this area, 4QInstruction and the Wisdom of Solomon are indebted to apocalyptic constructs, although the latter text also borrows heavily from the Greek world to present a contrast between righteous and sinful behavior and the hope for immortality. The corollaries between the two sapiential documents are a matter of great consequence for Second Temple Wisdom studies, pointing to an ongoing reevaluation of older ideas, a break with many of the standard frameworks, and an "eschatologizing" of Wisdom that brought fundamental change to the tradition.

---

[180] There is no explicit reference to fellowship with the angels in Wis. Sol.

[181] This means a more unfavorable conclusion for the wicked in 4QInstruction, since their end involves eternal punishment in Sheol, the "dark regions."

[182] For the Wisdom of Solomon, it is necessary for the righteous to understand the divine plan (2:21–24), and this constitutes a striking parallel with 4QInstruction. In addition, the later text builds on Gen 1:27 to explain the created order. God created Adam and all of humanity "in the image of his own eternity" (Wis 2:23). Collins, "Mysteries of God," 300–1, also associates Wis 7:1 ("I also am mortal, like everyone else, a descendant of the first-formed child of earth") with the mortal body of Gen 2:7.

# CONCLUSION

This study has pointed to a profound shift in certain Second Temple instructions, from an earthly to an otherworldly focus. The content of 4QInstruction and the Wisdom of Solomon indicates a reconfiguration of the traditional model: a righteous person's "inheritance" no longer consisted of "gladness and joy and long life" (Sir 1:12), but "glory everlasting and peace eternal" (4Q418 126 ii 8). Those who adopted such a belief system drew from a variety of sources and ideas in order to construct this vision of reality. We have discussed the synthesis of sapiential and apocalyptic concepts in 4QInstruction, which permitted a direct link between the cautious ethic of traditional Wisdom and access to the heavenly realm. A person's success was contingent upon understanding the mysteries of God and leading a virtuous life. Such a perspective challenged the tradition to move beyond the earthly sphere for retribution. This eschatological vision made a permanent imprint: later figures, both Jewish and Christian, would provide more developed understandings of ultimate reward and punishment that built on the ideas of earlier works.[1] Our discussion has also shown that many sapiential figures (e.g., Qoheleth, Ben Sira) opposed such a move.

This discussion has demonstrated that a preoccupation with death characterizes many of the later instructions, but not the earlier material. Societies differ in terms of their explicit interest in human mortality: we need only contrast the elaborate place of death and the afterlife in Egyptian religion with the paucity of references to this topic in the Hebrew Bible. It should be acknowledged that the earthly focus of earlier Wisdom and much of the biblical material does not represent the diversity of religious beliefs in ancient Israel, as studies in recent years have demonstrated. It would be erroneous to assume that death only became a topic of importance during the third-century B.C.E.[2] Yet the content of the Hebrew Bible presents a fairly unified understanding of

---

[1] For example, the parallels between 4QInstruction and the Synoptics are intriguing and worthy of further study. A heavenly reward for the righteous (e.g., Matt 5:12) and an interest in the angelic realm in the context of judgment (Matt 16:27) are two important examples.

[2] For example, Saul's consultation of the medium at Endor (1 Sam 28:7) and the appearance of Samuel indicate an interest in the realm of the dead. The legal material

the heavens as an impenetrable realm, a location that is not the ultimate destination of righteous individuals.[3] In the presentation of the biblical writers, the heavens function as the domain of God and cannot be traversed by ordinary mortals, even at the end of a person's life.[4] The earthly realm remains the arena for human actions, and this is especially true for instructional texts. In this study, we have cited the emphasis on daily life and immediate possibilities in the Egyptian instructions. The compilers of Proverbs adopted their Egyptian predecessors' concern for present justice and piety, including the characteristic lack of interest in death and speculation about the afterlife. The focus on a "qualitative" death for the foolish is a didactic move designed to influence pupils' current behavior. "Life" and "death" constitute binary opposites in Proverbs, useful categories for the ethical dualism of this collection (like the "two paths" language and the contrast between Lady Wisdom and the Strange Woman). Only in later instructions is there a more serious engagement with the possibility of an afterlife. This marked distinction suggests a chronological separation between the book of Proverbs and an emergent discussion during the Hellenistic period. It is highly unlikely that a comprehensive collection like Proverbs would be detached from a major debate over retribution and the finality of death. In contrast, the book of Qoheleth almost certainly derives from a later era, probably the Ptolemaic period. This author uses incisive reasoning to answer the pioneering suggestions of his contemporaries and refute any belief in the afterlife (e.g., 3:16–22).[5]

The likely reasons for this shift are diverse and in many respects related to the *Zeitgeist* of the later period. It seems clear from Qoheleth, Job, and even Ben Sira that various figures began to see weaknesses in the standard retributive model. Even if certain commentators have

---

in the Hebrew Bible frequently discourages such speculative beliefs and practices (e.g., Deut 18:9–12).

[3] John J. Collins, "Journeys to the World Beyond in Ancient Judaism," in *Apocalyptic and Eschatological Heritage* (ed. M. McNamara; Dublin: Four Courts, 2003), 20–36, who includes a survey of the scattered Mesopotamian ascent stories (e.g., Gilgamesh, the account of Enmeduranki).

[4] The visions of various prophets concerning the heavens are of course a major exception (e.g., Isa 6:1–13; Ezek 1:1–3:15). Yet as Collins ("Journeys to the World Beyond") notes, the details of the divine realm are sparsely recounted, the actual ascent of the prophets is not described, and there is even skepticism among some figures about the authenticity of such trips (Jer 23:18; Ezek 28:2). In addition, these descriptions do not involve a belief in the immortality of the individual soul.

[5] For this same reason, our discussion has suggested a postexilic date for the final version of Job, perhaps as late as the book of Qoheleth.

tended to overstate the facile outlook in Proverbs, this collection does reflect the perspective of entrenched scribal administrators ("learned clerks") promising present justice. Their "deliberate and programmatic construal of reality" (Fox) became insufficient at a certain point after the exile. Frustration *and* a pastiche of new influences led to innovative departures from the former understanding of the *Tun-Ergehen-Zusammenhang*. Among the important factors, the Hellenistic traditions about the ascent of the soul provided a logical belief for assimilation. Such a perspective survives in Plato's account of Er, Greek epitaphs, and in the writings of Euripides (where the righteous go to the αἰθήρ of the gods). We have argued that the "return" of the divine breath to God, which had traditionally signified physical death (e.g., Qoh 12:7), was transformed into a belief in the survival/ascent of the human spirit and that popular beliefs about astral immortality undoubtedly played a role in this development.

The popularity of apocalyptic descriptions like the ones in *1 Enoch* also influenced the "eschatologizing" of Wisdom in 4QInstruction and other texts. The use of "mystery" language and such terms as קץ and פקודה are absent from earlier instructions, but such elements do appear in apocalyptic works like *1 Enoch*, Daniel, and many passages from the Scrolls. The Book of the Watchers and Daniel do not find harmony or the potential for it in the earthly sphere; rather, the world is in at least a partial state of anomie.[6] Political persecution and a marginalized status led many communities (in varying degrees) to this otherworldly perspective. The wisdom tradition was clearly influenced by the new set of constructs for addressing divine revelation and retribution. While some sages held fast to traditional, earthly Wisdom (Ben Sira), those responsible for 4QInstruction sought to combine practical advice with an appeal to divine mysteries *and* salvation at the end of days. It is no coincidence that this interpretive leap coincided with the spread of apocalyptic literature. If we place 4QInstruction in the latter part of the second-century B.C.E. (a date for which we have argued in this discussion), then the development of this perspective continued after the Maccabean revolt, when Daniel and other apocalyptic texts won increasing acceptance. Stuckenbruck seems on the mark in claiming

---

[6] John J. Collins, "Cosmos and Salvation: Jewish Wisdom and Apocalypticism in the Hellenistic Age," in *Seers, Sibyls, and Sages in Hellenistic-Roman Judaism* (Leiden: Brill, 1997), 336. The level of discord can differ from one text to the other: some apocalyptic texts (e.g., the Epistle of Enoch) are not as dramatic in their presentation.

that the Enochic complex of traditions, Daniel, and 4QInstruction were able to "cross-fertilise as their distinct forms of apocalyptic wisdom took shape" during the second-century.[7] The adoption of such ideas challenged the standard paradigm for instructional literature: the otherworldly framework for reward and punishment, the emphasis on divine mystery, and the use of heavenly imagery involving angels demonstrate indebtedness to ideas that had become available for sapiential reflections. The late second-century is the most likely setting for such a shift as we find in 4QInstruction.

The promise of an otherworldly inheritance would have been a hopeful message for pupils who were forced to accept difficult circumstances and "live in the world as it is." This discussion has highlighted the importance of social context in assessing various instructions and the authors' act-consequence understanding. The reflections of more entrenched sages generally present a "locative" model for prosperity, where the preservation of social structures and the hope for solidarity are emphasized. Ben Sira, who was dependent on the priestly authorities, and the "independent" conclusions of 4QInstruction are a useful contrast on this point. If communities responsible for texts like 4QInstruction wanted to offer a consistent principle of causality, then they had to present an alternative model. Their peripheral status did not afford them the opportunities of the retainer class, and this is why J.Z. Smith's definition of apocalypticism as *"wisdom lacking a royal patron"* is so helpful for understanding a text like 4QInstruction and why it includes an eschatological component.

Other influences, including textual traditions, also had an impact on this new model. The emergence of the Genesis creation narratives as grist for discussion of divine majesty, theodicy, and the different types of people in the world marks an important development. Both Ben Sira and 4QInstruction (and to a lesser extent Qoheleth) wrestle with the language of these stories and interpret freely from them in order to construct theological arguments. For example, Sirach glosses over the disobedience of Adam and Eve and instead emphasizes moral discernment as a positive gift rather than a forbidden fruit (Sir 17:6–7). For his part, the author of 4QInstruction uses the terminology and

---

[7] Loren Stuckenbruck, "4QInstruction and the Possible Influence of Early Enochic Traditions: An Evaluation," in *The Wisdom Texts from Qumran and the Development of Sapiential Thought* (ed. C. Hempel et al.; BETL 159; Leuven: Leuven University Press/Peeters, 2002), 261.

ideas in the creation stories to differentiate two categories of people: those who are privy to the "mystery that is to be" and the bulk of the population from whom the Lord has denied access. The accounts in Genesis became important tools for highlighting the duality in creation, an interpretive move that had not occurred in earlier generations. Much of this engagement relates to the theodicy question. The origins of evil became a topic of great concern during this period, as evidenced by the references to sin and human accountability in the Book of the Watchers, Ben Sira, and 4QInstruction.

Ancient Near Eastern Wisdom texts from all periods represent an effort to make sense of human existence in relation to divine majesty and the finitude of earthly existence. We have discussed the unresolved tension between divine determinism and human initiative in many of these texts and the genuine efforts at explaining the diversity of individual experiences. For example, the Jewish sage Qoheleth declares that God "has put a sense of past and future (העלם)" into the minds of humanity, "yet they cannot find out what God has done from the beginning to the end" (3:11). This sapiential author emphasizes the gulf between God and humanity and our inability to understand the machinations of the universe. During the course of Qoheleth's lifetime and in subsequent generations, various authors and groups began to address this gulf more directly, by asking difficult questions about act and consequence, death, and the possibility of individual immortality. Some looked to the heavens for their ultimate reward, and the tradition was forever changed.

# BIBLIOGRAPHY

Aitken, James K., "Divine Will and Providence," in *Ben Sira's God: Proceedings of the International Ben Sira Conference - Ushaw College 2001* (ed. R. Egger-Wenzel; BZAW 321; Berlin: de Gruyter, 2002), 282–301.

Aletti, Jean-Noël, "Séduction et parole en Proverbes I–IX," *Vetus Testamentum* 27 (1977): 129–44.

Argall, Randal A., *1 Enoch and Sirach: A Comparative Literary and Conceptual Analysis of the Themes of Revelation, Creation, and Judgment* (SBLEJL 8; Atlanta: Scholars Press, 1995).

Assmann, Jan, *Death and Salvation in Ancient Egypt* (trans. David Lorton; Ithaca: Cornell University Press, 2005).

———, *Maât, l'Égypte pharaonique et l'idée de justice sociale* (Paris: Julliard, 1989).

———, *Ma'at: Gerechtigkeit und Unsterblichkeit im alten Ägypten* (Munich: Beck, 1990).

———, "State and Religion in the New Kingdom," in *Religion and Philosophy in Ancient Egypt* (ed. W.K. Simpson; YES 3; New Haven: Yale University Press, 1989), 55–88.

———, "Weisheit, Loyalismus, und Frömmigkeit," in *Studien zu altägyptischen Lebenslehren* (ed. E. Hornung and O. Keel; OBO 28; Fribourg/Göttingen: Universitätsverlag/Vandenhoeck & Ruprecht, 1979), 11–72.

Auwers, Jean-Marie, "Problèmes d'interprétation de l'épilogue de Qohèlèt," in *Qohelet in the Context of Wisdom* (ed. A. Schoors; BETL 136; Leuven: Leuven University Press/Peeters, 1998), 267–82.

Backhaus, Franz-Josef, *'Denn Zeit und Zufall trifft sie alle': Studien zur Komposition und zum Gottesbild im Buch Qohelet* (BBB 83; Frankfurt: Anton Hain, 1993).

Barthélemy, D., and J.T. Milik, *Qumran Cave 1* (DJD 1; Oxford: Clarendon Press, 1955).

Beentjes, Pancratius C., *The Book of Ben Sira in Hebrew* (VTSup 68; Leiden: Brill, 1997).

———, "Theodicy in the Wisdom of Ben Sira," in *Theodicy in the World of the Bible* (ed. A. Laato and J.C. de Moor; Leiden: Brill, 2003), 509–24.

Berlin, Andrea M., "Between Large Forces: Palestine in the Hellenistic Period," *Biblical Archaeologist* 60 (1997): 2–51.

Blackman, Aylward M., *The Story of King Cheops and the Magicians Transcribed from Papyrus Westcar (Berlin Papyrus 3033)* (ed. W.V. Davies; Reading: J.V. Books, 1988).

Blenkinsopp, Joseph, "Ecclesiastes 3.1–15: Another Interpretation," *Journal for the Study of the Old Testament* 66 (1995): 55–64.

———, *Wisdom and Law in the Old Testament* (Oxford: Oxford University Press, 1995).

Blumenthal, Elke, "Ptahhotep und der 'Stab des Alters'," in *Form und Mass: Beiträge zur Literatur, Sprache, und Kunst des alten Ägypten: Festschrift für Gerhard Fecht zum 65. Geburtstag am 6. Februar 1987* (ed. J. Osing and G. Dreyer; ÄUAT 12; Wiesbaden: O. Harrassowitz, 1987), 84–97.

Boccaccini, Gabriele, *Middle Judaism: Jewish Thought, 300 B.C.E. to 200 C.E.* (Minneapolis: Fortress Press, 1991).

Bolin, Thomas, "Rivalry and Resignation: Girard and Qoheleth on the Divine-Human Relationship," *Biblica* 86 (2005): 245–59.

Boström, Lennart, *The God of the Sages: The Portrayal of God in the Book of Proverbs* (CBOTS 29; Stockholm: Almqvist and Wiksell International, 1990).

Braun, Rainer, *Kohelet und die frühhellenistische Popularphilosophie* (BZAW 130; Berlin: de Gruyter, 1973).

Brooke, George J., "Biblical Interpretation in the Wisdom Texts from Qumran," in *The Wisdom Texts from Qumran and the Development of Sapiential Thought* (ed. C. Hempel et al.; BETL 159; Leuven: Leuven University/Peeters, 2002), 201–20.

Brunner, Hellmut, "Der freie Wille Gottes in der ägyptischen Weisheit," in *Les Sagesses du Proche-Orient Ancien, Colloque de Strasbourg, 17–19 mai 1962* (Paris: Presses Universitaires de France, 1963), 103–20.

——, *Das hörende Herz: kleine Schriften zur Religions- und Geistesgeschichte Ägyptens* (OBO 80; Fribourg/Göttingen: Universitätsverlag/Vandenhoeck & Ruprecht, 1988).

——, "Die religiöse Wertung der Armut im alten Ägypten," *Saeculum* 12 (1961): 319–44.

Burkes, Shannon, *Death in Qoheleth and Egyptian Biographies of the Late Period* (SBLDS 170; Atlanta: Society of Biblical Literature, 1999).

——, *God, Self, and Death: The Shape of Religious Transformation in the Second Temple Period* (JSJSup 79; Leiden: Brill, 2003).

Camp, Claudia, "Understanding a Patriarchy: Women in Second-Century Jerusalem through the Eyes of Ben Sira," in *'Women like This': New Perspectives on Jewish Women in the Greco-Roman World* (ed. A.J. Levine; Atlanta: Scholars Press, 1991), 1–39.

——, *Wisdom and the Feminine in the Book of Proverbs* (Bible and Literature Series 11; Decatur, Ga.: Almond Press, 1985).

Carasik, Mark, "Who Were the 'Men of Hezekiah' (Proverbs XXV 1)?" *Vetus Testamentum* 44 (1994): 289–300.

Carr, David M., *Writing on the Tablet of the Heart: Origins of Scripture and Literature* (Oxford: Oxford University Press, 2005).

Clifford, Richard J., *Proverbs* (OTL; Louisville: Westminster John Knox Press, 1999).

Coggins, Richard J., *Sirach* (Sheffield: Sheffield Academic Press, 1998).

Collins, John J., "The Afterlife in Apocalyptic Literature," in *Judaism in Late Antiquity. Part 4: Death, Life-After-Death, Resurrection and the World-to-Come in the Judaisms of Late Antiquity* (ed. J. Neusner and A.J. Avery-Peck; Leiden: Brill, 2000), 119–38.

——, *The Apocalyptic Imagination* (2d ed.; Grand Rapids: Eerdmans, 1998).

——, *Apocalypticism in the Dead Sea Scrolls* (London: Routledge, 1997).

——, "Before the Fall: The Earliest Interpretations of Adam and Eve," in *The Idea of Biblical Interpretation: Essays in Honor of James L. Kugel* (ed. H. Najman and J.H. Newman; JSJSup 83; Leiden: Brill, 2004), 293–308.

——, "The Biblical Precedent for Natural Theology," in *Encounters with Biblical Theology* (Minneapolis: Fortress Press, 2005), 91–104; originally published in *Journal of the American Academy of Religion* 45 (1977): 35–67.

——, "Cosmos and Salvation: Jewish Wisdom and Apocalypticism in the Hellenistic Age," in *Seers, Sibyls, and Sages in Hellenistic-Roman Judaism* (Leiden: Brill, 1997), 317–38; originally published in *History of Religions* 17 (1977): 121–42.

——, *Daniel* (Hermeneia; Minneapolis: Fortress Press, 1993).

——, "The Eschatologizing of Wisdom in the Dead Sea Scrolls," in *Sapiential Perspectives: Wisdom Literature in Light of the Dead Sea Scrolls. Proceedings of the Sixth International Symposium of the Orion Center for the Study of the Dead Sea Scrolls and Associated Literature, 20–22 May, 2001* (ed. J.J. Collins et al.; STDJ 51; Leiden: Brill, 2004), 49–65.

——, "Genre, Ideology, and Social Movements in Jewish Apocalypticism," in *Mysteries and Revelations: Apocalyptic Studies since the Uppsala Colloquium* (ed. J.J. Collins and J.H. Charlesworth; Sheffield: Journal for the Study of the Old Testament, 1991), 11–32.

——, "In the Likeness of the Holy Ones: The Creation of Humankind in a Wisdom Text from Qumran," in *The Provo International Conference on the Dead Sea Scrolls* (ed. D.W. Parry and E. Ulrich; STDJ 30; Leiden: Brill, 1999), 609–19.

——, *Jewish Wisdom in the Hellenistic Age* (OTL; Louisville: Westminster John Knox Press, 1997).

——, "Journeys to the World Beyond in Ancient Judaism," in *Apocalyptic and Eschatological Heritage* (ed. M. McNamara; Dublin: Four Courts, 2003), 20–36.

——, "Messianism in the Maccabean Period," in *Judaisms and Their Messiahs at the Turn of the Christian Era* (ed. J. Neusner et al.; Cambridge: Cambridge University Press, 1987), 97–109.

——, "The Mysteries of God: Creation and Eschatology in 4QInstruction and the Wisdom of Solomon," in *Wisdom and Apocalypticism in the Dead Sea Scrolls and in the Biblical Tradition* (ed. F. García Martínez; BETL 168; Leuven: Leuven University Press/Peeters, 2003), 287–305.

——, "The Nature and Aims of the Sect Known from the Dead Sea Scrolls," in *Flores Florentino: Dead Sea Scrolls and Other Early Jewish Studies in Honour of Florentino García Martínez* (ed. E.J.C. Tigchelaar; Leiden: Brill, forthcoming).

——, "The Origin of Evil in Apocalyptic Literature," in *Seers, Sibyls and Sages in Hellenistic-Roman Judaism* (Leiden: Brill, 1997), 287–99; originally published in *Congress Volume: Paris* (ed. J.A. Emerton; Leiden: Brill, 1995).

——, "Proverbial Wisdom and the Yahwist Vision," in *Encounters with Biblical Theology* (Minneapolis: Fortress Press, 2005), 105–16; originally published in *Semeia* 17 (1980): 1–17.

——, "The Root of Immortality: Death in the Context of Jewish Wisdom," *Harvard Theological Review* 71 (1978): 177–92.

——, "The Time of the Teacher: An Old Debate Renewed," in *Studies in the Hebrew Bible, Qumran, and the Septuagint Presented to Eugene Ulrich* (ed. P.W. Flint et al.; VTSup 101; Leiden: Brill, 2006), 212–29.

——, "Wisdom, Apocalypticism, and Generic Compatibility," in *In Search of Wisdom: Essays in Memory of John G. Gammie* (ed. L.G. Perdue et al.; Louisville: Westminster John Knox Press, 1993), 165–85.

——, "Wisdom Reconsidered, in Light of the Scrolls," *Dead Sea Discoveries* 4 (1997): 265–81.

Cook, Johann, "Apocalyptic Terminology in the Septuagint of Proverbs," *Journal of Northwest Semitic Languages* 25 (1999): 251–61.

——, *The Septuagint of Proverbs: Jewish and/or Hellenistic Proverbs?* (VTSup 69; Leiden: Brill, 1997).

Corley, Jeremy, *Ben Sira's Teaching on Friendship* (BJS 316; Providence: Brown Judaic Studies, 2002).

——, "An Intertextual Study of Proverbs and Ben Sira," in *Intertextual Studies in Ben Sira and Tobit: Essays in Honor of Alexander A. Di Lella, O.F.M.* (ed. J. Corley and V. Skemp; CBQMS 38; Washington, D.C.: Catholic Biblical Association of America, 2005), 155–82.

——, "Seeds of Messianism in Hebrew Ben Sira and Greek Sirach," in *The Septuagint and Messianism* (BETL 195; Leuven: Leuven University Press/Peeters, 2006), 301–12.

Crenshaw, James L., *Defending God: Biblical Responses to the Problem of Evil* (New York: Oxford University Press, 2005).

——, *Ecclesiastes* (OTL; Philadelphia: Westminster Press, 1987).

——, *Education in Ancient Israel: Across the Deadening Silence* (ABRL; New York: Doubleday, 1998).

——, "The Expression *mî yôdēaʿ* in the Hebrew Bible," *Vetus Testamentum* 36 (1986): 274–88.

——, "Method in Determining Wisdom Influence upon 'Historical Literature'," *Journal of Biblical Literature* 88 (1969): 129–42.

——, *Old Testament Wisdom: An Introduction* (rev. and enl. ed.; Louisville: Westminster John Knox Press, 1998).

——, "The Problem of Theodicy in Sirach: On Human Bondage," in *Theodicy of the Old Testament* (ed. J.L. Crenshaw; IRT 4; Philadelphia: Fortress Press, 1983), 119–40; originally published in *Journal of Biblical Literature* 94 (1975): 47–64.

——, "Proverbs, Book of," in *The Anchor Bible Dictionary* (ed. D.N. Freedman; 6 vols.; New York: Doubleday, 1992), 5:513–20.

——, "The Shadow of Death in Qoheleth," in *Israelite Wisdom: Theological and Literary Essays in Honor of Samuel Terrien* (ed. J.G. Gammie; New York: Scholar's Press, 1979), 205–16.

Crüsemann, Frank, "The Unchangeable World: The 'Crisis of Wisdom' in Koheleth," in *God of the Lowly: Socio-Historical Interpretations of the Bible* (trans. M.J. O'Connell; ed. W. Schottroff and W. Stegemann; Marynoll: Orbis Books, 1984), 57–77.

Cumont, Franz V.M., *After life in Roman Paganism* (New Haven: Yale University Press, 1922).

Dahood, Mitchell, "Immortality in Proverbs 12, 28," *Biblica* 41 (1960): 176–181.

Delitzsch, Franz, *Das Salomonisches Sprüchbuch: Biblischer Commentar über das AT* (Leipzig: Brunnen-Verlag, 1873).

Dell, Katharine J., *The Book of Proverbs in Social and Theological Context* (Cambridge: Cambridge University Press, 2006).

Demaree, R.J., *The ꜣḥ jḳr n Rꜥ Stelae: On Ancestor Worship in Ancient Egypt* (Leiden: Nederlands Institut voor het Nabije Oosten, 1983).

Dijk, Jacobus van, "The Amarna Period and the Later New Kingdom," in *The Oxford History of Ancient Egypt* (ed. I. Shaw; Oxford: Oxford University Press, 2000), 272–313.

Di Lella, Alexander A., "Wisdom of Ben-Sira," in *The Anchor Bible Dictionary* (ed. D.N. Freedman; 6 vols.; New York: Doubleday, 1992), 6:931–45.

Eichler, Eckhard, "Zur Datierung und Interpretation der Lehre des Ptahhotep," *Zeitschrift für ägyptische Sprache und Altertumskunde* 128 (2001): 97–107.

Elgvin, Torleif, "Admonition Texts from Cave 4," in *Methods of Investigation of the Dead Sea Scrolls and the Khirbet Qumran Site: Present Realities and Future Prospects* (ed. M.O. Wise et al.; Annals of the New York Academy of Sciences 722; New York: New York Academy of Sciences, 1994), 179–96.

——, "An Analysis of 4QInstruction" (Ph.D. diss., Hebrew University of Jerusalem, 1997).

——, "Early Essene Eschatology: Judgment and Salvation according to Sapiential Work A," in *Current Research and Technological Development on the Dead Sea Scrolls: Conference on the Texts from the Judean Desert, Jerusalem, 30 April 1995* (ed. D.W. Parry and S.D. Ricks; STDJ 20; Leiden: Brill, 1996), 126–65.

——, "The Mystery to Come: Early Essene Theology of Revelation," in *Qumran Between the Old and New Testaments* (ed. F.H. Cryer and T.L. Thompson; JSOTSup 290; Sheffield: Sheffield Academic Press, 1998), 113–50.

——, "Priestly Sages? The Milieus of Origin of 4QInstruction and 4QMysteries," in *Sapiential Perspectives: Wisdom Literature in Light of the Dead Sea Scrolls, Proceedings of the Sixth International Symposium of the Orion Center for the Study of the Dead Sea Scrolls and Associated Literature, 20–22 May, 2001* (ed. J.J. Collins et al.; STDJ 51; Leiden: Brill, 2004), 67–89.

——, "The Reconstruction of Sapiential Work A," *Revue de Qumran* 16 (1995): 559–80.

——, "Wisdom and Apocalypticism in the Early Second Century BCE—The Evidence of 4QInstruction," in *The Dead Sea Scrolls Fifty Years After Their Discovery: Proceedings of the Jerusalem Congress, July 20–25, 1997* (ed. L.H. Schiffman et al.; Jerusalem: Israel Exploration Society/Shrine of the Book, Israel Museum, 2000), 226–47.

——, "Wisdom With and Without Apocalyptic," in *Sapiential, Liturgical and Poetical Texts from Qumran: Proceedings of the Third Meeting of the International Organization for Qumran Studies, Oslo 1998* (ed. D. Falk et al.; STDJ 35; Leiden: Brill, 2000), 15–38.

Elgvin, Torleif, et al., *Qumran Cave 4.XV: Sapiential Texts, Part I* (DJD 20; Oxford: Clarendon Press, 1997).

Fecht, Gerhard, *Der Habgierige und die Maat in der Lehre des Ptahhotep (5. und 19. Maxime)* (ADAI.K 1; Glückstadt: J.J. Augustin, 1958).

Finkelstein, Israel, and Neil A. Silberman, *The Bible Unearthed: Archaeology's New Vision of Ancient Israel and the Origin of its Sacred Texts* (New York: The Free Press, 2001).

Fischer, A.A., "Kohelet und die frühe Apokalyptik: eine Auslegung von Koh 3,16–21," in *Qohelet in the Context of Wisdom* (ed. A. Schoors; BETL 136; Leuven: Leuven University Press/Peeters, 1998), 339–57.

Fischer, Stefan, *Die Aufforderung zur Lebensfreude im Buch Kohelet und seine Rezeption der ägyptischen Harfnerlieder* (WAS 2; Frankfurt: Peter Lang, 1999).

———, "Qohelet and 'Heretic' Harpers' Songs," *Journal for the Study of the Old Testament* 98 (2002): 105–21.

Fletcher-Louis, Crispin, *All the Glory of Adam: Liturgical Anthropology in the Dead Sea Scrolls* (STDJ 42; Leiden: Brill, 2002).

Fox, Michael V., "Aspects of Religion in the Book of Proverbs," *Hebrew Union College Annual* 39 (1968): 55–69.

———, "Frame Narrative and Composition in the Book of Qohelet," *Hebrew Union College Annual* 48 (1977): 83–106.

———, "The Inner Structure of Qohelet's Thought," in *Qohelet in the Context of Wisdom* (ed. A. Schoors; BETL 136; Leuven: Leuven University Press/Peeters, 1998), 225–39.

———, "LXX-Proverbs as a Text-Critical Resource," *Textus* 22 (2005): 95–128.

———, *Proverbs 1–9* (AB 18A; New York: Doubleday, 2000).

———, *Qohelet and His Contradictions* (JSOTSup 71; Sheffield: Almond Press, 1989).

———, "The Social Location of the Book of Proverbs," in *Texts, Temples, and Traditions: A Tribute to Menahem Haran* (ed. M.V. Fox et al.: Winona Lake, Ind.: Eisenbrauns, 1996), 227–39.

———, *A Time to Tear Down and a Time to Build Up: A Rereading of Ecclesiastes* (Grand Rapids: Eerdmans, 1999).

———, "Two Decades of Research in Egyptian Wisdom Literature," *Zeitschrift für ägyptische Sprache und Altertumskunde* 107 (1980): 120–35.

———, "Wisdom in Qoheleth," in *In Search of Wisdom: Essays in Memory of John G. Gammie* (ed. L.G. Perdue et al.; Louisville: Westminster/John Knox Press, 1993), 115–31.

———, "World Order and Ma'at: A Crooked Parallel," *Journal of the Ancient Near Eastern Society* 23 (1995): 37–48.

Fraade, Steven D., *Enosh and His Generation: Pre-Israelite Hero and History in Postbiblical Interpretation* (SBLMS 30; Chico, Ca.: Scholars Press, 1984).

———, "Hagu, Book of," in *Encyclopedia of the Dead Sea Scrolls* (ed. L.H. Schiffman and J.C. VanderKam; 2 vols.; New York: Oxford University Press, 2000): 1:327.

Frankfort, Henri, *Ancient Egyptian Religion: An Interpretation* (New York: Columbia University Press, 1948).

Freuling, Georg, „*Wer eine Grube gräbt…* " *Der Tun-Ergehen-Zusammenhang und sein Wandel in den alttestamentliche Weisheitliteratur* (WMANT 102; Neukirchen-Vluyn: Neukirchener Verlag, 2004).

Frey, Jörg, "Flesh and Spirit in the Palestinian Jewish Sapiential Tradition and in the Qumran Texts: An Inquiry into the Background of Pauline Usage," in *The Wisdom Texts from Qumran and the Development of Sapiential Thought* (ed. C. Hempel et al.; BETL 159; Leuven: Leuven University Press/Peeters, 2002), 367–404.

Galling, Kurt, *Die Fünf Megilloth* (2d ed.; HAT 18; Tübingen: Mohr, 1969).

Gammie, John G., "From Prudentialism to Apocalypticism: The Houses of the Sages amid Varying Forms of Wisdom," in *The Sage in Israel and the Ancient Near East* (ed. J.G. Gammie and L.G. Perdue; Winona Lake, Ind.: Eisenbrauns, 1990), 479–97.

———, "Spatial and Ethical Dualism in Jewish Wisdom and Apocalyptic Literature," *Journal of Biblical Literature* 93 (1974): 356–85.

———, "Stoicism and Anti-Stoicism in Qoheleth," *Hebrew Annual Review* 9 (1985): 169–187.

García Martínez, Florentino, "Marginalia on 4QInstruction," *Dead Sea Discoveries* 13 (2006): 24–37.

——, "Wisdom at Qumran: Worldly or Heavenly?" in *Wisdom and Apocalypticism in the Dead Sea Scrolls and in the Biblical Tradition* (ed. F. García Martínez; BETL 168; Leuven: Leuven University Press/Peeters, 2003), 1–17.

García Martínez, Florentino, and Eibert J.C. Tigchelaar, *The Dead Sea Scrolls Study Edition* (2 vols.; Leiden: Brill, 1997–98).

Gerleman, Gillis, "The Septuagint Proverbs as a Hellenistic Document," *Oudtestamentische Studien* 8 (1950): 15–27.

——, *Studies in the Septuagint, III, Proverbs* (Lund: Gleerup, 1956).

Gese, Hartmut, "The Crisis of Wisdom in Koheleth," trans. L.L. Grabbe, in *Theodicy in the Old Testament* (ed. J.L. Crenshaw; IRT 4; Philadelphia: Fortress Press, 1983), 141–153; originally published as "Die Krisis der Weisheit bei Koheleth," in *Les Sagesses du Proche-Orient Ancien, Colloque de Strasbourg 17–19 mai 1962* (Paris: Presses Universitaires de France, 1963), 139–51.

——, *Lehre and Wirklichkeit in der alten Weisheit: Studien zu den Sprüchen Salomos und zu dem Buche Hiob* (Tübingen: Mohr, 1958).

Gladson, Jerry, "Retributive Paradoxes in Proverbs 10–29" (Ph.D. diss., Vanderbilt University, 1975).

Goedicke, Hans, "The Teaching of Amenemope, Chapter XX. (Amenemope 20, 20–21, 20)," *Revue d'Égyptologie* 46 (1995): 99–106.

Goering, Gregory Schmidt, "To Whom Has Wisdom's Root Been Revealed?: Ben Sira and the Election of Israel" (Ph.D. diss., Harvard University, 2006).

Goff, Matthew J., "Discerning Trajectories: 4QInstruction and the Sapiential Background of the Sayings Source Q," *Journal of Biblical Literature* 124 (2005): 657–73.

——, *Discerning Wisdom: The Sapiential Literature of the Dead Sea Scrolls* (VTSup 116; Leiden: Brill, 2007).

——, "Hellenistic Instruction in Palestine and Egypt: Ben Sira and Papyrus Insinger," *Journal of Jewish Studies* 36 (2005): 147–72.

——, "The Mystery of Creation in 4QInstruction," *Dead Sea Discoveries* 10 (2003): 163–86.

——, *The Worldly and Heavenly Wisdom of 4QInstruction* (STDJ 50; Leiden: Brill, 2003).

Goldstein, Jonathan A., "The Syriac Bill of Sale from Dura-Europos," *Journal of Near Eastern Studies* 25 (1966): 1–16.

Golka, Friedemann W., *The Leopard's Spots: Biblical and African Wisdom in Proverbs* (Edinburgh: T&T Clark, 1993).

Gordis, Robert, *Koheleth-The Man and His World* (TS 19; New York: Bloch, 1955).

Gropp, Douglas M., "The Origin and Development of the Aramaic *Šallīṭ* Clause," *Journal of Near Eastern Studies* 52 (1993): 31–36.

Grumach, Irene, *Untersuchungen zur Lebenslehre des Amenope* (MÄSt 23; Munich: Deutscher Kunstverlag, 1972).

Hadot, Jean, *Penchant Mauvais et Volonté Libre dans la Sagesse de Ben Sira (L'Ecclésiastique)* (Brussels: University Press, 1970).

Harrington, Daniel J., "Mystery," in *Encyclopedia of the Dead Sea Scrolls* (ed. L.H. Schiffman and J.C. VanderKam; 2 vols.; New York: Oxford University Press, 2000): 1:589–91.

——, "Two Early Jewish Approaches to Wisdom: Sirach and Qumran Sapiential Work A," *Journal for the Study of the Pseudepigrapha* 16 (1997): 25–38.

——, "Wisdom and Apocalyptic in 4QInstruction and 4 Ezra," in *Wisdom and Apocalypticism in the Dead Sea Scrolls and in the Biblical Tradition* (ed. F. García Martínez; BETL 238; Leuven: Leuven University Press/Peeters, 2003), 343–57.

——, *Wisdom Texts from Qumran* (London: Routledge, 1996).

Harrison, C. Robert, "Hellenization in Syria-Palestine: The Case of Judea in the Third Century B.C.E.," *Biblical Archaeologist* 57 (1994): 98–108.

——, "Qoheleth in Social-Historical Perspective" (Ph.D. diss., Duke University, 1991).

Haspecker, Josef, *Gottesfurcht bei Jesus Sirach* (AnBib 30; Rome: Pontifical Biblical Institute, 1967).

Heim, Knut Martin, *Like Grapes of Gold Set in Silver: An Interpretation of Proverbial Clusters in Proverbs 10:1–22:16* (BZAW 23; Berlin: de Gruyter, 2001).

Hempel, Johannes, *Die althebräische Literatur und ihr hellenistisch-jüdisches Nachleben* (Wildpark-Potsdam: Akademische Verlagsgesellschaft Athenaion, 1930).

Hengel, Martin, *Judaism and Hellenism: Studies in their Encounter in Palestine during the Early Hellenistic Period* (2 vols.; Philadephia: Fortress Press, 1974).

Hermisson, Hans-Jurgen, *Studien zur israelitischen Spruchweisheit* (WMANT 28; Neukirchen-Vluyn: Neukirchener Verlag, 1968).

Hertzberg, Hans-Wilhelm, *Der Prediger* (2d ed.; KAT XVII.4; Gütersloh: Mohn, 1963).

Hölbl, Günther, *A History of the Ptolemaic Empire* (trans. T. Saavedra; New York: Routledge, 2001).

Hornung, Erik, *Conceptions of God in Ancient Egypt: The One and the Many* (trans. J. Baines; Ithaca: Cornell University Press, 1982).

——, "Lehren über das Jenseits?" in *Studien zu altägyptischen Lebenslehren* (ed. E. Hornung and O. Keel; OBO 28; Fribourg/Göttingen: Universitätsverlag/Vandenhoeck & Ruprecht, 1979), 217–24.

Horsley, Richard, and Patrick Tiller, "Ben Sira and the Sociology of the Second Temple" in *Second Temple Studies III: Studies in Politics, Class, and Material Culture* (JSOTSup 340; London: Sheffield Academic Press, 2002), 74–108.

Hultgård, Anders, "Persian Apocalypticism," in *The Encyclopedia of Apocalypticism, Volume 1: The Origins of Apocalypticism in Judaism and Christianity* (ed. J.J. Collins; New York: Continuum, 2000), 39–83.

Humbert, Paul, *Recherches sur les sources égyptiennes de la littérature sapientiale d'Israel* (Neuchâtel: Secrétariat de l'Université, 1929).

Hurvitz, Avi, "The Chronological Significance of 'Aramaisms' in Biblical Hebrew," *Israel Exploration Journal* 18 (1968): 234–40.

——, "The Date of the Prose Tale of Job Linguistically Reconsidered," *Harvard Theological Review* 67 (1974): 17–34.

Huwiler, Elizabeth, "Control of Reality in Israelite Wisdom" (Ph.D. diss., Duke University, 1988).

Jamieson-Drake, D.W., *Scribes and Schools in Monarchic Judah* (SWBA 9; Sheffield: Almond Press, 1991).

Janowski, Bernd, "Die Tat kehrt zum Täter zurück: Offene Fragen im Umkreis des 'Tun-Ergehen-Zusammenhangs,'" *Zeitschrift für Theologie und Kirche* 91 (1994): 247–71.

Jokiranta, Jutta M., "'Sectarianism' of the Qumran 'Sect': Sociological Notes," *Revue de Qumran* 78 (2001): 223–39.

Kaiser, Otto, "Die Furcht und die Liebe Gottes. Ein Versuch, die Ethik Ben Siras mit der des Apostels Paulus zu vergleichen," in *Ben Sira's God: Proceedings of the International Ben Sira Conference-Ushaw College 2001* (ed. R. Egger-Wenzel; BZAW 321; Berlin: de Gruyter, 2002), 39–75.

Kamano, Nate, *Cosmology and Character: Qoheleth's Pedagogy from a Rhetorical-Critical Perspective* (BZAW 312; Berlin: de Gruyter, 2002).

Kaminsky, Joel S., *Corporate Responsibility in the Hebrew Bible* (JSOTSup 196; Sheffield: Sheffield Academic Press, 1995).

Kayatz, Christa, *Studien zu Proverbien 1–9: Eine form- und motivgeschichtliche Untersuchung unter Einbeziehung ägyptischen Vergleichsmaterials* (WMANT 22; Neukirchen-Vluyn: Neukirchener Verlag, 1966).

Kearns, Conleth, "Ecclesisasticus, or the Wisdom of Jesus the Son of Sirach," in *A New Catholic Commentary on Holy Scripture* (ed. R.C. Fuller; London: Thomas Nelson Publishers, 1969), 541–62.

Keller, Carl-A., "Zum sogenannten Vergeltungsglauben im Proverbienbuch," in *Beiträge zur alttestamentlichen Theologie: Festschrift für Walther Zimmerli zum 70. Geburtstag* (ed. H. Donner and R. Hanart; Göttingen: Vandenhoeck & Ruprecht, 1977), 223–38.

Kitchen, Kenneth A., "The Basic Literary Forms and Formulations of Ancient Instructional Writings in Egypt and Western Asia," in *Studien zu altägyptischen Lebenslehren* (ed. E. Hornung and O. Keel; OBO 28; Fribourg/Göttingen: University Press/Vandenhoeck & Ruprecht, 1979), 235–82.

Klotz, David, "The Use of *jb*-Compounds in Ptahhotep," (paper presented at Yale University Near Eastern Languages and Civilizations panel, 5 December 2001).

Koch, Klaus, "Is There a Doctrine of Retribution in the Old Testament," trans. T.H. Trapp, in *Theodicy in the Old Testament* (ed. J.L. Crenshaw; IRT 4; Philadelphia: Fortress Press, 1983), 57–87; originally published as "Gibt es ein Vergeltungsdogma im Alten Testament?" *Zeitschrift für Theologie und Kirche* 52 (1955): 1–42.

Koch, Roland, *Die Erzählung des Sinuhe* (BAe 17; Brussels: Fondation Égyptologie Reine Elisabeth, 1990).

Krüger, Thomas, *Qoheleth* (trans. O.C. Dean; Hermeneia; Minneapolis: Fortress Press, 2004).

Kugel, James, "Qohelet and Money," *Catholic Biblical Quarterly* 51 (1989): 32–49.

Lange, Armin, "Eschatological Wisdom in Qoheleth and in the Dead Sea Scrolls," in *The Dead Sea Scrolls Fifty Years After Their Discovery: Proceedings of the Jerusalem Conference, July 20–25, 1997* (ed. L. Schiffman et al.; Jerusalem: Israel Exploration Society/Shrine of the Book, Israel Museum, 2000), 817–24.

——, "In Diskussion mit dem Tempel: zur Auseinandersetzung zwischen Kohelet und weisheitlichen Kreisen am Jerusalemer Tempel," in *Qohelet in the Context of Wisdom* (ed. A. Schoors; BETL 136; Leuven: Leuven University Press/Peeters, 1998), 113–60.

——, *Weishseit und Prädestination: Weisheitliche Urordnung und Prädestination in den Textfunden von Qumran* (STDJ 18; Leiden: Brill, 1995).

Lange, Hans O., *Das Weisheitbuch des Amenemope aus dem Papyrus 10,474 des British Museum herausgeben und erklärt* (Copenhagen: Andr. Fred Høst, 1925).

Lauha, Aarre, *Kohelet* (BKAT 19; Neukirchen-Vluyn: Neukirchener Verlag, 1978).

Lee, Thomas R., *Studies in the Form of Sirach 44–50* (SBLDS 75; Atlanta: Scholars Press, 1986).

Leeuwen, Raymond C. van, "Liminality and Worldview in Proverbs 1–9," *Semeia* 50 (1990): 111–44.

Lemaire, André, *Les écoles et la formation de la Bible dans l'ancien Israel* (Göttingen: Vandenhoeck & Ruprecht, 1981).

Lichtheim, Miriam, *Ancient Egyptian Literature* (3 vols.; Berkeley: University of California Press, 1973–80).

——, "Didactic Literature," in *Ancient Egyptian Literature: History and Forms* (ed. A. Loprieno; PÄ 10; Leiden: Brill, 1996), 243–63.

——, *Late Egyptian Wisdom Literature in the International Context: A Study of Demotic Instructions* (OBO 52; Fribourg/Göttingen: University Press/Vandenhoeck & Ruprecht, 1983).

——, *Maat in Egyptian Autobiographies and Related Studies* (OBO 120; Fribourg/Göttingen: University Press/Vandenhoeck & Ruprecht, 1992).

——, "The Songs of the Harpers," *Journal of Near Eastern Studies* 4 (1945): 178–212.

Liesen, Jan, *Full of Praise: An Exegetical Study of Sir 39,12–35* (JSJSup 64; Leiden: Brill, 2000).

Loader, J.A., *Polar Structures in the Book of Qohelet* (BZAW 152; Berlin: de Gruyter, 1979).

Lohfink, Nobert, *Qoheleth* (trans. S. McEvenue; Continental; Minneapolis: Fortress Press, 2003).

Loretz, Oswald, *Qohelet und der alte Orient: Untersuchungen zu Stil und theologischer Thematik des Buches Qohelet* (Freiburg: Herder, 1964).

Lorton, David, "The Expression *šms-jb*," *Journal of the American Research Center in Egypt* 7 (1968): 41–54.

Macaskill, Grant, *Revealed Wisdom and Inaugurated Eschatology in Ancient Judaism and Early Christianity* (JSJSup 115; Leiden: Brill, 2007).

Machinist, Peter, "Fate, *miqreh*, and Reason: Some Reflections on Qohelet and Biblical Thought," in *Solving Riddles and Untying Knots* (ed. Z. Zevit et al.; Winona Lake, Ind.: Eisenbrauns, 1995), 159–75.

Mack, Burton, *Wisdom and the Hebrew Epic: Ben Sira's Praise of the Fathers* (CSHJ; Chicago: University of Chicago Press, 1985).

Magness, Jodi, *The Archaeology of Qumran and the Dead Sea Scrolls* (Grand Rapids: Eerdmans, 2002).

Maier, Christl, *Die 'fremde Frau' in Proverbien 1–9: eine exegetische sozialgeschichtliche Studie* (OBO 144; Göttingen: Vandenhoeck & Ruprecht, 1995).

Maier, Gerhard, *Mensch und freier Wille* (WUNT 12; Tübingen: Mohr, 1971).

Marböck, Johannes, "Das Gebet um die Rettung Zions Sir 36,1–22 (G 33,1–13a; 36,16b–22) im Zusammenhang der Geschichtsschau ben Siras," in *Memoria Jerusalem. Freundesgabe Franz Sauer* (ed. J.B. Bauer and J. Marböck; Graz/Jerusalem: Akademische Druck und Verlagsanstalt, 1977), 93–115.

———, *Gottes Weisheit Unter Uns: zur Theologie des Buches Sirach* (HBS 6; Freiburg: Herder, 1995).

———, *Weisheit im Wandel: Untersuchungen zur Weisheitstheologie bei Ben Sira* (Bonn: Hanstein, 1971).

Mattila, Sharon, "Ben Sira and the Stoics: A Reexamination of the Evidence," *Journal of Biblical Literature* 119 (2000): 473–501.

McKane, William, *Prophets and Wise Men* (SBT 44; London: SCM Press, 1965).

———, *Proverbs* (OTL; Philadelphia: Westminster, 1970).

Metzger, Bruce M., "The Fourth Book of Ezra," in *The Old Testament Pseudepigrapha Volume 1: Apocalyptic Literature and Testaments* (ed. J.H. Charlesworth; Garden City, NY: Doubleday, 1983), 517–59.

Michel, Diethelm, *Qohelet* (EdF 258; Darmstadt: Wissenschaftliche Buchgesellschaft, 1988).

———, *Untersuchungen zur Eigenart des Buches Qohelet* (BZAW 183; Berlin: de Gruyter, 1989).

Middendorp, Theophil, *Die Stellung Jesu Ben Siras zwischen Judentum und Hellenismus* (Leiden: Brill, 1973).

Morenz, Siegfried, *Egyptian Religion* (trans. A.E. Keep; London: Methuen and Co., 1973).

Moxnes, Halvor, "Honor and Shame," *Biblical Theology Bulletin* 23 (1993): 167–76.

Murphy, Catherine M., *Wealth in the Dead Sea Scrolls and in the Qumran Community* (Leiden: Brill, 2002).

Murphy, Roland E., *Ecclesiastes* (WBC 23A; Dallas: Word Books, 1992).

———, *The Tree of Life: An Exploration of Biblical Wisdom Literature* (3d ed.; Grand Rapids: Eerdmans, 1990).

———, "Wisdom and Yahwism," in *No Famine in the Land: Studies in Honor of John L. McKenzie* (ed. J.A. Flanagan and A.W. Robinson; Missoula, Mo.: Scholars Press, 1975), 117–26.

———, "Wisdom Theses," in *Wisdom and Knowledge: Essays in Honour of Joseph Papin* (ed. J. Armenti; 2 vols.; Villanova: Villanova University Press, 1976).

Newsom, Carol A., "'Sectually Explicit' Literature from Qumran," in *The Hebrew Bible and Its Interpreters* (ed. W.H. Propp et al.; Winona Lake, Ind.: Eisenbrauns, 1990), 167–87.

———, "Woman and the Discourse of Patriarchal Wisdom: A Study of Proverbs 1–9," in *Gender and Difference in Ancient Israel* (ed. P.L. Day; Minneapolis: Fortress Press, 1989), 142–60.

Nickelsburg, George W.E., *1 Enoch 1: A Commentary on the Book of 1 Enoch, Chapters 1–36; 81–108* (Hermeneia; Fortress Press: Minneapolis, 2001).

———, *Jewish Literature between the Bible and the Mishnah* (2d ed.; Minneapolis: Fortress Press, 2005).

———, *Resurrection, Immortality, and Eternal Life in Intertestamental Judaism: Revised and Expanded Edition* (HTS 56; Cambridge: Harvard University Press, 2006).

———, "Wisdom and Apocalypticism in Early Judaism: Some Points for Discussion," in *Conflicted Boundaries in Wisdom and Apocalypticism* (ed. B.G. Wright and L.W. Wills; SBLSymS 35; Atlanta: Society of Biblical Literature, 2005), 17–39.

Nickelsburg, George W.E., and James C. VanderKam, *1 Enoch: A New Translation* (Minneapolis: Fortress Press, 2004).

Nitzan, Bilhah, "The Ideological and Literary Unity of 4QInstruction and Its Authorship," *Dead Sea Discoveries* 12 (2005): 257–79.

Oesterly, W.O.E., "The Teaching of Amen-em-ope and the Old Testament," *Zeitschrift für die alttestamentliche Wissenschaft* 45 (1927): 9–24.

Olyan, Saul, "Ben Sira's Relationship to the Priesthood," *Harvard Theological Review* 80 (1987): 261–86.

Perdue, Leo G., "Liminality as a Social Setting for Wisdom Instructions," *Zeitschrift für die alttestamentliche Wissenschaft* 93 (1981): 114–26.

———, "Wisdom and Apocalyptic: The Case of Qoheleth," in *Wisdom and Apocalypticism in the Dead Sea Scrolls and in the Biblical Tradition* (ed. F. García Martínez; BETL 168; Leuven: Leuven University Press/Peeters, 2003), 231–58.

———, *Wisdom and Creation: The Theology of Wisdom Literature* (Nashville: Abingdon, 1994).

Piankoff, Alexandre, *Le «cœur» dans les Textes égyptiens depuis l'Ancien jusqu'à la Fin du Nouvel Empire* (Paris: Libraire orientaliste Paul Geuthner, 1930).

Plöger, Otto, *Sprüche Salomos (Proverbia)* (BKAT 17; Neukirchen-Vluyn: Neukirchener Verlag, 1984).

Podechard, E., *L'Ecclésiaste* (EtB; Paris: Gabalda, 1912).

Posener, Georges, "Le chapitre IV d'Aménémopé," *Zeitschrift für ägyptische Sprache und Altertumskunde* 99 (1973): 129–135.

Prato, Gian Luigi, *Il Problema della Teodicea in Ben Sira* (AnBib 65; Rome: Pontifical Biblical Institute, 1975).

Preuss, Horst Dietrich, "Das Gottesbild der alteren Weisheit Israels," in *Studies in the Religion of Ancient Israel* (VTSup 23; Leiden: Brill, 1972), 117–45.

Puech, Émile, "Ben Sira 48:11 et la Résurrection," in *Of Scribes and Scrolls: Studies on the Hebrew Bible, Intertestamental Judaism and Christian Origins* (ed. H.W. Attridge et al.; Lanham, Md.: University Press of America, 1990), 81–91.

———, *La Croyance des Esséniens en la Vie Future: Immortalité, Résurrection, Vie Éternelle?* (2 vols. Paris: Gabalda, 1993).

———, "Les Fragments Eschatologiques de 4QInstruction (4Q416 1 et 4Q418 69 ii, 81–81a, 127)," *Revue de Qumran* 22 (2005): 89–119.

Quack, Joachim-Friedrich, *Studien zur Lehre für Merikare* (GOF 23; Wiesbaden: O. Harrassowitz, 1992).

Rad, Gerhard von, *Old Testament Theology* (trans. D.M.G. Stalker; 2 vols.; OTL; Louisville: Westminster John Knox Press, 2001).

———, *Wisdom in Israel* (trans. J. D. Martin; London/Harrisburg, Pa.: SCM Press Ltd./ Trinity Press International, 1972).

Ranston, Harry, *The Old Testament Wisdom Books and Their Teaching* (London: Epworth Press, 1930).

Reiterer, Friedrich V., "Deutung und Wertung des Todes durch Ben Sira," in *Die alttestamentliche Botschaft als Wegweisung* (ed. J. Zmijewski; Stuttgart: Verlags Katholisches Bibelwerk GmbH, 1990), 203–36.

———, "Review of Recent Research on Ben Sira (1980–1996)" in *The Book of Ben Sira in Modern Research: Proceedings of the First International Ben Sira Conference, 28–31 July 1996, Soesterberg, Netherlands* (BZAW 255; Berlin: de Gruyter, 1997), 23–61.

Rickenbacker, Otto, *Weisheitsperikopen bei Ben Sira* (Göttingen: Vandenhoeck & Ruprecht, 1973).

Robinson, Patricia A., "The Conception of Death in Judaism and in the Hellenistic and Early Roman Period" (Ph.D. diss., The University of Wisconsin-Madison, 1978).

Rofé, Alexander, "Revealed Wisdom: From the Bible to Qumran," in *Sapiential Perspectives: Wisdom Literature in Light of the Dead Sea Scrolls, Proceedings of the Sixth International Symposium of the Orion Center for the Study of the Dead Sea Scrolls and Associated Literature, 20–22 May, 2001* (ed. J.J. Collins et al.; STDJ 51; Leiden: Brill, 2004), 1–11.

Römheld, Diethard, *Wege der Weisheit: die Lehren Amenemopes und Proverbien 22,17–24,22* (BZAW 184; Berlin: de Gruyter, 1989).

Roth, Wolfgang, "The Gnomic-Discursive Wisdom of Jesus Ben Sirach," *Semeia* 17 (1980): 35–79.

Rudman, Dominic, "A Note on the Dating of Ecclesiastes," *Catholic Biblical Quarterly* 61 (1999): 47–53.

Rylaarsdam, J. Coert, *Revelation in Jewish Wisdom Literature* (Chicago: University of Chicago Press, 1946).

Sanders, E.P., *Paul and Palestinian Judaism* (Philadelphia: Fortress Press, 1977).

Sanders, Jack, *Ben Sira and Demotic Wisdom* (SBLMS 28; Chico, Ca.: Scholars Press, 1983).

———, "Ben Sira's Ethic of Caution," *Hebrew Union College Annual* 50 (1979): 73–106.

Schiffman, Lawrence H., "Halakhic Elements in the Sapiential Texts from Qumran," in *Sapiential Perspectives: Wisdom Literature in Light of the Dead Sea Scrolls, Proceedings of the Sixth International Symposium of the Orion Center for the Study of the Dead Sea Scrolls and Associated Literature, 20–22 May, 2001* (ed. J.J. Collins et al.; STDJ 51; Leiden: Brill, 2004), 89–100.

Schmid, Hans Heinrich, *Gerechtigkeit als Weltordnung* (BHT 40; Tübingen: Mohr, 1968).

———, *Wesen und Geschichte der Weisheit: eine Untersuchung zur altorientalische Weisheitsliteratur* (BZAW 101; Berlin: Töpelmann, 1966).

Schnabel, Eckhard J., *Law and Wisdom from Ben Sira to Paul: A Tradition Historical Inquiry into the Relation of Law, Wisdom, and Ethics* (WUNT 16; Tübingen: Mohr, 1985).

Schneidau, Herbert N., *Sacred Discontent* (Berkeley: University of California Press, 1976).

Schniedewind, William M., *How the Bible Became a Book* (Cambridge: Cambridge University Press, 2004).

Schoors, Antoon, "Koheleth: A Perspective of Life After Death?" *Ephemerides theologicae lovanienses* 61 (1985): 295–303.

———, *The Preacher Sought to Find Pleasing Words: A Study of the Language of Qoheleth* (2 vols.; OLA 41; Leuven: Peeters Press and Department of Oriental Studies, 1992–2004).

Schwienhorst-Schönberger, Ludger, "Kohelet: Stand und Perspectiven der Forschung," in *Das Buch Kohelet: Studien zur Struktur, Geschichte, Rezeption und Theologie* (ed. L. Schwienhorst-Schönberger; BZAW 254; Berlin: de Gruyter, 1997).

———, *'Nicht im Menschen Gründet das Glück' (Koh 2,24): Kohelet im Spannungsfeld jüdischer Weisheit und hellenistischer Philosophie* (HBS 2; Freiburg: Herder, 1994).

Scott, Alan, *Origen and the Life of the Stars: A History of an Idea* (Oxford: Clarendon Press, 1991).

Segal, M.H., *Sēper ben-Sîrāʾ haššālēm* (4th ed.; Jerusalem: Bialik Institute, 1997).

Seow, C.L., *Ecclesiastes* (AB 18C; New York: Doubleday, 1997).
——, "Linguistic Evidence and the Dating of Qoheleth," *Journal of Biblical Literature* 115 (1996): 643–66.
Setzer, Claudia, *Resurrection of the Body in Early Judaism and Early Christianity* (Boston: Brill, 2004).
Sharp, Carolyn J., "Ironic Representation, Authorial Voice, and Meaning in Qohelet," *Biblical Interpretation* 12 (2004): 37–68.
Sheppard, Gerald T. "The Epilogue to Qoheleth as Theological Commentary," *Catholic Biblical Quarterly* 39 (1977): 182–189.
——, *Wisdom as a Hermeneutical Construct* (BZAW 180; Berlin: de Gruyter, 1980).
Shields, Martin A., *The End of Wisdom: A Reappraisal of the Canonical Function of Ecclesiastes* (Winona Lake, Ind.: Eisenbrauns, 2006).
Shupak, Nili, "The Instruction of Amenemope and Proverbs 22:17–24:22 from the Perspective of Contemporary Research," in *Seeking Out the Wisdom of the Ancients: Essays Offered to Honor Michael V. Fox on the Occasion of His Sixty-Fifth Birthday* (Winona Lake, Ind.: Eisenbrauns, 2005), 203–20.
——, *Where Can Wisdom Be Found? The Sage's Language in the Bible and in Ancient Egyptian Literature* (OBO 130; Fribourg/Göttingen: Universitätsverlag/Vandenhoeck & Ruprecht, 1993).
Simpson, William K., ed., *The Literature of Ancient Egypt* (3d ed.; New Haven: Yale University Press, 2003).
——, *The Literature of Ancient Egypt* (New Haven: Yale University Press, 1972).
Skehan, Patrick W., and Alexander A. Di Lella, *The Wisdom of Ben Sira* (AB 39; New York: Doubleday, 1987).
Smend, Rudolph, *Die Weisheit des Jesus Sirach erklärt* (Berlin: Reimer, 1906).
Smith, J.Z., *Map is Not Territory* (Chicago: University of Chicago Press, 1978).
Stadelmann, Helge, *Ben Sira als Schriftgelehrter: Eine Untersuchung zum Berufsbild des vormakkabäischen Sofer unter Berücksichtigung seines Verhältnisses zu Priester-, Propheten- und Weisheitslehrertum* (WUNT 2; Tübingen: Mohr, 1981).
Steiert, Franz-Josef, *Die Weisheit Israels: ein Fremdkörper im alten Testament?: eine Untersuchung zum Buch der Sprüche auf dem Hintergrund der ägyptischen Weisheitslehren* (FThSt; Freiburg: Herder, 1990).
Strugnell, John, and Daniel J. Harrington, *Qumran Cave 4.XXIV: Sapiential Texts, Part 2. 4QInstruction (Mûsār Lĕ Mēvin): 4Q415ff. With a re-edition of 1Q26* (DJD 34; Oxford: Clarendon Press, 1999).
Stuckenbruck, Loren, "4QInstruction and the Possible Influence of Early Enochic Traditions: An Evaluation," in *The Wisdom Texts from Qumran and the Development of Sapiential Thought* (ed. C. Hempel et al.; BETL 159; Leuven: Leuven University Press/Peeters, 2002), 245–61.
Tcherikover, Victor, *Hellenistic Civilization and the Jews* (Philadelphia: Jewish Publication Society, 1959; repr., Peabody: Hendrickson Publishers, 1999).
Tigchelaar, Eibert J.C., "The Addressees of 4QInstruction," in *Sapiential, Liturgical, and Poetical Texts from Qumran: Proceedings of the Third Meeting of the International Organization for Qumran Studies, Olso 1998* (ed. D. Falk et al.; STDJ 35; Leiden: Brill, 2000), 62–75.
——, *To Increase Learning for the Understanding Ones: Reading and Reconstucting the Fragmentary Early Jewish Sapiential Text 4QInstruction* (STDJ 44; Leiden: Brill, 2001).
——, "Towards a Reconstruction of the Beginning of 4QInstruction (4Q416 Fragment 1 and Parallels)," in *The Wisdom Texts from Qumran and the Development of Sapiential Thought* (ed. C. Hempel et al.; BETL 159; Leuven: Leuven University Press/Peeters, 2002), 99–126.
Tiller, Patrick, "The Sociological Context of the Dream Visions of Daniel and Enoch," in *Enoch and Qumran Origins: New Light on a Forgotten Connection* (ed. G. Boccaccini; Grand Rapids: Eerdmans, 2005), 23–26.

Tobin, Vincent A., Introduction to "The Teaching for King Merikare," in *The Literature of Ancient Egypt* (ed. William K. Simpson; 3d ed. New Haven: Yale University Press, 2003), 152–53.

Tov, Emmanuel, "Recensional Differences between the Masoretic Text and the Septuagint of Proverbs," in *Of Scribes and Scrolls: Studies on the Hebrew Bible, Intertestamental Judaism, and Christian Origins Presented to John Strugnell* (ed. H.W. Attridge et al.; Lanham, Md.: University Press of America, 1990), 43–56.

Uehlinger, Christoph, "Qohelet im Horizont mesopotamischer, levantischer und ägyptischer Weisheitliteratur der perischen und hellenistischen Zeit," in *Das Buch Kohelet: Studien zur Struktur, Geschichte, Rezeption und Theologie* (ed. L. Schwienhorst-Schönberger; BZAW 254; Berlin: de Gruyter, 1997), 155–247.

VanderKam, James C., *The Dead Sea Scrolls Today* (Grand Rapids: Eerdmans, 1994).

———, Review of M.J. Goff, *The Worldly and Heavenly Wisdom of 4QInstruction. Catholic Biblical Quarterly* 67 (2005): 117–18.

Vattioni, Francesco, *Ecclesiastico: Testo ebraico con apparato critico e versioni greca, latina e siraica* (Naples: Istituto Orientale di Napoli, 1968).

Vawter, Bruce, "Intimations of Immortality and the Old Testament," *Journal of Biblical Literature* 91 (1972): 158–71.

Vergote, Joseph, "La notion de Dieu dans les Livres de sagesse égyptiens," in *Les Sagesses du Proche-Orient Ancien, Colloque de Strasbourg 17–19 mai 1962* (Paris: Presses Universitaires de France, 1963), 159–90.

Vermes, Geza, and Martin Goodman, eds., *The Essenes According to the Classical Sources* (Sheffield: Journal for the Study of the Old Testament, 1989).

Vernus, Pascal, "Le discours politique de l'*Enseignement de Ptahhotep*," in *Literatur und Politik im pharaonischen und ptolemäischen Ägypten* (ed. J. Assmann and E. Blumenthal; Paris: Institut Français D'Archéologie Orientale, 1999), 139–52.

———, *Sagesses de l'Égypte pharaonique/Présentation, traduction et notes* (Paris: Imprimerie nationale, 2001).

Volten, Aksel, "Der Begriff der Maat in den ägyptischen Weisheitstexten," in *Les Sagesses du Proche-Orient Ancien, Colloque de Strasbourg 17–19 mai 1962* (Paris: Presses Universitaires de France, 1963), 73–101.

Wacholder, Ben Zion, and Martin G. Abegg, *A Preliminary Edition of the Unpublished Dead Sea Scrolls: The Hebrew and Aramaic Texts from Cave Four* (2 vols.; Washington, D.C.: Biblical Archaeology Society, 1992).

Washington, Harold C., *Wealth and Poverty in the Instruction of Amenemope and the Hebrew Proverbs* (SBLDS 142; Atlanta: Scholars Press, 1994).

Weinfeld, Moshe, *Deuteronomy and the Deuteronomic School* (Oxford: Clarendon Press, 1972).

Werman, Cana, "What is the *Book of Hagu?*" in *Sapiential Perspectives: Wisdom Literature in Light of the Dead Sea Scrolls, Proceedings of the Sixth International Symposium of the Orion Center for the Study of the Dead Sea Scrolls and Associated Literature, 20–22 May, 2001* (ed. J.J. Collins et al.; STDJ 51; Leiden: Brill, 2004), 125–40.

Westermann, Claus, *Roots of Wisdom: The Oldest Proverbs of Israel and Other Peoples* (trans. J.D. Charles; Louisville: Westminster John Knox, 1995).

———, "Weisheit im Sprichwort," in *Schalom. Studien zu Glaube und Geschichte Israels, Alfred Jepsen zum 70. Geburtstag* (Stuttgart: Calwer Verlag, 1971), 73–85.

Whitley, Charles Francis, *Koheleth: His Language and Thought* (Berlin: de Gruyter, 1979).

Whybray, R.N., *The Book of Proverbs: A Survey of Modern Study* (HBI 1; Leiden: Brill, 1995).

———, *The Composition of the Book of Proverbs* (JSOTSup 168; Sheffield: JSOT Press, 1994).

———, "The Sage in the Israelite Royal Court," in *The Sage in Israel and the Ancient Near East* (ed. J.G. Gammie and L.G. Perdue; Winona Lake, Ind.: Eisenbrauns, 1990), 133–39.

——, *Wealth and Poverty in the Book of Proverbs* (JSOTSup 99; Sheffield: JSOT Press, 1990).

Wicke-Reuter, Ursel, "Ben Sira und die frühe Stoa. Zum Zusammanehang von Ethik und dem Glauben an eine göttliche Providenz," in *Ben Sira's God: Proceedings of the International Ben Sira Conference-Ushaw College 2001* (ed. R. Egger-Wenzel; BZAW 321; Berlin: de Gruyter, 2002), 268–81.

——, *Göttliche Providenz und menschliche Verantwortung bei Ben Sira und in der frühen Stoa* (BZAW 298; Berlin: de Gruyter, 2000).

Williams, Ronald J., "The Alleged Semitic Original of the *Wisdom of Amenemope*," *Journal of Egyptian Archaeology* 47 (1961): 100–106.

——, "The Sages of Ancient Egypt in the Light of Recent Scholarship," *Journal of the American Oriental Society* 101 (1981): 1–13.

Wilson, Frederick, "Sacred and Profane? The Yahwistic Redaction of Proverbs Reconsidered," in *The Listening Heart: Essays in Wisdom and the Psalms in Honor of Roland E. Murphy, O. Carm.* (JSOTSup 58; Sheffield: JSOT Press, 1987), 313–34.

Wilson, Gerald H., "'The Words of the Wise': The Intent and Significance of Qohelet 12:9–14," *Journal of Biblical Literature* 103 (1984): 175–92.

Winston, David, "Theodicy in Ben Sira and Stoic Philosophy," in *Of Scholars, Savants, and their Texts: Studies in Philosophy and Religious Thought* (ed. R. Link-Salinger; New York: Peter Lang, 1989), 239–50.

——, *The Wisdom of Solomon* (AB 43; New York: Doubleday, 1979).

Wischmeyer, Oda, *Die Kultur des Buches Jesus Sirach* (BZNW 77; Berlin: Walter de Gruyter, 1995).

Wold, Benjamim G., *Women, Men, and Angels: The Qumran Document Musar leMevin and its Allusions to Genesis Creation Traditions* (Tübingen: Mohr Siebeck, 2005).

Wolters, Al, "*Sôpiyyâ* (Prov 31:27) as Hymnic Participle and Play on *Sophia*," *Journal of Biblical Literature* 104 (1985): 577–87.

Wright, A.D.G., "Additional Numerical Patterns in Qoheleth," *Catholic Biblical Quaterly* 45 (1983): 32–43.

——, "The Riddle of the Sphinx: The Structure of the Book of Qoheleth," *Catholic Biblical Quarterly* 30 (1968): 331–34.

——, "The Riddle of the Sphinx Revisited: Numerical Patterns in the Book of Qoheleth," *Catholic Biblical Quaterly* 42 (1980): 35–51.

Wright, Benjamin G., "The Categories of Rich and Poor in the Qumran Sapiential Literature," in *Sapiential Perspectives: Wisdom Literature in Light of the Dead Sea Scrolls, Proceedings of the Sixth International Symposium of the Orion Center for the Study of the Dead Sea Scrolls and Associated Literature, 20–22 May, 2001* (ed. J.J. Collins et al.; STDJ 51; Leiden: Brill, 2004), 101–25.

——, "'Fear the Lord and Honor the Priest': Ben Sira as Defender of the Jerusalem Priesthood," in *The Book of Ben Sira in Modern Research: Proceedings of the First International Ben Sira Conference, 28–31 July 1996, Soesterberg, Netherlands* (BZAW 255; Berlin: de Gruyter, 1997), 189–222.

——, *No Small Difference: Sirach's Relationship to Its Hebrew Parent Text* (SCS 26; Atlanta: Scholars Press, 1989).

——, "'Put the Nations in Fear of You': Ben Sira and the Problem of Foreign Rule," *Society of Biblical Literature Seminar Papers* 38 (Atlanta: Scholars Press, 1999), 77–93.

——, "Putting the Puzzle Together: Some Suggestions Concerning the Social Location of the Wisdom of Ben Sira," in *Conflicted Boundaries in Wisdom and Apocalypticism* (ed. B.G. Wright and L. Wills; SBLSymS 35; Atlanta: Society of Biblical Literature, 2005), 89–113.

——, Review of Matthew J. Goff, *The Worldly and Heavenly Wisdom of 4QInstruction. Journal of Biblical Literature* 124 (2005): 548–53.

Wright, N.T., *The Resurrection of the Son of God: Christian Origins and the Question of God, Volume 3* (Minneapolis: Fortress Press, 2003).

Würthwein, Ernst, "Egyptian Wisdom and the Old Testament," in *Studies in Ancient Israelite Wisdom* (trans. B.W. Kovacs; ed. J.L. Crenshaw; New York: KTAV, 1976), 113–34.

Wyatt, Nicolas, *Religious Texts from Ugarit* (2d ed.; London: Sheffield, 2002).

Yoder, Christine R., *Wisdom as a Woman of Substance: A Socioeconomic Reading of Proverbs 1–9 and 31:10–31* (BZAW 304; Berlin: de Gruyter, 2001).

Žába, Zybnek, *Les Maximes de Ptahhotep* (Prague: Editions de l'Académie Tchécoslovaque des Sciences, 1956).

Zimmerli Walther, "Das Buch Qohelet-Traktat oder Sentenzensammlung?" *Vetus Testamentum* 24 (1974): 221–30.

——, *Das Buch des Predigers Salomo* (3d ed.; ATD 16; Göttingen: Vandenhoeck & Ruprecht, 1980), 123–253.

# INDEX OF AUTHORS

# INDEX OF TEXTS

NEW TESTAMENT

## PSEUDEPIGRAPHA

## Dead Sea Scrolls And Related Literature

## JOSEPHUS AND PHILO